OSGi and Equinox

OSGi and Equinox

Creating Highly Modular Java™ Systems

Jeff McAffer
Paul VanderLei
Simon Archer

✦✦ Addison-Wesley

Upper Saddle River, NJ • Boston • Indianapolis • San Francisco
New York • Toronto • Montreal • London • Munich • Paris • Madrid
Capetown • Sydney • Tokyo • Singapore • Mexico City

Many of the designations used by manufacturers and sellers to distinguish their products are claimed as trademarks. Where those designations appear in this book, and the publisher was aware of a trademark claim, the designations have been printed with initial capital letters or in all capitals.

The authors and publisher have taken care in the preparation of this book, but make no expressed or implied warranty of any kind and assume no responsibility for errors or omissions. No liability is assumed for incidental or consequential damages in connection with or arising out of the use of the information or programs contained herein.

The publisher offers excellent discounts on this book when ordered in quantity for bulk purchases or special sales, which may include electronic versions and/or custom covers and content particular to your business, training goals, marketing focus, and branding interests. For more information, please contact:

U.S. Corporate and Government Sales
(800) 382-3419
corpsales@pearsontechgroup.com

For sales outside the United States please contact:

International Sales
international@pearson.com

Visit us on the Web: informit.com/aw

Library of Congress Cataloging-in-Publication Data
OSGi and Equinox : creating highly modular Java systems / Jeff McAffer,
Paul VanderLei, Simon Archer.
        p.   cm.
   Includes index.
   ISBN 0-321-58571-2 (pbk. : alk. paper)
   1. Java (Computer program language) 2. Computer software—Development.
   I. VanderLei, Paul. II. Archer, Simon (Simon J.) III. Title.
   QA76.73.J38M352593 2010
   005.2'762—dc22
                                                        2009047201

ISBN-13: 978-0-321-58571-4
ISBN-10:   0-321-58571-2
Text printed in the United States on recycled paper at RR Donnelley in Crawfordsville, Indiana.
Second printing September 2010

To my brother Ray
—Jeff McAffer

To Elizabeth and our four bundles:
Andrew, Bryant, Maria, and Josie
—Paul VanderLei

To my parents for their continual support
and encouragement in all my endeavors
—Simon Archer

Contents

22.4 Bundling by Reference   392

22.5 Bundling Using bnd   394

22.6 Troubleshooting Class Loading Problems   394

    22.6.1 Issues with Class.forName()   395

    22.6.2 Issues with Context Class Loaders   399

    22.6.3 Managing JRE Classes   401

    22.6.4 Serialization   402

22.7 Summary   403

Chapter 23   **Advanced Topics**   **405**

23.1 The Equinox Console   406

    23.1.1 Extending the Equinox Console   407

23.2 Roles in OSGi   409

23.3 The Shape of Bundles   411

23.4 Fragments   413

23.5 Singletons   415

23.6 Bundle Lifecycle   416

    23.6.1 Lifecycle States   416

    23.6.2 BundleActivator   418

    23.6.3 The Downside of Activators   418

    23.6.4 Uses for Activators   419

23.7 Bundle Activation Policy   419

23.8 Controlling Bundle Start   421

    23.8.1 Persistent Starting   422

    23.8.2 Enabling the Activation Policy   422

    23.8.3 osgi.bundles   422

23.9 Class Loading   423

    23.9.1 Class Lookup Algorithm   424

    23.9.2 Declaring Imports and Exports   424

    23.9.3 Importing versus Requiring   426

    23.9.4 Optionality   426

    23.9.5 The uses Directive   426

Foreword

My role as the Chief Technology Officer of SpringSource brings me into frequent contact with companies building enterprise applications: many familiar names from the Fortune 500, and a whole host of others besides. If there is one thing you quickly learn, it is that the world of enterprise applications is messy and complex. Even four to five years ago, customers adopting Spring were asking us for ways to help them manage the size and complexity of the applications they were building. Large team sizes and applications with hundreds or thousands of internal components (Spring beans) were not uncommon. The pressures on enterprises to deliver increasingly sophisticated applications, in shorter and shorter time frames, have only been growing since then. In many cases applications are now always live and are constantly evolving. The move to deliver software "as a service"—internally or externally—can only accelerate this trend.

In the enterprise Java landscape, the traditional unit of deployment for an enterprise application is a web application archive (WAR) file. A number of common themes arise in my discussions with enterprise development teams:

- The WAR file as a single large unit of packaging and deployment is slowing down development processes and making it more difficult to structure large development teams since everything must come together in a single packaging step before anything can be deployed.

- WAR files are getting too large and unwieldy—a typical enterprise application may have literally hundreds of third-party dependencies, all packaged inside the WAR file. This has an adverse effect on upload and deployment times.

- Attempting to tackle complexity by deploying multiple WAR files side by side in the same container leads to problems with heap usage in the JVM since each WAR file has its own copy of all the dependencies, even though many of them could in theory be shared.

- When deploying WAR files side by side, there is no easy way to share common services.

○ The WAR file as the smallest unit of change means that changes in large enterprise applications cannot be easily isolated and contained.

○ Attempts to introduce "self-policed" (i.e., unenforced) modularity constraints into a design typically fail, despite best intentions.

To help manage the large team sizes and complex requirements of modern enterprise applications, it is clear that we need a more principled way to "divide and conquer." Something that lets us encapsulate well-defined parts of the system as modules with hidden internals and carefully managed externals. Something that enables those modules to be packaged and deployed individually without forcing us to revise the whole universe. Something that provides a principled mechanism for bringing those modules together in a running system, and that can cope with the changes introduced by continuous evolution.

Facing these requirements back in 2005, it was an easy decision at Spring-Source (then Interface21) to turn to OSGi, the "dynamic module system for Java," as the foundation technology for modular enterprise applications. Even then, the OSGi Service Platform was already mature and proven in industrial settings, as well as being lightweight through its heritage in embedded systems.

The modularity layer of OSGi provides a mechanism for dividing a system into independent modules, known as bundles, that are independently packaged and deployed and have independent lifecycles. This solved a part of the problem for us—helping to keep the implementation types of a module private, and exposing only types that form part of the public interface of a module. We wanted enterprise developers to continue developing their applications using Spring, of course, and through the Spring Dynamic Modules' open-source project created a simple model whereby each module had its own set of components (Spring beans). Some of those components are private to the module, but some should be made public so that components in other modules can use them. The OSGi service layer provides an answer to this problem, promoting an in-memory service-oriented design. Components from a module can be published in the OSGi service registry, and from there other modules can find and bind to those services. OSGi also provides the necessary primitives to track services that may come and go over time as modules are installed, uninstalled, and upgraded.

The next stage in our journey with OSGi was the introduction of the Spring-Source dm Server: an enterprise application server that is not only built on top of OSGi, but critically also supports the deployment of applications developed as a set of OSGi bundles. Spring Dynamic Modules works with any compliant OSGi Service Platform implementation, but for the dm Server we had to choose an OSGi Service Platform as the base on which to build. We chose to build on Equinox, the Eclipse implementation of the OSGi Service Platform, and also the reference implementation for the core OSGi specification. The open-source nature of Equinox fit well with our own open-source philosophy and has been invaluable in enabling us to work closely with the developers of Equinox and submit patches and change requests over time. The widespread adoption of Equinox (as the underpinnings of Eclipse, to name but one example) gave us confidence that it would be battle-hardened and ready for enterprise usage.

I am seeing a strong and growing serious interest in OSGi among companies large and small. Building on OSGi will provide a firm foundation for dividing your application into modules, which in turn will help you structure the team(s) working on it more effectively. "Organization follows architecture" in the sense that your ability to divide a complex application into independent pieces also facilitates the structuring of team responsibilities along the same lines. In other scenarios, your teams may be fixed, and you need an architecture that enables those teams to work together most effectively. Again, a principled basis for dividing a system into modules can facilitate that. With OSGi as a basis, your unit of packaging and deployment can become a single module, removing bottlenecks in the process and helping to minimize the impact of change. OSGi is also incredibly well suited to product-line engineering, and to situations where you need to provide an extension or plug-in mechanism to enable third parties to extend your software.

The future for OSGi looks bright. Version 4.2 of the specification has just been released, and the OSGi Core Platform and Enterprise Expert Groups are very active. A glance at the membership of the OSGi Alliance and the composition of the expert groups tells you just how seriously enterprise vendors are taking it. I am confident that the investment of your time in reading and studying this book will be well rewarded. It is my belief that OSGi is here to stay. A firm grasp of the strengths—and the weaknesses—of the OSGi Service Platform will prove invaluable to you on your journey toward creating agile, modular software.

—Adrian Colyer
   CTO, SpringSource
   October 2009

Preface

OSGi is a hot topic these days; all the major Java application server vendors have adopted OSGi as their base runtime, Eclipse has been using OSGi as the basis of its modularity story and runtime for at least the past five years, and countless others have been using it in embedded and "under the covers" scenarios. All with good reason.

The success of Eclipse as a tooling platform is a direct result of the strong modularity enshrined in OSGi. This isolates developers from change, empowers teams to be more agile, allows organizations to change the way that they develop software, and lubricates the formation and running of ecosystems. These same benefits can be realized in any software domain.

The main OSGi specification is remarkably concise—just 27 Java types. It is well designed, and specified to be implemented and used in real life. Adoption of OSGi is not without challenges, however. Make no mistake: Implementing highly modular and dynamic systems is hard. There is, as they say, no free lunch. Some have criticized OSGi as being complicated or obtuse. In most cases it is the problem that is complex—the desire to be modular or dynamic surfaces the issues but is not the cause. Modularizing existing monolithic systems is particularly challenging.

This book is designed to both highlight such topics and provide knowledge, guidance, and best practices to mitigate them. We talk heavily of modularity, components, and dynamism and show you techniques for enhancing your system's flexibility and agility.

Despite using OSGi for many years, participating in writing the OSGi specifications, and implementing Equinox (the OSGi framework specification reference implementation), during the writing of this book we learned an incredible amount about OSGi, Equinox, and highly modular dynamic systems. We trust that in reading it you will, too.

About This Book

This book guides up-and-coming and established OSGi developers through all stages of developing and delivering an example OSGi-based telematics and fleet management system called *Toast*.

We develop Toast from a blank workspace into a full-featured client and server system. The domain is familiar to most everyone who has driven a car or shipped a package. Telematics is, loosely speaking, all the car electronics—radio, navigation, climate control, and so on. Fleet management is all about tracking and coordinating packages and vehicles as they move from one place to another.

The set of problems and opportunities raised allows us to plausibly touch a wide range of issues from modularity and component collaboration to server-side programming and packaging and delivery of highly modular systems. We create stand-alone client applications, embedded and stand-alone server configurations, and dynamic enhancements to both. This book enables you to do the same in your domain.

Roughly speaking, the book is split into two sections. The first half, Parts I and II, sets the scene for OSGi and Equinox and presents a tutorial-style guide to building Toast. The tutorial incrementally builds Toast into a functioning fleet management system with a number of advanced capabilities. The tutorial is written somewhat informally to evoke the feeling that we are there with you, working through the examples and problems. We share some of the pitfalls and mishaps that we experienced while developing the application and writing the tutorial.

The second half of the book looks at what it takes to "make it real." It's one thing to write a prototype and quite another to ship a product. Rather than leaving you hanging at the prototype stage, Part III is composed of chapters that dive into the details required to finish the job—namely, the refining and refactoring of the first prototype, customizing the user interface, and building and delivering products to your customers. This part is written as a reference, but it still includes a liberal sprinkling of step-by-step examples and code samples. The goal is both to dive deep and cover most of the major stumbling blocks reported in the community and seen in our own development of professional products.

A final part, Part IV, is pure reference. It covers the essential aspects of OSGi and Equinox and touches on various capabilities not covered earlier in the book. We also talk about best practices and advanced topics such as integrating third-party code libraries and being dynamic.

OSGi, despite being relatively small, is very comprehensive. As such, a single book could never cover all possible topics. We have focused on the functions and services that we use in the systems we develop day to day under the assumption that they will be useful to you as well.

OSGi, Equinox, and EclipseRT

The OSGi community is quite vibrant. There are at least three active open-source framework implementation communities and a wide array of adopters and extenders. The vast majority of this book covers generic OSGi topics applicable to any OSGi system or implementation. Throughout the book we consistently use Equinox, the OSGi framework specification reference implementation, as the base for our examples and discussions. From time to time we cover features and facilities available only in Equinox. In general, these capabilities have been added to Equinox to address real-world problems—things that you will encounter. As such, it is prudent that we discuss them here.

Throughout the book we also cover the Eclipse Plug-in Development Environment (PDE) tooling for writing and building OSGi bundles. PDE is comprehensive, robust, and sophisticated tooling that has been used in the OSGi context for many years. If you are not using PDE to create your OSGi-based systems, perhaps you should take this opportunity to find out what you are missing.

Finally, Eclipse is a powerhouse in the tooling domain. Increasingly it is being used in pure runtime, server-side, and embedded environments. This movement has come to be known as *EclipseRT*. EclipseRT encompasses a number of technologies developed at Eclipse that are aimed at or useful in typical runtime contexts. The Toast application developed here has been donated to the Eclipse Examples project and is evolving as a showcase for EclipseRT technologies. We encourage you to check out http://wiki.eclipse.org/Toast to see what people have done to and with Toast.

Audience

This book is targeted at several groups of Java developers. Some Java programming experience is assumed, and no attempt is made to introduce Java concepts or syntax.

For developers new to OSGi and Equinox, there is information about the origins of the technology, how to get started with the Eclipse OSGi bundle tooling, and how to create your first OSGi-based system. Prior experience with Eclipse as a development tool is helpful but not necessary.

For developers experienced with writing OSGi bundles and systems, the book formalizes a wide range of techniques and practices that are useful in creating highly modular systems using OSGi—from service collaboration approaches to server-side integration and system building as part of a release engineering process, deployment, and installation.

For experienced OSGi developers, this book includes details of special features available in Equinox and comprehensive coverage of useful facilities such as

Declarative Services, buddy class loading, Google Earth integration, and the Eclipse bundle tooling that make designing, coding, and packaging OSGi-based systems easier than ever before.

Sample Code

Reading this book can be a very hands-on experience. There are ample opportunities for following along and doing the steps yourself as well as writing your own code. The companion download for the book includes code samples for each chapter. Instructions for getting and managing these samples are given in Chapter 3, "Tutorial Introduction," and as needed in the text. In general, all required materials are available online at either http://eclipse.org or http://equinoxosgi.org. As mentioned previously, a snapshot of Toast also lives and evolves as an open-source project at Eclipse. See http://wiki.eclipse.org/Toast.

Conventions

The following formatting conventions are used throughout the book:

> **Bold**—Used for UI elements such as menu paths (e.g., **File > New > Project**) and wizard and editor elements
>
> *Italics*—Used for emphasis and to highlight terminology
>
> `Lucida`—Used for Java code, property names, file paths, bundle IDs, and the like that are embedded in the text
>
> `Lucida Bold`—Used to highlight important lines in code samples

Notes and sidebars are used often to highlight information that readers may find interesting or helpful for using or understanding the function being described in the main text. We tried to achieve an effect similar to that of an informal pair-programming experience where you sit down with somebody and get impromptu tips and tricks here and there.

Feedback

The official web site for this book is http://equinoxosgi.org. Additional information and errata are available at informit.com/title/0321585712. You can report problems or errors found in the book or code samples to the authors at book@equinoxosgi.org. Suggestions for improvements and feedback are also very welcome.

Acknowledgments

It is impossible to write a book such as this without the cooperation and help of a vast number of people. In our case, virtually the entire Equinox team contributed directly to the end result through conversations, help with code and concepts, bug fixes, manuscript review, or just general support.

A few individuals contributed exceptional amounts of time and brain-power to this project, and we extend our heartfelt thanks to them here:

Tom Watson—Tom is the driving force behind Equinox and is very active in the OSGi specification community. His pragmatic approach and level head have brought you Equinox and us a guiding hand in the creation of this material.

Chris Aniszyzck—Chris has brought his diverse passions to bear on PDE, the tooling that makes OSGi and Equinox a pleasure to program. The creation of this book drove many new use cases and requirements. Chris eagerly pushed PDE to be even more of a bundle development environment, making life easier for all of us.

Ian Bull—Ian applied his pedagogical skill and attention to detail on all things related to p2, packaging, and building, making the whole process of building and delivering OSGi functionality tractable.

Stoyan Boshev—Stoyan is the guiding hand behind the Equinox Declarative Services implementation. DS figures heavily in this book and the sample code. Stoyan spent countless hours implementing DS and working with us to bring its power to you.

A number of people provided portions of the book's sample code or in-depth review and guidance on technical elements of the content. In particular, DJ Houghton and Scott Admiraal completed exhaustive testing and review of the tutorial sections, saving our behinds in the process. Rafael Oliveira Nóbrega and Chris Aniszyzck contributed hugely to the creation of Declarative Services tooling, making DS usable by mere mortals. Andrew Niefer, Pascal Rapicault, Simon Kaegi, and Scott Lewis all contributed fixes, samples, and guidance on technologies ranging from PDE Build and p2 to server-side OSGi to ECF. Patrick Dempsey contributed the Crust code and offered tireless support on all things Mac-related. BJ Hargrave, the steady hand of OSGi, patiently discussed any number of design points, best practices, and coding approaches.

We were also fortunate to have the Eclipse community and a number of people who reviewed chapters or provided valuable input and help. These include Joel Rosi-Schwartz, Benjamin Muskalla, Kevin Barnes, Grant Gayed and the SWT team, Ralf Sternberg, Matt Flaherty, the readers of the early drafts on Rough Cuts, and all the people involved in developing the Toast example code.

Of course, no book project is possible without a publishing team. We were lucky to have Greg Doench as the enduring editor of the Eclipse Series along with Michelle Housley, Barbara Wood, Elizabeth Ryan, and the whole crew at Addison-Wesley who made this a relatively painless and quite enjoyable experience.

The authors would like to individually acknowledge the following people:

Jeff McAffer: Nancy, Sydney, and Toby, you are the loves of my life. Mom, Dad, and Val, I love you fiercely; you made me what I am today and I am thankful. The entire EclipseSource team, thanks for giving me the room to move and being generally enthusiastic around Toast and this project.

Paul VanderLei: I'd like to thank my partners at Band XI International—John Cunningham, Brett Hackleman, Patrick Dempsey, and James Branigan—for generously providing me the time to complete this project. Thanks, too, to my wife and children for their patience and love. Finally, I'm forever grateful to my father, whose encouragement and sage counsel have shaped my entire career.

Simon Archer: Undertaking to write a book such as this involves a huge amount of time, dedication, and sacrifice. While I am grateful for my coauthors, Jeff and Paul, for their time and dedication to this project, it is to my wife, Lisa, and my children, Thomas and Emma, that I owe the most gratitude since they are the ones who made all the sacrifices. Thank you for your constant love and support and for allowing me the time to work on the book—I am forever in your debt.

Beyond this book, OSGi would not be what it is today without the following people:

BJ Hargrave—BJ is the CTO at the OSGi Alliance and has been driving the technology since the beginning. He was the lead for the IBM OSGi implementation, SMF, that was donated to Eclipse as the forerunner of Equinox. He continues to promote and guide OSGi as it evolves beyond its original domain.

Peter Kriens—Peter is the OSGi Evangelist and a longtime leader of the OSGi community. He fulfills his evangelical role with style and energy that are inspiring. The continuity and clarity that we see in the OSGi specifications are a direct result of Peter's editorial and design skill.

Tom Watson—Tom is the co-lead and heavy lifter in the Equinox OSGi project at Eclipse and a valued member of the OSGi expert groups. He is responsible for the entire framework implementation and many of the add-on facilities. His pragmatism and thoroughness have made Equinox what it is today.

Richard Hall—Richard is the lead of the Apache Felix project and is very active in the OSGi specification process. Felix is an evolution of the Oscar project, the first open-source OSGi framework implementation and an inspiration to the Equinox team as they looked to adopt OSGi. The alternative viewpoint provided by the Felix project continues to enrich the specification and implementation process.

About the Authors

Jeff McAffer co-leads the Eclipse RCP and Equinox OSGi projects and is CTO and cofounder of EclipseSource. He is one of the architects of the Eclipse Platform and a coauthor of *The Eclipse Rich Client Platform* (Addison-Wesley). He co-leads the RT PMC and is a member of the Eclipse Project PMC, the Tools Project PMC, and the Eclipse Architecture Council and a former member of the Eclipse Foundation Board of Directors. Jeff is currently interested in all aspects of Eclipse components, from developing and building bundles to deploying, installing, and ultimately running them. Previous lives include being a Senior Technical Staff Member at IBM; being a team lead at Object Technology International covering work in Smalltalk, distributed/parallel OO computing, expert systems, and metalevel architectures; and getting a Ph.D. from the University of Tokyo.

Paul VanderLei is a partner at Band XI International. He has more than twenty-five years of software engineering experience with an emphasis on object-oriented design and agile practices. He is well known for his innovative yet straightforward engineering solutions to complex problems. After earning his M.S. in computer science from Arizona State University, he joined Object Technology International and worked on a wide range of Smalltalk-based systems. After OTI's acquisition by IBM, Paul developed embedded Java applications and user interfaces for the automotive and medical industries as a founding member of IBM's Embedded Java Enablement Team. He has been using OSGi in commercial applications for over ten years. He lives in Grand Rapids, Michigan, with his wife and four children.

Simon Archer has more than sixteen years of software engineering experience with an emphasis on object-oriented design, agile practices, and software quality. After earning his B.Sc. in computer science from the University of Portsmouth, UK, he worked as a Smalltalk developer at Knowledge System Corporation and later at Object Technology International. While at OTI in 2000, Simon began working with and teaching OSGi in areas such as telematics and RFID. Today he works for IBM Rational, using OSGi to build collaborative development tools for the Jazz Foundation project. He lives in Cary, North Carolina, with his wife and two children.

PART I

Introduction

This first part of the book introduces OSGi and Equinox, Eclipse's implementation of the OSGi standard. Chapter 1 outlines the history and context of OSGi. Its usefulness and applicability are illustrated with real-world examples of OSGi and Equinox in action. Chapter 2 gives an overview of OSGi concepts, terminology, and architecture to ensure that all readers have a common understanding.

CHAPTER 1

OSGi, Equinox, and Eclipse

As this book goes to press, both OSGi and Eclipse are celebrating their tenth birthdays as Java technologies. Though they were developed independently in completely different domains, their lineage can be traced back to teams in the same organization with a similar need to provide componentized Java solutions. In the case of OSGi it was home gateways and set-top boxes. For Eclipse, that need was in the tooling space. Both, however, had very similar needs for modularity and extensibility.

In this first chapter of a book dedicated to OSGi and Equinox, we look at some of the history behind these technologies, how they are used, what they are good for, and what they can do for you.

1.1 A Bit of History

For the first few years, OSGi and Eclipse technologies grew up in parallel with only a few passing encounters. The OSGi organization was a loose consortium of embedded and home gateway vendors. Its modular runtime specifications evolved quickly with several major revisions, new services, and expert groups in different domains, particularly vehicle software. Adoption ramped up, and more and more framework implementations appeared. The OSGi community maintained its focus on the embedded market, and those needs continued to be reflected in concise and honed APIs and design.

At the same time, Eclipse was a loose consortium of software tool vendors looking to create a comprehensive tooling platform. Its technology was maturing and quickly dominating the tooling market. Eclipse-based offerings with thousands of components were shipping as flagship products from major software companies. Modularity and the open community, two key ingredients, were working as a powerful pair to drive a revolution in the tooling world. Eclipse also began to reach beyond tools and into rich client applications. This shift drove the need for a more robust modularity mechanism, support for dynamic behavior, and, moreover, standardization.

In 2003 the Equinox project was created at Eclipse. The initial goal was to address the runtime-related issues seen in the Eclipse of the day—static behavior, a nonstandard markup and execution model, and, as a result, the inability to leverage the work of others in areas such as provisioning and management. OSGi was not the only contender.

After a public survey of the available technologies (e.g., Avalon, JMX, and, of course, OSGi), OSGi was identified as the most promising approach—its clear component model and strong execution specification were seen as great assets. The potential for leveraging the standardization and creating an even broader community was clearly evident.

Having decided on OSGi, the team had to get, write, borrow, or co-opt an open-source implementation. At the time there were relatively few choices: the open-source Oscar project at ObjectWeb—now the Felix project at Apache—and IBM's Service Management Framework (SMF), a shipping commercial framework. Knopflerfish, now an open-source implementation, was not yet open-source and was unknown to the team.

Oscar had lots of great characteristics, not the least of which was its internal simplicity. SMF had the benefit of being an industrial-strength implementation that had been in production for some years and had the backing of a team of developers. In the end SMF was selected as the starting point. IBM donated the code to Equinox, and the transformation began in earnest.

Marrying the two mind-sets and approaches was not easy, but working closely with the OSGi Core Platform Expert Group, the Equinox team helped evolve a number of changes and additions to the OSGi framework specification to cover the new use cases. Lazy activation, bundle fragments, bundle name and version semantics, and bundle dependencies are all fruits of this very successful and productive collaboration. Within six months the original Eclipse runtime was seamlessly replaced with the new Equinox OSGi implementation. From there Equinox evolved to be the reference implementation for the newly minted OSGi R4 framework specification, and the future of both communities changed forever.

1.2 Collaboration

In the years since then, one thing has become clear: The benefits of collaboration are immense. It is no overstatement that Eclipse's adoption of OSGi put the technology on the map. Google hits on "OSGi" increased by two orders of magnitude in the time around Eclipse's adoption of OSGi. Most of the hard work was done before Eclipse came along, but with a few additions and some implicit marketing, OSGi was in front of millions of software developers in a new context.

The benefits flow both ways. Equinox is seeing a surge in its use in runtime scenarios from servers to embedded. In that context the shoe is now on the other foot. All of the major Java application server vendors are adopting OSGi. Many of those are using Equinox. Suddenly OSGi is the technology to watch, and Equinox is one of the key implementations.

On a more technical level we have seen a massive transition in the way software systems are put together. Eclipse really showed that componentized software ecosystems work—it changed the tooling landscape. OSGi, Equinox, Felix, and associated projects are now fueling similar transformations in adjacent spaces in the runtime world.

The software industry has a long history of producing component models for various domains—CORBA, SOM, SOA, SCA, to name just a few. Some have gained a persistent following in particular computing categories, but few have a following that spans the computing landscape. What is it about OSGi that makes it interesting in such a wide range of computing environments and application domains?

Perhaps the key factor is that it started in a constrained environment with some hard requirements. The original focus of the OSGi effort can be seen in the organization's original name—the Open Services Gateway initiative. The initial work was done in the late 1990s to facilitate smart homes, home gateways, set-top boxes, and the like. The requirements of that domain forced an ethic of modularity, compactness, and dynamism on the API design.

While the home gateway industry may yet take off, it did not do so as hoped a decade ago. The core design points have, however, come to be appreciated and are applicable in almost every computing domain.

Modularity, it turns out, is the lubricant of collaboration.

1.3 Modularity and Freedom of Action

Like it or not, the world needs boundaries. The saying "Good fences make good neighbors" has variations in many languages with good reason. Boundaries set expectations and form the basis of contracts between the parties. Defining these boundaries in a formal way enables development-time and runtime monitoring and enforcement of the boundaries.

OSGi has robust boundary mechanisms. Through a series of mechanisms, software components define themselves, what they offer to others, and what they need of others. A component must clearly state a dependency on what some other component is offering before collaboration can happen.

This directly supports implementation and information hiding. Hiding is great because it limits the assumptions you can make and forces the decoupling of system elements. With no knowledge to the contrary, you have to assume anything—or nothing—can happen. With hiding you can do whatever you like in your own yard.

Even the most robust fences have gates. Whereas a fence stops people from traversing the boundary, a gate declares that there is a boundary but allows people to pass, understanding that there are new rights and obligations.

With a formal definition of the fences and gates, components are decoupled and freedom of action is increased. But it is not just the components that are liberated. The development teams, system integrators, and product designers have newfound independence and power. This manifests itself in a number of ways:

Concrete abstraction—Modules add another granularity of abstraction. Just as subroutine calls, separate source files, and classes enable functional abstraction, modules raise the level of abstraction and enable reuse and sharing.

Granular equivalence—Modules add a layer of insulation that makes it easier to substitute equivalent components. The idea of implementation substitution is not new—interfaces, mock objects, and polymorphism are in the same vein. The clear API definition inherent in modularity cranks this up a notch and facilitates the substitution of whole components. This in turn frees teams to act independently, removes bottlenecks, and reduces risk in the software lifecycle. Teams are largely decoupled and can evolve their components independently.

The death of the wad—API and packaging boundaries drive developers to stay in bounds. Similarly, because the API surface area of their bundle is explicit, developers think harder about the contracts they are making with others. This in turn discourages the creation of amorphous wads of tightly coupled code.

Getting there fast—*Flexibility* and *time to market* are cool buzzwords, but they are also real assets. Developing business logic and then deploying in a stand-alone server, rich clients, or integrated with existing web infrastructure is a tangible benefit, especially if little change is required. This cuts both ways, too. It's easier to describe and deploy different functional sets on the same platform.

1.4 Platforms

Modularity brings freedom, but it also enables platforms. The notion of platform is a well-known phenomenon in many domains outside computers. Cars, for example, are very expensive to develop. Manufacturers have long since updated their businesses to develop platforms and then outfit them separately. Initially it was just trim quality and tuning levels—Pontiac and Buick, Ford and Mercury, Honda and Acura. These different product lines shared common designs, components, and assembly-line tooling. With the diversification of the auto market, platforms now extend across "markets"—Accord sedan and Odyssey minivan, Taurus car and Flex crossover—same platform, different market.

One way to think of platforms is as a specialization on the underlying modules. Platforms aggregate a set of components and configure them in a way that is ideal for a particular domain or market. They address the parts of the solution that are largely commoditized. Other teams then build real added value on top of the platform.

Platforms allow companies to move quickly to develop new offerings because they don't have to develop each from the ground up. End users benefit as well since the underlying technology is generally more widely used and better tested. These effects are magnified as platforms evolve with new capabilities and characteristics and communities of extenders emerge.

1.5 Ecosystems

Popular platforms develop ecosystems—communities of consumers and contributors—that work with a platform and apply it in more specific ways. In the vehicle example the immediate platform ecosystem is internal to the manufacturer and associated companies. Aftermarket parts vendors benefit to a certain degree but have less influence.

With heavy trucks, however, the ecosystem is much closer to the platform. Heavy truck makers produce a modest number of different chassis and drivetrain combinations. In many cases, these roll off the assembly line in forms that are not roadworthy—they lack taillights and other safety equipment. The trucks go to dealers and customers who then customize the platform as a dump truck, goods hauler, tow truck, and so on. In this case the ecosystem is more open and extensive.

Open ecosystems drive innovation. Because everyone has access to the common platform, offerings stand on the merits of their added value. Ecosystem members can compete or collaborate, or both—"co-opetition." End users can choose how they interact with and consume ecosystems' output.

1.6 OSGi in Context

What does all this really have to do with OSGi and you? In short, OSGi enables these effects in the software world. We have seen Eclipse evolve as a tooling platform that dominates the overall development environment market. In Section 1.7.1, "NASA's Maestro and Ensemble," we look at how the NASA Ensemble project builds on top of Eclipse in the rich client and server space to create a space mission software platform. As of this writing, all major Java application server vendors have adopted OSGi, and in many cases Equinox, as the basis for their flagship offerings.

All of this is possible because of the deep modularity promoted, supported, and enforced by OSGi.

1.6.1 The Java Lie

One of the early slogans of the Java community was "Write once. Run anywhere." In a certain context that is true, but unfortunately the Java world has been divided in three by Java ME, SE, and EE. These address different computing environments and promote different modularity and execution models. While it is true that the Java code itself likely works everywhere, the overall system does not.

OSGi, on the other hand, makes very few assumptions about the surrounding environment or the context in which it is used. This enables its use in a wide range of scenarios with one consistent programming model. Components written for the server can be run on the client and vice versa. Moreover, the tooling and developer skills are the same across all execution environments. We will see how this works later in the book.

1.6.2 Reality Check

If all this sounds too good to be true, it is. Well, sort of. There is, as they say, no free lunch. Modularity is not easy. It forces you to express your expectations, add rigor, maintain additional metadata, and negotiate contracts. It is simple human nature that every time you draw a box there ensues a discussion about what is in the box and what is not. This is not entirely unhealthy. Most of these discussions result in a deeper understanding of the problem, a more coherent team view of the system, and, indeed, better software.

As always, it is possible to do something bad with something good. Your first, second, and third component sets will be tightly coupled, brittle, and inconveniently granular. You will struggle to identify the players, their roles, and how they interact. These are not problems of OSGi or even modularity—these are

design challenges present in any system. OSGi, through its modularity requirements, both forces you and enables you to think about these problems in concrete
and tangible terms.

We have encountered a number of teams that, in their adoption of OSGi, have
said, "OSGi is hard" or "OSGi does not work for us because <insert some reason
why software design best practices do not apply to them>." This is shooting the
messenger. Certainly some OSGi facilities could be better, and no one tool is
appropriate in all situations. However, if you view OSGi as a framework for describing the elements of your system, it actually does not even matter if you run OSGi.

One example of this is the Apache Harmony project. This is an effort to create
an open-source Java SE 5 implementation. The Java class libraries are a large and
complicated software system with many intertwined pieces. To enable multiple
independent teams to work on the project, the Harmony team turned to OSGi
markup and tooling. The library was broken up into a number of OSGi components with clear API boundaries. OSGi tooling was used to enforce the boundaries
at development time. In this context it does not matter that at runtime OSGi is
not present.

1.6.3 OSGi Longevity

The OSGi specifications are produced by the OSGi Alliance, an industry consortium of mostly software and embedded systems vendors. It operates as a series of
Expert Groups (EGs) focused on particular computing domains: Core, Enterprise,
Vehicle, and Mobile. While participation in the specification process is limited to
members, the specifications produced are freely implementable. Specification
compliance certification is a managed, for-fee service.

Overall the organization has a robust governance structure and a relatively
rigorous specification process. The specifications produced are complete and very
readable. Each specification has an accompanying reference implementation (RI).
In many cases the RI is open-source. For example, the core framework RI is Equinox. In other cases the RI is proprietary to the alliance.

In addition to their own self-proclaimed standards, the OSGi Alliance has
been the driver behind Java Community Process standards such as JSRs 232 and
291—OSGi in Java ME and Java SE, respectively.

The current core specifications are widely implemented in a range of open-
source and commercial offerings. Adoption is strong and growing. Some new
specifications coming out of the Enterprise EG show great promise but are only
just released.

The main challenge for OSGi as a specifications body is to maintain relevance as
the computing world shifts from Java to so-called dynamic languages. Currently

OSGi is firmly fixed as a Java-based technology. Of course the concepts and approaches translate to other languages, and modularity is sorely lacking in those environments—there is ample room for OSGi value to be added; it just needs to be done.

1.7 OSGi and Equinox in Practice

The canonical example of widespread OSGi and Equinox use is the Eclipse Integrated Development Environment (IDE). It is used by millions of software developers around the world. There are thousands of developers writing bundles to extend the platform and hundreds of companies shipping products based on these capabilities. It has revolutionized the tooling market largely on the back of the underlying modularity infrastructure.

Nonetheless, people still do not relate to Eclipse as an example of OSGi's power because they are not writing large, tooling-related systems. They are writing small to medium end-user or server-side systems. Eclipse, the development environment, is a large and complicated platform that has nothing to offer them. They can, however, still benefit massively from the effects described in this chapter—the same effects that drove the success of Eclipse. Here we look at some uses of these technologies in other domains.

1.7.1 NASA's Maestro and Ensemble

One of the more appealing uses of OSGi is in NASA's Maestro and Ensemble projects. Some years ago NASA adopted the Eclipse Rich Client Platform (RCP) as the base for its Maestro space mission software platform. They are using it today to manage the *Spirit* and *Opportunity* missions on Mars. Their experience with Eclipse, OSGi, and, moreover, modular software development was so positive that Maestro spawned Ensemble.

Ensemble is a broader effort involving many NASA teams in the creation and use of a space mission software platform. Each mission is made up of many different elements, and each element has its own set of software for planning and executing the required steps. While the domain and content of this software may be quite varied, there is a common set of functions, UIs, and other facilities that are useful across the board. Ensemble captures these commodity components and makes them available to mission software teams.

In the evolution of NASA's platform there has come to be a rather large element of server-side work. The team has expanded to use Equinox on the server and developed their own RESTlet infrastructure to address scaling and flexibility issues. In their EclipseCon 2008 tutorial on the topic they summarize the approach as follows:

Eclipse RCP + Server-side Equinox = "Tierless Computing"

○ Develop many bundles independent of deployment environment.

○ Share some capabilities between server and client.

○ Freely migrate capabilities back and forth as needed.

○ Use a consistent development environment (Eclipse) and component model (OSGi) throughout.

○ Debug clients and servers simultaneously!

These directly mirror the benefits and effects discussed earlier in this chapter. The NASA team is living the OSGi effect.

1.8 Summary

OSGi is a powerful, robust modularity framework and runtime. Equinox is a robust, scalable, and comprehensive implementation of the key OSGi specifications. Both the specifications and the implementations are open and driven by multi-vendor organizations with a long track record of delivering innovation.

The value that these technologies deliver enables individual developers, teams, and organizations to change the way they develop and deliver software. This grand claim has been substantiated by numerous examples in open-source and commercial software settings, including the NASA team building Maestro and Ensemble.

As this pair evolves, OSGi coming up from the embedded world and Equinox coming down from the tooling domain, they are spreading into the more traditional server runtime space where Java application server vendors are adopting the approach with gusto. No wonder analysts are calling OSGi one of the hottest technologies to watch.

Throughout the rest of this book we walk you through the details of OSGi, real-world examples of its benefits, and best practices for leveraging these in your projects.

CHAPTER 2

OSGi Concepts

The OSGi Alliance[1] (http://osgi.org) is an independent consortium with the mission "to create a market for universal middleware." This manifests itself as a set of specifications, reference implementations, and test suites around a dynamic module system for Java. The module system forms the basis for a "service platform" that in turn supports the creation and execution of loosely coupled, dynamic modular systems. Originating in the embedded space, OSGi retains its minimalist approach by producing a core specification of just 27 Java types. This ethic of simplicity and consistency is pervasive in the OSGi specifications.

In this chapter we explore the basic concepts around OSGi and look at how they fit together. You will learn about

- The OSGi framework, its key parts and operation
- Bundles, their structure, and their lifecycle
- Services, extensions, and component collaboration

2.1 A Community of Bundles

An OSGi system is a community of components known as *bundles*. Bundles executing within an OSGi service platform are independent of each other, yet they collaborate in well-defined ways. Bundles are fully self-describing, declaring their public API, defining their runtime dependencies on other bundles, and hiding their internal implementation.

---

1. The OSGi Alliance was founded as the Open Services Gateway initiative. They have since rebranded as the "OSGi Alliance."

Bundle writers, *producers*, create bundles and make them available for others to use. System integrators or application writers, *consumers*, use these bundles and write still more bundles using the available API. This continues until there is enough functionality available to solve a given problem. Bundles are then composed and configured to create the desired system.

As shown in Figure 2-1, an OSGi application has no top and no bottom—it is simply a collection of bundles. There is also no *main* program; some bundles contribute code libraries; others start threads, communicate over the network, access databases, or collaborate with still others to gain access to hardware devices and system resources. While there are often dependencies between bundles, in many cases bundles are peers in a collaborative system.

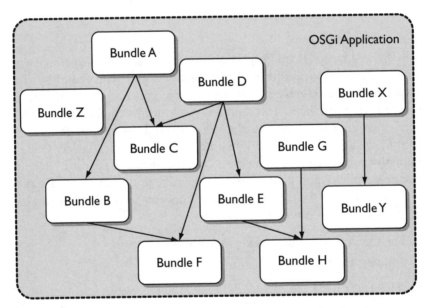

Figure 2–1   An OSGi application as a collection of interdependent bundles

OSGi-based systems are dynamic in that the bundles in the community can change over the lifetime of the application. A bundle can be installed, uninstalled, and updated at any time. To facilitate this, bundles must be implemented to gracefully handle being uninstalled, as well as to respond to the addition, removal, and possible replacement of collaborating bundles.

These characteristics lead to a fundamentally simple but powerful module system upon which other systems can be built. Indeed, modularity and OSGi bundles are among the secrets to the success of Eclipse as a platform and as an ecosystem. In any suitably large system it is increasingly unlikely that all components will be written by the same producer. In fact, in an OSGi system such as an Eclipse application, it is common for bundles to come from a variety of producers, such as open-source projects, corporations, and individuals. The strong modularity promoted and supported by OSGi dramatically increases the opportunity for code reuse and accelerates the delivery of applications.

2.2 Why OSGi?

If OSGi is so small and simple, what makes it so special? To understand more, let's first look at a traditional Java application. A Java system is composed of *types*—*classes* and *interfaces*. Each type has a set of members—*methods* and *fields*—and is organized into *packages*. The set of Java packages defines a global type namespace, and the Java language defines the visibility rules used to manage the interactions between types and members. As shown in Figure 2-2, types and packages are typically built and shipped as Java Archives (JARs). JARs are then collected together on one *classpath* that is linearly searched by the Java virtual machine (JVM) to discover and load classes.

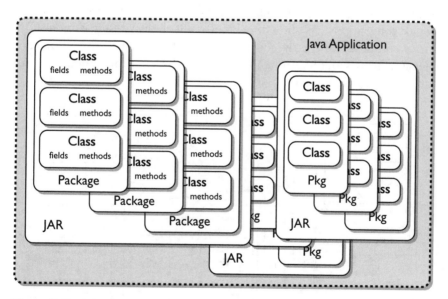

Figure 2–2 A Java application

So far it sounds pretty good—packages feel modular and there are visibility rules to enable information hiding. At the low level the story is reasonable, but things break down at the system and collaboration level. There are two main issues: Packages are too granular to be modules, and JARs are simply a delivery mechanism with no runtime semantics.

The Java type and member visibility rules allow developers to hide elements within a package, so it feels natural to say that packages == modules. In practice this forces either packages to be too large or modules to be too numerous. Experience tells us that modules are often themselves composed of code from various sources and that it is a best practice to use fine-grained package naming to enable later refactoring. Mixing packages with modularity is counter to both experiences.

The JAR concept is very useful. It could be argued that the JAR as a delivery vehicle was one of the drivers of the original success of Java. Producers create JARs of useful function, and consumers use these JARs to build systems. Unfortunately, JARs really are just a delivery vehicle and have minimal impact on the running of the system. Delivered JARs simply go on a flat classpath with no control over the accessibility of their contents.

Combined, these characteristics mean that Java has no support for defining or enforcing dependencies. Without dependencies, modularity is not possible. You end up with systems where JARs fight for position on the classpath, JAR content has more to do with who wrote the code rather than its functionality, APIs are unclear, and the relationships between JARs are at best managed by weak conventions. As shown in Figure 2-3, the net result is monolithic applications composed of tightly coupled JARs with multidirectional and even cyclical dependencies. Collaboration and sharing between teams is impacted and application evolution hindered.

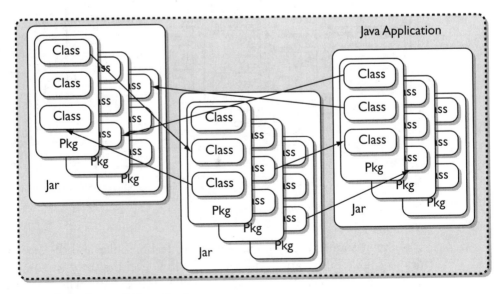

Figure 2–3 A monolithic application

OK, so what makes OSGi better? It's still Java, right? True. OSGi builds on the basic Java mechanisms just outlined but adds a few key elements. In particular, rather than talking about JARs, OSGi talks about bundles. A bundle is typically implemented as a JAR, but with added identity and dependency information; that is, bundles are self-describing JARs. This simple idea has two effects: Producers and consumers have an opportunity to express their side of the contract, and the runtime has the information it needs to enforce these expectations.

By default the packages in a bundle are hidden from other bundles. Packages containing API must, by definition, be available to other bundles and so must be explicitly *exported*. Bundles including code that uses this API must then have a matching *import*. This visibility management is similar in concept to Java's package visibility but at a much more manageable and flexible level.

The OSGi runtime enforces these visibility constraints, thus forming the basis of a strong but loosely coupled module system. Importing a package simply states that the consuming bundle depends on the specified package, regardless of the bundles that provide it. At runtime a bundle's package dependencies are resolved and bundles are wired together, based on rules that include package names, versions, and matching attributes. This approach effectively eliminates the *classpath hell* problem while simultaneously providing significant class loading performance improvements and decreased coupling.

No code is an island. All this loose coupling comes at a price. In a traditional Java system, if you wanted to use some functionality, you would simply reference the required types. The tightly coupled approach is simple but limiting. In a scenario that demands more flexibility this is not possible. The Java community is littered with ad hoc and partial solutions to this: Context class loaders, `Class.forName`, "services" lookup, log appenders—all are examples of mechanisms put in place to enable collaboration between loosely coupled elements.

While the importing and exporting of packages express static contracts, *services* are used to facilitate dynamic collaboration. A service is simply an object that implements a contract, a type, and is registered with the OSGi service registry. Bundles looking to use a service need only import the package defining the contract and discover the service implementation in the service registry. Note that the consuming bundle does not know the implementation type or producing bundle since the service interface and implementation may come from different bundles—the system is collaborative yet remains loosely coupled.

Services are dynamic in nature: A bundle dynamically registers and unregisters services that it provides, and it dynamically acquires and releases the services that it consumes. Some bundles are service providers, some are service consumers, and others are both providers and consumers.

In many ways OSGi can be thought of as an extension to the Java programming language that allows package visibility and package dependency constraints to be specified at development time and enforced at runtime. Through these constraints it is easier to build applications that are composed of loosely coupled and highly cohesive components.

2.3 The Anatomy of a Bundle

A bundle is a self-describing collection of files, as shown in Figure 2-4.

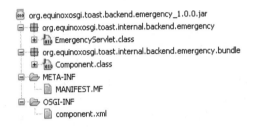

Figure 2–4 Bundle anatomy

The specification of a bundle's contents and requirements is given in its manifest file, META-INF/MANIFEST.MF. The manifest follows the standard JAR manifest syntax but adds a number of OSGi-specific headers. The manifest for the org.equinoxosgi.toast.backend.emergency bundle from the figure looks like this:

```
org.equinoxosgi.toast.backend.emergency/MANIFEST.MF
Manifest-Version: 1.0
Bundle-ManifestVersion: 2
Bundle-SymbolicName: org.equinoxosgi.toast.backend.emergency
Bundle-Version: 1.0.0
Import-Package: javax.servlet;version="2.4.0",
  javax.servlet.http;version="2.4.0",
  org.equinoxosgi.toast.core;version="1.0.0",
  org.equinoxosgi.toast.core.emergency;version="1.0.0",
  org.osgi.service.component;version="1.0.0",
  org.osgi.service.http;version="1.2.0"
Export-Package: org.equinoxosgi.toast.backend.emergency.internal;
  version="1.0.0";x-internal:=true,
  org.equinoxosgi.toast.backend.emergency.internal.bundle;
  version="1.0.0";x-internal:=true
Bundle-RequiredExecutionEnvironment: J2SE-1.4
Bundle-Copyright: Copyright (c) 2009 equinoxosgi.org
Bundle-Name: Toast Back End Emergency
Bundle-Vendor: equinoxosgi.org
```

All bundle manifests must have the headers Bundle-SymbolicName and Bundle-Version. The combination of these headers uniquely identifies the bundle to

OSGi frameworks, developers, and provisioning systems. A bundle also expresses its modularity through headers such as `Export-Package`, `Import-Package`, and `Require-Bundle`. Additional headers such as `Bundle-Copyright`, `Bundle-Name`, and `Bundle-Vendor` are purely documentation. Throughout the book we'll introduce additional headers as they arise in the tutorial.

A bundle can contain Java types, native libraries, or other, nonexecutable files. The content and structure of a bundle depend entirely on what it is delivering and how it is being used. Most bundles deliver Java code to be executed by a Java runtime. These are structured as JARs with the Java code in a package-related folder structure (e.g., `org/equinoxosgi/toast/core/Delay.class`).

Bundles that deliver non-Java content (e.g., source, documentation, or static web content) are structured to suit the mechanism consuming their content. For example, native executables and files being accessed from other programs must reside directly on disk rather than nested inside JAR files. OSGi framework implementations such as Equinox facilitate this by supporting *folder-based* bundles. Folder-based bundles are essentially just JAR bundles that have been extracted.

2.4 Modularity

An OSGi bundle provides a clear definition of its modularity—this includes its identity, its requirements, and its capabilities. The `Bundle-SymbolicName` and `Bundle-Version` manifest headers take care of defining identity. A bundle can have a number of different capabilities and requirements. The most common pattern is to express these dependencies in terms of Java packages. Bundle developers can also specify dependencies on whole bundles.

2.4.1 Exporting a Package

To give access to Java types in a bundle, the bundle must export the package containing the types; that is, OSGi's unit of Java dependency is the Java package. Bundles can export any number of packages. By exporting a package, the bundle is saying that it is able and willing to supply that package to other bundles. Exported packages form the public API of the bundle. Packages that are not exported are considered to be private implementation details of the bundle and are not accessible to others. This is a powerful concept and one of the reasons that OSGi's component model is so appealing.

A bundle that uses the `Export-Package` header to export several packages is shown in the following manifest snippet. Notice that the packages are specified in a comma-separated list and that a version number can be specified for each package. Each package is versioned independently.

```
org.equinoxosgi.toast.core/MANIFEST.MF
Bundle-SymbolicName: org.equinoxosgi.toast.core
Bundle-Version: 1.0.0
Export-Package: org.equinoxosgi.toast.core;version=1.2.3,
 org.equinoxosgi.toast.core.services;version=8.4.2
```

2.4.2 Importing a Package

Exporting a package makes it visible to other bundles, but these other bundles must declare their dependency on the package. This is done using the `Import-Package` header.

The following manifest snippet shows a bundle that imports several packages. As with exports, the set of imported packages is given as a comma-separated list. Notice here that the import for each package can be qualified with a *version range*. The range specifies an upper and lower bound on exported versions that will satisfy the requirements of this bundle. Versions, version ranges, and dependency management are discussed throughout the book as they form a key part of developing, maintaining, and deploying modular systems.

```
org.equinoxosgi.toast.core/MANIFEST.MF
Bundle-SymbolicName: org.equinoxosgi.toast.core
Bundle-Version: 1.0.0
Import-Package: org.osgi.framework;version="[1.3,2.0.0)"
 org.osgi.service.cm;version="[1.2.0,2.0.0)"
```

2.4.3 Requiring a Bundle

It is also possible to specify a dependency on an entire bundle using a `Require-Bundle` header, as shown in the following manifest fragment:

```
org.equinoxosgi.toast.dev.airbag.fake/MANIFEST.MF
Bundle-Name: Toast Fake Airbag
Bundle-SymbolicName: org.equinoxosgi.toast.dev.airbag.fake
Bundle-Version: 1.0.0
Import-Package: org.eclipse.core.runtime.jobs,
 org.equinoxosgi.toast.core;version="[1.0.0,2.0.0)",
 org.equinoxosgi.toast.dev.airbag;version="[1.0.0,2.0.0)"
Require-Bundle: org.eclipse.equinox.common; bundle-version="3.5.0"
```

With this approach, a bundle is wired directly to the prerequisite bundle and all packages it exports. This is convenient but reduces the ability to deploy bundles in different scenarios. For example, if the required bundle is not, or cannot be, deployed, the bundle will not resolve, whereas the actual package needed may be available in a different bundle that can be deployed.

Requiring bundles can be useful when refactoring existing systems or where one bundle acts as a façade for a set of other bundles. Requiring a bundle also allows for the specification of dependencies between modules that do not deliver Java code and so do not export or import packages.

THE HISTORY OF Require-Bundle

Historically, Eclipse projects use Require-Bundle because that is what the original Eclipse runtime supported. Now that Eclipse is OSGi-based, many of these bundles would be better off using Import-Package. This is happening over time as the need for this additional flexibility is recognized.

2.4.4 Enforcing Modularity

Given these capability and requirements statements, the OSGi framework *resolves* the dependencies and wires bundles together at runtime. Modularity in an OSGi system is enforced through a combination of wires and standard Java language visibility rules. To manage this, the framework gives each bundle its own class loader. This keeps separate the classes from the different bundles. When a bundle is uninstalled or updated, its class loader, and all classes loaded by it, are discarded. Having separate class loaders allows the system to have multiple versions of the same class loaded simultaneously. It also enforces the standard Java type visibility rules, such as package visible and public, protected and private, in a bundle world.

2.5 Modular Design Concepts

Given these constructs, how do we talk about OSGi-based applications? One way is to look at the abstraction hierarchy:

Application > Bundle > Package > Type > Method

This shows that a bundle is an abstraction that is bigger than a package but smaller than an application. In other words, an application is composed of bundles; bundles are composed of packages; packages are composed of types; and types are composed of methods. So, just as a type is composed of methods that implement its behavior, an application is composed of bundles that implement its behavior. The task of decomposing an application into bundles is similar to that of decomposing an application into types and methods.

Another way to talk about OSGi-based systems is to talk about decomposition. Key to high-quality design at all levels is the decomposition used. We talk about and measure decomposition along three axes: granularity, coupling, and cohesion. Here we relate these terms to the OSGi environment:

Granularity—Granularity is the measure of how much code and other content is in a bundle. Coarse-grained bundles are easy to manage but are inflexible and bloat the system. Fine-grained bundles give ultimate control but require more attention. Choosing the right granularity for your bundles is a balance of these tensions. Big is not necessarily bad, nor small, good. In some ways granularity is the overarching consequence of coupling and cohesion.

Coupling—Coupling is an outward view of the number of relationships between a bundle and the rest of the system. A bundle that is highly coupled requires many other bundles and generally makes many assumptions about its surrounding context. On the other hand, loosely coupled bundles operate independently and offer you the flexibility to compose your application to precisely meet your changing requirements without dragging in unnecessary dependencies.

Cohesion—Cohesion is an inward view of the relevance of the elements of a bundle to one another. In a highly cohesive bundle, all parts of the bundle are directly related to, and focused on, addressing a defined, narrowly focused topic. Low-cohesion bundles are ill-defined dumping grounds of random content. Highly cohesive bundles are easier to test and reuse, and they enable you to deliver just the function you need and nothing more. A common pitfall is to consider a bundle to be either an entire subsystem or an entire layer in the application's architecture, for example, the domain model or the user interface. A highly cohesive bundle often provides a solution to part, but not all, of a problem.

These ideas are not unique to OSGi—they are tenets of good design practices and fundamental to object-oriented and agile approaches. In the case of OSGi, however, the system is designed to expose and enforce key aspects of coupling, cohesion, and granularity, making the benefits directly tangible. OSGi encourages you to decompose your application into right-grained bundles that are loosely coupled and highly cohesive.

2.6 Lifecycle

OSGi is fundamentally a dynamic technology. Bundles can be installed, started, stopped, updated, and uninstalled in a running system. To support this, bundles must have a clear lifecycle, and developers need ways of listening to and hooking into the various lifecycle states of a bundle (see Fig. 2-5).

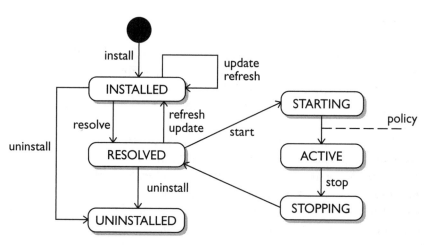

Figure 2–5   Bundle lifecycle

Every bundle starts it runtime life in the *installed* state. From there it becomes *resolved* if all of its dependencies are met. Once a bundle is resolved, its classes can be loaded and run. If a bundle is subsequently started and transitions to the *active* state, it can participate in its lifecycle by having an *activator*. Using the activator, the bundle can initialize itself, acquire required resources, and hook in with the rest of the system. At some point—for example, on system shutdown—active bundles get stopped. Bundles with activators have a chance to free any resources they may have allocated. Bundles transition back to the resolved state when they are stopped. From there they may be restarted or *uninstalled*, at which time they are no longer available for use in the system.

All of this state changing surfaces as a continuous flow of events. Bundles support dynamic behavior by listening to these events and responding to the changes. For example, when a new bundle is installed, other bundles may be interested in its contributions.

The OSGi framework dispatches events when the state of the bundles, the services, or the framework itself changes.

Service events—Fired when a service is registered, modified, or unregistered

Bundle events—Fired when the state of the framework's bundles changes, for example, when a bundle is installed, resolved, starting, started, stopping, stopped, unresolved, updated, uninstalled, or lazily activated

Framework events—Fired when the framework is started; an error, warning, or info event has occurred; the packages contributing to the framework have been refreshed; or the framework's start level has changed

2.7 Collaboration

OSGi-based systems are composed of self-describing bundles as outlined previously. Bundles can collaborate by directly referencing types in other bundles. That is a simple pattern familiar to all Java programmers, but such systems are tightly coupled and miss out on the real power of modularity—loose coupling and dynamic behavior.

To loosen the coupling between modules, there must be a collaboration mechanism, a third party, that acts as an intermediary and keeps the collaborators at arm's length. The typical OSGi mechanism for this is the *service registry*. Equinox, of course, supports the service registry but also adds the *Extension Registry*. These complementary approaches are outlined in the following sections and discussed in more detail throughout the book.

2.7.1 Services

The OSGi service registry acts like a global bulletin board of functions coordinating three parties: bundles that define service interfaces, bundles that implement and register service objects, and bundles that discover and use services. The service registry makes these collaborations anonymous—the bundle providing a service does not know who is consuming it, and a bundle consuming a service does not know what provided it. For example, Figure 2-6 shows Bundle C that declares an interface used by Bundle B to register a service. Bundle A discovers and uses the service while remaining unaware of, and therefore decoupled from, Bundle B. Bundle A depends only on Bundle C.

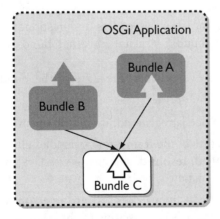

Figure 2–6   Service-based collaboration

Services are defined using a Java type, typically a Java interface. The type must be public and reside in a package that is exported. Other bundles—and perhaps even the same bundle—then implement the service interface, instantiate it, and register the instance with the service registry under the name of the service interface. The classes that implement the service, being implementation details, generally are not contained in packages that are exported.

Finally, a third set of bundles consumes the available services by importing the package containing the service interface and looking up the service in the service registry by the interface name. Having obtained a matching service object, a consuming bundle can use the service until done with it or the service is unregistered. Note that multiple bundles can consume the same service object concurrently, and multiple service objects may be provided by one or more bundles.

The dynamic aspect of service behavior is often managed in conjunction with the lifecycle of the bundles involved. For example, when a bundle is started, it discovers its required services and instantiates and registers the services it provides. Similarly, when a bundle is stopped, its bundle activator unregisters contributed services and releases any services being consumed.

2.7.2 Extensions and Extension Points

The Equinox Extension Registry is a complementary mechanism for supporting inter-bundle collaboration. Under this model, bundles can open themselves for extension or configuration by declaring an *extension point*. Such a bundle is essentially saying, "If you give me the following information, I will do . . . ." Other bundles then *contribute* the required information to the extension point in the form of *extensions*.

In this book we use the example of an extensible web portal that allows actions to be contributed and discovered via the Extension Registry. In this approach the portal bundle declares an `actions` extension point and a contract that says,

> "Bundles can contribute `actions` extensions that define portal actions with a path, a label, and a class that implements the interface `IPortalAction`. The portal will present the given label to the user organized according to the given path and such that when the user clicks on the label, a particular URL will be accessed. As a result of the URL request, the portal will instantiate the given action class, cast it to `IPortalAction`, and call its `execute` method."

Figure 2-7 shows this relationship graphically.

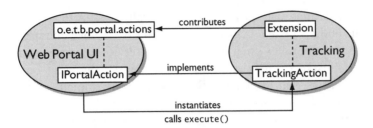

Figure 2–7   Extension contribution and use

Extension-to-extension-point relationships are defined using XML in a file called `plugin.xml`. Each participating bundle has one of these files. As bundles are resolved in the system, their extensions and extension points are loaded into the Extension Registry and made available to other bundles. A full set of Extension Registry events is broadcast to registered listeners along the way. Extension and extension points can also be managed programmatically.

2.8 The OSGi Framework

The modularity mechanisms described previously are largely implemented by the *OSGi Framework*. As such, an OSGi application is a collection of one or more bundles executing in an OSGi framework. The framework takes care of all the dependency resolution, class loading, service registrations, and event management.

TERMINOLOGY

The phrases "the OSGi framework," "the OSGi runtime," and "the service platform" are often used interchangeably and are typically abbreviated to just "the framework," "the runtime," or "the platform."

The framework is reified in a running system as the *System Bundle*. Representing the OSGi framework as a bundle allows us to view the entire platform consistently as a collection of collaborating bundles. While the System Bundle is clearly special, it contains a manifest, exports packages, provides and consumes services, and broadcasts and listens to events like any other bundle.

The System Bundle differs from other bundles in that its lifecycle cannot be managed. It is started automatically when the framework is started and continues in the active state until the framework is stopped. Stopping the System Bundle causes the framework to shut down. Similarly, the System Bundle cannot be uninstalled while running, since doing so would cause the framework to terminate.

The other bundles in an OSGi system are installed into the framework and started as needed. The set of installed bundles in a framework is persisted from run to run—when the framework is shut down and relaunched, the same set of bundles is present and started in the new framework. As such, bundles need to be installed and started only once.

Interestingly, the framework specification does not say how the framework itself is started or how the initial set of bundles is installed. In general it is envisioned that there is an external management agent installing and uninstalling, and starting and stopping, bundles. This may be a central service provider, systems integrator, provisioning agent, or the end user. This approach is powerful, as it makes the framework equally applicable in a wide range of scenarios.

The framework also supplies some rudimentary data management facilities. Each bundle is given its own data area to use as required. The data written in this area is persisted for as long as the bundle is installed in the framework.

2.9 Security

The OSGi specifications include security as a fundamental element. In addition to the standard Java 2 permissions, OSGi-specific permissions are defined throughout the framework and supplemental services. For example, with the system running in secure mode, bundles require distinct permissions to register and look up services and access properties.

The permissions in a system are managed by special-purpose services such as the Conditional Permissions Admin service. This service can be used to manage permissions on a per-bundle basis by, for example, giving bundles certain permissions if they are digitally signed by particular parties. In addition, the User Admin service facilitates the management of user-level or application permissions based on the current user's identity and role.

The real value of the OSGi permission model is that it is used throughout the entire framework and service set.

2.10 OSGi Framework Implementations

At the time of this writing there have been four major revisions of the OSGi specifications. Over the ten-year history of OSGi there have been many implementations. The current R4.x specifications are implemented by several open-source and commercial entities:

Equinox—Perhaps the most widely used open-source OSGi implementation, Equinox is the base runtime for all Eclipse tooling, rich client, server-side, and embedded projects. It is also the reference implementation for the core framework specification, several service specifications, and JSR 291. It is available under the Eclipse Public License from http://eclipse.org/equinox.

Felix—Originally the Oscar project, the Felix open-source project at Apache supplies a framework implementation as well as several service implementations. It is available under the Apache License v2 from http://felix.apache.org.

Knopflerfish—The Knopflerfish open-source project supplies an R4.x framework implementation as well as several service implementations. It is available under a BSD-style license from http://knopflerfish.org.

mBedded Server—This commercial R4.x implementation from ProSyst is used in a number of embedded application areas. ProSyst offers several additional service implementations. It is available under commercial terms from http://prosyst.com.

Concierge—Concierge is an open-source highly optimized and minimized R3.0 specification implementation that is suitable for use in small embedded scenarios. It is available under a BSD-style license from http://concierge .sourceforge.net.

Despite the many features and functions included in the base framework, implementations are very small and run on minimal JVM implementations. Concierge weighs in at a mere 80K disk footprint. The base specification-compliant parts of R4.x implementations tend to have a 300–600K disk footprint. Implementations such as Equinox include considerable additional functionality such as enhanced flexibility, advanced signature management, and high scalability in their base JARs but still stay under 1M on disk.

2.11 Summary

The OSGi framework specification is a good example of power through simplicity and consistency. The technology is based on a small number of simple but general notions such as modularity and services. OSGi's origins in the embedded world drive a minimalist approach that is present throughout the specification.

It is this simplicity that allows the framework to be extended and applied in a wide range of situations. This is the key value in OSGi—its universality. The Eclipse adoption of OSGi and its subsequent spread to use in the rich client and now server world bring real power to Java developers and system integrators.

PART II

OSGi by Example

The best way to learn about the power of OSGi and Equinox is to build a real system. This part of the book guides you through just that. Starting with a blank machine, we walk through setting up Eclipse for OSGi development and then creating, running, debugging, and enhancing a reasonably full-featured fleet management system called Toast. The screen shots here show an example of the Toast in-vehicle client you will build.

The material in Part II is presented in an informal tutorial style—as if we were sitting with you and guiding you through Toast's development. You are encouraged to follow along and do the steps described. If you would rather not follow the steps, or are having difficulties, the completed code for each section is also available in an easy-to-use Samples Manager. Even though the chapters are very development oriented, the text for each chapter is complete and can be read without following the steps or looking at the supplied code.

CHAPTER 3

Tutorial Introduction

This chapter guides you on the journey of developing a fully functional OSGi-based application, Toast. Using the same application throughout the book adds to the coherence of the samples and more closely matches the situations encountered in real-world software development. The principles and practices discussed throughout are applicable in a wide range of application domains and execution scenarios. Before getting down to the nuts and bolts of Toast development, we set the stage for the application by outlining its nature and evolution. We also ensure that you are set up with a working development environment.

This chapter focuses on three major issues:

○ Outlining the sample application and sketching its evolution

○ Setting up your Eclipse IDE so you can develop the code yourself

○ Getting and using the Samples Manager to compare and manage the sample code

3.1 What Is Toast?

Toast is a sample application in the *telematics* and fleet management domain. If you're unfamiliar with the term, you're almost certainly familiar with the concept. Wikipedia has the following to say about telematics:

> [Telematics is] the integrated use of telecommunications and informatics. More specifically it is the science of sending, receiving and storing information via telecommunication devices.

You will have seen this in car navigation and *infotainment* devices. A typical telematics system interfaces to the devices in the vehicle and provides a user interface for interacting with or managing the devices. More sophisticated systems connect to a fleet management control center over a wireless network and allow remote control of the devices.

In its finished form, Toast covers all of these bases—it interfaces to a simulated GPS and airbag, integrates with Google Earth, and communicates with an OSGi-based fleet management control center using a variety of protocols.

At a high level, Toast consists of a *client* and a *back end*. The Toast Client provides a variety of functionality, including an emergency application that notifies the control center of the vehicle's GPS location when the airbag deploys, an application that tracks the vehicle's GPS location and periodically notifies the control center, a touch screen interface to control the vehicle's audio and climate systems, and a turn-by-turn navigation system.

The Toast Back End is developed over the course of the book from a simple emergency monitoring station to an extensible fleet management platform for managing and controlling vehicles. This includes vehicle discovery, tracking, and software management or provisioning.

The attractiveness of Toast as an example goes beyond the familiarity of telematics, fleet management, and the functionality of the various applications. It is compellingly extensible—we can reasonably explore a number of technologies without *making it up*. More important, this range of scenarios enables us to discuss a variety of real-world OSGi-related challenges:

Bundle granularity—A deployed Toast system, including the in-vehicle client, the device simulators, and the control center, amounts to over 100 bundles. That may seem like a lot, but this architecture both is representative of real systems and allows us to demonstrate a number of best practices in dealing with large numbers of interdependent bundles.

Third-party libraries—Most real-world applications make use of third-party code; Toast is no exception. The full Toast application uses libraries from Eclipse, Apache, the broader Java open-source community, as well as Google JavaScript. We walk you through the process of incorporating non-OSGi-aware third-party libraries into an OSGi-based application and detail the issues to watch for.

Dynamic installation and removal of functionality—Toast is a highly dynamic application with functionality being installed and removed, servers and clients interacting, and user input being handled. Through this example we show how to write bundles that adapt to the appearance of new functionality and to the removal or updating of dependencies. We also show how to use p2, the latest deployment implementation in Equinox, to manage executable Equinox profiles.

Extensibility and collaboration—As you walk through the development of Toast, you'll see a number of approaches to extensibility and collaboration, including services, Declarative Services, the Whiteboard Pattern, the Equinox Extension Registry, and more. Writing new functionality is relatively straightforward, and Toast combines this with support for the dynamic installation and removal of applications to create a powerful software platform.

Testing and simulation strategies—Throughout the book, Toast develops into a reasonably complex application. Accordingly, we provide examples and best practices for automated testing, from POJO (plain old Java object) development to using mock objects and JUnit in OSGi-based system tests. We also show how to test against simulated devices for situations where real device hardware is either unavailable or cannot be used economically. Deploying real airbags can get very expensive!

Off-board communications—Very few systems today stand alone. Most eventually communicate to off-board servers, peers, or subsystems. For example, Toast clients use HTTP to communicate with the control center running the Jetty web server. The device simulator uses a similar approach but embeds a small web server in the vehicle itself. Provisioning is done using the Eclipse Communications Framework (ECF) to talk to software repositories.

Graphical and web-based user interfaces—Using OSGi certainly does not require a user interface; many real-world applications are "headless." Nevertheless, Toast provides a number of UI examples—the graphical user interface intended for an in-vehicle touch screen, a simple web UI for the control center, and JavaScript web-based UI for the device simulator.

Finally, Toast is fun. It is simple and easily understood, yet rich enough to provide a basis for a variety of applications and technology integrations. The lessons learned in developing Toast are readily applicable to other domains and applications.

TOAST IS ALSO AT ECLIPSE

Putting together Toast has been very informative and gratifying. As we show it to other people at Eclipse, they have lots of great ideas for how to extend and improve it. To facilitate this we have donated a snapshot of Toast, the code as of Chapter 14, to the Examples project at Eclipse. We fully hope and expect that it will evolve beyond the example you see here. See http://wiki.eclipse.org/Toast for more information.

3.2 The Evolution of Toast

In Part II we develop Toast over a number of tutorial chapters. Each chapter presents a new concept and makes incremental progress over the preceding chapter. As development progresses, we supply the code for each iteration. Where it helps to clarify the discussion, the chapter text includes code snippets. The Samples Manager, available from http://equinoxosgi.org, contains the complete code for each chapter and allows you to perform each step on your own, browse the code, or simply read the text.

Hello, Toast (Chapter 4)—The tutorial starts with an empty workspace and walks you through creating a simple emergency application—whenever the airbag deploys, the GPS location is read and displayed along with an emergency message. This simple example is then split into three bundles and the reasoning and tooling explained. By the end of this section, you will have a running application based on a collection of OSGi bundles.

Services (Chapter 5)—This chapter moves beyond the notion of bundles and presents the concept of services and inter-bundle collaboration. More than just code libraries, bundles can register services with the OSGi service registry, allowing other bundles to make use of their provided functionality without being tightly coupled.

Dynamic Services (Chapter 6)—Here we introduce the idea that bundles and services can come and go throughout the lifetime of a running system. This dynamic behavior is one of the hallmarks of OSGi-based systems and figures heavily in many of the design and implementation decisions you make. In this discussion we first present OSGi Service Trackers, followed by a review of a third-party toolkit for service management called the Service Activator Toolkit (SAT). Finally, we present OSGi's Declarative Services (DS). DS is adopted for the remainder of the tutorial. At the end of this section, Toast embraces the dynamic nature of the scenario.

Client/Server Interaction (Chapter 7)—At this point Toast operates as a stand-alone OSGi application. To fully implement the emergency scenario, we need a control center to receive emergency notifications. In this chapter we implement the control center as a separate OSGi system. We use HTTP for the communication between the client system and the control center. By chapter's end, Toast runs on separate machines, and the emergency application sends emergency information to the control center.

Testing (Chapter 8)—Even though there is little complex domain logic in Toast at this point, we can begin to write tests for what we do have. This chapter uses EasyMock and JUnit to test the domain logic in the emergency scenario. This demonstrates that when domain logic is clearly separated from the OSGi plumbing, the barrier to creating a suite of automated tests is significantly lowered. We also show how to write OSGi-based system tests.

Packaging (Chapter 9)—It's time to snip the strings and export Toast so it runs outside the workspace and can be distributed to others. In this chapter you will learn how to build, publish, and zip signed and otherwise exported bundles from your workspace. We also show you how to combine them with prebuilt bundles from others and ultimately distribute your system.

Pluggable Services (Chapter 10)—At this point in Toast, we have only mocked up the devices in our application. In this chapter we add a device simulator that presents a simple web user interface, allowing you to virtually operate the vehicle devices (e.g., GPS and airbag) and thus interact with Toast subsystems. This chapter demonstrates how to structure your system to allow for the pluggability of alternate implementations of the same service.

Extensible User Interface (Chapter 11)—From an end-user perspective Toast is pretty boring so far. Here we add a Standard Widget Toolkit (SWT)-based graphical user interface that allows users to operate the installed Toast Client subsystems. We also add support for audio and climate control and integrate Google Earth for navigation mapping and guidance support. These additions demonstrate a number of interesting OSGi topics, and we are careful to point these out.

Dynamic Configuration (Chapter 12)—Toast is designed to be highly configurable. In this chapter you will learn how to manage this configurability using the OSGi Configuration Admin service by way of an example. We add to Toast a new application that tracks the vehicle's location and periodically reports to the control center. It uses OSGi's Configuration Admin service to determine how often the tracking application reports to the control center.

Web Portal (Chapter 13)—In this chapter we add a web UI to the control center. While the web UI itself is quite simple, we create an extensible portal to demonstrate how to effectively use Declarative Services and the Whiteboard Pattern.

System Deployment with p2 (Chapter 14)—A key aspect of OSGi-based systems is their flexibility in deployment. Telematics systems in particular benefit from the ability to remotely manage the software and information. This chapter introduces and demonstrates the use of the Equinox p2 provisioning platform to install, configure, update, and remove functionality from a Toast system.

3.3 Development Environment Installation

The code in this book has been developed and tested using the Galileo SR1 release of Eclipse. You can get this from http://eclipse.org/downloads. Since Eclipse is a tooling platform, several different configurations are available. The Eclipse team has put together a tooling configuration specifically for people building bundle-based applications—people like you—the "Eclipse for RCP/Plug-in Developers" package. Despite the name, this is a comprehensive set of tools for writing OSGi bundles. More generally, any of the packages that include the Java Development Tools (JDT) or Plug-in Development Environment (PDE) will work fine.

Each package is available for a variety of machine configurations and is mirrored across the globe. Choose the appropriate package, platform, and mirror and download the tooling.

Having downloaded Eclipse, extract the file to a location of your choosing. In the examples we assume you have extracted it to `c:\ide`.

OBTAINING A JAVA RUNTIME ENVIRONMENT

The Eclipse downloads do not include a Java Runtime Environment (JRE) or Java Software Development Kit (SDK). Many systems include an acceptable JRE. If yours does not, http://eclipse.org/downloads/moreinfo/jre.php provides information on getting a suitable JRE.

For the work in this book, it is convenient to have a Java SDK (sometimes called a JDK), as it includes much of the Java source, convenient for debugging, and a couple of handy tools such as `jarsigner`.

To start Eclipse, run the Eclipse application launcher (`eclipse.exe` or `eclipse`, depending on your operating system). As Eclipse starts, you'll be prompted for a workspace location. The workspace is the place your development artifacts are stored. It is typically a good idea to locate the workspace somewhere separate from the Eclipse installation. This simplifies the management of multiple workspaces as well as changing versions of Eclipse. By default a location in your user directory (e.g., `c:\Documents and Settings\Administrator\workspace`) will be suggested. This is a fine choice if you are just starting out.

3.4 Sample Code

As mentioned earlier, Toast ultimately ends up including many bundles. Many of these evolve quite a bit as the tutorial and deep-dive chapters progress. It turns out that managing a dozen different versions of the same bundles in coherent sets is quite complicated. To help with this, we supply a *Samples Manager* tool to help you both manage the sample code and move from sample to sample.

The Samples Manager includes all of the code and resources for each sample. To install the Samples Manager, run your Eclipse IDE and follow these steps:

○ Open the **Software Updates** dialog using **Help > Install New Software....**

○ On the **Available Software** page click the **Add...** button to add a new software site.

○ In the dialog, enter `http://equinoxosgi.org`, the location of the book's software site, and click **OK**.

○ Expand the tree for the **Equinox OSGi Book** site and select the **Samples Manager**. Pick the most recent version available. (You may need to uncheck the **Group Items by Category** option to see it.)

○ Click **Next** and go through the following pages of the wizard, carefully reading and accepting the licenses and warnings. After the Samples Manager is installed, a restart dialog appears. Select **Restart**.

3.4.1 *Moving from Chapter to Chapter*

When the Samples Manager is installed, an **OSGi/Equinox** menu appears on the main menu bar. Run the tool by selecting **OSGi/Equinox > Samples Manager**, and the Samples Manager view as shown in Figure 3-1 will appear.

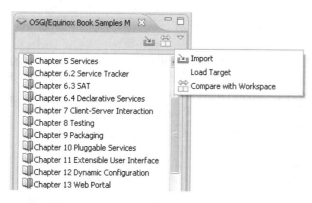

Figure 3–1 Samples Manager

The list shows all chapters of the book that have associated sample code. Note that some chapters have multiple samples. Select a sample and click **Import** on the toolbar or in the context menu to load all projects related to the selected sample into the workspace.

One goal of the Samples Manager is to ensure that you can move from sample to sample smoothly and with a clean slate. If you have a problem, you can simply reload. As such, the Samples Manager deletes all sample projects that it previously loaded before loading the new projects. It also cleans up the launch configurations related to the samples. This ensures that your workspace contains only the projects for one sample and is in a known state.

YOUR CONTENT MAY BE DISCARDED

When moving to a new sample, the Samples Manager deletes old sample projects even if you have changed them. So your intermediate results may be discarded.

The **Samples Manager** view highlights the chapter that you have loaded to remind you what is in the workspace. The Samples Manager's Help content includes the most recent instructions and tips for its use.

3.4.2 Comparing

The Samples Manager also supports comparing the workspace to the set of projects for a sample. This is extremely useful when you are following the tutorial steps. For example, while doing Chapter 7, you may find that something is not working or the steps are unclear. Comparing the workspace to the Chapter 7 sample tells you what is left to do or where your setup is different from the expected outcome.

Similarly, you can selectively load parts of a solution into the workspace. Several chapters require sets of resources or large chunks of code that you are not expected to create on your own. Use the Samples Manager's comparison tool, as shown in Figure 3-2, and the **Copy into Workspace** action to select files and folders and copy them into the workspace.

Notice that the compare editor distinguishes between files that have changes and those that exist in only one location. Changes are highlighted in the lower area, and there is a minus sign (-) if a file does not exist in the workspace but does exist in the comparison chapter. Conversely, a plus sign (+) is shown if a file exists only in the workspace. So in this example, the Bundle-Activator header was removed when moving to Sample 6.4 and the Service-Component header was added.

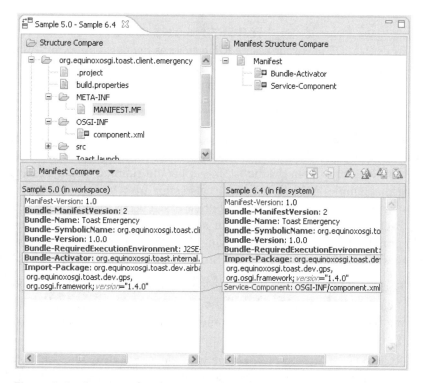

Figure 3–2   Comparing Sample 5 to Sample 6.4

THINK THIS IS BACKWARDS?

Some readers may think that this is backwards. Think of the compare editor as telling you what the workspace has or does not have compared to the other sample you selected.

3.5 Target Platform Setup

Before starting to write code, you need to set up the workspace's *target platform*. The target platform is the set of bundles against which your code is compiled and from which you will create your systems. The target is distinct from the bundles that happen to make up your Eclipse tooling. In our case, the target includes mostly just the Equinox bundles needed to implement Toast. We can add and remove bundles in the target without affecting the tools.

TARGETING THE IDE

By default PDE uses your Eclipse IDE bundles as the target platform. This is convenient and sufficient for the initial stages of Toast but will quickly become unwieldy. As such, we recommend using a distinct target platform.

PDE includes comprehensive support for defining and managing target platforms. The Samples Manager you installed also includes a predefined target suitable for the examples in this book. To get up and running quickly, load the target using the Samples Manager. You can also start from scratch and assemble your own target definition. We describe both workflows in the following sections.

Eventually Toast will have client and server parts. In the examples you will add graphical UIs and do some testing. The target must have all the supporting bundles needed for these activities. Broadly speaking, you need four things:

Equinox SDK—The Equinox team has put together an all-in-one SDK that includes all the Equinox bundles, along with their source and a few supporting bundles such as Jetty and some Apache pieces. This is the core of what Toast needs.

RCP SDK—Later on in Toast we will add a graphical UI. Although the UI will not technically be an Eclipse RCP application, it will use the Eclipse SWT. We will also use a few utility bundles from the base Eclipse platform. It is easiest just to add the whole RCP SDK to the target.

Delta pack—Equinox supports many different hardware and OS platforms. The binary executable and graphical libraries are platform specific. To ease consumption, the Eclipse team has put together a *delta pack* that contains all of the parts of the basic Eclipse infrastructure that are platform specific. This is of use to Toast when exporting and building.

Testing stuff—In Chapter 8, "Testing," we use libraries such as JUnit and EasyMock. These need to be in the target as well.

3.5.1 *The Predefined Target*

The Samples Manager comes with a handy target that includes all of the components just listed. Carry out the following steps to load the predefined target:

○ Use the **Load Target** entry in the Samples Manager's toolbar menu as shown in Figure 3-1 to initiate the target load. This should show a progress dialog while the target contents are copied into the workspace. When it completes, there will be a project called ToastTarget that contains the target definition and some of the target content.

○ Open the **Target Platform** preferences page, **Window > Preferences > Plug-in Development > Target Platform,** and look for the entry called **Toast Target.** Select the check box beside that entry and click **Apply** or **OK** to use the Toast target.

DO NOT SET THE TARGET THROUGH THE TARGET EDITOR

Targets are defined in .target files. The Toast target is in toast.target in the ToastTarget project you just loaded. We will talk about editing this file in the next section, but here you should be aware of a bug in PDE as of Galileo SR1 (September 2009).

When a target file is opened, the target editor attempts to *resolve* its contents. To do this, it attempts to open all of the bundles in the target. The Toast target refers to some remote software repositories at eclipse.org for some of its bundles. The net result is that when the target file is opened, PDE starts downloading the constituents of the target from some remote server. This can be many megabytes. In many cases this is a bonus—pre-caching the content. However, there is a bug.

Do not click on the **Set as target platform** link in the target editor while the editor is resolving. Doing this causes a race condition that ultimately prevents the target definition from loading.

If you do this by mistake, you will see a dialog reporting a locking or synchronization error. When this happens, close the target editor and restart Eclipse. Then follow the steps for loading the target using the target preferences, or open the editor and wait for it to complete resolving before clicking the link.

Targets in the Workspace

The workflow described in this section results in at least part of the Toast target living in a project in your workspace. In a sense this is strange—the target is all the stuff *not* in your workspace?! It turns out to be very convenient to treat the content of the target as a resource that you can put into source control and share. In the development of the book samples and our work with product teams it is quite common to have a project in the workspace and Software Configuration Management (SCM) system to contain the content and target definition. New team members can simply check out the target. When one team member changes the target, the others need only update. This is complementary to the target platform Software Site facilities described in the following section.

3.5.2 Defining Target Platforms

We recommend that you use the predefined target from the previous section, since it will make things easier later on when we add to the target. But at some point you will have to define your own target for your own projects. This section describes how that is done. If you are up and running with the predefined target, skip this section and treat it as a reference to come back to.

A target platform is just a list of bundles and features from various locations. Sources of content include the following:

Directories—Specifying a directory adds to the target all bundles and features found in that directory. Directories of bundles can be acquired by downloading archives from the web, for example, from eclipse.org.

Installations—Pointing the target at an existing Eclipse install adds all elements of the install to the target platform. This includes linked folders, drop-ins, and any other bundles and features that make up the install.

Features—Adding features is similar to adding a directory but with the added ability to select a subset of features found in the directory. All bundles indicated by the selected features are also added to the target.

Software sites—There are many software repositories around the world. Adding a software site allows you to identify a repository from which bundles and features are loaded.

The predefined Toast target uses directories and software sites in its definition. We will next walk you through the steps we used to create the target platform. In a sidebar in the previous section we talked about having targets in the workspace. We illustrate that approach here. If you would rather not, you can put the target content wherever you like, but the target definition file still has to go somewhere in the workspace.

- ○ Create a simple project using **File > New > Project... > General > Project**. We have called our target project ToastTarget.
- ○ Create a target platform definition using the **File > New > Other > Plug-in Development > Target Definition** wizard.
- ○ Enter a name for the target file and situate it in the new project.
- ○ Notice at the bottom of the wizard that there are several options for initializing your new target. Select the **Nothing** option, as we are building this target from scratch. In other scenarios you may wish to prime your new target with content listed elsewhere.
- ○ Click **Finish** to complete the wizard and open the target editor on the new target definition, as shown in Figure 3-3.

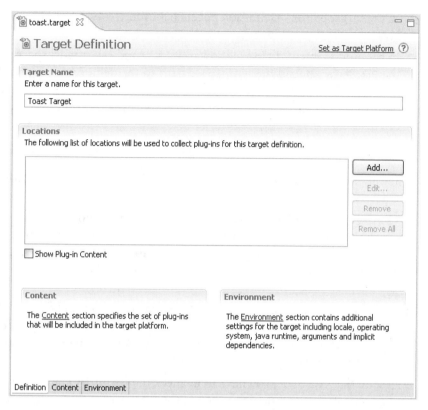

Figure 3–3 Target definition editor

In the editor you can fill in a useful name for the target definition, but the really interesting part is the **Locations** section. For the Toast target we will need to add a directory for the delta pack and a software site for the Equinox and RCP SDKs. Let's do the delta pack first:

○ Get the delta pack by downloading it from the Eclipse project download site, http://download.eclipse.org/eclipse. Choose **Latest Release** from the options given. As of this writing it is 3.5.1.

○ On the subsequent download page, select **Delta Pack** on the left navigation bar. This scrolls the page to the delta pack download link. Notice there is only one link since, by definition, it is all the pieces that are platform dependent. Select the link and save the archive to a convenient spot on your local drive.

○ When the download is complete, create a new folder called delta.pack in the target project and import the downloaded content into the folder using **File > Import... > General > Archive File**.

○ In the target editor's **Definition** page, click **Add...** and select **Directory**. Click **Next**.

○ In the **Add Content** dialog, click **Variables...** and select **workspace_loc** from the list. Now append the workspace path to the delta pack content. For example, the location should look like the following, assuming you called your project `ToastTarget`: `${workspace_loc}/ToastTarget/delta.pack/eclipse`

Next we'll add a software site and get the Equinox and RCP SDKs:

○ In the target editor's **Definition** page, click **Add...** and select **Software Site**. Click **Next**.

○ On the subsequent **Add Software Site** wizard page, choose **Galileo** in the **Work with** drop-down. If there is a more recent release repository available, feel free to choose it. If the site you want is not listed, click the **Add...** button and enter the **Name** and URL **Location** for the site. For example, the Galileo site is at http://download.eclipse.org/releases/galileo.

○ Once the site is selected, the content area of the wizard should fill in as shown in Figure 3-4. Select the **Equinox Project SDK** either by expanding the **EclipseRT Target Platform Components** category or by typing its name in the filter area above the content.

○ To add the RCP SDK, you have to uncheck the **Group by Category** box under the content area and then type RCP in the filter area. Select **Eclipse RCP SDK**.

MULTI-SELECTION MAY NOT WORK

There is a bug in some versions of Eclipse where using the filter can clear the current selection. You may need to add the SDKs individually or not use the filter.

○ **Important! You must uncheck the "Include required software" box** at the bottom left of the wizard. Failure to do this will result in a bloated target that may not work for the Toast scenario.

After you click **Finish**, PDE resolves the target. This may take some time as the content is downloaded from the software site. Once the resolution is com-

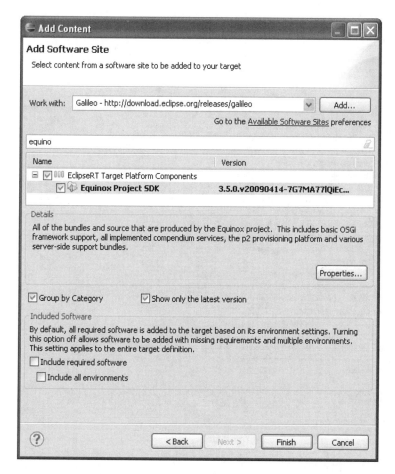

Figure 3–4 Galileo software site content

plete, take a look at the **Content** page of the target editor. You should see something similar to the editor shown in Figure 3-5. Notice that we have left the addition of the testing-related bundles as a further exercise for the reader. Basically you add a directory to the target definition and target and then collect the bundles and features you want. Once the target definition is completed, save the file and click **Set as Target Platform** at the top right.

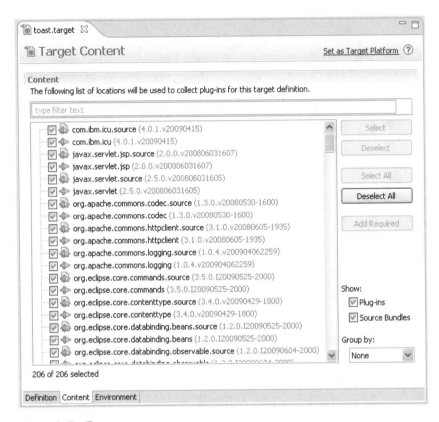

Figure 3–5   Toast target content

3.6 Learning by Example

One of the most efficient and effective ways of figuring out how to program a system is by browsing examples. We can't emphasize this enough. It can be overwhelming, but there are various shortcuts and mechanisms you can use to help follow the code. Here is a short list of the workspace navigation operations we use on a day-to-day basis:

Navigate > Open Type... (**Ctrl+Shift+T**)—Opens the Java type with the name you enter. Wildcards and case-sensitive acronyms, CamelCasing, are supported. Use this to discover where a type is or if it exists.

Navigate > Open Resource... (**Ctrl+Shift+R**)—Opens a resource with the name you enter. Wildcards and case-sensitive acronyms, CamelCasing, are supported. Use this to discover resources and their location.

Open Plug-in Artifact (Ctrl+Shift+A)—Opens the artifact that defines the plug-in or bundle element that you enter. For example, enter the ID of an extension and the `plugin.xml` defining the extension is opened.

Ctrl-3—Presents a condensed list of commands, views, preferences, and other facilities. Simply type some words related to what you need and the list is filtered. For example, typing `targ` finds the target preference page.

Navigate > Quick Type Hierarchy (Ctrl+T)—Pops up a type hierarchy rooted by the type associated with the selection in the current Java editor. For example, if the selection is on a type, a normal type hierarchy is opened. If the selection is on or in a method, all implementers of that method in the hierarchy are shown. Press **Ctrl+T** again to invert the hierarchy.

Search > References > Workspace (Ctrl+Shift+G)—Searches for references to the selected Java element (e.g., type, method, field) in the Java editor. **Ctrl+Shift+U** does the same search but local to the file.

Navigate > Open Declaration (F3)—Opens the declaration of the Java element selected in the current Java editor.

OSGi systems are quite decoupled. That's the whole point! This can, however, make it hard to figure out how various pieces interact. PDE offers various tools and mechanisms for navigating these interconnections. The **Plug-in Development** perspective (**Window > Open Perspective > Other... > Plug-in Development**) includes a Plug-ins view. From this you can easily navigate the dependencies and references. From the PDE plug-in editor you can discover the extension-to-extension-point interconnections, navigate to the classes defined in various extensions, and browse extension point documentation.

ADDING TYPES TO JAVA SEARCH

In the Plug-ins view, select all plug-ins and use the **Add to Java Search** context menu entry or the ✻ view toolbar button to add all known plug-ins to the Java search scope. This is helpful because Java search looks only in projects in the workspace and their dependent projects. This means that if you open an empty workspace and try to open a type, say, using **Ctrl+Shift+T**, the type selection dialog will be empty. By adding all plug-ins in your target platform to the search, you can more easily navigate example code and classes that you do not reference from your projects.

3.7 Summary

Once set up, Eclipse and PDE make it easy to create and run OSGi systems. The setup detailed here is robust in that you can use the IDE to work on many different workspaces, the target platform can be updated independently of the IDE or the workspaces, and the IDE itself can be updated without affecting the workspaces or the target platform.

By adding Samples Manager support, you can jump to any chapter and set up your workspace in seconds. You can also validate the tutorial steps as you go and get quick summaries of all the changes done so far and those left to do.

CHAPTER 4

Hello, Toast

The temptation with any project is to start big. We could architect an entire complex of bundles, fully proving how our application will function before we write a single line of code. But that's not how agile projects evolve. And evolve they do. So much so that often the initial code might be totally unrecognizable by the time the project is finished.

So rather than start with architecture, we'll start with a humble understanding of one simple scenario in the telematics domain. In fact, the first pass at the Toast application will not even concern itself with OSGi at all. By the time this chapter concludes, however, Toast will be built of bundles. In subsequent chapters we'll add functionality to Toast in terms of both telematics and OSGi.

The goals of this chapter are to

○ Create a group of very simple classes that implement one simple telematics scenario

○ Create three bundle projects derived from this initial code base using the PDE tooling

○ Run our three-bundle application using an OSGi launch configuration

4.1 A Simple Scenario

Our first telematics scenario covers the case of emergency notification. Here the vehicle has two devices—an airbag and a GPS. If the airbag deploys, an emergency monitor is notified. The monitor queries the GPS for the vehicle location and notifies an off-board service center about the emergency. For now, we'll just print the vehicle's location on the console.

4.1.1 The Project

Our first foray into creating a project for our code is not the typical path taken when developing for OSGi. We just want to get the function working before worrying about bundles and other OSGi things. As soon as this first non-OSGi iteration of Toast runs, we'll refactor and abandon it for a more modular approach.

As with all the samples in this book, if you'd rather not follow along with the step-by-step instructions, you can simply read along and later load the sample code for "Chapter 4.1 Hello, Toast" using the Samples Manager.

❍ Start by creating a normal Java project. From the workbench select **File > New > Project**, expand **Java**, and select **Java Project** to start the **New Java Project** wizard shown in Figure 4-1.

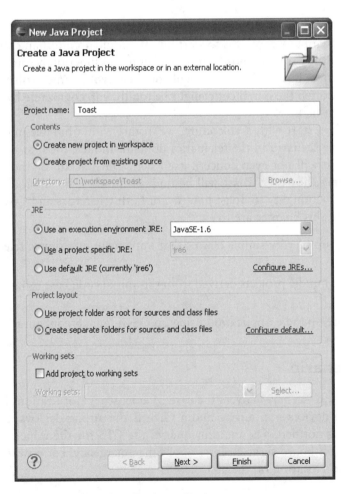

Figure 4–1   New Java Project wizard

○ For the project name, enter Toast. Accept all the other defaults and click **Finish**.

○ You may see a dialog asking you to switch to the Java perspective. If so, just click **Yes**.

4.1.2 Gps

Now we have to create a couple of devices—the GPS and the airbag. Let's create the Gps class first. The Gps class provides APIs for querying the vehicle's location. Since we don't have real GPS hardware with which to communicate, this Gps class will simply return hard-coded values.

○ Create the Gps class by selecting **File > New > Class** to start the **New Java Class** wizard shown in Figure 4-2. Enter Toast/src for the source folder and

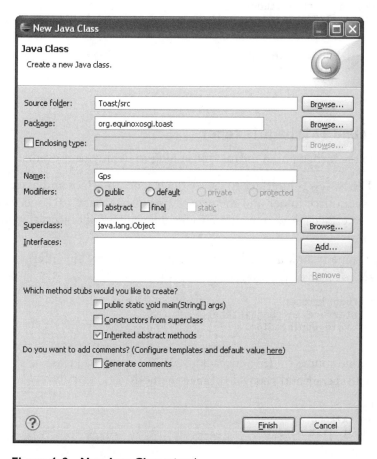

Figure 4–2   New Java Class wizard

org.equinoxosgi.toast for the package. For the class name, enter Gps. With all the other fields in their default values, click **Finish**.

The Gps class is created and a Java editor on the new class opens.

❍ Fill in the content of the Gps class as follows:

Toast/Gps
```
public class Gps {
  public int getHeading() {
    return 90; // 90 degrees (east)
  }

  public int getLatitude() {
    return 3776999; // 37.76999 N
  }

  public int getLongitude() {
    return -12244694; // 122.44694 W
  }

  public int getSpeed() {
    return 50; // 50 kph
  }
}
```

4.1.3 Airbag *and* IAirbagListener

Now define the airbag and a means of listening to deployment events:

❍ Select **File > New > Interface** to create the listener interface and place it in the Toast/src source folder and the org.equinoxosgi.toast package. Having a listener interface allows the airbag to be independent of objects that are interested in it.

❍ Use the same techniques as before, but this time create the interface IAirbagListener as follows:

Toast/AirbagListener
```
public interface IAirbagListener {
  public void deployed();
}
```

In the same source folder and package create an Airbag class as shown here that has addListener and removeListener methods:

Toast/Airbag
```
public class Airbag {
  private List listeners;
```

```
public Airbag() {
  super();
  listeners = new ArrayList();
}

public synchronized void addListener(IAirbagListener listener) {
  listeners.add(listener);
}

public synchronized void deploy() {
  for (Iterator i = listeners.iterator(); i.hasNext();)
    ((IAirbagListener) i.next()).deployed();
}

public synchronized void removeListener(IAirbagListener listener) {
  listeners.remove(listener);
}
}
```

○ To fix any compilation errors, organize Airbag's imports by selecting the file in the **Package Explorer** or opening it in a Java editor and using either **Ctrl+Shift+O** or **Source > Organize Imports** from the context menu. You'll make use of this operation often as you progress through the tutorial.

COMPILER WARNINGS

Having created the Airbag class, you might have noticed some compiler warnings regarding *raw types*. By default the Eclipse compiler's warnings are set to be aware of generic types such as List<E>, ArrayList<E>, and Iterator<E> and will issue warnings when a type is not specified.

○ Since Toast is targeting Java 1.4 and does not use generics, we can safely disable these compiler warnings. Open the preferences dialog by choosing **Window > Preferences,** and then select **Java > Compiler > Errors/Warnings.** Expand the **Generic types** section and change each compiler setting to **Ignore.** Upon clicking **OK,** you will be asked if you wish to perform a full build, to which you should answer **Yes.** (See Figure 4-3.)

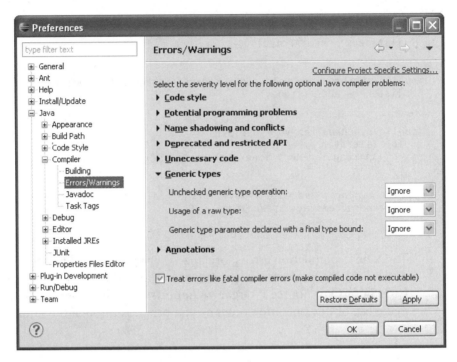

Figure 4–3   Workspace compiler preferences

4.1.4 EmergencyMonitor

With the Gps and Airbag classes and the IAirbagListener interface defined, the next step is to write the emergency monitor logic:

○ Create an EmergencyMonitor class that implements the IAirbagListener interface as follows:

Toast/EmergencyMonitor
```
public class EmergencyMonitor implements IAirbagListener {
  private Airbag airbag;
  private Gps gps;

  public void deployed() {
    System.out.println("Emergency occurred at lat=" + gps.getLatitude()
        + " lon=" + gps.getLongitude() + " heading=" + gps.getHeading()
        + " speed=" + gps.getSpeed());
  }

  public void setAirbag(Airbag value) {
    airbag = value;
  }
```

```
public void setGps(Gps value) {
  gps = value;
}

public void shutdown() {
  airbag.removeListener(this);
}

public void startup() {
  airbag.addListener(this);
}
}
```

The setGps and setAirbag methods allow us to use dependency injection to set the dependencies independent of instantiation. We could have done all of this in a constructor, but as we will see in later chapters, the separation of instantiation and initialization logic is quite useful.

Similarly, the separate startup and shutdown methods further decouple the monitor's lifecycle from the EmergencyMonitor class's instantiation. This, too, will prove to be a useful approach as Toast becomes more and more modular and dynamic.

Notice that the business logic of the monitor is contained mostly in the deployed method. This method satisfies the listener interface and implements the real emergency behavior. All the other methods are infrastructure in support of this code.

BEHAVIORAL SYMMETRY

It's a good practice to make the startup method and the shutdown method symmetrical; that is, whatever behavior startup does, shutdown should undo in *reverse order.*

4.1.5 Main

Now, to run this minimal non-OSGi Toast application, we need a main method that instantiates the three classes, binds them together, and forces the airbag to deploy:

❍ Define the Main class as follows:

Toast/Main
```
public class Main {
  public static void main(String[] args) {
    System.out.println("Launching");
    Gps gps = new Gps();
```

```
        Airbag airbag = new Airbag();
        EmergencyMonitor monitor = new EmergencyMonitor();
        monitor.setGps(gps);
        monitor.setAirbag(airbag);
        monitor.startup();
        airbag.deploy();
        monitor.shutdown();
        System.out.println("Terminating");
    }
}
```

4.1.6 Running

Running the example is simple:

❍ Select the Main class in the **Package Explorer** and use **Run As > Java Application** from the context menu to start Toast.

The Console view displays the following output:

```
Launching
Emergency occurred at lat=3776999 lon=-12244694 heading=90 speed=50
Terminating
```

4.1.7 Checkpoint

At this point Toast is very simple, but it is already starting to show the beginnings of some architectural patterns that will turn out to be very powerful as the system gets larger and more complex—keeping devices independent of business logic to increase cohesion and reduce coupling.

4.2 Slicing Toast into Bundles

At this point Toast is a single project with no OSGi awareness. This relates to what you might see in the real world—many applications start as monoliths or have some minimal homegrown modularity mechanism. As requirements and deployment scenarios grow, so grows the need for modularity. This is when the power of OSGi comes into play.

In this section we slice Toast up into a set of OSGi bundles. Even though Toast is very simple and moving it to OSGi is easy, the patterns and approaches we follow are useful when you are porting your more complex applications to OSGi.

The first step in modularizing an application is identifying its essential structure. This helps you understand the dependencies and identify interactions, and thus define the modules. Consider the diagram in Figure 4-4.

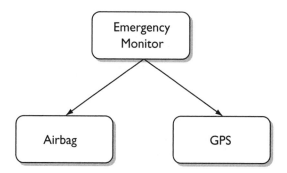

Figure 4–4 Bundle dependencies

Notice that the Emergency Monitor depends on both the GPS and Airbag and that the GPS and Airbag are independent of one another. This is a good clue that our system can be broken into three independent parts. Furthermore, we know the direction of the dependencies and can avoid circular dependencies.

Avoid Circular Dependencies

When designing a system of OSGi bundles, we recommend that you avoid circular dependencies. While OSGi supports circular dependencies, they increase the complexity of the design and can cause difficulties at build time and confusion in deployment.

Having identified some candidate components, the next step is to consider whether each should be in a bundle of its own or if parts can be packaged together. In many ways these become deployment questions: Does it make sense to have a GPS without an airbag or an airbag without a GPS? In this case, it does. Does it make sense to have an airbag or a GPS without an emergency monitor? Again, it does. So here we get ultimate flexibility, at the cost of modest additional complexity, by putting each function in its own bundle. This is another example of creating a design that favors components that exhibit high cohesion and loose coupling. We will leverage this several times in the evolution of Toast and talk more about this and other best practices for bundling code throughout the book.

To get going on the OSGi-based Toast, follow along with the step-by-step instructions here, or read along and load the sample code from "Chapter 4.2 Hello, Toast," using the Samples Manager.

4.2.1 GPS Bundle

Start by creating a new plug-in project for the GPS bundle:

○ Select **File > New > Project...** From the resulting dialog, expand **Plug-In Development**, select **Plug-in Project**, and click **Next** to get the **New Plug-in Project** wizard shown in Figure 4-5.

Figure 4–5   New Plug-in Project wizard

○ For the project name, enter org.equinoxosgi.toast.dev.gps. Under **Target Platform** choose the radio button labeled **an OSGi framework** and select **Equinox** from the drop-down list.

○ Match the remainder of the settings to the wizard shown in the figure and click **Next**.

Project and Bundle Names

Project names such as `org.equinoxosgi.toast.dev.gps` look a little strange at first—they look a lot like Java package names! In fact, that is deliberate. The bundle namespace is flat, so bundle IDs must be managed.

This management is done mostly through conventions rather than rules. We use the reverse domain name convention, similar to Java package naming, to identify bundles. This is a familiar approach to Java programmers; it addresses situations where, like packages, bundles are pooled and need to be uniquely identified. Using reverse domain names is a convenient, human-readable way of managing the namespace.

In the Eclipse tooling, each bundle is developed in a separate project. Given that the project namespace is also flat, it is convenient to match a project's name with the bundle's `Bundle-SymbolicName`.

○ On the **Content** page of the wizard, type `Toast Gps` for the **Name**, and select `J2SE-1.4` for the **Execution Environment**. Get in the habit of doing this for every bundle you create in this tutorial.

○ Make sure that all of the items in the **Options** section are not checked, accept the rest of the default values, and click **Finish**.

○ You may see a dialog asking you to switch to the Plug-In Development perspective. If so, just click **Yes**.

Once the project is created, the OSGi bundle manifest editor appears. Leave it open for now; we'll come back to it in a bit.

Since we already have a working `Gps` class from our first iteration, just move that class into this project:

○ Select the `Gps` class in the `Toast` project. From the context menu, select **Refactor > Move...**. Select the `src` folder under the `org.equinoxosgi.toast.dev.gps` project and press the **Create Package...** button.

○ Name the package the same as the project: `org.equinoxosgi.toast.dev.gps`.

○ Then select the newly created package and click **OK**.

Now the GPS bundle has the functionality it needs, but it is all inside the bundle—nothing outside the bundle can see it. In fact, the original `Toast` project now shows compile errors because of this. To make the code visible, the packages containing the functionality others can use must be *exported*.

❍ To do this, go back to the OSGi bundle manifest editor that opened earlier. If it's not still open, just double-click on the MANIFEST.MF file in the META-INF folder of the GPS project and open it.

❍ On the **Runtime** tab, in the **Exported Packages** section, click the **Add...** button.

❍ Select the org.equinoxosgi.toast.dev.gps package and click **OK**. Then save the editor.

While you are in the manifest editor, take some time to explore the bundle. The tabs on the manifest editor allow you to edit the various aspects of the bundle manifest, as summarized in textual form in the **MANIFEST.MF** tab. Let's review the details of the MANIFEST.MF file for the GPS bundle:

org.equinoxosgi.toast.dev.gps/MANIFEST.MF
```
Manifest-Version: 1.0
Bundle-ManifestVersion: 2
Bundle-Name: Toast Gps
Bundle-SymbolicName: org.equinoxosgi.toast.dev.gps
Bundle-Version: 1.0.0.qualifier
Bundle-RequiredExecutionEnvironment: J2SE-1.4
Export-Package: org.equinoxosgi.toast.dev.gps
```

Notice the Bundle-SymbolicName and Bundle-Version headers. These are mandatory, and together they uniquely identify the bundle. Many of the other headers appear as a result of the answers we provided when filling out the wizard for creating this bundle. The Export-Package header lists the one package in this bundle as exported so other bundles can use it.

That does it for your first bundle. Certainly as you progress through the subsequent chapters, your bundles will get more complex, but a bundle really needs only two things to qualify as a bundle: some interesting artifacts (in this case the Gps class) and a manifest.

4.2.2 Airbag Bundle

Rather than repeat the detailed instructions from the first bundle, here we give a list of steps you can follow to create the airbag bundle:

❍ Create a project for the bundle named org.equinoxosgi.toast.dev.airbag. Remember to use Toast Airbag for the **Name** and J2SE-1.4 for the **Execution Environment**.

❍ Move the existing Airbag class and the IAirbagListener interface into a new package named org.equinoxosgi.toast.dev.airbag in the new bundle.

❍ Open the bundle's manifest editor and export the package org.equinoxosgi.toast.dev.airbag.

A review of the **MANIFEST.MF** tab in the manifest editor shows similar content to that of the GPS bundle, with a single package being exported:

```
Org.equinoxosgi.toast.dev.airbag/MANIFEST.MF
Manifest-Version: 1.0
Bundle-ManifestVersion: 2
Bundle-Name: Toast Airbag
Bundle-SymbolicName: org.equinoxosgi.toast.dev.airbag
Bundle-Version: 1.0.0.qualifier
Bundle-RequiredExecutionEnvironment: J2SE-1.4
Export-Package: org.equinoxosgi.toast.dev.airbag
```

4.2.3 Emergency Monitor Bundle

Creating the emergency monitor bundle follows a similar pattern:

- ○ Create a project for the bundle named org.equinoxosgi.toast.client.emergency. Remember to use Toast Emergency for the **Name** and J2SE-1.4 for the **Execution Environment**.

- ○ Move the existing EmergencyMonitor class into a package named org.equinoxosgi.toast.client.emergency in the new bundle.

There is no need to export the new package as there is no code for other bundles to use. Instead, the emergency bundle needs to *import* packages from the other two bundles. In fact, if you are following along, you should have some compile errors in your workspace as the airbag- and GPS-related types are not visible to the emergency monitor bundle.

- ○ Open the emergency bundle's manifest editor and select the **Dependencies** tab.

- ○ Add the org.equinoxosgi.toast.dev.gps and org.equinoxosgi.toast.dev .airbag packages to the **Imported Packages** list on the right. This lets the emergency bundle see the GPS and airbag code from the other bundles.

- ○ While you are there, add org.osgi.framework to the **Imported Packages** list. The OSGi framework types will be needed in the next step.

PACKAGE FILTERING

An easy way to narrow the search for packages to add is to type *toast or *osgi into the search field at the top of the **Package Selection** dialog.

All that is left to do is the code from Main—the code that instantiates and starts the logic. In OSGi-based systems, applications do not have a main method.

Instead, applications are a community of bundles that hook into the OSGi framework lifecycle. One of the ways a bundle can participate in the framework lifecycle is by defining a *bundle activator.*

A bundle activator must implement the OSGi BundleActivator interface. That's why we needed to import the org.osgi.framework package previously. Now create a new bundle activator class in the emergency project:

❍ In the manifest editor, click on the **Activator** link on the **Overview** tab. This opens a partially completed **New Java Class** wizard.

❍ Fill in the package as org.equinoxosgi.toast.client.emergency and the class name as Activator. Click **Finish** to create a skeleton activator class containing stubs for the required start and stop methods.

❍ Fill in the rest of the code as follows:

```
org.equinoxosgi.toast.client.emergency/Activator
public class Activator implements BundleActivator {
  private Airbag airbag;
  private Gps gps;
  private EmergencyMonitor monitor;

  public void start(BundleContext context) throws Exception {
    System.out.println("Launching");
    gps = new Gps();
    airbag = new Airbag();
    monitor = new EmergencyMonitor();
    monitor.setGps(gps);
    monitor.setAirbag(airbag);
    monitor.startup();
    airbag.deploy();
  }

  public void stop(BundleContext context) throws Exception {
    monitor.shutdown();
    System.out.println("Terminating");
  }
}
```

Notice that the start method is basically the same as the original main method we wrote. The OSGi framework invokes this method as it starts the bundle. Similarly, the OSGi framework invokes stop when the framework is about to stop the bundle.

The emergency bundle is complete, so take a look at its manifest. Notice the Bundle-Activator header that identifies the bundle's entry point. Also, you can see that the bundle imports three packages but does not export any.

```
org.equinoxosgi.toast.client.emergency/MANIFEST.MF
Manifest-Version: 1.0
Bundle-ManifestVersion: 2
```

```
Bundle-Name: Toast Emergency
Bundle-SymbolicName: org.equinoxosgi.toast.client.emergency
Bundle-Version: 1.0.0.qualifier
Bundle-RequiredExecutionEnvironment: J2SE-1.4
Bundle-Activator: org.equinoxosgi.toast.client.emergency.Activator
Import-Package: org.equinoxosgi.toast.dev.airbag,
 org.equinoxosgi.toast.dev.gps,
 org.osgi.framework;version="1.5.0"
```

○ With the refactoring complete, you can now safely delete the original Toast project from your workspace.

4.2.4 Launching

Now that the three bundles are complete, the OSGi-based Toast is ready to run. Recall that in Section 4.1.6, "Running," we were able use the **Run As > Java Application** menu entry to run Toast. Under the covers that created a *launch configuration* describing how to run Toast. Here we show you how to do that for OSGi-based systems. Alternatively, you can use the Samples Manager to install the final code for this chapter and then use the launch configuration in the emergency project. Follow these steps to create a launch configuration as shown in Figure 4-6:

○ Select **Run > Run Configurations...** from the menu bar.

○ Select **OSGi Framework** and choose **New** from the context menu to create a new launch configuration.

○ Name the launch configuration Toast.

○ Click the **Deselect All** button at the right.

○ Select the three Toast bundles from the list of **Workspace** bundles by checking the box beside each one.

○ Scroll down to the **Target Platform** section and check the box beside the bundle org.eclipse.osgi.

○ Uncheck the box beside **Add new workspace bundles to this launch configuration automatically**.

○ On the **Common** tab, select the **Shared file** option and use /org.equinoxosgi .toast.client.emergency as the folder. This causes the launch configuration to be saved in the project, making it easier to share with other team members.

○ Finally, click the **Run** button.

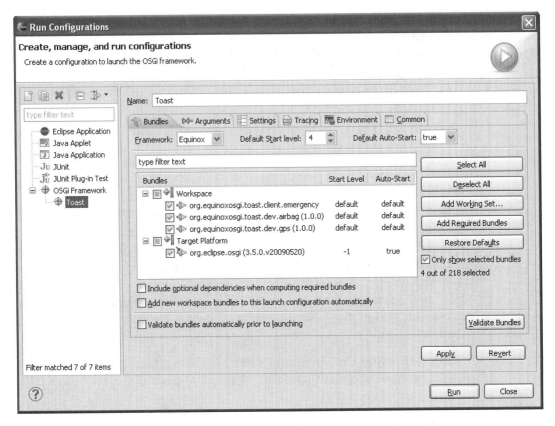

Figure 4–6　OSGi-based Toast launch configuration

Running this launch configuration causes the OSGi framework to start. The framework then installs and starts the bundles listed in the launch configuration. As a result, start on the emergency monitor's bundle activator is run, and you should see the following output on the Console view:

```
osgi> Launching
Emergency occurred at lat=3776999 lon=-12244694 heading=90 speed=50
```

The framework continues to run until you shut it down by typing close in the Console view. Shutting down the framework invokes the stop method on the emergency bundle's activator. The console will show the following:

```
Launching
Emergency occurred at lat=3776999 lon=-12244694 heading=90 speed=50
osgi> close
Terminating
```

4.3 Summary

We started this chapter with a simple telematics scenario. The first pass was done without regard for OSGi, focusing instead on a clean object-oriented design. This first iteration of Toast was then refactored into three bundles, one for each device and one for the emergency monitor, and the bundle dependencies were properly captured. OSGi's bundle lifecycle was hooked by writing a bundle activator in the emergency bundle. The system was run using an OSGi-based launch configuration, and system startup and shutdown were visible through application output on the console.

In this chapter you learned how to refactor a non-OSGi project into OSGi bundles. You learned how to create bundle manifests and how to run an OSGi application using a launch configuration.

There's still a long way to go to turn this simplistic system into a dynamic and fully functional telematics application, but the first steps of defining and running bundles are complete.

CHAPTER 5

Services

This chapter moves beyond the notion of bundles and presents the concept of *services*. Services further decouple bundles by allowing them to collaborate without depending on a particular implementation or packaging. This in turn makes your systems more flexible and opens the door to dynamic collaboration, updating, extension, and reconfiguration.

The goals of this chapter are to

○ Introduce services and their use

○ Refactor the implementation of Toast to use services

○ Discuss the dynamic behavior of services and show some of the application design points that promote and inhibit dynamism

5.1 Moving to Services

In Chapter 2, "OSGi Concepts," we talked about how modularizing your system gives you the power to compose functional pieces in different ways to suit the needs at hand. This is not without a cost, however. Decoupling leaves the individual modules isolated—that is part of the power—with no inherent means of interacting or collaborating with others. Since modules can be used in many different scenarios, they cannot rely on a particular scope or concrete context. Similarly, modules need a way of supplying function to other modules. This is where services come in.

Section 5.1.2 of the OSGi Service Platform Core Specification defines a service as

"An object registered with the service registry under one or more interfaces together with properties. This object can be discovered and used by bundles."

This is a simple yet powerful notion and one that should be familiar to Java programmers. OSGi uses Java interfaces to cleanly separate specification from implementation. For every interface there may be many implementations. Referencing interfaces rather than implementations provides the flexibility to use multiple implementations or change your mind regarding the implementation to use. Figure 5-1 depicts a Bundle A that requires a service, Bundle B that implements a service, and Bundle C that defines a service.

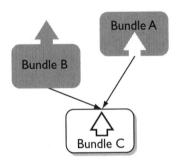

Figure 5–1   An OSGi service

So what advantages do OSGi services offer a little three-bundle application such as Toast? For starters, in our current implementation the emergency monitor logic is tightly coupled to the classes that implement the behavior of the airbag and the GPS. Those implementations are fake at the moment, and swapping in new classes would require modification to the emergency monitor. As we'll see in this chapter, OSGi services offer a better way to discover and acquire these underlying components.

In general, OSGi services should be favored over inter-bundle class dependencies. Whenever a bundle references a class defined in another bundle, a tight coupling is created.

When using a service, a bundle need depend only on the service interfaces required rather than any implementation classes. A service is obtained anonymously via the OSGi service registry and is referenced only via its interface. It is not even possible to cast a service back to its implementation class since that class is typically in a package that is not exported by the providing bundle. Simply put, OSGi services allow a bundle to dramatically reduce its dependencies by eliminating the ability to make assumptions.

Figure 5-2 contrasts the tight coupling created when Class A in Bundle X depends on Class B in Bundle Y with the loose coupling when services are used. In the former case, Bundle Y must *always* be resolved for Bundle X to be

Inter-bundle Dependencies   Service Dependencies

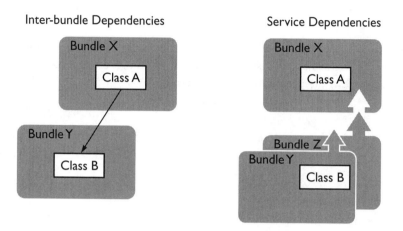

Figure 5-2 Using a service to achieve loose coupling between bundles

resolved—they are effectively a single functional unit. By contrast, if Class A in Bundle X depends only on an OSGi service interface, it is free to use any bundle, such as Y or Z, that provides the service.

This is precisely the case for how the emergency monitor instantiates and manages both the airbag and the GPS. The airbag and GPS bundles act merely as runtime libraries for the emergency monitor bundle. While this may be appropriate in some situations, making a bundle responsible for creating, starting, and shutting down its own functionality as services improve encapsulation of code and clarifies responsibilities. Instead of having the emergency monitor configure its own airbag and GPS, it would be better to use dependency injection and have it configured with an available airbag and GPS service. This is enabled using OSGi services.

Finally, the current implementation of the application is brittle. If we wanted to swap the implementation of any of the bundles with a newer version or an alternative implementation, it would require major surgery. Doing so on a live system is altogether impossible. The ability to dynamically replace implementation is a key advantage of using OSGi services.

5.2 Registering the GPS Service

Let's start taking advantage of OSGi services by refactoring the GPS bundle to instantiate its own GPS object and register it as a service. The first step is to create an interface for the GPS and use it to register a GPS service.

SERVICE CLASSES?

Strictly speaking, OSGi allows you to register services under class names rather than interface names. This is sometimes useful, but registering interfaces as services maintains the decoupling and is preferred.

With this point in mind, use some of the handy Java refactoring tools in Eclipse to create the IGps interface and update the GPS-related classes and packages:

- ○ Open a Java editor on the Gps class. From the context menu, select **Refactor > Extract Interface....**
- ○ Type IGps for the interface name.
- ○ Select all four members in the list.
- ○ Deselect the **Generate method comments option** and press **OK.**

The net result of these steps is to create the IGps interface and to update the Gps class to implement IGps and EmergencyMonitor to use the new interface where possible.

```
org.equinoxosgi.toast.dev.gps/IGps
public interface IGps {
    public int getHeading();
    public int getLatitude();
    public int getLongitude();
    public int getSpeed();
}
```

USE REFACTORING

Notice that refactoring did more than just rename. It can also change the uses of the original class to use the new interface. This saves much time and pain.

To support future alternative implementations and to clarify the real state of the GPS service, the name of the current Gps class should more accurately reflect that it is just a trivial and fake implementation, not one that is connected to real GPS hardware:

- ○ Select the **Gps class** in the Package Explorer and use the **Refactor > Rename...** option from the context menu to rename **Gps** to be **FakeGps.** Note that you can also use **Alt+Shift+R** or **F2** to invoke the rename refactoring.

It's a good practice to distinguish between API and non-API—that is, code that is intended to be used by others and code that is internal implementation detail. Since OSGi manages code visibility at the package level, you should keep implementation classes in a separate package and clearly indicate that they are not APIs. In the case of the GPS bundle, this means the IGps interface should be in an API package and the FakeGps class in a non-API package.

○ Select the **Refactor > Move...** option from the context menu on FakeGps in the Package Explorer.

○ Press the **Create Package...** button in the top right of the **Move** dialog and create a package called org.equinoxosgi.toast.internal.dev.gps.fake by entering the name and clicking **Finish**.

○ Complete the refactoring by pressing **OK** in the **Move** dialog.

Naming Convention for Internal Packages

Including the word internal in the names of internal packages is a good practice because it makes it easy to identify non-API packages. We prefer to place internal immediately after org.equinoxosgi.toast because it ensures that internal packages are sorted together within the project.

The next step is to create a bundle activator for the GPS bundle. The activator will act as the entry point for the bundle similarly to what we saw in Section 4.2.3, "Emergency Monitor Bundle." In this case the activator needs to create and *register* the GPS service.

All bundle activators must implement the BundleActivator interface. This interface is defined in the org.osgi.framework package. In the previous chapter you manually listed the packages that the emergency monitor bundle imported. This is convenient for small numbers of packages but can be overbearing for even modest code bases. Fortunately, the PDE tooling provides a handy feature that automates the management of your bundle's dependencies. Instead of listing individual packages to be imported, you can list a set of bundles from which your bundle's dependencies can be computed. Let's try that out here:

○ Open the MANIFEST.MF file in the GPS bundle.

○ From the **Dependencies** tab in the manifest editor, expand the **Automated Management of Dependencies** section at the bottom left, as shown in Figure 5-3.

Figure 5–3   Automated Management of Dependencies section

❍ Make sure that the **Import-Package** radio button is selected as opposed to the **Require-Bundle** radio button. We'll talk more about that later.

❍ Add the bundle `org.eclipse.osgi` to the **Automated Management of Dependencies** list and save the editor. Notice that the project's code can now reference types in the bundle `org.eclipse.osgi`.

❍ Later we'll return here and click the **add dependencies** link to compute the bundle's imported packages and ensure that its runtime dependencies are satisfied.

In the preceding chapter you created a bundle activator for the emergency monitor bundle. Now, create one for the GPS bundle so it can control its own lifecycle:

❍ Go to the **Overview** tab on the GPS bundle manifest editor.

❍ In the **Activator** field in the **General Information** section, type `Activator` as the name of the bundle activator class.

❍ Click the **Activator** link to the left of the field to bring up the **New Java Class** wizard.

❍ Type `org.equinoxosgi.toast.internal.dev.gps.fake.bundle` in the **Package** field and press **Finish**. This creates the new bundle activator class with stubs for the `start` and `stop` methods.

❍ Update the stubs to create and register the service in `start` and unregister the service in `stop`. They should look something like the code shown in the next snippet. Note that you will likely have to add some Java package import statements to the `Activator`. Select **Source > Organize Imports** from the context menu or **Ctrl+Shift+O** to generate the necessary package import statements.

`org.equinoxosgi.toast.dev.gps/Activator`

```
public class Activator implements BundleActivator {
  private ServiceRegistration registration;

  public void start(BundleContext context) {
    FakeGps gps = new FakeGps();
    registration = context.registerService(
        IGps.class.getName(), gps, null);
  }

  public void stop(BundleContext context) {
    registration.unregister();
  }
}
```

When the GPS bundle starts, the OSGi framework creates the bundle activator and calls its `start` method. This instantiates a `FakeGps` object and registers it with the OSGi service registry as an `IGps` service. Similarly, when the bundle stops, the bundle activator unregisters the service.

Notice that the bundle activator uses the fully qualified name of `IGps` to register the service. This is the name that other bundles will use to discover the service. The activator also caches the `ServiceRegistration` returned by the `registerService` method so that the service can later be unregistered when the bundle is stopped.

The last thing to do for the GPS bundle is to ensure that the bundle manifest accurately captures the imported and exported packages. First check the imported packages:

○ Go to the **Dependencies** tab of the bundle manifest editor for the GPS bundle.

○ In the **Automated Management of Dependencies** section, click the **add dependencies** link.

○ Save the editor.

Clicking this link analyzes the code in the bundle and determines the subset of available packages that need to be imported by the bundle at runtime. Notice in Figure 5-4 that the list of **Imported Packages** now shows all of the external packages referenced in the code. See the sidebar titled "Automatically Updating Runtime Dependencies" for how to have each bundle's dependencies automatically updated prior to launching the OSGi framework.

For the exported packages list, notice that `IGps` is the only type in this bundle that other bundles need to see. Check the manifest to make sure that its package is exposed as API and the other implementation and OSGi-related packages are not.

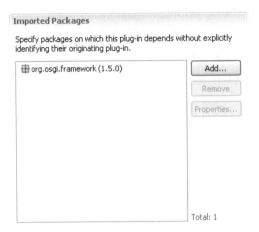

Figure 5–4   Imported Packages section

❍ From the bundle manifest editor for the GPS bundle, go to the **Runtime** tab.

❍ The **Exported Packages** list should contain only `org.equinoxosgi.toast.dev.gps`. If you select that package, the **visible to downstream plug-ins** option on the right should be selected.

HIDE OSGi CODE

Keep the bundle activator and other OSGi-related code in a separate package that is not visible to other bundles. It is internal detail, and separating the OSGi-related code from the domain logic is a best practice that makes it easier to understand the domain code and reuse it in a non-OSGi deployment.

Automatically Updating Runtime Dependencies

Any code changes you make to a bundle might require that you update its runtime dependencies. Since this happens so often and is so easy to forget, consider enabling the **Plug-in Development** preference to automatically recompute bundle dependencies.

Prior to launching, each bundle's runtime dependencies are calculated exactly as if you had manually clicked the **add dependencies** link in the **Automated Management of Dependencies** section of the manifest editor.

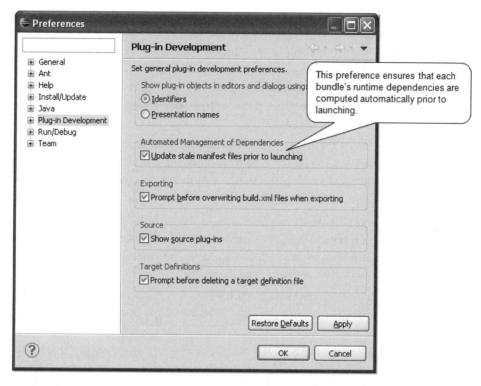

Figure 5–5 Automated Management of Dependencies preferences

At this point, you may notice some compiler errors on the org.equinoxosgi .toast.client.emergency project. We'll clean those up later on.

5.3 Registering the Airbag Service

Like the GPS bundle, the airbag bundle sits at the bottom of the food chain, and the process for exposing it as a service is similar. You may want to refer to the details in Section 5.2, "Registering the GPS Service," as you follow these abbreviated steps:

- ○ Extract a new interface called IAirbag from the Airbag class. Don't include the deploy method in the interface, since we'll be making that method private later on.
- ○ Rename the Airbag class to be FakeAirbag.
- ○ Move the FakeAirbag class into a new internal package called org.equinoxosgi.toast.internal.dev.airbag.fake.

○ In the **Dependencies** tab of the bundle manifest editor, under the **Automated Management of Dependencies** section, select the **Import-Package** radio button and add `org.eclipse.osgi` to the list.

○ Also add `org.eclipse.core.jobs` to the list since we'll need that later. Rather than implementing our own concurrency utility classes, we make use of the `org.eclipse.core.jobs` bundle. It is well tested and supports the concurrency function that we need.

○ The Jobs API requires types from another bundle, `org.eclipse.equinox.common`. Add this bundle to the **Required Plug-ins** section rather than the **Automated Management of Dependencies** section we've used previously. See "Dealing with Split Packages" for an explanation.

○ Save the editor.

○ In the **Overview** tab, type `Activator` into the **Activator** field and click the **Activator** link to the left. Create it in the package `org.equinoxosgi.toast` `.internal.dev.airbag.fake.bundle`.

○ Add code to the activator to create and register the airbag service on start and unregister the service on stop. You can copy and modify the code from the GPS bundle if you like.

○ In the **Runtime** tab of the bundle manifest editor, ensure that only the `org.equinoxosgi.toast.dev.airbag` package is exported by the bundle.

○ In the **Dependencies** tab under the **Automated Management of Dependencies** section, click the **add dependencies** link to recompute the imported packages.

○ Save the editor.

DEALING WITH SPLIT PACKAGES

Normally it's recommended that you add required bundles to the **Automated Management of Dependencies** and let the tooling determine the list of packages that you actually need. For historical reasons, the package needed from the Equinox common bundle in this case is split across three different bundles, a so-called *split package*. Without delving into the details of split packages, the simplest way to resolve this ambiguity is to explicitly specify the bundle containing the split of the package we need in the **Required Plug-ins** section.

To complete the airbag bundle, let's make it more stand-alone. It does not make sense for an airbag to have a `deploy` method that others can call—real airbags deploy all by themselves. To make things handy for testing and demonstration, update FakeAirbag to deploy and notify its listeners every five seconds, as shown in the following code snippet:

```
org.equinoxosgi.toast.dev.airbag/FakeAirbag
public class FakeAirbag implements IAirbag {
  private List listeners = new ArrayList();
  private Job job;
  private boolean isRunning;

  public synchronized void addListener(IAirbagListener listener) {
    listeners.add(listener);
  }

  private synchronized void deploy() {
    for (Iterator i = listeners.iterator(); i.hasNext();)
      ((IAirbagListener) i.next()).deployed();
  }

  public synchronized void removeListener(IAirbagListener listener) {
    listeners.remove(listener);
  }

  public synchronized void shutdown() {
    isRunning = false;
    job.cancel();
    try {
      job.join();
    } catch (InterruptedException e) {
      // shutting down, safe to ignore
    }
  }

  public synchronized void startup() {
    isRunning = true;
    job = new Job("FakeAirbag") {
      protected IStatus run(IProgressMonitor monitor) {
        deploy();
        if (isRunning)
          schedule(5000);
        return Status.OK_STATUS;
      }
    };
    job.schedule(5000);
  }
}
```

USE join TO ENSURE THE COMPLETION OF JOBS

The join call in the shutdown method is necessary to ensure that we wait for the Job to terminate. To comply with the OSGi specification, a bundle being stopped must ensure that it disposes of all consumed system resources.

Favor Import-Package over Require-Bundle

The manifest headers Import-Package and Require-Bundle are used to describe a bundle's dependencies.

Import-Package—This header is used to express a bundle's dependency upon packages that are exported by other bundles. At runtime the framework analyzes the constraints and wires the bundles together.

Require-Bundle—This header is used to express a bundle's explicit dependency upon other bundles by specifying a list of bundle symbolic names. A bundle that uses this header automatically has access to the packages exported by its required bundles.

Importing packages is recommended over requiring bundles as it results in a more flexible and loosely coupled system, offering system designers the ability to swap out implementations and deployments of function to suit their needs.

Since FakeAirbag now has a Job that deploys the airbag every five seconds, modify the airbag's bundle activator to call startup to schedule the Job and shutdown to cancel it:

```
org.equinoxosgi.toast.dev.airbag/Activator
public class Activator implements BundleActivator {
  private FakeAirbag airbag;
  private ServiceRegistration registration;

  public void start(BundleContext context) {
    airbag = new FakeAirbag();
    airbag.startup();
    registration = context.registerService(
      IAirbag.class.getName(), airbag, null);
  }

  public void stop(BundleContext context) {
    registration.unregister();
    airbag.shutdown();
  }
}
```

BUNDLE ACTIVATOR METHODS MUST BE QUICK

It is vital that the bundle activator's start and stop methods finish as quickly as possible, since the framework cannot start or stop any other bundles until they return.

5.4 Acquiring Services

If the GPS and airbag bundles can be said to reside at the bottom of the food chain, then the emergency monitor bundle sits at the top of the food chain; that is, it acquires services but doesn't register any.

Hooking the emergency monitor into the service mechanism requires very little change to EmergencyMonitor since it was already built to inject the airbag and GPS dependencies via its setGps and setAirbag methods. As we refactored the other elements of Toast, the Gps and Airbag classes were split into interfaces and internal implementation classes, FakeGps and FakeAirbag, which are not API. So the only change needed in EmergencyMonitor is to reference the new interfaces in the setGps and setAirbag signatures and in private fields. But wait, these changes were automatically made by the **Refactor > Extract Interface...** operation. The result looks like this:

org.equinoxosgi.toast.client.emergency/EmergencyMonitor
```
public class EmergencyMonitor implements IAirbagListener {
  private IAirbag airbag;
  private IGps gps;

  public void deployed() {
    System.out.println("Emergency occurred at lat=" + gps.getLatitude()
        + " lon=" + gps.getLongitude() + " heading=" + gps.getHeading()
        + " speed=" + gps.getSpeed());   }

  public void setAirbag(IAirbag value) {
    airbag = value;
  }

  public void setGps(IGps value) {
    gps = value;
  }

  public void shutdown() {
    airbag.removeListener(this);
  }

  public void startup() {
    airbag.addListener(this);
  }
}
```

Also, since the airbag and GPS bundles are now responsible for registering their respective services, the bundle activator for the emergency monitor bundle no longer needs to do this. Refactor the bundle activator to look like this snippet:

org.equinoxosgi.toast.client.emergency/Activator
```
public class Activator implements BundleActivator {
  private IAirbag airbag;
  private ServiceReference airbagRef;
```

```
private IGps gps;
private ServiceReference gpsRef;
private EmergencyMonitor monitor;

public void start(BundleContext context) throws Exception {
  System.out.println("Launching");
  monitor = new EmergencyMonitor();
  gpsRef = context.getServiceReference(IGps.class.getName());
  airbagRef = context.getServiceReference(IAirbag.class.getName());
  if (gpsRef == null || airbagRef == null) {
    System.err.println("Unable to acquire GPS or airbag!");
    return;
  }
  gps = (IGps) context.getService(gpsRef);
  airbag = (IAirbag) context.getService(airbagRef);
  if (gps == null || airbag == null) {
    System.err.println("Unable to acquire GPS or airbag!");
    return;
  }
  monitor.setGps(gps);
  monitor.setAirbag(airbag);
  monitor.startup();
}

public void stop(BundleContext context) throws Exception {
  monitor.shutdown();
  if (gpsRef != null)
    context.ungetService(gpsRef);
  if (airbagRef != null)
    context.ungetService(airbagRef);
  System.out.println("Terminating");
}
}
```

In the revised code, the bundle starts, instantiates an EmergencyMonitor, and then injects the airbag and GPS dependencies. Now that we are using services, the bundle discovers the required services using the OSGi service registry. The BundleContext supplied to start is the bundle's means of interacting with the OSGi framework.

Using the BundleContext, the activator tries to get a ServiceReference for both the IGps and IAirbag services. A ServiceReference is a handle to a service object rather than the service itself. The activator may fail to acquire a ServiceReference if the service has not yet been registered. Given a ServiceReference, you can use the BundleContext's getService method to dereference it and get the service object it represents. Note that getService may return null if the service has been unregistered since the ServiceReference was acquired. We talk more about this race condition in Chapter 6, "Dynamic Services."

Having acquired service references and implementations for both the IGps and IAirbag services, the bundle's activator initializes and starts the emergency monitor using the setGps, setAirbag, and startup methods.

When the bundle stops, the emergency monitor's shutdown method is called, and the emergency monitor stops using the GPS and airbag services it was given. The activator then calls the BundleContext's ungetService method to release the services. This is important because the service registry reference counts the bundles using each service. Ungetting the service when you are done with it keeps the system running smoothly.

This refactoring greatly clarifies the modularity boundaries and inter-module interactions. There are a few tweaks we can do to clean things up:

- First, notice that EmergencyMonitor is not API. To reflect this, rename the EmergencyMonitor's package to org.equinoxosgi.toast.internal.client.emergency.

- Similarly, refactor the emergency monitor bundle's activator to be consistent with the other bundle activators; that is, move the Activator class to a new internal package called org.equinoxosgi.toast.internal.client.emergency.bundle.

- Since the emergency monitor bundle has no API, ensure that the bundle manifest does not export any packages.

- Use the **Automated Management of Dependencies** section of the bundle manifest editor to compute the bundle's imported packages rather than adding them manually. Remove all the packages from the **Imported Packages** list on the right, then add the following bundles to the **Automated Management of Dependencies** list:

```
org.equinoxosgi.toast.dev.airbag
org.equinoxosgi.toast.dev.gps
org.eclipse.osgi
```

- Save the bundle manifest editor.

- Finally, click the **add dependencies** link to compute the bundle's imported packages, and save the bundle manifest editor again.

5.5 Launching

With the three bundles refactored to make use of OSGi services, it's time to launch the application again:

- Select **Run > Run Configurations...** from the menu bar.

- Select the Toast run configuration from beneath **OSGi Framework** in the list at the left.

- Add the two new bundles by checking the box beside the following bundles in the **Target Platform** section of the list:

```
org.eclipse.core.jobs
org.eclipse.equinox.common
```

❍ Click the **Run** button.

The OSGi framework is launched and installs and starts the bundles listed in the launch configuration. You should see the following output on the Console view:

```
Launching
Emergency occurred at lat=3776999 lon=-12244694 heading=90 speed=50
Emergency occurred at lat=3776999 lon=-12244694 heading=90 speed=50
...
```

5.6 Troubleshooting

Given the way the code is written, there is also a chance that when you launch, you might see this output in the Console view instead:

```
Launching
Unable to acquire GPS or airbag!
```

In some cases this version of Toast will fail because the emergency monitor's bundle activator is dependent on the order in which the bundles are started. If the GPS and airbag bundles happen to be started before the emergency monitor bundle, everything works perfectly. If the emergency monitor bundle is started before either or both of the others, the services it needs will not be registered yet and the startup will fail. We structured the exercise to illustrate the pitfalls of decoupling—you can no longer make as many assumptions. Fortunately, there are several facilities in OSGi and Equinox for handling this situation, and the next chapter, "Dynamic Services," covers this topic in detail.

If you encounter this problem, you can hack around it temporarily by changing the start level of the emergency bundle in the launch configuration to be a number greater than Equinox's default start level of 4. Don't set it higher than 6, since the Equinox framework will only activate bundles up to that level by default.

DON'T DO THIS

Using start levels to manually control the start order of your bundles is fraught with problems for a large, dynamic application, so we certainly do not recommend you use them for anything beyond making this one example run.

5.7 Summary

At the outset of this chapter, the Toast sample application was made up of three bundles that were tightly coupled—they did not take advantage of OSGi services. We refactored Toast so the airbag and GPS were bona fide OSGi services with the emergency monitor requiring them both. This allowed the three bundles to collaborate, but the emergency monitor optimistically assumes that the GPS and airbag services are available at the time the application started—a first taste of the challenges of dynamic behavior.

In this chapter we saw how to register services and how to acquire them. We also talked about how to write a bundle activator for every bundle that registers or acquires services. Finally, we learned that writing bundles that depend on a specific start order is not a good idea. Simply registering and acquiring services does not take into account the potential dynamic nature of services.

In the next chapter we show you three approaches for handling dynamic services: Service Tracker, Service Activator Toolkit, and Declarative Services.

CHAPTER 6

Dynamic Services

This chapter addresses the notion that bundles and services can come and go throughout the lifetime of a running system. Dynamic behavior is one of the hallmarks of OSGi-based systems and is central to many of the design and implementation decisions you make. Here we present three mechanisms for dealing with the dynamic nature of services: OSGi's Service Trackers, a third-party mechanism called the Service Activator Toolkit (SAT), and finally OSGi's Declarative Services.

The goals of this chapter are to

○ Modify the bundle activators in Toast to use OSGi Service Trackers so they can handle dynamic services

○ Present the Service Activator Toolkit as a very simple way to write bundle activators that handle dynamic services

○ Present OSGi's Declarative Services and adopt it as the mechanism to be used throughout the remainder of Toast development

6.1 Introduction to Dynamic Services

At the end of Chapter 5, "Services," we had Toast implemented in terms of services but noted that the system may not work depending on the order in which the bundles are started. Ironically, this is a symptom of the power of OSGi. OSGi systems are loosely coupled and may not have a central thread of control—they are composed of cooperating functional pieces, or services. These services have to discover each other and cannot depend on one being installed and started before the other.

While it is possible to use OSGi's startLevel service to control the order in which bundles are started, it is not a recommended practice. As the number of bundles in the application increases, the start order interdependencies become complex, and this approach becomes a maintenance nightmare. The StartLevel service is discussed in more detail in Section 21.7.1, "Start Levels."

A better approach is to make our application independent of bundle start order altogether. OSGi provides several mechanisms for achieving this. First, the framework fires service events as bundles register and unregister services. Using *service listeners*, a bundle can receive these events and track the services it requires. When all the services are available, the activator can acquire them and start its operation—perhaps registering even more services. This approach requires a fair amount of complex code to handle concurrency and the varying order in which services come and go. As such we do not cover it in detail here.

The complexity of service listeners and the fact that this was the only option in early releases of OSGi gave rise to third-party frameworks such as the Service Activator Toolkit (SAT). SAT provides an abstract BundleActivator with a set of helper methods that listen and react to service events. Using SAT, an application inherits the complex functionality it needs to properly handle the coming and going of services.

Since those early days, OSGi has evolved two additional mechanisms for dealing with dynamic services: Service Trackers and Declarative Services. This chapter covers both of these mechanisms and gives you a chance to try them in the Toast sample application.

The Evolution of the OSGi Service Model

Services are an inherent part of the overall OSGi architecture and have been there from the beginning. Over time the facilities around services have evolved.

Release 1: service registration and event listening—The initial release of the OSGi specification provided service registration and listening APIs as the way to work with the OSGi service model. This typically required the bundle developer to create and register services in the bundle's activator. A bundle requiring another service adds a service event listener and responds to service registration, unregistration, and modification events fired by the OSGi framework.

Release 2: Service Tracker—Release 2 of the OSGi specification introduced the Service Tracker. As the name implies, a Service Tracker tracks the addition, removal, and modification of services being used by a bundle and eliminates much of the duplicate listener code and race conditions.

Release 4: Declarative Services—Release 4 of the OSGi specification introduced Declarative Services, which makes handling the dynamic acquisition and release

> of services easier for bundle developers by eliminating all service management code. In addition, using Declarative Services makes using OSGi services more scalable by delaying class loading and object creation. See Chapter 15, "Declarative Services," and Chapter 24, "Declarative Services Reference," for coverage of Declarative Services.

6.2 Using Service Trackers

A Service Tracker, as the name implies, is a mechanism for tracking the comings and goings of services matching a specification. At any point you can ask a Service Tracker to give you the service objects it is tracking. Service Trackers are highly customizable and can be made to update the state of other services based on the changes they see. In this chapter we refactor the emergency monitor's bundle activator to use Service Trackers and show how they are used to make Toast safely dynamic. We also examine the advantages and disadvantages of this approach.

In this section we suggest that you load the sample code for "Chapter 6.2 Service Tracker" using the Samples Manager and read along rather than trying to do the modifications manually. There are a number of changes and we are really just trying to illustrate the use of Service Trackers.

6.2.1 Modifying the Bundle Activator

All of the changes needed to use Service Trackers happen in the emergency monitor's bundle activator in `org.equinoxosgi.toast.client.emergency.bundle`. The following code snippet shows the entire content of the new activator class. Following that is a description of the changes.

BENEFITS OF DEPENDENCY INJECTION

This is another example where the dependency injection approach is beneficial—all of the infrastructure code is concentrated in one OSGi-specific class rather than being peppered across the business logic of Toast. Changing the service acquisition technique does not affect the "real" application code.

```
org.equinoxosgi.toast.client.emergency/Activator
public class Activator implements BundleActivator {
    private IAirbag airbag;
```

```java
private ServiceTracker airbagTracker;
private BundleContext context;
private IGps gps;
private ServiceTracker gpsTracker;
private EmergencyMonitor monitor;

private void bind() {
  if (gps == null) {
    gps = (IGps) gpsTracker.getService();
    if (gps == null)
      return; // No IGps service.
  }
  if (airbag == null) {
    airbag = (IAirbag) airbagTracker.getService();
    if (airbag == null)
      return; // No IAirbag service.
  }
  monitor.setGps(gps);
  monitor.setAirbag(airbag);
  monitor.startup();
}

private ServiceTrackerCustomizer createAirbagCustomizer() {
  return new ServiceTrackerCustomizer() {
    public Object addingService(ServiceReference reference) {
      Object service = context.getService(reference);
      synchronized (Activator.this) {
        if (Activator.this.airbag == null) {
          Activator.this.airbag = (IAirbag) service;
          Activator.this.bind();
        }
      }
      return service;
    }

    public void modifiedService(ServiceReference reference,
        Object service) {
      // No service property modifications to handle.
    }

    public void removedService(ServiceReference reference,
        Object service) {
      synchronized (Activator.this) {
        if (service != Activator.this.airbag)
          return;
        Activator.this.unbind();
        Activator.this.bind();
      }
    }
  };
}

private ServiceTrackerCustomizer createGpsCustomizer() {
  return new ServiceTrackerCustomizer() {
    public Object addingService(ServiceReference reference) {
```

```
           Object service = context.getService(reference);
           synchronized (Activator.this) {
             if (Activator.this.gps == null) {
               Activator.this.gps = (IGps) service;
               Activator.this.bind();
             }
           }
           return service;
         }

         public void modifiedService(ServiceReference reference,
             Object service) {
           // No service property modifications to handle.
         }

         public void removedService(ServiceReference reference,
             Object service) {
           synchronized (Activator.this) {
             if (service != Activator.this.gps)
               return;
             Activator.this.unbind();
             Activator.this.bind();
           }
         }
       };
   }

   public void start(BundleContext context) throws Exception {
     this.context = context;
     monitor = new EmergencyMonitor();
     ServiceTrackerCustomizer gpsCustomizer = createGpsCustomizer();
     gpsTracker = new ServiceTracker(context, IGps.class.getName(),
         gpsCustomizer);
     ServiceTrackerCustomizer airbagCustomizer =
         createAirbagCustomizer();
     airbagTracker = new ServiceTracker(context,
         IAirbag.class.getName(), airbagCustomizer);
     gpsTracker.open();
     airbagTracker.open();
   }

   public void stop(BundleContext context) throws Exception {
     airbagTracker.close();
     gpsTracker.close();
   }

   private void unbind() {
     if (gps == null || airbag == null)
       return;
     monitor.shutdown();
     gps = null;
     airbag = null;
   }
}
```

Notice that, as before, the start method begins by instantiating the EmergencyMonitor. Then, instead of trying to acquire the GPS and airbag services directly, it creates a ServiceTracker for each. When the required airbag and GPS services are available, the trackers call bind and the emergency monitor's setGps, setAirbag, and startup methods. To be safe, bind and unbind are called from inside synchronized blocks to make sure that service changes are handled atomically.

The new stop method simply closes the two Service Trackers. Since a Service Tracker is implemented using service event listeners, it is important that they be closed. Failure to close the trackers results in listener leaks. See Chapter 22, "Dynamic Best Practices," for more information on leaks and other issues as a result of dynamic behavior. Note that closing a tracker causes its tracked services to be removed and thus the emergency monitor to be unbound.

The big change in the activator comes in the creation of the ServiceTracker and ServiceTrackerCustomizer objects. The key here is in the ServiceTrackerCustomizers. These are a means of adding lifecycle functionality to the trackers. The customizers in this example react to IAirbag and IGps services coming and going by triggering the binding or unbinding of the emergency monitor as appropriate. A customizer has to handle special cases, for example, where there are multiple instances of the same service type. When unbinding one service instance, there may be alternative service implementations of the same type—the customizer should try to rebind to ensure uninterrupted execution. Similarly, it must ensure that it deactivates and unbinds the emergency monitor only when the service in use is removed, not just when services are removed.

The activator creates two Service Trackers, one for each of the IAirbag and IGps services, and each Service Tracker has its own customizer. Each Service Tracker is opened, causing it to start listening to the relevant events from the OSGi framework.

6.2.2 Launching

The Service Tracker–based version of Toast is ready to run:

○ Select **Run > Run Configurations...** from the menu bar.

○ Select the **Toast** run configuration from beneath **OSGi Framework** in the list at the left.

○ Finally, click the **Run** button.

ADDING THE NEW DEPENDENCY

The only new dependency in this sample is on the org.osgi.util.tracker package. Assuming you have the **Update stale manifest files prior to launching**

PDE preference selected as discussed in Section 5.2, "Registering the GPS Service," the import for this package is automatically added to the emergency monitor's bundle manifest prior to launching Toast. Since this package comes from a bundle that is already in the launch configuration, there is nothing to do but run. If that option is not set, you'll need to add the new package by clicking the **add dependencies** link under **Automated Management of Dependencies** on the **Dependencies** tab of the emergency bundle manifest editor.

You should see the following output on the Console view, repeating every five seconds:

```
Emergency occurred at lat=3776999 lon=-12244694 heading=90 speed=50
Emergency occurred at lat=3776999 lon=-12244694 heading=90 speed=50
...
```

Toast runs every time now, regardless of the bundle start order, because the bundle activator uses Service Trackers to defer starting the emergency monitor until it has successfully acquired both the GPS and the airbag services. To play around with how this works, try manually stopping and restarting the various services in the application:

❍ In the Console view, press **Enter** to see the osgi> prompt. Then type the ss command to display a *short status* of the installed bundles. You should see the following output, although the bundle IDs and the order of the bundles might not be the same:

```
osgi> ss

Framework is launched.

id      State           Bundle
0       ACTIVE          org.eclipse.osgi_3.5.0.v20090520
1       ACTIVE          org.equinoxosgi.toast.dev.gps_1.0.0.qualifier
2       ACTIVE          org.eclipse.core.jobs_3.4.100.v20090429-1800
3       ACTIVE          org.eclipse.equinox.common_3.5.0.v20090520-1800
4       ACTIVE          org.equinoxosgi.toast.dev.airbag_1.0.0.qualifier
5       ACTIVE          org.equinoxosgi.toast.client.emergency_1.0.0
```

❍ Stop the airbag bundle by typing stop 4 at the prompt. (Note that the ID number for the airbag may be different for you.) Stopping the bundle triggers its activator's stop method, causing it to stop and unregister the airbag service. As a result, the airbag no longer deploys every five seconds and the emergency monitor is unbound. To confirm that the services are gone, type bundle 4 and note that the list of registered services is empty.

○ Restart the airbag bundle by typing start 4 at the prompt. The bundle's activator starts and registers the airbag service, thus satisfying the dependencies of the emergency monitor bundle. As a result, an emergency monitor is created and registered as a listener of the airbag service. At this point you will see the airbag deploying again every five seconds. To confirm that the service is back, type bundle 4 and note the airbag service in the list of registered services.

○ Stop the GPS bundle by typing stop 1. Here the GPS service is unregistered, in turn causing the emergency monitor to be unbound until a GPS service is reregistered. Note that the airbag service continues as usual, deploying and notifying its listeners every five seconds. Since the emergency monitor has removed itself as a listener, there is no response to the deployment of the airbag.

○ Restart the GPS bundle by typing start 1. This causes a GPS service to be registered and the requirements of the emergency monitor to be satisfied. The emergency monitor starts up and adds itself again as a listener of the airbag. The emergency notifications start appearing again on the console.

○ Terminate the OSGi framework by typing close at the prompt or by pressing the **Stop** button at the top of the Console view to terminate the OSGi framework.

BUNDLE SYMBOLIC NAMES IN THE CONSOLE

Console commands such as start and stop accept both bundle IDs and bundle symbolic names as parameters. While typing a bundle's symbolic name is clearly verbose and error-prone, it can be a useful alternative to using bundle IDs when you know the bundles you wish to start and stop instead of having to use the ss command to find their bundle IDs.

6.2.3 Service Tracker Summary

Service Trackers are a nice abstraction of the service management requirements. Even with this relatively simple example, however, it is apparent that writing a customizer is quite complicated. In fact, while putting together the code for this section, the authors and other experts went through several iterations attempting to perfect the code. No matter what we did, a good balance of simplicity and scalability could not be found. For example, in the code presented here, acquiring more than just two services requires the addition of several conditionals across several methods. It's very easy to get this code wrong, and testing, fixing, and verifying such changes is a chore.

Service Trackers can, however, be useful when getting and using services periodically throughout your code. Many OSGi developers use Service Trackers in an à la carte manner to acquire services whenever they may be needed—trackers help by doing all the accounting for you and giving you easy access to the service object. This is simple and useful but has the downside that it forces references to OSGi into your application's domain logic. This in turn ties your implementation to OSGi such that it cannot be run or tested in a non-OSGi environment. In keeping with our POJO style, using Service Trackers outside the bundle activator is not a recommended practice.

All in all, Service Trackers are a somewhat less than optimal solution for handling dynamic bundles.

6.3 Using the Service Activator Toolkit

Long before OSGi provided Declarative Services or even the Service Tracker, listening to service events was the only way to handle dynamic services. A bundle activator that thoroughly handled dynamic services was an impressive, if difficult-to-maintain, piece of code. From this complexity the Service Activator Toolkit (SAT) was born.

SAT is not a framework, but rather it provides an abstract bundle activator that your bundle activator can subclass. This allows you to reuse the complex but well-tested service listener behavior rather than implementing and maintaining it yourself. SAT also provides some tooling for the initial construction of your bundle activators as well as for the runtime analysis of your bundles.

6.3.1 Installing SAT into the Target Platform

Before we can use SAT, we must add it to the target platform. If you followed our recommendation in Chapter 3, "Tutorial Introduction," and loaded the predefined target, you can follow the steps given here. If you built your own target, we recommend you return to Chapter 3, "Tutorial Introduction," and load the predefined target before continuing.

- ○ Open the `toast.target` file in the `ToastTarget` project.
- ○ On the **Definition** tab, click the **Add...** button to add a location.
- ○ In the **Add Content** dialog, choose **Directory** from the list and click the **Next** button.
- ○ Type ${workspace_loc}/ToastTarget/org.eclipse.soda.sat/eclipse as the location and click **Finish**.
- ○ Save the contents of the editor.
- ○ Click the **Set as Target Platform** link in the top right corner of the editor.

To apply the SAT approach to Toast, we need to tweak the bundle activators from Chapter 5, "Services," to use the SAT abstract `BaseBundleActivator` and take advantage of its facilities. The following code snippets and explanations walk you through that process. The final code for this section is in the sample called "Chapter 6.3 SAT" in the Samples Manager. Note that to see the changes, you must compare this new code to that of Chapter 5, "Services," as the changes here are not based on the Service Tracker work of the previous section.

6.3.2 Modifying the GPS Bundle Activator

As you may recall, the GPS bundle is at the bottom of the food chain. As such, all we have to do is create and supply the GPS service when the bundle is activated. Before we modify the bundle activator, however, we first need to make the core SAT bundle visible to the GPS bundle:

○ Open the GPS bundle's manifest and add `org.eclipse.soda.sat.core` to the list of bundles under **Automated Management of Dependencies** on the **Dependencies** tab.

○ Save the bundle manifest editor.

○ Now update the activator to match the following snippet:

```
org.equinoxosgi.toast.dev.gps/Activator
public class Activator extends BaseBundleActivator {
  protected void activate() {
    IGps gps = new FakeGps();
    addExportedService(IGps.class.getName(), gps, null);
  }
}
```

○ Run **Organize Imports** before saving this file.

The main change is the addition of the `activate` method. This method is called by SAT when the activator has acquired its required imported services. SAT hooks into the OSGi lifecycle by implementing `start` and `stop` and then calling `activate` when all the stated constraints are met and `deactivate` when the constraints cease to be satisfied. Since the GPS bundle is at the bottom of the food chain, there are no constraints, and `activate` can be called immediately.

6.3.3 Modifying the Airbag Bundle Activator

The airbag bundle activator is a little more interesting in that the airbag service needs to be started via its `startup` method so that it can deploy periodically and stopped via its `shutdown` method when the bundle is stopped. You'll need to repeat the same steps listed in the preceding section to add the SAT core bundle to the airbag bundle's dependencies. Then update the airbag activator to match the following snippet:

org.equinoxosgi.toast.dev.airbag/Activator

```
public class Activator extends BaseBundleActivator {
  private FakeAirbag airbag;

  protected void activate() {
    airbag = new FakeAirbag();
    airbag.startup();
    addExportedService(IAirbag.class.getName(), airbag, null);
  }

  protected void deactivate() {
    airbag.shutdown();
    airbag = null;
  }
}
```

6.3.4 *Modifying the Emergency Monitor Bundle Activator*

Finally, the emergency monitor is at the top of the food chain and so needs to specify some service dependencies. These dependencies must be satisfied before the emergency monitor is started. Again, don't forget to repeat the steps listed in the earlier GPS section to add the SAT core bundle to this bundle's dependencies. Then update the activator as outlined here:

org.equinoxosgi.toast.client.emergency/Activator

```
public class Activator extends BaseBundleActivator {
  private IAirbag airbag;
  private IGps gps;
  private EmergencyMonitor monitor;

  protected void activate() {
    monitor = new EmergencyMonitor();
    gps = (IGps) getImportedService(IGps.class.getName());
    airbag = (IAirbag) getImportedService(IAirbag.class.getName());
    monitor.setGps(gps);
    monitor.setAirbag(airbag);
    monitor.startup();
  }

  protected void deactivate() {
    monitor.shutdown();
    monitor = null;
  }

  protected String[] getImportedServiceNames() {
    return new String[] {
        IAirbag.class.getName(), IGps.class.getName()};
  }
}
```

The key to this activator is the `getImportedServiceNames` method. This is called by the SAT infrastructure and must return an array containing the fully qualified type names of the services that the bundle requires. SAT then ensures that services matching these names are acquired from the service registry before calling `activate`. While the `activate` method is executing, you can be assured that all the required imported services are available.

Conversely, the `deactivate` method is called when one of the acquired services is being unregistered with the service registry. Upon returning from `deactivate`, the SAT infrastructure attempts to reacquire the lost service, which, if successful, will cause the `activate` method to be called once more.

In effect, these few methods replace the use of the `ServiceTracker` and the `ServiceTrackerCustomizer` from Section 6.2.

6.3.5 Launching

Running the SAT version of Toast is very much like all other cases. Here, of course, you must ensure that the SAT core bundle is in the launch configuration:

❍ Select **Run > Run Configurations...** from the menu bar.

❍ Select the **Toast** run configuration from beneath **OSGi Framework** in the list at the left.

❍ Add the bundles `org.eclipse.osgi.services` and `org.eclipse.soda.sat.core` to the launch. You'll need to uncheck the **Only show selected bundles** option to add more bundles. Then you can find them under the **Target Platform** heading in the bundles list.

❍ Click the **Run** button.

You should see the familiar output on the Console view:

```
Emergency occurred at lat=3776999 lon=-12244694 heading=90 speed=50
Emergency occurred at lat=3776999 lon=-12244694 heading=90 speed=50
...
```

If you like, you can experiment with stopping and starting the various bundles as in the previous section. When you are done, remember to terminate the OSGi framework before moving on. Type the `close` command into the Console view or press the **Stop** button at the top of the view.

6.3.6 SAT Summary

As you can see, the bundle activator code is significantly simpler with SAT when compared to the original implementation or even the Service Tracker implementation. SAT does a rigorous job of safely activating and deactivating your application bundles based on the availability of the services they need to acquire.

Among its other benefits, SAT provides support for optional services, managed services, managed service factories, and even for delayed creation of domain logic using proxies. SAT comes with a rich set of tooling, including a bundle activator wizard that could have helped with the conversions you just did, as well as some useful runtime tooling to help you analyze the dependencies that bundles have on other bundles.

SAT does introduce some modest performance overheads. For example, it requires a certain amount of work per bundle at startup time. Specifically, even if a bundle's required services are not available, SAT must still load and run the bundle activator to make that determination. Therefore, for very large applications with thousands of bundles, many of which are not active initially, SAT is less than optimal.

At the other end of the spectrum, developers of tiny systems may balk at adding more "utility" bundles to their configurations. SAT's physical footprint is quite modest, and if you are going to write a well-behaved dynamic system of any complexity, you are going to have multiple copies of similar code. At a certain point you win by having just one general-purpose, well-tested implementation.

USING BUNDLES FROM OUTSIDE OSGi

Some people see the fact that SAT and other parts of Equinox are not included in the OSGi specification as a drawback. This is frankly a shortsighted view. There are many useful bundles out there from many sources. Your own domain bundles may be useful to others inside and outside your organization. Like most Equinox bundles, SAT is fully framework independent and can be used in any OSGi-based system.

On the whole, SAT is quite useful and offers very real improvements over using Service Trackers. You should consider using SAT for systems with bundles numbering in the hundreds, especially those whose bundles are likely to be started anyway.

6.4 Using Declarative Services

Release 4 of the OSGi specification brought an altogether new way to solve the dynamic services issue—Declarative Services (DS). Having just read the SAT section of this chapter, you might consider DS to support a declarative form of the

SAT `getImportedServiceNames` and `addExportedService` methods; that is, DS is a way for a bundle to declare, in an XML file, the services it provides and references. DS binds and unbinds these services at the appropriate time.

SERVICE COMPONENT RUNTIME

Although the runtime portion of Declarative Services is technically called the Service Component Runtime, we use the term *Declarative Services*, or DS for short, to refer to both the specification and its runtime implementation.

Because Declarative Services is—as the name implies—declarative, no bundle code needs to be loaded to determine whether a bundle's prerequisites have been met. In fact, bundles that use DS generally do not need to have an activator at all.

Chapter 15, "Declarative Services," and Chapter 24, "Declarative Services Reference," discuss Declarative Services in detail. In this section we look at using DS in our prototype Toast application. As with the SAT example, start with the code from the sample for Chapter 5, "Services," and for each of our three bundles update the activator and associated files. The final code for this section is in the sample called "Chapter 6.4 Declarative Services" in the Samples Manager. Note that to see the changes, you must compare this new code to that of Chapter 5, "Services," as the changes here are not based on the Service Tracker or SAT work of the previous sections.

6.4.1 Modifying the GPS Bundle

The GPS bundle is a great place to start because it is the simplest of the bundles and it lies at the bottom of the food chain.

DS works in terms of *components*. A component is an entity that references zero or more services and provides zero or more services. A component consists of two parts: an XML file describing the DS component and the services that it references and provides, and a class that implements the component's provided services and receives referenced services.

As a convention, the XML file that describes the component is called `component.xml` and is located in the bundle in a folder called `OSGI-INF`. Carry out the following steps to add the component specification to the GPS bundle:

❍ Select the GPS project and choose **New > Other...** from the context menu. Under **Plug-in Development**, select **Component Definition** and press **Next**.

❍ For the folder name, use `org.equinoxosgi.toast.dev.gps/OSGI-INF`. This creates a folder inside the project where the `component.xml` file will reside.

○ Use the default file name of `component.xml`.

○ Press the **Browse...** button, start typing `FakeGps` for the class of the component, select it once it appears in the list, and press **Finish**.

The tooling generates a file called `component.xml` in the `OSGI-INF` folder and opens an editor as show in Figure 6-1.

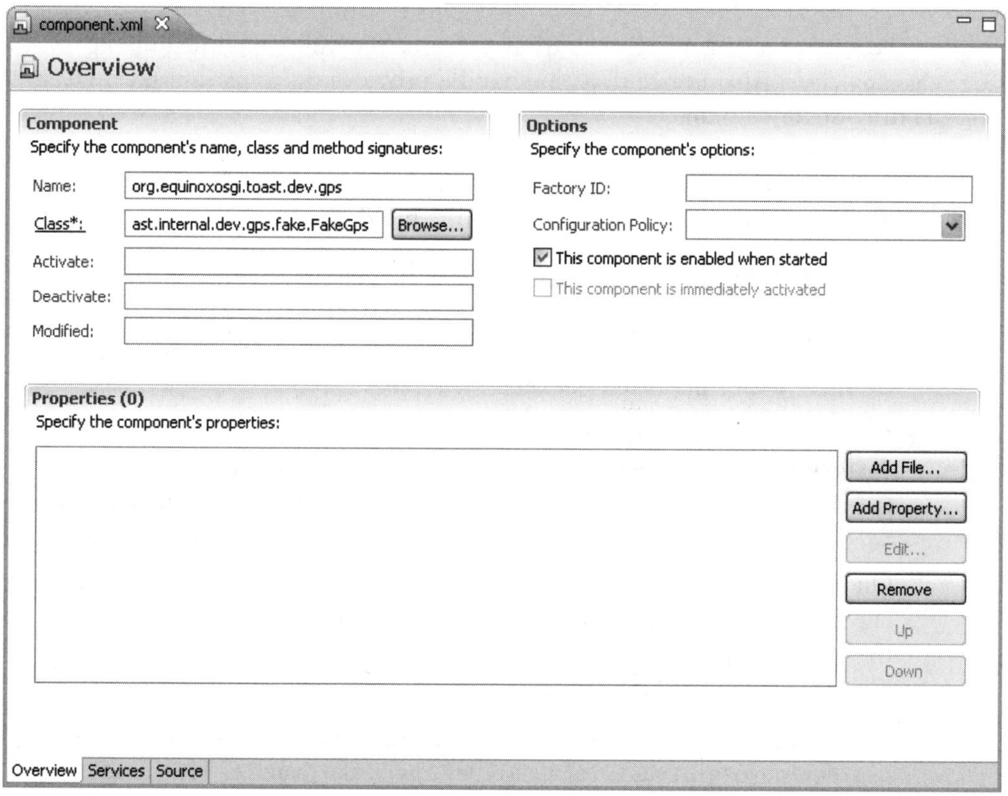

Figure 6–1 Declarative Services editor

Poke around in the editor and make the following modification to expose the bundle's GPS implementation as a service:

○ On the **Services** tab, press the **Add...** button in the **Provided Services** section, and type in `IGps` for the interface name. Press **OK**.

○ Save the contents of the editor.

Now look on the **Source** tab of the editor where you can see the contents of the generated `component.xml` file. It should look like this:

```
org.equinoxosgi.toast.dev.gps/component.xml
<?xml version="1.0" encoding="UTF-8"?>
<scr:component xmlns:scr="http://www.osgi.org/xmlns/scr/v1.1.0"
    name="org.equinoxosgi.toast.dev.gps">
  <implementation
      class="org.equinoxosgi.toast.internal.dev.gps.fake.FakeGps"/>
  <service>
    <provide interface="org.equinoxosgi.toast.dev.gps.IGps"/>
  </service>
</scr:component>
```

Notice that the implementation class is the fully qualified name of the FakeGps class. Also notice that this bundle provides the IGps interface, given by its fully qualified name.

With the component.xml complete, all that remains is to update the bundle to delete the activator, tell DS where to find the component description file, and ensure that the new files are included in the build:

- ○ Starting on the **Overview** tab of the bundle manifest editor for the GPS bundle, select and delete the previous bundle activator from the **Activator** field.

- ○ On the **Dependencies** tab, remove org.eclipse.soda.sat.core.framework from the list of **Imported Packages**.

- ○ Also remove org.eclipse.soda.sat.core from the list of **Automated Management of Dependencies**.

- ○ On the **MANIFEST.MF** tab, notice that the DS tooling already added the Service-Component header to declare the location of the component.xml file.

- ○ On the **Build** tab, in the **Binary Build** section, notice that the DS tooling already checked the box beside the OSGI-INF folder to include the component.xml in the build of the bundle.

- ○ Save the contents of the manifest editor.

- ○ Finally, delete the package that contains the old bundle activator: org.equinoxosgi.toast.internal.dev.gps.fake.bundle. The bundle no longer has any OSGi-specific code.

MULTIPLE COMPONENTS

A bundle may contain many components. This simply means that there would be either many component XML files or many <component> elements inside a single component XML file. See Chapter 15, "Declarative Services," for more information.

6.4.2 Modifying the Airbag Bundle

Updating the airbag bundle to use DS follows largely the same set of steps: Add the component.xml, create the component implementation of IAirbag, and update the manifest definition. These steps are detailed here:

- ○ Select the airbag project and choose **New > Other...** from the context menu. Under **Plug-in Development**, select **Component Definition** and press **Next**.

- ○ For the folder name, use org.equinoxosgi.toast.dev.airbag/OSGI-INF.

- ○ Press the **Browse...** button, start typing FakeAirbag for the class of the component, select it once it appears in the list, and press **Finish**.

- ○ Once the editor opens on component.xml, fill in startup and shutdown for the **Activate** and **Deactivate** fields, respectively.

- ○ On the **Services** tab, press the **Add...** button in the **Provided Services** section, and type in IAirbag for the interface name. Press **OK**.

- ○ Save the contents of the editor.

- ○ Delete the package that contains the bundle activator, since it is no longer needed.

- ○ Finally, remove the bundle activator reference from the bundle manifest itself on the **Overview** tab, and remove the two SAT references from the **Dependencies** tab.

Look on the **Source** tab of the editor where you can see the contents of the generated component.xml file. It should look like this:

```
org.equinoxosgi.toast.dev.airbag/component.xml
<?xml version="1.0" encoding="UTF-8"?>
<scr:component xmlns:scr="http://www.osgi.org/xmlns/scr/v1.1.0"
    name="org.equinoxosgi.toast.dev.airbag"
    activate="startup" deactivate="shutdown">
  <implementation class=
      "org.equinoxosgi.toast.internal.dev.airbag.fake.FakeAirbag"/>
  <service>
    <provide interface="org.equinoxosgi.toast.dev.airbag.IAirbag"/>
  </service>
</scr:component>
```

Notice that the activate and deactivate attributes of this component refer to the startup and shutdown methods on FakeAirbag. In this case, the startup method is called by DS when another component requests the service provided by this component. The deactivate method is called when the bundle is stopped.

6.4.3 Modifying the Emergency Bundle

Finally, let's adapt the emergency monitor bundle to use DS. The steps are for the most part the same as for the other two bundles, but because the emergency monitor bundle sits at the top of the food chain, there are a few differences:

○ Select the emergency monitor project and choose **New > Other...** from the context menu. Under **Plug-in Development**, select **Component Definition** and press **Next**.

○ For the folder name, use `org.equinoxosgi.toast.client.emergency/OSGI-INF`.

○ Use the default file name of `component.xml`.

○ Press the **Browse...** button, start typing `EmergencyMonitor` for the class of the component, select it once it appears in the list, and press **Finish**.

○ Again, fill in `startup` and `shutdown` for the **Activate** and **Deactivate** fields, respectively.

○ Flip over to the **Services** tab in the editor. In the **Referenced Services** section, press the **Add...** button, type in `IAirbag`, and press **OK**. Then, with `IAirbag` still highlighted, press the **Edit...** button. In the **Name** field, type in `airbag`. In the **Bind** field, type in `setAirbag`. This means that when the airbag becomes available to the emergency monitor component, DS calls the `setAirbag` method.

○ Now repeat these steps to add a referenced service for the GPS. Use `gps` for the **Name** field. Use `setGps` for the **Bind** field so DS can link in the `IGps` service when it becomes available.

○ Save the contents of the editor.

○ Delete the package that contains the bundle activator, since it is no longer needed.

○ Finally, remove the bundle activator reference from the bundle manifest itself on the **Overview** tab, and remove the two references to SAT from the **Dependencies** tab.

UNBIND METHODS ARE OFTEN NOT NEEDED

Typical DS components do not need an `unbind` method as DS itself takes care of freeing references to bound services. We recommend that you not specify an entry in that field unless you have a specific requirement to hook that aspect of the component lifecycle, for example, when using dynamic components. Chapter 15, "Declarative Services," includes considerable detail on related topics, and Chapter 13, "Web Portal," shows an example of `unbind` methods in action.

It's worth taking a closer a look at the generated `component.xml` file for this component. Select the **Source** tab to see the content shown in the following snippet:

```
org.equinoxosgi.toast.client.emergency/component.xml
<?xml version="1.0" encoding="UTF-8"?>
<scr:component xmlns:scr="http://www.osgi.org/xmlns/scr/v1.1.0"
    name="org.equinoxosgi.toast.client.emergency"
    activate="startup" deactivate="shutdown">
  <implementation class=
    "org.equinoxosgi.toast.internal.client.emergency.EmergencyMonitor"
    />
  <reference bind="setAirbag" cardinality="1..1"
    interface="org.equinoxosgi.toast.dev.airbag.IAirbag" name="airbag"
    policy="static"/>
  <reference bind="setGps" cardinality="1..1"
    interface="org.equinoxosgi.toast.dev.gps.IGps" name="gps"
    policy="static"/>
</scr:component>
```

Naming Conventions

There are several things that need naming when working with DS: the component and its lifecycle methods, and the referenced services and their lifecycle methods.

○ **Component name**—The component name must be globally unique. This name is not particularly important, so we suggest deriving it from the name of the bundle contributing the component. For example, here we used `org.equinoxosgi.toast.client.emergency`.

○ **Component lifecycle methods**—By default, `activate` and `deactivate` methods are called on the component as it changes state. We prefer, and use here, the more generic `startup` and `shutdown` naming convention.

○ **Referenced service names**—As with all naming, we recommend semantic naming such as `gps` over type-based names when identifying referenced services. Using a type-based name implies a relationship that likely does not exist and a maintenance burden that is guaranteed to require work. Semantic names are more flexible and more clearly identify the role that the referenced service plays. Note that referenced service names are optional. A name is needed only for debugging purposes and when using the `ComponentContext`'s `locateService` and `locateServices` methods.

○ **Referenced service lifecycle methods**—We also recommend that you derive the `bind` and `unbind` method names from the semantics of the service being referenced and the role it plays in your component. This should relate to the referenced service name. So, if the referenced service name is `gps`, the bind and unbind method names should be `setGps` and `clearGps`.

There are a few interesting things to note in this component declaration. First, this component requires the GPS and airbag services to work. This is captured in the two <reference> elements. Here the interface must be the fully qualified name of the service interface, but the reference name, if specified, need be unique only within the component. Notice also that, unlike the other two cases, this component does not provide any services—it is at the top of the food chain.

The activation portion of the lifecycle for this component under DS matches the earlier implementation. The EmergencyMonitor expects that DS will invoke the setGps and setAirbag methods as those required services become available. Once all the required services are available and their corresponding bind methods have been invoked, it expects DS to invoke its startup method.

The deactivation portion of the lifecycle is now a mirror image of the activation. When any required service becomes unavailable, DS first invokes the shutdown method followed by the relevant unbind methods if specified.

6.4.4 Launching

With the three bundles refactored to use DS, let's launch the application again:

❍ Select **Run > Run Configurations...** from the menu bar.

❍ Select the **Toast** run configuration from beneath **OSGi Framework** in the list at the left.

❍ Scroll down into the **Target Platform** bundles and check the box beside the bundles org.eclipse.equinox.ds and org.eclipse.equinox.util. These bundles are Equinox's DS implementation and prerequisite.

❍ Also, remove the org.eclipse.soda.sat.core bundle from this list.

❍ On the **Arguments** tab, add this to the **VM Arguments** so we can see any DS errors on the console:

```
-Dequinox.ds.print=true
```

---

eclipse.ignoreApp and osgi.noShutdown

You'll notice two VM arguments that are in the list by default:

```
-Declipse.ignoreApp=true -Dosgi.noShutdown=true
```

When the eclipse.ignoreApp argument is set to true, the main launching thread will not start the default application. This makes sense in our case because we are running a plain OSGi system rather than an Eclipse application.

> Setting the `osgi.noShutdown` argument to `true` causes the OSGi framework to keep running even when the main thread has completed. In many cases, there is no work to be done on the main thread, so we need this option to make sure the framework stays alive.

When you click the **Run** button, you should see the familiar output on the Console view:

```
Emergency occurred at lat=3776999 lon=-12244694 heading=90 speed=50
Emergency occurred at lat=3776999 lon=-12244694 heading=90 speed=50
...
```

6.4.5 Declarative Services Summary

By making Toast run on Declarative Services, you learned how to declare, both in XML and using the DS tooling, the services that a bundle references and those that it provides. You did this for bundles both at the top and at the bottom of the food chain.

Moving from bundle activators to Declarative Services was not a difficult task. That ease of migration comes from the nature of DS but also in large part as a side effect of the principle maintained throughout Toast—keeping the domain logic separate from the plumbing and maintaining a unidirectional bundle dependency graph.

6.5 Summary

When the lifecycle and discovery of services are kept out of the domain logic, the domain logic can be used with Service Trackers, SAT, Declarative Services, and even in non-OSGi deployments. In fact, you might have noticed that in exploring all three dynamic service mechanisms, you barely modified the domain logic.

It's also important to point out that a well-structured OSGi-based system can be written using any of the three approaches shown in this chapter. While all three approaches have their advantages and disadvantages, we don't consider them equally useful in all situations. In fact, we don't recommend basing your system on Service Trackers at all.

SAT works well for systems with bundles numbering in the hundreds or fewer, not in the thousands. The price SAT pays to determine if each bundle is ready to activate becomes insignificant if all your bundles end up getting started anyhow. SAT's tooling makes it easy to create and refactor your bundles.

Declarative Services, because of its declarative nature, scales up to systems with thousands of bundles, and it shines particularly in systems where many of the bundles run only occasionally. Not relying on a bundle running code to determine whether it is ready has definite performance advantages. But those advantages come at a cost. Debugging is more difficult when using DS than when using SAT, although the tooling mitigates this to some degree. So while all three approaches are valid, we've chosen to implement the remainder of Toast using Declarative Services, as it offers the most benefits and the simplest programming model.

CHAPTER 7

Client/Server Interaction

At this point Toast operates as a stand-alone application. To fully implement the emergency scenario, however, we need a service center to which we can report emergencies. In this chapter we implement a separate OSGi runtime to be that service center. By chapter's end, the client's emergency application is sending emergency information to the service center using simple HTTP for communications.

Since Toast is growing in size and complexity, it's also the right time to introduce some effective patterns for handling configurable runtime parameters as well as logging.

The goals of this chapter are to

○ Implement the service center as a separate runtime, using OSGi and servlets

○ Enhance the client side to allow the emergency monitor to communicate with the service center over HTTP

○ Present mechanisms for logging and handling command-line parameters

○ Launch both the service center and the client and test their interaction

In previous tutorial chapters, we showed every line of code and every change. In this and subsequent chapters, however, the volume of code makes that approach infeasible. Instead we'll ask you to use the Samples Manager to load each project and then we provide you with detailed instructions for building the rest of the code in the chapter. If you prefer, you still have the option to load all the finished code for the chapter and just read along with the tutorial sections.

7.1 The Back End

Back end is the term Toast uses for the server side. It's important to understand that the implementation of the Toast Back End assumes that it is running as an entirely separate OSGi runtime on an entirely separate Java VM. It might even be running on an entirely separate computer. It's also headless; that is, it has no user interface.

The back end is a server that listens for clients to report emergencies. The simplest way to handle messaging of this sort is to use HTTP. The OSGi specification defines an HTTP service that allows applications like Toast to register servlets. Interchangeable implementations of that service are available from a variety of sources. We use the one provided by Equinox.

7.1.1 The Core Bundles

Before we implement the back end emergency functionality, we need to set up two core bundles. The `org.equinoxosgi.toast.core` bundle provides a set of utility classes used by both the back end and the client runtimes. The details of the various utility classes in this bundle are covered in Section 7.3, "Utility Classes," and are not important here. You can just load the `org.equinoxosgi.toast.core` bundle using the Samples Manager as discussed in Section 3.4.2, "Comparing."

The other bundle we need is `org.equinoxosgi.core.emergency`. It contains a set of constants that are used by both the back end and the client runtimes to implement the emergency scenario.

○ Create a new bundle project called `org.equinoxosgi.toast.core.emergency`. Refer to Section 4.2.1, "GPS Bundle," for detailed instructions on creating a bundle project.

Next create the package and the interface:

○ Create a new interface in this bundle called `IEmergencyConstants` and place it in a new package called `org.equinoxosgi.toast.core.emergency`. Fill in the code with the following snippet:

```
org.equinoxosgi.toast.core.emergency/IEmergencyConstants
public interface IEmergencyConstants {
    public static final String EMERGENCY_FUNCTION = "emergency";
    public static final String HEADING_PARAMETER = "heading";
    public static final String LATITUDE_PARAMETER = "latitude";
    public static final String LONGITUDE_PARAMETER = "longitude";
    public static final String SPEED_PARAMETER = "speed";
}
```

○ On the **Runtime** tab of the bundle's manifest, add the newly created package to the list of exported packages. Then save the manifest.

7.1.2 The Back End Emergency Bundle

With the two core bundles in place, let's create the bundle with the back end's application logic. It consists of a servlet to handle emergency notifications from the client and a component to register the servlet with the servlet container implemented by HttpService.

○ Create a new plug-in project for the bundle named `org.equinoxosgi.toast` `.backend.emergency`.

○ In the manifest editor, add the following bundles to the **Automated Management of Dependencies** list, making sure the **Import-Package** button is selected:

```
javax.servlet
org.eclipse.osgi.services
org.equinoxosgi.toast.core
org.equinoxosgi.toast.core.emergency
```

The `javax.servlet` bundle contains the necessary packages for HTTP communications. The `org.eclipse.osgi.services` bundle contains the interface HttpService.

Now create the servlet to handle incoming HTTP requests from clients. For now, each time it receives an emergency message, it simply logs the emergency information to the console.

○ Create a class called `EmergencyServlet` in a package called `org.equinoxosgi.toast.internal.backend.emergency` with the class `HttpServlet` as its superclass. Use the following snippet to complete the class:

```
org.equinoxosgi.toast.backend.emergency/EmergencyServlet
public class EmergencyServlet extends HttpServlet {
    protected void doGet(
        HttpServletRequest request, HttpServletResponse response)
        throws ServletException, IOException {
        String id = getParameter(request, response,
            ICoreConstants.ID_PARAMETER);
        int latitude = Integer.parseInt(getParameter(request, response,
            IEmergencyConstants.LATITUDE_PARAMETER));
        int longitude = Integer.parseInt(getParameter(request, response,
            IEmergencyConstants.LONGITUDE_PARAMETER));
        int heading = Integer.parseInt(getParameter(request, response,
            IEmergencyConstants.HEADING_PARAMETER));
        int speed = Integer.parseInt(getParameter(request, response,
            IEmergencyConstants.SPEED_PARAMETER));
        double lat = latitude / 100000.0;
        double lon = longitude / 100000.0;
```

```
        LogUtility.logInfo(this, "Emergency: " + id + " (" + lat + "N, "
            + lon + "E) " + heading + "deg " + speed + "kph");
        PrintWriter writer = response.getWriter();
        writer.print("Help is on its way!");
        response.setContentType(ICoreConstants.CONTENT_TYPE_PLAIN);
    }

    private String getParameter(
        HttpServletRequest request, HttpServletResponse response,
        String parameter) throws ServletException, IOException {
        String value = request.getParameter(parameter);
        if (value == null || value.length() == 0) {
            response.sendError(HttpServletResponse.SC_NOT_ACCEPTABLE,
                ICoreConstants.MISSING_PARAMETER + parameter);
            throw new ServletException(ICoreConstants.MISSING_PARAMETER
                + parameter);
        }
        return value;
    }
}
```

The key code here is the standard servlet doGet method. The method simply gathers the parameters from the HTTP request, logs the emergency event to the console, and responds to the client with a text message. In a more complete application the emergency event would go into a database and trigger any number of follow-on actions, but here this is enough to paint the picture.

Notice that the EmergencyServlet class is pure domain code; that is, it is unaware of OSGi. As a generic subclass of HttpServlet, it can be reused in a server setup that does not involve OSGi. In the Toast scenario, however, we are using OSGi and we need to register the generic EmergencyServlet with the HttpService. We need to create a component to achieve this:

○ Create a class called Component in a package called org.equinoxosgi.toast .internal.backend.emergency.bundle. Use this snippet to complete the class:

org.equinoxosgi.toast.backend.emergency.bundle/Component
```
public class Component {
    private HttpService http;
    private String servletAlias;

    public void setHttp(HttpService value) {
        http = value;
    }

    protected void shutdown() {
        http.unregister(servletAlias);
    }

    protected void startup() {
        try {
```

```
    String servletRoot = PropertyManager.getProperty(
        ICoreConstants.BACK_END_URL_PROPERTY,
        ICoreConstants.BACK_END_URL_DEFAULT);
    UrlBuilder urlBuilder = new UrlBuilder(servletRoot);
    urlBuilder.appendPath(IEmergencyConstants.EMERGENCY_FUNCTION);
    servletAlias = urlBuilder.getPath();

    EmergencyServlet servlet = new EmergencyServlet();
    http.registerServlet(servletAlias, servlet, null, null);
    LogUtility.logDebug(this, "Registered EmergencyServlet at "
        + servletAlias);
    } catch (Exception e) {
    LogUtility.logError(this,
        "Error registering servlet with HttpService", e);
    }
  }
}
```

Here the bulk of the work is in the startup component lifecycle method. startup creates the alias for the emergency servlet, instantiates the actual servlet, and then registers it with the HttpService. The shutdown method then takes care of unregistering the servlet when the component is deactivated. The setHttp method provides the hook that DS needs to inject the HttpService into the component.

All that remains is to describe the emergency component to DS by following these steps:

- ○ Create a new service component for this bundle called component.xml in the OSGI-INF folder of this bundle. Refer to Section 6.4.1, "Modifying the GPS Bundle," for detailed instructions.

- ○ Use Component as the class for the component.

- ○ Fill in startup and shutdown for the **Activate** and **Deactivate** fields, respectively.

- ○ Add HttpService as a referenced service. Use http as the **Name** and setHttp as the **Bind** method. This means that when the HTTP service becomes available to the back end emergency component, DS invokes the setHttp method.

The back end emergency bundle is a typical top-of-the-food-chain bundle. It references one service, the HttpService, and provides no services. With the back end in place, we're ready to make changes to the client side and hook them together.

7.2 The Client Side

Recall from the previous chapter that the emergency monitor bundle listens for the airbag to deploy, obtains the vehicle's location from the GPS bundle, and then writes this information to the console. Now we want the emergency monitor to notify the back end we just created. The first step is a mechanism that handles the communication from the client to the back end. Once this is completed, we can modify the emergency monitor bundle to use this mechanism and talk to the back end.

7.2.1 *The Channel Bundle*

Since a mechanism that acts as a communication channel for clients to send messages to servers using HTTP is useful for more than just the emergency scenario, let's expose it as a service and put it in a separate bundle:

○ Create a new project for the bundle named `org.equinoxosgi.toast` `.core.channel.sender`.

○ Add `org.equinoxosgi.toast.core` to the **Automated Management of Dependencies** list, making sure the **Import-Package** button is selected.

Now create the interface to define the channel service:

○ Create an interface called `IChannel` in a package called `org.equinoxosgi` `.toast.core.channel.sender`. Use the following snippet to complete the interface:

`org.equinoxosgi.toast.core.channel.sender/IChannel`
```
public interface IChannel {
   public InputStream send(ChannelMessage message) throws IOException;
}
```

The `IChannel` interface defines a single method that allows the client to send a message to the back end and to receive an `InputStream` containing the back end's response.

The `ChannelMessage` class is a simple data structure that captures the idea of a *function* and a set of *parameters*. It is logically part of the `IChannel` service API because any consumer that invokes the `send` method needs to create a `ChannelMessage` first. As such, it should go in the same package as `IChannel`.

○ Create a class called `ChannelMessage` in the same package as `IChannel`. Use the following snippet to complete the class:

`org.equinoxosgi.toast.core.channel.sender/ChannelMessage`
```
public class ChannelMessage {
   private String function;
   private Map parameters;

   public ChannelMessage(String function) {
      super();
      this.function = function;
```

```java
    parameters = new HashMap(11);
  }

  public void addParameter(String parameter, int value) {
    addParameter(parameter, Integer.toString(value));
  }

  public void addParameter(String parameter, String value) {
    parameters.put(parameter, value);
  }

  public boolean equals(Object obj) {
    if (this == obj)
      return true;
    if (obj == null)
      return false;
    if (getClass() != obj.getClass())
      return false;
    ChannelMessage other = (ChannelMessage) obj;
    if (function == null) {
      if (other.function != null)
        return false;
    } else if (!function.equals(other.function))
      return false;
    if (parameters == null) {
      if (other.parameters != null)
        return false;
    } else if (!parameters.equals(other.parameters))
      return false;
    return true;
  }

  public String getFunction() {
    return function;
  }

  public Iterator getParametersIterator() {
    return parameters.keySet().iterator();
  }

  public int hashCode() {
    final int prime = 31;
    int result = 1;
    result = prime * result
        + ((function == null) ? 0 : function.hashCode());
    result = prime * result
        + ((parameters == null) ? 0 : parameters.hashCode());
    return result;
  }

  public String valueForParameter(String parameter) {
    return (String) parameters.get(parameter);
  }
}
```

Now that the service interface is complete, make sure that the service package is visible to other bundles:

○ In the **Runtime** tab of the manifest editor, add `org.equinoxosgi.toast.core` `.channel.sender` to the list of exported packages.

Now we are set to implement the `IChannel` service, but we first need to decide where the implementation will go. Should the implementation go in its own bundle or in the same bundle as the service interface? If we expect there to be more than one implementation of the service, it makes sense to put the service definition in one bundle and place each implementation in its own separate bundle. In this case, we don't expect more than this one implementation, so putting the interface and the implementation together is OK. If we decide later to add another implementation of `IChannel`, we can refactor our original implementation to be in a separate package from the service interface. This is one of the powers of OSGi's modularity—clients of a service are isolated from the implementations, so implementers have more freedom.

○ To create the implementation, make a new class called `UrlChannel` that implements `IChannel` and put it in a package called `org.equinoxosgi.toast` `.internal.core.channel.sender`. Complete the body of the class using this snippet:

`org.equinoxosgi.toast.internalcore.channel.sender/UrlChannel`

```
public class UrlChannel implements IChannel {
  private final String urlSpec;

  public UrlChannel() {
    super();
    urlSpec = PropertyManager.getProperty(
        ICoreConstants.BACK_END_URL_PROPERTY,
        ICoreConstants.BACK_END_URL_DEFAULT);
  }

  private URL createUrl(String urlSpec, ChannelMessage message)
      throws MalformedURLException {
    UrlBuilder builder = new UrlBuilder(urlSpec);
    builder.appendPath(message.getFunction());
    for (Iterator i = message.getParametersIterator(); i.hasNext();) {
      String parameter = (String) i.next();
      String value = message.valueForParameter(parameter);
      builder.addParameter(parameter, value);
    }
    URL url = builder.toUrl();
    String value = builder.toString();
    LogUtility.logDebug(this, value);
    return url;
  }
```

```
public InputStream send(ChannelMessage message) throws IOException {
  URL url = createUrl(urlSpec, message);
  LogUtility.logDebug(this, "Sending message: " +
      message.getFunction());
  return url.openStream();
  }
}
```

The last step in completing the bundle is to create a component definition that exposes UrlChannel as an IChannel service:

○ Create a new service component for this bundle called component.xml in the OSGI-INF folder of this bundle.

○ Use the UrlChannel for the class of the component.

○ Add IChannel as a provided service.

Notice that this bundle lies at the bottom of the food chain since it registers a service but requires none. Notice also that the service implementation class can be used directly as the component implementation class—a demonstration of DS's POJO capabilities.

ECLIPSE COMMUNICATION FRAMEWORK

The Eclipse Communication Framework (ECF) project has a vast array of facilities for interprocess communication over many different protocols. Here communication is not our focus, so we are using a very simplistic approach. For building more robust systems, however, we recommend using ECF infrastructure.

Bundle API Surface Area

A bundle's API surface area is the total number of packages that the bundle exports via its Export-Package manifest header. As previously mentioned, less is more in this regard, and ideally a bundle has a small API surface area upon which other bundles can depend.

Minimize exported types—A bundle should minimize the number of types that it exports. A bundle should always divide its package namespace into API packages and internal packages. A common convention is to name internal packages by including a segment called internal. As new types are added to the bundle, a decision must always be made as to whether the type is API and should reside in an exported package, or is private implementation and should reside in an internal package that is not exported.

Favor exporting interfaces over classes—Ideally an exported package should contain only interfaces. When a class must be exported, it should be a simple data type that does not dictate how a service interface is implemented. If the bundle provides an OSGi service, the implementation of the service should reside in a private internal package.

Package names are API, too—Do not forget that an export package is part of the bundle's public API upon which other bundles can depend. Special attention should be given to the naming of such packages. Keeping packages highly cohesive is recommended, and exported packages should contain small sets of closely related types and should have intention-revealing names.

`Bundle-SymbolicName` **is API, too**—A bundle's `Bundle-SymbolicName` manifest header should also be treated as API. Not only does the `Bundle-SymbolicName` uniquely identify a bundle, but other bundles can use the `Require-Bundle` manifest header to declare a dependency upon the bundle by specifying its `Bundle-SymbolicName`. A bundle's `Bundle-SymbolicName` is also accessible programmatically via the `Bundle` method `getSymbolicName`. `Bundle` objects can be accessed in a variety of ways, such as via the `BundleContext`, via the `PackageAdmin` service, and via `BundleEvents` that are fired to `BundleListeners`.

Artifacts should be placed, by default, in a bundle's internal package. Artifacts that are placed in an exported package should be carefully scrutinized and reviewed since they contribute to the bundle API surface area. Packages are exported using the `Export-Package` manifest header.

As with all public APIs, renaming and refactoring packages breaks bundles that depend upon them and should therefore be avoided. For this reason it is important to structure and name exported packages carefully.

7.2.2 The Emergency Monitor Bundle

Now that we have a means of communicating to the back end, the emergency monitor on the client needs to be updated to use the channel support and tell the server about emergencies.

Let's start by adding the necessary bundles to the client's emergency monitor project:

○ Open the manifest editor for `org.equinoxosgi.toast.client.emergency` and add the following bundles to the **Automated Management of Dependencies** list:

```
org.equinoxosgi.toast.core.channel.sender
org.equinoxosgi.toast.core
```

```
org.equinoxosgi.toast.core.emergency
org.eclipse.core.jobs
```

❍ In the **Required Plug-ins** list, add `org.eclipse.equinox.common`. Section 5.3, "Registering the Airbag Service," provides a detailed discussion of the rationale for using `Require-Bundle` in this case.

With the necessary packages now available, we can modify the `EmergencyMonitor` class to talk to the back end via a channel. The following snippet outlines the changes needed. As with the other snippets, you can load this from the Samples Manager.

org.equinoxosgi.toast.client.emergency/EmergencyMonitor
```
public class EmergencyMonitor implements IAirbagListener {
  private IAirbag airbag;
  private IChannel channel;
  private IGps gps;
  private Job job;

  public void deployed() {
    startJob();
  }

  private void runEmergencyProcess() {
    ChannelMessage message = new ChannelMessage(
        IEmergencyConstants.EMERGENCY_FUNCTION);
    String id = PropertyManager.getProperty(
        ICoreConstants.ID_PROPERTY, ICoreConstants.ID_DEFAULT);
    message.addParameter(ICoreConstants.ID_PARAMETER, id);
    message.addParameter(IEmergencyConstants.LATITUDE_PARAMETER,
        gps.getLatitude());
    message.addParameter(IEmergencyConstants.LONGITUDE_PARAMETER,
        gps.getLongitude());
    message.addParameter(IEmergencyConstants.HEADING_PARAMETER,
        gps.getHeading());
    message.addParameter(IEmergencyConstants.SPEED_PARAMETER,
        gps.getSpeed());
    InputStream stream = null;
    try {
      stream = channel.send(message);
      InputStreamReader reader = new InputStreamReader(stream);
      try {
        BufferedReader buffer = new BufferedReader(reader);
        String reply = buffer.readLine();
        LogUtility.logDebug(this, "Received reply: " + reply);
      } finally {
        stream.close();
      }
    } catch (IOException e) {
      LogUtility.logError(this, "Unable to send to back end: ", e);
    }
    job = null;
  }
```

```
public void setAirbag(IAirbag value) {
  airbag = value;
}

public void setChannel(IChannel value) {
  channel = value;
}

public void setGps(IGps value) {
  gps = value;
}

public void shutdown() {
  stopJob();
  airbag.removeListener(this);
}

private void startJob() {
  if (job != null) {
    return;
  }
  job = new Job("EmergencyMonitor") {
    protected IStatus run(IProgressMonitor monitor) {
      runEmergencyProcess();
      return Status.OK_STATUS;
    }
  };
  job.schedule();
}

public void startup() {
  airbag.addListener(this);
}

private void stopJob() {
  if (job != null) {
    job.cancel();
    try {
      job.join();
    } catch (InterruptedException e) {
      // shutting down, ok to ignore
    }
    job = null;
  }
}
}
```

This class has three major parts: lifecycle and job management, setters for
dependency injection, and the code for sending messages over a channel. Notice
the setChannel method was introduced to accept the IChannel service when it
becomes available.

The most significant change to EmergencyMonitor is in the domain logic.
Now, when the airbag deploys and the deployed method is invoked, instead of

simply printing the emergency message to the console, the monitor gathers readings from the GPS, instantiates a `ChannelMessage`, and sends it to the back end via the channel.

The emergency monitor uses a `Job` to communicate with the back end because it is a potentially long-running operation. Since `deploy` is called as a listener notification, it would be bad form to block the notifier thread with remote communications and prevent other listeners from hearing about the events.

Finally, we need to modify the component definition for the emergency monitor bundle to require the `IChannel` service:

○ Open the `component.xml` in the `OSGI-INF` folder of this bundle.

○ On the **Services** tab, in the **Referenced Services** section, press the **Add...** button, type in `IChannel`, and press **OK**.

○ Then, with `IChannel` still highlighted, press the **Edit...** button. In the **Name** field, type in `channel`.

○ In the **Bind** field, type in `setChannel`. Then save the file.

7.3 Utility Classes

Scattered throughout the code snippets on both the back end and the client-side implementations in this chapter you may have noticed references to a few new utility classes. Specifically, constants interfaces `ICoreConstants` and `IEmergencyConstants` have been introduced along with `PropertyManager` and `LogUtility`.

7.3.1 Constants

Toast uses Java interfaces to define constants that are shared between different bundles. `ICoreConstants` lives in the `org.equinoxosgi.toast.core` bundle and is intended to be used by any Toast bundle. `IEmergencyConstants` is broken out into a separate bundle called `org.equinoxosgi.toast.core.emergency`. The constants it defines are intended to be used only by the parts of Toast that implement the emergency scenario, both on the client and on the back end.

In later chapters, when Toast is divided into deployable features, it will be very handy that the constants needed by the emergency scenario can easily be installed and removed along with the rest of the code that implements the emergency scenario.

7.3.2 Properties

The `PropertyManager` class resides in the `org.equinoxosgi.toast.core` bundle. It is a simple helper class that exposes Java system properties and logs property accesses for debugging purposes. For example, in the code in the previous section, the `EmergencyMonitor` used the `PropertyManager` to fetch the value used to identify itself in messages to the back end.

For now the easiest way to define system properties is to use VM arguments when launching. To do this you place the key/value pairs in the **VM Arguments** section of the **Arguments** tab of your run configuration where each is preceded by –D. For example, to define the `toast.id` argument to have a value of `Kevin131`, add the following to the **VM Arguments**:

```
-Dtoast.id=Kevin131
```

In later chapters we introduce the notion of a product and two configuration files: `config.ini` and `launcher.ini`. Any of these can also be used to set up system properties.

7.3.3 Logging

Toast defines a class called `LogUtility` in `org.equinoxosgi.toast.core`. `LogUtility` provides a simple API for logging messages at various levels to both the OSGi Log Service and to the console. Chapter 17, "Logging," provides a deep dive on logging.

`LogUtility` is used throughout Toast. The `EmergencyMonitor`, for example, uses `LogUtility` in two places, first when it receives a reply from the back end. It logs it at debug level, which makes it easy to suppress by setting the `LogUtility`'s log level to be `LOG_INFO` or higher. It uses `LogUtility` again if a communication error occurs. In this case it logs it at error level and passes along the exception as well as a descriptive message.

Why a Singleton and Not a Service?

It is not always obvious whether certain functionality should be implemented as a service or as a singleton. In the case of `LogUtility` and `PropertyManager`, one could argue both ways.

In this example it was a conscious decision to implement them as singletons. We decided that requiring users of these utilities to acquire them as services would often be more trouble than it was worth. For example, often the very reason for property fetching or logging is to report a situation concerning services. In other words, the utilities need to operate at a level even below services.

Also, had we chosen to make them services, any bundle that needed to fetch properties or do logging would need to acquire that service and then pass it down into the depths of the domain logic or contrive to make it available internally. This can needlessly clutter otherwise simple implementations and APIs.

For our needs, the LogUtility insulates Toast from the details of the logging configured into the system.

7.4 Running Toast

Now that Toast consists of two separate runtimes, we need two launch configurations. The original client launch configuration from the previous chapter still resides in org.equinoxosgi.toast.client.emergency. We'll need to modify it to include the new bundles created in this chapter. We'll also need to make another launch configuration to run the back end.

7.4.1 Running the Back End

Start by creating a new launch configuration for the back end:

○ Create a new run configuration named backend. You can refer to Section 4.2.4, "Launching," for detailed instructions.

○ Select the following three bundles from the workspace:

```
org.equinoxosgi.toast.backend.emergency
org.equinoxosgi.toast.core
org.equinoxosgi.toast.core.emergency
```

○ Select the following six bundles from the target platform:

```
javax.servlet
org.eclipse.equinox.ds
org.eclipse.equinox.http
org.eclipse.equinox.util
org.eclipse.osgi
org.eclipse.osgi.services
```

The org.eclipse.equinox.http bundle contains an implementation of HttpService. Without it, there would be no server, and Toast's back end servlet would not be able to register. The org.eclipse.equinox.ds and org.eclipse.equinox.util bundles provide the DS implementation.

○ Add the following VM arguments:

```
-Dequinox.ds.print=true
-Dtoast.core.util.logLevel=DEBUG
-Dorg.osgi.service.http.port=8080
```

The last two arguments are new in this chapter. The first of these configures the LogUtility to log all messages, including debug messages, to the console. The last argument sets the port for the HTTP server to 8080. If you use port 8080 for some other server on your computer, change this argument or shut down the conflicting program.

- ○ On the **Common** tab, select the **Shared file** option and use `/org.equinoxosgi.toast.backend.emergency` as the folder.
- ○ Run the backend launch configuration.

You should see the following log messages on the Console view:

```
Property: -Dtoast.backend.url=http://localhost:8080/toast
Component: Registered EmergencyServlet at /toast/emergency
```

The first message indicates that the `PropertyManager` has accessed the `toast.backend.url` system property. The second message indicates that the `EmergencyServlet` has been registered. You can check the servlet by pointing your web browser at http://localhost:8080/toast/emergency.

If the server is running properly, you should see a reply in your web browser such as `406 - Missing parameter: id`. You'll also see a stack trace in the Console view.

7.4.2 Running the Client

The client launch configuration needs to be updated to include three new bundles:

- ○ Rename the `Toast` launch configuration to be `client`.
- ○ In addition to the original bundles listed, add the following three bundles:

```
org.equinoxosgi.toast.core
org.equinoxosgi.toast.core.channel.sender
org.equinoxosgi.toast.core.emergency
```

- ○ With the backend launch configuration still running, run the `client` launch configuration.

On the Console view for the client, the first things to appear are two messages from the `PropertyManager` indicating that it has obtained properties for the client ID and for the back end URL:

```
Property: -Dtoast.id=ABC123
Property: -Dtoast.backend.url=http://localhost:8080/toast
```

After about five seconds, the airbag deploys and the `URLChannel` logs two further messages. The first one indicates the HTTP request that it sends to the back end. The second message shows the logical content of the message it sends. Finally, the `EmergencyMonitor` logs the reply it receives from the back end. This sequence repeats every five seconds.

```
UrlChannel: http://localhost:8080/toast/emergency?speed=50&longitude=
-12244694&latitude=3776999&heading=90&id=ABC123
UrlChannel: Sending message: emergency
EmergencyMonitor: Received reply: Help is on its way!
```

In the meantime, take a look at the back end's console by clicking the 🖥▾ icon in the Console view. Notice that the back end logs a message each time it receives an emergency notification from the client:

```
EmergencyServlet: Emergency: ABC123 (37.76999N, -122.44694E) 90deg 50kph
```

7.5 Summary

In this chapter we added a server-side runtime to the overall Toast application. The client and back end runtimes even share some common bundles. The client now notifies the back end when an emergency occurs. These two runtimes are both based on OSGi and can run independently on different workspaces or even different machines.

We created a variety of bundles along the way, some providing services, some referencing services, and some utility bundles that neither provide nor reference any services. Most significantly, this chapter covered the registration of a servlet into a server.

The power of modularity and concern with separation was once again evident. Toast now consists of seven bundles, up from three at the end of Chapter 6, "Services." Figure 7-1 shows the three original bundles along with the four new

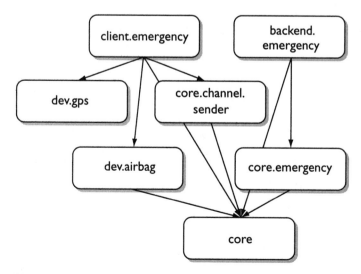

Figure 7–1   Bundle dependencies

bundles. The original three bundles are still present but have been updated to clearly separate domain logic from the client-server communications. We have also separated out two bundles that provide shared infrastructure for both client and server. The result is a system of seven highly cohesive bundles. We will see the advantages to this approach as we look at testing in the next chapter.

CHAPTER 8

Testing

Despite the best efforts of software engineers, defects occur in even the most carefully crafted applications. And so an entire subset of the software industry has arisen from the need for testing. Books, courses, tools, frameworks, even large teams of seasoned software professionals have been dedicated to the craft of software testing.

Toast needs testing, too. Until now in the development of Toast, we have not paid much attention to testing. We have been careful to make sure that it is possible to test Toast, but we have written no test cases.

Many software developers embrace the notion of writing test cases first (or at least early). While we count ourselves among them, it's worth noting that we have chosen to take a tutorial-based approach to building Toast as opposed to a test-driven approach. This is because while taking a test-driven approach is a good development practice, it is not necessarily the best way to learn or teach. Now that you have a basic understanding of creating OSGi-based systems, we can cover the elements of OSGi development that relate to testing. In particular, we cover

- General issues around testing Toast that can be applied to OSGi-based applications in general
- The principles and practices around making bundles and systems testable
- Implementing a unit test for one piece of Toast domain logic using the JUnit and EasyMock frameworks
- System-wide testing of Toast as an OSGi-based system

8.1 Making Toast Testable

Before we launch into implementing automated tests for Toast, let's review some of the practices we have introduced in Toast that enable us to create clean test cases. These points relate to all kinds of software development.

POJOs—The most important practice to make sure your code is testable is to write your domain logic as pure POJOs. Allowing OSGi-specific dependencies into your domain logic makes writing and running simple JUnit tests significantly more difficult.

Dependency injection—In an effort to decouple and allow elements to be reused, we have been using setter-based dependency injection. This allows us to provide alternative implementations and, as we will see, mock objects with relative ease.

Clear APIs—APIs support black-box testing. When your domain logic is defined by an API, it's clear exactly what needs to be tested. Similarly, if your domain logic references other facilities only by their APIs, it makes it clear what needs to be mocked up as part of the test harness.

8.2 Unit-Testing Toast

Before we take on writing a system-wide test for all of Toast, let's start by writing a unit test for the `EmergencyMonitor`. We'll take a black-box approach, injecting the airbag and GPS that it needs and verifying that it invokes the APIs of its required services properly.

Our testing will use JUnit and EasyMock, both of which conveniently reside in the target platform. We'll show only enough of these two frameworks as is necessary to get the tests running.

The tests should also abide by the best practices of test-driven development. Specifically, the tests should run quickly with no unnecessary delays. Also, the tests should not rely on any human interaction either in setting up the test or in verifying that the test passed.

8.2.1 Test Strategy

Since the `EmergencyMonitor` is the unit under test, we'll need to mock up all the services with which it interacts. With a mock airbag, a mock GPS, and a mock channel in place, we can simulate an airbag deployment. We'll expect the `EmergencyMonitor` to gather the location information from the mock GPS and then to invoke the send API on the mock channel.

Mocking

Many people have not heard of mocking or the use of mock objects. As the name implies, mocking involves the creation of objects that look, smell, and taste like the real thing but are in fact hollow shells that answer only enough of the right questions to fool the test subject. Mocking also allows you to set up complicated and very controlled scenarios because you have direct control over the behavior of the mock objects.

There are many different mock object frameworks such as EasyMock, JMock, and others. Fundamentally they all work by creating a proxy object for the object being mocked and allowing you to effectively record some desired behavior. You can then inject the mock object into the test subject and replay the behavior. The mock object also allows you to monitor its interaction with others by recording values supplied or counting method calls. For anyone who has suffered through creating comprehensive test suites for complicated systems, mocking is manna from heaven.

We refer to the mock objects collectively as the test harness. Figure 8-1 shows the EmergencyMonitor with the three mock objects comprising the test harness.

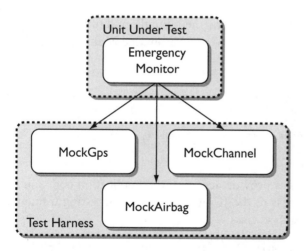

Figure 8–1   EmergencyMonitor with the test harness

8.2.2 Writing the Test Case

It makes sense to put the test code in a separate project from the emergency monitor code that it tests. But notice that the EmergencyMonitor class itself is not visible to other projects. We can solve this dilemma by using a fragment bundle.

Fragment Bundles

Fragment bundles allow optional functionality to be added to another bundle, known as the host. At runtime a fragment is merged with its host and has full visibility of all the packages in its host, so it is ideal for containing unit tests.

Since JUnit does not require OSGi, you can run tests as simple Java applications and use normal Java projects. Were you to do that, you'd need to manage the classpath yourself to gain access to `EmergencyMonitor`.

Since we're using PDE to manage our classpath in every other project, we use the same mechanism for our test projects here. It also gives you the chance to try out fragments.

Follow these steps to create the fragment project that will contain the new test:

○ Select **File > New > Project**. Then expand **Plug-in Development** and select **Fragment Project** to create a fragment project called `org.equinoxosgi.toast.client.emergency.test`.

○ On the last page of the wizard, select `org.equinoxosgi.toast.client.emergency` as the **Host Plug-in,** and select `J2SE 1.5` as the execution environment. Easy-Mock requires Java 1.5.

○ Open the manifest editor on the fragment bundle and turn to the **Dependencies** tab. Add the following bundles to the **Automated Management of Dependencies** section:

```
org.equinoxosgi.toast.core
org.equinoxosgi.toast.core.emergency
org.equinoxosgi.toast.dev.gps
org.equinoxosgi.toast.dev.airbag
org.equinoxosgi.toast.core.channel.sender
org.junit
org.easymock
```

The five Toast bundles provide access to the application code, and the other two bundles provide access to the JUnit and EasyMock testing frameworks. Next, create the test case class:

○ Create an `EmergencyMonitorTestCase` class in a package called `org.equinoxosgi.toast.client.emergency.test` with `junit.framework.TestCase` as its superclass. Use the following snippet to complete the class:

org.equinoxosgi.toast.client.emergency.test/EmergencyMonitorTestCase
```
public class EmergencyMonitorTestCase extends TestCase implements
```

```
          IEmergencyConstants, ICoreConstants {
        public void testAirbagDeploy() throws Exception {
          EmergencyMonitor emergencyMonitor = new EmergencyMonitor();
          IGps gps = createMock(IGps.class);
          expect(gps.getLatitude()).andReturn(123).once();
          expect(gps.getLongitude()).andReturn(456).once();
          expect(gps.getHeading()).andReturn(789).once();
          expect(gps.getSpeed()).andReturn(10).once();

          IAirbag airbag = createMock(IAirbag.class);
          airbag.addListener(emergencyMonitor);
          expectLastCall().once();
          airbag.removeListener(emergencyMonitor);
          expectLastCall().once();

          IChannel channel = createMock(IChannel.class);
          final ChannelMessage message = new
              ChannelMessage(EMERGENCY_FUNCTION);
          message.addParameter(ID_PARAMETER, ID_DEFAULT);
          message.addParameter(LATITUDE_PARAMETER, 123);
          message.addParameter(LONGITUDE_PARAMETER, 456);
          message.addParameter(HEADING_PARAMETER, 789);
          message.addParameter(SPEED_PARAMETER, 10);
          ByteArrayInputStream reply = new ByteArrayInputStream(
              "Help is on its way!".getBytes());
          expect(channel.send(message)).andReturn(reply).once();

          replay(gps, airbag, channel);
          emergencyMonitor.setGps(gps);
          emergencyMonitor.setAirbag(airbag);
          emergencyMonitor.setChannel(channel);
          emergencyMonitor.startup();
          emergencyMonitor.deployed();
          Delay.seconds(1); // wait for emergency monitor thread to complete
          emergencyMonitor.shutdown();
          verify(channel, gps, airbag);
        }
      }
```

MANAGING STATIC IMPORTS

Because Eclipse's organize imports feature does not bring in static imports, you'll need to add the following line to the compilation unit's import statements and organize imports again:

```
import static org.easymock.EasyMock.*;
```

Once you organize imports, this line will be expanded into an individual line for each imported function.

The test creates an EmergencyMonitor and then mocks up a GPS, airbag, and channel using EasyMock. The first three sections of the testAirbagDeploy method set the expectations for the test. This consists of telling each mock object how many API invocations to expect as well as what values to return.

The final section is where the actual testing takes place. The call to replay sets the stage by telling the mock objects that future calls are *for real*. Next it injects the mock objects into the EmergencyMonitor and triggers its deployed method to simulate an airbag deploy. Along the way, EasyMock compares the results against the original expectations, catching any discrepancies that occur. Finally, the verify call makes sure that all the expectations of the mock objects were met. Any exceptions or unmet expectations that occur cause the test case to fail.

Notice the one-second delay before the test case shuts down the EmergencyMonitor. This delay is necessary because the EmergencyMonitor performs its processing in a separate thread from the thread on which deployed is called. Without a delay, there is a chance that the test case would call shutdown before the emergency processing completed in the other thread. In general, using a delay in a test case is discouraged, since it can lead to situations where the test case may pass on a fast machine and fail on a slower machine. Exercise extreme caution when using a delay in this fashion.

8.2.3 Running the Unit Test

With the EmergencyMonitorTestCase written, it's easy to run:

○ From the context menu on the test case class, select **Run As > JUnit Test,** and the results will be shown in the JUnit view. The view should show a green solid bar with zero failures, as seen in Figure 8-2, indicating that the test case passed.

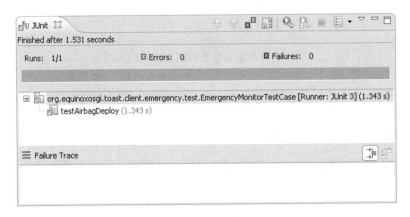

Figure 8–2 Successful test run in the JUnit view

8.3 System-Testing Toast

If the advantage of unit testing is that it can test POJOs outside of OSGi, the advantage of system testing is that it does just the opposite. In other words, unit tests focus on small units of the application functionality, but system tests put the entire application through its paces with all the components in place.

8.3.1 Test Strategy

The strategy in system testing is the opposite of the unit-testing strategy. In this case, to test as much of the application as possible implies mocking up as little of the application as possible.

To get an idea of how the system test should work, think about how we've been testing the application in prior chapters. We started with a fake airbag that deployed on its own every five seconds. Then we added some logging to the channel implementation and to the back end so we could verify that the application had reacted correctly by looking at the console.

We can make an automated system test that operates in much the same way but with two changes. First, instead of an airbag that deploys itself, we'll build our own mock airbag that deploys when commanded by the test case. Similarly, instead of reading the logged messages on the console with our eyes, we'll create a mock LogService that allows the test case to verify that what was logged matches its expectations. Figure 8-3 shows the system being tested along with the test harness.

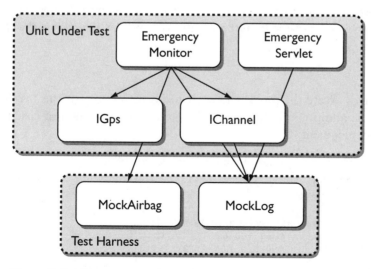

Figure 8–3 The system test harness

Furthermore, to take advantage of the fact that our test system will be running as a bundle, we'll programmatically stop and restart the GPS bundle to verify that the application responds correctly.

8.3.2 Creating the Test Harness

The test harness consists of the mock airbag and the mock Log Service. These need to be provided as services to the rest of the application, so we also need a DS component to provide each of those. To contain all of this, create the system test bundle with the proper dependencies:

○ Create a new project for the bundle named
  `org.equinoxosgi.toast.system.test`.

○ In the manifest editor, add the following bundles to the **Automated Management of Dependencies** list:

```
org.eclipse.osgi
org.eclipse.osgi.services
org.equinoxosgi.toast.dev.airbag
org.equinoxosgi.toast.dev.gps
org.junit
```

○ Save the contents of the editor.

MOCKING CAN BE DONE MANUALLY

You need not use a mocking framework like EasyMock to use mock objects in your tests. Sometimes it is easier just to create your own simple implementations of the required interfaces for test purposes. We take this approach in the system test here.

Next, let's create the mock airbag. It needs to implement the `IAirbag` interface plus one additional public method, `deploy`, to allow the test case to trigger an airbag deployment.

○ Create a class called `MockAirbag` in a package called
  `org.equinoxosgi.toast.system.test`. Use the following snippet to complete the class:

```
org.equinoxosgi.toast.system.test/MockAirbag
public class MockAirbag implements IAirbag {
  private List listeners = new ArrayList();

  public synchronized void addListener(IAirbagListener listener) {
    listeners.add(listener);
  }
```

```
public synchronized void deploy() {
  for (Iterator i = listeners.iterator(); i.hasNext();)
    ((IAirbagListener) i.next()).deployed();
}

public synchronized void removeListener(IAirbagListener listener) {
  listeners.remove(listener);
}
}
```

Since we want the rest of the system to use the mock airbag, we need to declare it as a component:

○ Create a new service component in OSGI-INF.

○ Since we plan to declare more than one component in this bundle, name it airbag.xml.

○ Use MockAirbag as the implementation class.

○ Add IAirbag as a provided service.

Now let's create a mock LogService. Chapter 17, "Logging," talks in detail about the OSGi LogService. Here all we need to know is that we have to implement the LogService interface and a public method that allows the test case to verify that an expected message has been logged.

The LogUtility class is designed to work with or without a LogService. So far we've been running without any LogService, so the LogUtility writes application messages to the console. If we include a mock LogService as part of the system test, the LogUtility will write any application messages to this mock LogService. And since the mock LogService is part of the test harness, the test case can verify that the application logs the messages that the test case expects.

○ Create a class called MockLog in the existing org.equinoxosgi.toast.system.test package. Use the following snippet to complete the class:

org.equinoxosgi.toast.system.test/MockLog
```
public class MockLog implements LogService {
  private List messages = new ArrayList(255);

  public void log(int level, String message) {
    record(message);
  }

  public void log(int level, String message, Throwable exception) {
    record(message);
  }

  public void log(ServiceReference sr, int level, String message) {
    record(message);
  }
```

```java
  public void log(ServiceReference sr, int level, String message,
      Throwable exception) {
    record(message);
  }

  private boolean findMessage(String messageFragment) {
    while (!messages.isEmpty()) {
      String message = (String) messages.remove(0);
      if (message.indexOf(messageFragment) != -1) {
        return true;
      }
    }
    return false;
  }

  private void record(String message) {
    synchronized (messages) {
      messages.add(message);
      messages.notifyAll();
    }
  }

  public boolean watchFor(String messageFragment, long maxWaitMs) {
    long deadline = System.currentTimeMillis() + maxWaitMs;
    try {
      synchronized (messages) {
        while (System.currentTimeMillis() < deadline) {
          if (findMessage(messageFragment))
            return true;
          messages.wait(deadline - System.currentTimeMillis());
        }
      }
    } catch (InterruptedException e) {
      // ignore
    }
    return false;
  }
}
```

The MockLog stores every message that gets logged. It provides the watchFor
method so the test case can easily verify that an expected message has been
logged. To make it convenient, it allows the test case to match against just a fragment of the message that was logged. It also provides a maximum wait time so
the test can fail if the expected message is not logged within that time window.

We now need to declare the mock log as a component just as we did for the
mock airbag:

  ○ Create another component for this bundle in OSGI-INF/log.xml. Use MockLog
    as the implementation class, and add LogService as a provided service.

8.3.3 Writing the Test Case

With the test harness in place, we move on to writing the test case. Unlike other JUnit test cases, the system test case need not concern itself with starting up the system or even the mock objects. Instead, everything is running as components under DS, so we really only need to think about the test case itself.

The test case needs access to three things. First, it needs the MockAirbag so it can command it to be deployed. Second, it needs the BundleContext so it can locate and stop the GPS bundle as part of its test. Finally, it needs the MockLog so it can verify that the system responded as expected.

To obtain these three objects, the test case must also be a component under DS. It can obtain the bundle context in its startup method and can obtain the mock objects in setAirbag and setLog via the familiar DS dependency injection mechanism.

○ Create a class called SystemTestCase in the org.equinoxosgi.toast.system.test package with the class TestCase as its superclass. Use the following snippet to complete the class:

org.equinoxosgi.toast.system.test/SystemTestCase
```
public class SystemTestCase extends TestCase {
  private static BundleContext context;
  private static MockLog log;
  private static MockAirbag airbag;
  private static boolean isActivated;
  private static Object lock = new Object();

  public void startup(BundleContext context) {
    SystemTestCase.context = context;
    synchronized (lock) {
      isActivated = true;
      lock.notifyAll();
    }
  }

  protected void setUp() throws Exception {
    super.setUp();
    synchronized (lock) {
      if (!isActivated)
        lock.wait();
    }
  }

  public void setAirbag(IAirbag value) {
    SystemTestCase.airbag = (MockAirbag) value;
  }

  public void setLog(LogService value) {
    SystemTestCase.log = (MockLog) value;
  }
```

```
public void testEmergency() throws Exception {
    log.watchFor("Registered EmergencyServlet", 5000);
    airbag.deploy();
    boolean success = log.watchFor("Sending message: emergency", 5000);
    assertTrue("Never sent emergency", success);
    success = log.watchFor("Emergency: ABC123", 500);
    assertTrue("Never received emergency", success);
    success = log.watchFor("Help is on its way!", 500);
    assertTrue("Never received reply", success);

    ServiceReference ref = context
        .getServiceReference(IGps.class.getName());
    assertTrue("No IGps service available", ref != null);
    Bundle bundle = ref.getBundle();
    assertTrue("Could not get GPS bundle", bundle != null);
    context.ungetService(ref);
    bundle.stop();
    airbag.deploy();
    boolean failure = log.watchFor("Sending message: emergency", 1000);
    assertFalse("Should not have sent emergency", failure);

    bundle.start();
    airbag.deploy();
    success = log.watchFor("Sending message: emergency", 500);
    assertTrue("Never sent emergency", success);
    success = log.watchFor("Emergency: ABC123", 500);
    assertTrue("Never received emergency", success);
    success = log.watchFor("Help is on its way!", 500);
    assertTrue("Never received reply", success);
    }
}
```

If you take a close look at this code, you may notice some deviations from the typical pattern. The first clue that something is different is that the fields are all declared as static. Also notice the synchronized blocks in startup and setUp. The reasoning for this is a bit tricky.

In essence, our system test uses two competing programming models, OSGi service and Equinox extensions. The PDE JUnit test infrastructure uses Equinox extensions. It instantiates the test case and invokes setUp before invoking testEmergency. But this instance has no way of obtaining the BundleContext, MockAirbag, or MockLog.

Meanwhile, DS has its own way of starting things up. It instantiates a separate instance of the test case as a component and calls setAirbag, setLog, and startup. So while this instance does have access to the BundleContext, MockAirbag, and MockLog, it is never used to actually run any tests.

To solve this dueling instance problem, DS's test case instance stashes the BundleContext, MockAirbag, and MockLog in static fields while JUnit's test case instance obtains them from these same static fields.

But this gives us a synchronization problem. If JUnit's test case tries to access the static fields before DS's instance sets them, the test will fail. So we use the two synchronized blocks in setup to make JUnit's test case instance wait until DS's test case instance has a chance to set the static fields.

The actual system test resides in the testEmergency method. After waiting for the back end to come up, it deploys the MockAirbag and verifies that the rest of the system responds as expected by watching for specific messages to be logged. It then locates and stops the bundle containing the GPS service. Again, it deploys the airbag, but this time it expects that no messages are logged, since the emergency monitor will have shut down without a GPS. Finally, the GPS bundle is started again and the airbag deployed for a third time. The test verifies that the system correctly logs the emergency.

The last thing we need to do is to declare the test case as a component:

- Create another new component for this bundle in OSGI-INF/test.xml. Use SystemTestCase as the implementation class.
- Use startup as the activate method.
- Add a referenced service called airbag with IAirbag as its interface and setAirbag as its bind method.
- Add a referenced service called log with LogService as its interface and setLog as its bind method.

8.3.4 Running the System Test

With the test and harness code complete, we can turn our attention toward running the test. Running a system test is quite different from running a unit test where the POJO is in isolation. In the case of the system test, we need the entire OSGi platform running along with all the required bundles. So before we can run the system test suite, we need to create a launch configuration.

Follow these steps to create the system test launch configuration:

- Open the **Run Configurations** dialog and create a plug-in test configuration using **Run > Run Configurations...** and selecting **JUnit Plug-in Test**.
- On the **Test** tab, give it a name, say, Toast System Tests, check the **Run all tests in the selected project, package or source folder** option, and select the org.equinoxosgi.toast.system.test project.
- Flip to the **Arguments** tab and enter the following **VM Arguments**:

```
-Dequinox.ds.print=true
-Dtoast.core.util.logLevel=DEBUG
-Dorg.osgi.service.http.port=8080
```

- On the **Plug-ins** tab, select **plug-ins selected below only** for the **Launch with** option.

○ Then select the following eight **Workspace** bundles:

```
org.equinoxosgi.toast.backend.emergency
org.equinoxosgi.toast.client.emergency
org.equinoxosgi.toast.core
org.equinoxosgi.toast.core.channel.sender
org.equinoxosgi.toast.core.emergency
org.equinoxosgi.toast.dev.airbag
org.equinoxosgi.toast.dev.gps
org.equinoxosgi.toast.system.test
```

○ And select the following 16 **Target Platform** bundles:

```
javax.servlet
org.eclipse.core.contenttype
org.eclipse.core.jobs
org.eclipse.core.runtime
org.eclipse.equinox.app
org.eclipse.equinox.common
org.eclipse.equinox.ds
org.eclipse.equinox.http
org.eclipse.equinox.preferences
org.eclipse.equinox.registry
org.eclipse.equinox.util
org.eclipse.jdt.junit.runtime
org.eclipse.osgi
org.eclipse.osgi.services
org.eclipse.pde.junit.runtime
org.junit
```

○ Ensure that the **Default Auto-Start** option is set to `true` on the **Plug-ins** tab and the **Auto-Start** entry for the `org.equinoxosgi.toast.dev.airbag` bundle is set to `false`. The test uses a mock airbag implementation, so the standard airbag implementation is not needed. We still need the bundle, however, because it supplies the `IAirbag` interface.

SEPARATING INTERFACE FROM IMPLEMENTATION

This situation seems awkward because the `IAirbag` interface and the `FakeAirbag` implementation reside in the same bundle. Once we add a second implementation of `IAirbag` as we have done with `MockAirbag`, it gets difficult to include the interface we need while excluding the `FakeAirbag` implementation we do not need.

Chapter 10, "Pluggable Services," addresses this situation in more detail, splitting out many of the service interfaces from their implementations.

○ On the **Common** tab, select the **Shared file** option and use `/org.equinoxosgi.toast.system.test` as the folder.

Now that the launch configuration is complete, press the **Run** button in the **Run Configuration** dialog. The JUnit view appears, and when the test is completed, a solid green bar indicates that no failures occurred.

8.4 Summary

In this chapter we finally got around to writing some tests for Toast. We presented two mechanisms for testing: unit testing and system testing. Both are vitally important to the quality of the overall application.

The tests in this chapter are certainly far from comprehensive. Many aspects of Toast are not covered. The goal of the chapter was to demonstrate the steps to making both unit and system tests run. Fleshing out test cases to cover the remaining functionality of Toast as well as the additional functionality presented in the rest of the tutorial is left as an exercise for the reader.

CHAPTER 9

Packaging

Even though our Toast system is fully functioning with a client and server part, you still can't send it to your friends because it lives in your workspace. In this chapter we show you how to package that configuration and export it in various forms. The goal is to take Toast from a laboratory prototype to a complete and ready-to-install OSGi system.

As part of this process we also look at increasing the rigor of the Toast component specifications by better managing package imports and exports and through the use of version numbers, version ranges, and privacy mechanisms supported by Equinox.

By the end of this chapter you will have learned about

○ Creating product configurations

○ Exporting Toast and running it outside the workspace

○ Branding the Toast executable

○ Exporting Toast for other platforms

○ Version numbers, version ranges, and managing package imports and exports

9.1 Defining a Toast Product

So far we have been running Toast directly from the workspace using launch configurations. To get Toast out of the workspace, you have to define some *product configurations*. A product configuration gathers together all of the information needed to create a complete system in one convenient place. This includes the list of bundles and features as well as the information about splash screens, executable icons, and so on.

Product configurations themselves are not defined by OSGi, nor are they part of your deployed application. They are development-time artifacts used by the tooling to help you describe the system you want to create. They are somewhat like launch configurations on steroids. Here we will take the two launch configurations used to run the client and the back end and convert them to product definitions. Let's start with the back end.

9.1.1 Creating a Product Configuration

First we will create the product configuration using the following steps. Then the subsequent sections take you on a guided tour of the product editor and highlight points of interest.

- Use **File > New > Project > General > Project** to create a new project called ToastBackEnd. It is a good idea to create a separate project to hold these higher-level artifacts. Since products are really configurations of function, they stand apart from the function—bundles and features—and have a home of their own.

- Select the new org.equinoxosgi.toast.product.backend project, and if you are in the **Plug-in Development** perspective, use **File > New > Product Configuration** to start the **New Product Configuration** wizard, as shown in Figure 9-1. Otherwise, use **File > New > Other... > Plug-in Development > Product Configuration** to get the wizard.

- Fill in the wizard fields as shown in the figure by setting the product definition file name to backend.product.

- Next, choose a technique for initializing the configuration. The wizard can extract information from an existing product or launch configuration or simply create a basic product. If you have been following along, you already have a launch configuration called backend. The currently defined configurations are listed in the **Use a launch configuration** drop-down. Enable this option and pick a configuration you have already used and which you know launches the back end.

YOU CAN START WITH NOTHING

If you don't have a suitable launch configuration, use the **Create a configuration file with basic settings** option and add in the relevant bundles as discussed in Chapter 8, "Testing."

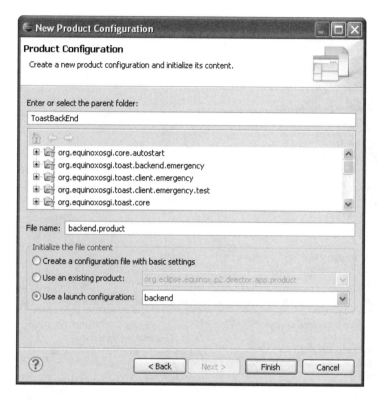

Figure 9–1 New Product Configuration wizard

○ Click **Finish**.

The wizard reads the launch configuration and uses it to build a product definition. In particular, it gets the list of bundles and any configuration information and command-line arguments used. The new product configuration is opened in an editor, similar to that shown in Figure 9-2.

9.1.2 The Overview Page

As with the bundle editor, the product configuration editor gathers together information from many different files and presents it all in one place. The configuration information is grouped onto several tabs within the editor. The **Overview** page in Figure 9-2 shows the **General Information** section at the top.

This gives access to the **ID, Version,** and **Name** of the product. None of these fields is mandatory for running the product, but when exporting or building, the **ID** and **Version** will be particularly useful.

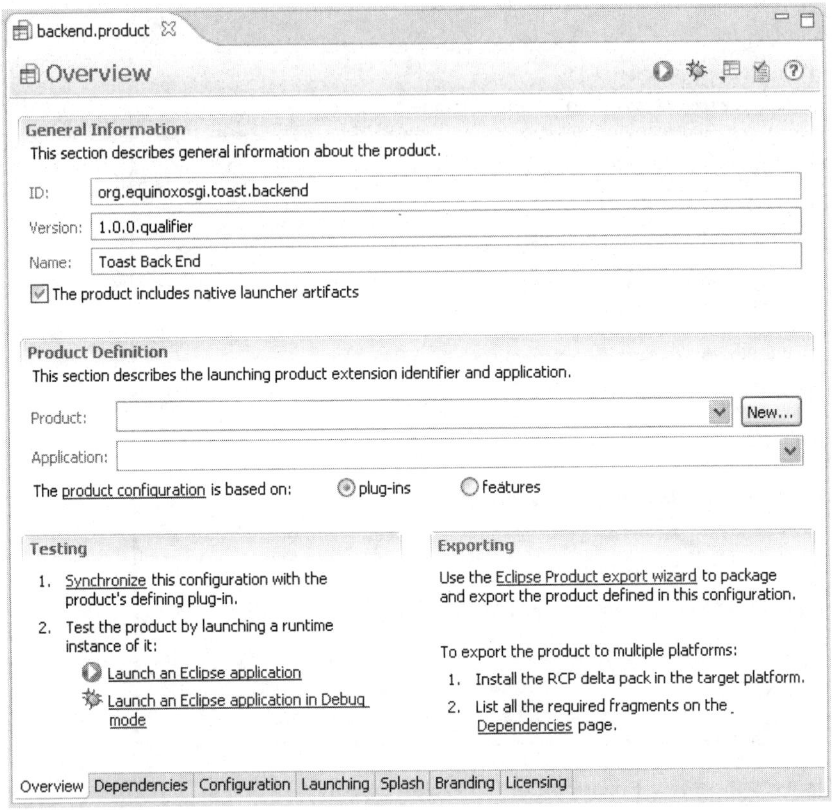

Figure 9–2   Back end product overview

○ Set the **ID** to org.equinoxosgi.toast.backend. The wizard filled in the version. For completeness, fill in the **Name**, Toast Back End.

The **Product Definition** section is next. It exposes the **Product** and **Application** values. These identify runtime branding and system entry point information, respectively. Leave these fields blank for now. We will use them in a later chapter.

Notice the two radio buttons beside **The product configuration is based on** at the bottom of the section. This allows you to say how you want to list the contents of the product—as either a list of bundles (plug-ins) or a list of features. For now we will use bundles, so ensure the **plug-ins** button is selected.

9.1.3 The Dependencies Page

Next take a look at the **Dependencies** page of the product editor, as shown in Figure 9-3. Here there is a simple list of bundles, since we decided to have a bundle-

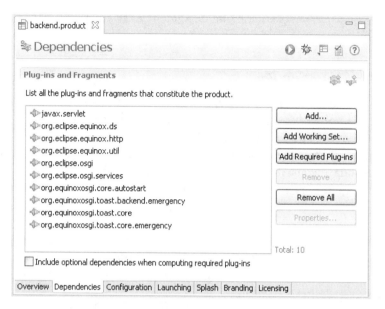

Figure 9–3 Back end product dependencies

based product definition. You can add and remove bundles from the list using workflows similar to those seen in the launch configuration dialog.

The **Add Required Plug-ins** button on the **Dependencies** page looks very attractive. The faith that you can click this one little button and magically all your requirements will be met, however, is sadly misplaced. In general, this button does more harm than good. It can be useful for getting an initial start or "just getting something running," but it can also wreak havoc on your bundle list and add all manner of unnecessary entries.

A better, though sometimes laborious, approach is to use the validate button in the top right of the editor to check for missing dependencies. This enables the same workflow as in the launch configuration dialog by showing you a list of all bundles with missing dependencies along with what those dependencies are. You can then add the needed bundles manually. Following this workflow, you get a good understanding of the requirements of your system and avoid lots of extra stuff being added just because it is available.

If you decide to use a feature-based product, as we will in later chapters, the list on the **Dependencies** page will include just features. This can be very convenient for readily seeing the structure and content of your product as it gets more complex. Whole collections of functions can be manipulated simply by adding or removing features. Validation continues to function, but you can no longer add individual bundles to satisfy missing dependencies. Rather, you have to find and add appropriate features that contain bundles that address the problem.

9.1.4 The Configuration Page

Flip over to the **Configuration** page. Here you see a list of bundles that are included or implied by the content of the **Dependencies** page. For each bundle listed, you can set whether or not it should be **Auto-Start**ed and at which **Start Level**. These are the same concepts we have seen in the launch configuration dialog. **Auto-Start** means that the associated bundle is both installed and started when the system is run. The start level helps define the order of starting. Start levels are discussed in more detail in Chapter 22, "Dynamic Best Practices."

In previous chapters we set up the launch configurations to ensure that the **Default Auto-Start** setting on the **Bundles** page was set to true. This ensured that all bundles listed in the launch configuration would be installed and started. While somewhat brute-force, it also avoids the tedious and error-prone listing of individual bundles to be started.

Unfortunately the current product editor **Configuration** page does not expose similar capability. Users are forced to explicitly list the bundles to start. To address this shortcoming, we've implemented an "auto-starter" bundle, `org.equinoxosgi.core.autostart`. A project containing the bundle is included in the Samples Manager for this chapter. The bundle simply starts and waits for other bundles to become resolved. On discovering a resolved bundle, the auto-starter starts the bundle. Using this you can get the effect of the launch configuration setup as follows:

○ Use the Samples Manager to load the auto-starter bundle from the Chapter 9 solution.

○ On the **Dependencies** tab, add `org.equinoxosgi.core.autostart` to the list of bundles in the product configuration.

○ Flip over to the **Configuration** tab and mark it as **Auto-Start = true** and set the **Start-level = 1** to ensure it is started before any bundles it may be starting. Having done that, there is no need to list any other bundles in the configuration—all bundles will be started upon becoming resolved.

For those familiar with the Equinox `config.ini` file, the **Configuration** page allows you to essentially manipulate the contents of the `osgi.bundles` entry in that file. In fact, given this capability and the various **Arguments** entry fields on the **Launching** page, the `config.ini` file is largely obsolete at development time—it can now be fully generated from the information in the product file. As such, you can ignore the contents of the **Configuration File** section on the **Configuration** page.

9.1.5 The Launching Page

The executable is the program that end users run when they want to start Toast, such as `toast.exe` on Windows. Having an executable more tightly integrates with the underlying system. For example, the application shows up correctly in the process lists, the Windows Taskbar, the Mac Dock, and so on.

You could just use the executable that comes with Eclipse, but of course you don't want to tell users to "double-click on `eclipse.exe`" to run Toast—you want a `toast.exe` for them to run. Furthermore, the Eclipse executable has Eclipse icons associated with it. It makes more sense for these icons to be specific to your system.

The **Program Launcher** section shown in Figure 9-4 allows you to set this up.

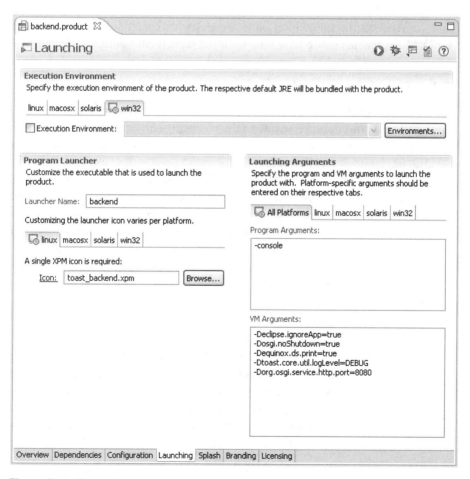

Figure 9–4 Executable branding

The **Launcher Name** box allows you to enter the simple name of the executable. You should not append .exe. That information is platform dependent, and PDE takes care of it when the product is exported. Here we entered backend for the launcher name.

Below the **Launcher Name** is a series of entry fields for identifying the icons associated with Toast's executable. It turns out that each OS requires different image sizes and formats, so the product editor has a section for the supported OSs. You need to fill in the image names only for the OSs in which you are interested. The Toast images are in the sample files for this chapter in the ToastBackEnd/branding folder. These images are used in the process of exporting Toast. During export, PDE creates an executable program that behaves exactly like the standard Eclipse executable but is renamed and branded with the icons you specified. You can add these to the product definition if desired.

Also on the **Launching** page are areas for specifying **Program Arguments** and **VM Arguments** as we have seen with the launch configurations in previous chapters.

9.1.6 *Running the Product*

Finally, launch the product using the links in the **Testing** section of the **Overview** or the run and debug buttons in the top right corner of the editor. The Toast Back End should start up as before. You can launch the client as before to verify that the back end is working correctly.

You may not have noticed, but launching the product caused a new launch configuration to be created. Open up the launch configuration dialog (**Run > Run...**) and take a look at the list. There is backend, the one you used as a base for the product configuration, and a new one called backend.product (assuming that is the name you used for your product configuration file). This new configuration is used by the product editor to launch your product. Since it is a normal launch configuration, you can run or debug it directly and use keyboard shortcuts such as **F11** to debug the last launched configuration.

LAUNCH FROM THE PRODUCT

PDE keeps the launch configuration and product configuration synchronized. If you change the list of bundles in the product configuration and save, the launch configuration is updated. This relationship is one-way—launching from or changing the launch configuration does not trigger any synchronization of the product configuration. When in doubt, launch Toast from the product editor.

9.1.7 Productizing the Client

Converting the client to be defined as a product is exactly the same as converting the back end. Here is a capsule summary of the steps required:

- ○ Create a ToastClient project and client.product product configuration. Base the product configuration on the client launch configuration you have been using to date.
- ○ Add the org.equinoxosgi.toast.core.autostart bundle to the product dependencies and ensure it is marked to auto-start.
- ○ Export the product and run it against the exported back end.

9.2 Exporting Toast

To get Toast out of the workspace, you have to export it. To do this, you identify what parts of the various projects should get packaged up into the corresponding binary bundles. For example, the org.equinoxosgi.toast.backend.emergency project has several development-time artifacts that should not go into the final bundle. Since we have been running from the workspace up until now, this has not been an issue. To export, you need to make this explicit.

The **Build** page in the bundle editor for the back end bundle helps with this. The **Binary Build** section shown in Figure 9-5 lists the set of development-time files and folders that are also part of the bundle's structure. Notice that several files are already selected. PDE takes care of adding things like the compiled Java classes, the META-INF directory, and other elements that are known to be required at runtime. Your bundle may require additional files such as icons, messages, or web content.

Take the time now to go through each of the bundles and ensure that the OSGI-INF directory is selected in the **Binary Build** section of the bundle editor's **Build** page.

CHECK THE BINARY BUILD LIST

Failure to correctly set up the **Binary Build** list is a very common source of errors. Typically, the bundle works fine when run from the workspace, but when exported, various images, text messages, and other elements are missing. If this happens to you, first check the **Binary Build** list.

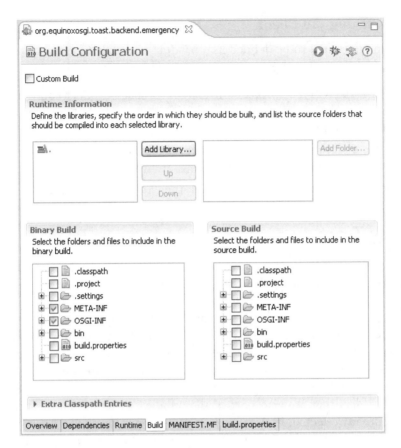

Figure 9–5   Binary Build specification

You can export the product by running the export wizard as outlined here:

○ Find the backend.product file in the **Package Explorer** or **Navigator**. Right-click and choose **Export... > Plug-in Development > Eclipse product**. Alternatively, open the product editor, select the **Overview** page, and click on the **Product Export** wizard link. There is also a convenient export button at the top right of all product editor pages. Either way, you should see the **Product Export** wizard, as shown in Figure 9-6.

○ First, ensure that backend.product is selected in the **Configuration** drop-down.

○ Fill in the **Root directory**, the top-level directory that is embedded in the export output. For example, it is useful to set this to be the name of your product with the version number. This way, people can extract the product

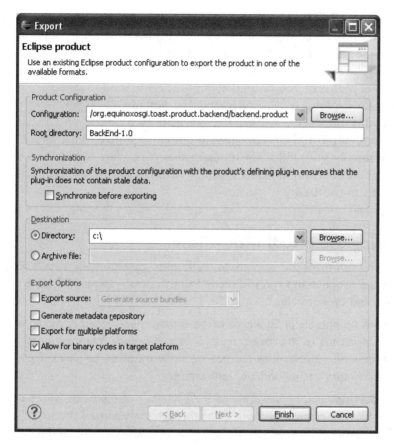

Figure 9–6   Product Export wizard

and it gets laid out on disk in a descriptive directory structure. For now, use
BackEnd-1.0 in this field.

○ In the **Synchronization** section, uncheck the **Synchronize before exporting**
box. We did not define a product extension for this product, so we don't need
to synchronize. PDE will complain if you leave the box checked.

○ Next, pick the export **Destination** and set the shape of the export **Archive file**
or **Directory**. This setting does not affect the content of the output, just the
layout. For now choose **Directory** so you can easily test what you are exporting. Later you can export as an archive to make Toast easier to distribute. Put
the output in any convenient location, but remember that the root directory
entered earlier is appended to the location specified. We use c:\ in the example here.

After you click **Finish**, PDE starts the export. It should run in the background, so you can continue using Eclipse while the export completes. First, it compiles the code from the workspace according to the configuration you described. The export wizard then gathers the compiled code and required parts of the target platform and outputs them to the specified location.

When the export is done, `c:\BackEnd-1.0` contains a fully functional Toast Back End that runs outside the workspace. Navigate to `c:\BackEnd-1.0\backend.exe`. Run the executable and enjoy your stand-alone Equinox-based server!

Undoubtedly you will want to share this with your friends and coworkers. Go back and export the product again. This time, specify an **Archive file** output and mail them the archive.

Cleaning the Install with `-clean`

When you run from the workspace, PDE takes care of many details. Once you export the product and run it directly from the file system, PDE is no longer in the loop and cannot help.

This crops up notably in Equinox's cache management. Typically, Equinox keeps a number of caches to improve startup time and reduce memory footprint. Since most production installations are not manually modified by users, Equinox does only rudimentary cache validation on startup.

During development, however, there are a number of scenarios where previously installed files are changed without going through the standard channels. For example, if you export Toast on top of a previous installation, some of the bundle content may change, but the bundle was never formally "updated" or "uninstalled." As such, Equinox does not notice the change. To you it appears as though your changes are not being picked up.

The easiest way around this is to avoid overwriting or tweaking previous installs. Failing that, however, you can run Equinox using the `-clean` program argument.

Running this way during development is useful as it tells Equinox to flush all of its caches and rebuild its state. Startup is a little slower, but you are guaranteed to get the latest content.

9.3 Packaging for Other Platforms

But what about your friends who use different operating or window systems or run on different hardware? They can't run the Toast elements you just exported because they contain platform-specific code—at least the executable. To package for other platforms, either you need to run the IDE on that platform, which is hard to manage, or you must have the code for those platforms on your machine and cross-deploy. This is much easier.

First you need to acquire all the platform-specific code needed for these other platforms. Fortunately, Eclipse supplies a *delta pack* for every build. The delta pack contains all parts of the Eclipse SDK, including Equinox, that are platform-specific. This includes the launchers as well as graphics libraries and other support for various platforms. So, for example, if you are on Windows and want to export the Toast Client for Linux/GTK, the delta pack has everything you need.

PLATFORM-SPECIFIC CODE IS NOT ALWAYS NEEDED

The issue of platform-specific code shows up for several bundles in the Eclipse platform. SWT, for example, has considerable amounts of essential platform-specific code. Several other bundles have platform-specific fragments that deliver natives and Java code to support optimizations. In these cases the bundles work fine without the platform fragments, but with the fragments they are faster or support enhanced function.

We included the delta pack in the target platform setup in Chapter 3, "Tutorial Introduction," and described how to get it if needed.

For now the Toast Client is relatively simple, and all we need from the delta pack is the executables. In later chapters we will add a GUI to the client and will need various SWT bundles.

SEPARATE TARGETS ARE USEFUL

In Chapter 3, "Tutorial Introduction," we talked about the importance of keeping your target and development Eclipse installs separate. Using the delta pack is a fine example that motivates that practice.

If you were using the development Eclipse install as a target, the simple default setup, the steps just described would have added the delta pack to the development install. As a result, the development environment would be cluttered with extra and irrelevant bundles.

With the delta pack in the target you can export for multiple platforms as follows:

○ Open the **Export** wizard and complete the first page of the wizard as before. This time check the **Export for multiple platforms** option, and then click **Next** to get to the **Cross-platform export** page shown in Figure 9-7.

○ Select the set of platforms for which you want to export and click **Finish**.

Figure 9–7   Cross-platform export

The export output goes to archives or directories specific to the related platform. For example, the Windows output appears in the directory named `c:\win32.win32.x86\client-1.0`.

9.4 Getting Serious about Component Definition

Now that you have Toast exported and running independently of your workspace, others can start to build on your fleet management platform. To facilitate this, we need to get more serious about the rigor of our component definitions. Many cultures have a saying akin to "Good fences make good neighbors." It is the same with components. Having a clear definition of what is in and out of bounds helps set expectations and smooths collaboration. Defining these boundaries in a formal way enables the tooling to help you write conformant code and the runtime to enforce the boundaries. In this section we talk about versions and version ranges and best practices for exporting packages as the key elements of component definition.

9.4.1 Versions and Version Ranges

In OSGi, bundles and packages are uniquely identified by a combination of their identifiers, `Bundle-SymbolicName` and package name respectively, and their version numbers. When you specify a dependency on a bundle or package, you can give a *version range* to narrow the set of content you are willing to accept. This is an extremely useful mechanism, but its value depends on the policy used around setting version numbers in the first place—if version numbers change randomly, ranges cannot help.

Since the IDs used for a given entity never change, the version number must change whenever the content of the entity changes. Version numbers in OSGi are made up of four parts: `major.minor.service.qualifier`:

Major—Differences in the major part indicate significant differences such that backward compatibility is not guaranteed.

Minor—Changes in the minor part indicate that the newer version of the entity is backward compatible with the older version, but it includes additional functionality and/or API.

Service—The service part indicates the presence of bug fixes and minor implementation (i.e., hidden) changes over previous versions.

Qualifier—The qualifier is not interpreted by the system. Qualifiers are compared using standard string comparison.

Following these numbering semantics is important. As parts of the system come to depend on one another, they need to know about changes in the compatibility contract as well as updating their requirements. For example, the following package import declaration claims that the back end bundle works with *any* version of the Toast core package. This is likely incorrect.

```
org.equinoxosgi.toast.backend.emergency/MANIFEST.MF
Bundle-SymbolicName: org.equinoxosgi.toast.backend.emergency
Import-Package: org.equinoxosgi.toast.core
```

A more likely scenario is that the back end is buying into the Toast core API at a specific minimum level, for example:

```
org.equinoxosgi.toast.backend.emergency/MANIFEST.MF
Bundle-SymbolicName: org.equinoxosgi.toast.backend.emergency
Import-Package: org.equinoxosgi.toast.core;version="[1.0.0,2.0.0)"
```

In this case, the back end is happy with any core package from 1.0 to 2.0 (not including 2.0). Given the version number semantics described previously, the back end is saying that it likes the 1.0 level API and does not want to be broken. A future version of the bundle may use some new API added to core package version 1.1. In that case the back end would change its import version range to be [1.1.0,2.0.0).

Conservative teams who want only bug fixes might narrow this range to [1.1.0,1.2.0) with the goal of getting only bug fixes. Paranoid teams seek to lock down the exact version used and would narrow the range further to [1.1.0,1.1.0].

The challenge here is to specify the version dependencies loosely enough so that the dependents work in various settings but tightly enough that the required API contracts are guaranteed. Of course, this mechanism works only if producers update their version numbers according to the semantics and give their consumers a chance to get it right—it takes two to collaborate.

LOAD THE VERSIONS FROM THE SAMPLE

Rather than going through all the manifests and updating the imports and exports, consider loading the manifests from the Samples Manager.

9.4.2 Exporting Packages and Friendship

OSGi has very strong boundary enforcement—you must state an Import-Package or Require-Bundle dependency before you can see the contents of another bundle, and you will only ever see contents that the bundle decides to expose. OSGi fences are quite high and robust.

This can be good as it supports implementation and information hiding. Hiding is great because it limits the assumptions you can make. With no knowledge to the contrary, you have to assume that anything (or nothing) can happen. Unfortunately, this black-and-white view of the world is not always optimal. For example, standard OSGi does have the notion of private collaboration between bundles. Exported packages are exported to everyone and registered services are available to all. Over the years we have seen many cases where this was just too rigid.

Returning to our fence analogy, even the most robust fences have gates. Whereas a fence stops people from traversing the boundary, a gate declares that there is a boundary but allows people to pass, understanding that there are new rights and obligations. The OSGi standard itself has the binary Export-Package gate—the package is available either to all or to no one. In Equinox we extended Export-Package with the x-friends and x-internal directives:

x-internal—Use this to mark an exported package as containing internal implementation details that are not considered API.

x-friends—Use this to mark an exported package as accessible only to a list of named bundles.

---

x-* WILL BE IGNORED

Bundles that use x-internal and x-friends are still OSGi-compliant. The OSGi specification states that nonstandard manifest headers and directives must be ignored by framework implementations that do not support them.

PDE includes tooling for these directives in the **Package Visibility** section of the **Runtime** page of the manifest editor, as shown in Figure 9-8. Here the package org.equinoxosgi.toast.internal.core is hidden from all other bundles—it is marked as x-internal:=true.

Figure 9–8 Package visibility manipulation

9.4.2.1 The Equinox x-internal Directive

Marking a package internal is like putting an "Enter at your own risk" sign on the gate. It tells people that they can use the package but there are no guarantees about the suitability, robustness, or durability of the code.

For example, it is common for Eclipse platform bundles to export all internal packages but mark them as x-internal. This supports early adopters and people with novel use cases as they seek to push the limits of your function. The markup tells them where the limit is. PDE supports developers by marking uses of internal code with *discouraged access* warnings. Under this model, developers wanting to stay in bounds have a clear indication that they are outside of their policies, and more aggressive developers can exercise informed consent. The discouraged access feedback can be set to **ignore, warn,** or **error** in the Java compiler preferences by searching for "discouraged."

9.4.2.2 The Equinox x-friends Directive

Marking a package as internal is enough to enable access and denote API—if it is marked as internal, it is not API. Conversely, if it is not API, you should not use it. But what about closely related bundles that are collaborating at the implementation level? In this case we would like to list particular consumers as approved to use a package—we want to note them as friends.

The x-friends directive is a specialization of x-internal in that it marks the exported package as internal but allows undiscouraged use of the package by the listed bundles—they do not get errors or warnings when referencing the package. Adding friends to a package can be done by adding them to the **Package Visibility** list shown in Figure 9-8. This serves two purposes: It tells the consumer that it's OK to use the package, and it reminds the producer that there are approved consumers of what would otherwise be non-API types. It essentially notes that there is a private contract between the two parties around the evolution of the code in the package.

FRIENDS BRING YOU CLOSER

Care should be taken when using the x-friends directive as it results in tight couplings between bundles.

9.4.2.3 Strict Mode

Some teams have a very strong API ethic that drives them to reject all use of internal code from other bundles. This is a powerful, though sometimes hard-to-maintain, position. Nonetheless, to support these teams, Equinox includes a *strict mode*. When the framework runs in strict mode, all internal package exports are ignored and friends-only access is enforced. The net effect is that no one in the system can violate the API boundaries—API lockdown. By default the framework does not use strict mode. You can enable strict mode using the following VM argument:

```
-Dosgi.resolverMode=strict
```

9.5 Summary

Exporting Toast as described here is the first step toward making Toast an engineered system offering. Without exporting, Toast is just a wad of code in your workspace. Exported, Toast becomes a full-fledged stand-alone system. PDE's exporting facilities make it easy to create and brand these packages—even across platforms. Now you have something to send to others.

Rigorous component design is an integral part of collaboration. Strong API boundaries support and facilitate this. Key to the definition of API is the versioning and usage qualification. Here we showed that OSGi, Equinox, and PDE provide a number of powerful mechanisms and tools for defining and enforcing API boundaries.

Given a set of well-defined components that can be exported, further chapters describe how to automate component builds and how to compose and deploy components using Equinox's p2 provisioning technology in various scenarios.

CHAPTER 10

Pluggable Services

The previous chapters have focused on topics that are vital to the development of a production system. We have a bit of functionality, a client that interacts with a back end, and some rudimentary tests. We can even package up Toast and run it as a stand-alone application. To be certain, there is still a lot left to do to make Toast more useful and robust. Of all that remains to be done, there's one big thing that Toast still lacks: reality.

Toast is based on fake devices. No matter how far you throw your computer or how hard you smash it against the wall, the GPS won't change, and the airbag won't deploy. In a real telematics system, we need to interface to the GPS and airbag hardware in the vehicle by way of device drivers.

In the real world, developing device drivers can take quite a bit of time, sometimes longer than the remainder of the system. And deploying real airbags to test software can get pretty expensive. So it makes sense to try to develop the domain logic separate from and in parallel with the device drivers. This is an aspect of development where OSGi really shines. Using OSGi services, you can develop your application in parallel.

In this chapter, as we continue to develop Toast, you will learn

❍ How to separate the service interface from implementation to enable service pluggability

❍ How to use the simple simulator framework to create simulators for services

❍ How to use pluggable OSGi services to run Toast with simulators

10.1 Separating Interface from Implementation

So far in Toast we've been using "fake" devices. The FakeGps and FakeAirbag work well enough for us to develop the domain logic that depends on them. Each of these fake devices resides in its own bundle, and each bundle contains both the service interface as well as the fake implementation. This was convenient in the beginning, but there was a hint of awkwardness when we created a mock airbag implementation in our system test. We had to include the bundle in the product definition so that the IAirbag interface would be present, but we had to ensure that the bundle was not started so the test case did not mistakenly bind to the wrong airbag service.

The trouble arises whenever we try to put together a system with an alternative implementation of the service. But because the service interface and the fake implementation are in the same bundle, we cannot use just the service interface without the fake implementation tagging along.

The solution is simple enough—separate the service interface and the fake implementation into distinct bundles.

Separation or Duplication?

An alternative to separating the service interface from the implementation is to duplicate the interface in every bundle that provides a service object. The primary advantage of this approach is a reduction in the number of bundles both during development and at runtime—each bundle is self-contained. This simplifies system structuring and deployment.

Unfortunately, this shifts the problem to creating and maintaining all the copies at development and build time. There are some tools such as *bnd* that support the copying of code while assembling bundles. These can be quite useful. PDE itself does not directly support this workflow.

The runtime drawback of the duplication approach is that with the implementation and interface in the same bundle, updating or uninstalling the implementation updates or uninstalls the API. As a result, the bundles wired to the bundle for the API are also affected—the isolation is degraded. This can cause a stop/resolve/start ripple throughout the system. With the interface in a separate bundle, the prerequisites are isolated from the implementation and are unaffected.

While both approaches are valid, we favor isolation and use the separation approach here.

10.1.1 Separating the Fake Airbag from Its Interface

Follow these steps to separate the fake airbag implementation and the airbag service into two separate bundles:

❍ Since the name of the project containing the fake airbag implementation is better suited for the service interface, create a new project for the fake implementation called `org.equinoxosgi.toast.dev.airbag.fake`. Refer to Section 4.2.1, "GPS Bundle," for detailed instructions on creating bundle projects.

❍ In the manifest editor, add `org.equinoxosgi.toast.dev.airbag` and `org.eclipse.core.jobs` to the **Automated Management of Dependencies** list.

❍ In the **Required Plug-ins** list, add `org.eclipse.equinox.common`.

❍ Save the manifest.

❍ Drag the `org.equinoxosgi.toast.internal.dev.airbag.fake` package from the `src` folder of the `org.equinoxosgi.toast.dev.airbag` project and drop it into the `src` folder of the newly created project.

❍ Click the **add dependencies** link at the bottom of the manifest editor.

❍ Edit the version range on the imported package `org.equinoxosgi.toast .dev.airbag` to be 1.0.0 inclusive to 2.0.0 exclusive by clicking the **Properties...** button.

❍ Create a new service component for this bundle called `component.xml` in the `OSGI-INF` folder of this bundle. Refer to Section 6.4.1, "Modifying the GPS Bundle," for detailed instructions.

❍ Use `FakeAirbag` for the class of the component.

❍ Use `startup` and `shutdown` for the activate and deactivate methods, respectively.

❍ Add `IAirbag` as a provided service.

Now the new fake airbag bundle is complete. The original `org.equinoxosgi .toast.dev.airbag` bundle needs a little cleaning up, since it no longer acts as a service component. When we created the service component, the tooling did most of the work. To remove the service component, we need to manually remove the `OSGI-INF` folder that contains it, and we also need to modify the manifest to no longer declare the service component and the build configuration to no longer include the `OSGI-INF` folder. Follow these steps to complete the removal of the service component:

❍ In the manifest editor of the `org.equinoxosgi.toast.dev.airbag` project, go to the **Build** tab and uncheck the `OSGI-INF` folder. Then remove the `OSGI-INF` folder from the project.

○ On the **MANIFEST.MF** tab, remove the entire line that declares the `Service-Component`.

○ With the fake implementation no longer in this bundle, we can remove its dependencies from the manifest. On the **Dependencies** tab, remove all items from the **Required Plug-ins, Automated Management of Dependencies,** and **Imported Packages** lists.

10.1.2 Separating the Fake GPS from Its Interface

Now let's repeat the separation procedure for the GPS. Follow these abbreviated steps:

○ Create a new plug-in project for the fake implementation called `org.equinoxosgi.toast.dev.gps.fake`.

○ In the manifest editor, add `org.equinoxosgi.toast.dev.gps` to the **Automated Management of Dependencies** list.

○ Save the manifest.

○ Drag the `org.equinoxosgi.toast.internal.dev.gps.fake` package into the src folder of the newly created project.

○ Click the **add dependencies** link at the bottom of the manifest editor.

○ Edit the version range on the imported package `org.equinoxosgi.toast.dev.gps` to be 1.0.0 inclusive to 2.0.0 exclusive.

○ Create a new service component for this bundle called `component.xml` in the `OSGI-INF` folder of this bundle, with `FakeGps` for the class of the component and `IGps` as a provided service.

○ In the manifest editor of the `org.equinoxosgi.toast.dev.gps` project, go to the **Build** tab and uncheck the `OSGI-INF` folder. Then remove the `OSGI-INF` folder from the project.

○ On the **MANIFEST.MF** tab, remove the entire line that declares the `Service-Component`.

10.1.3 Regression Testing

With the device service interfaces now properly separated from the fake implementations, it's a good idea to run the system test to make sure nothing is broken. But we need to make a few modifications first. Follow these steps to update the system test case and run it:

○ Select **Run > Run Configurations…** and open the `Toast System Test` launch configuration.

○ On the **Plug-ins** tab, uncheck the **Only show selected plug-ins** option to see all the bundles in the workspace and target.

○ Notice that the new fake device bundles are now available. Check the fake GPS bundle, `org.equinoxosgi.toast.dev.gps.fake`. It is needed now since it is no longer in the service interface bundle, `org.equinoxosgi.toast.dev.gps`. Make sure it has **Auto-Start** set to `true`.

○ There is no need to check the fake airbag because the test case does not need it. Recall that the test case has its own mock airbag as part of the test harness. All it needs is the airbag service interface that resides in `org.equinoxosgi.toast.dev.airbag`.

○ Click the **Run** button to run the system test case.

10.2 Device Simulation

Separating interface from implementation is not just good architecture; it enables new scenarios. In the case of Toast, it means that the fake devices are no longer the only choice when assembling a system. In the real world, this separation combined with OSGi's modularity enables parallel development. One team can work on the real device bundles that talk to real hardware while another team works on the layers above the devices. OSGi services allow the consumers of a service to be blissfully unaware that the services upon which they depend are fake, mock, or real implementations.

10.2.1 Concepts

Another type of service that plays an important role in enabling parallel development is the *device simulator*. A simulator allows developers to control a service manually, usually by way of a user interface available only at development time. Using simulated services aids in development and demonstration of the system. For developing Toast, it would be nice to simulate driving around in the vehicle, with the GPS updating as we drive along. It would also be handy to be able to deploy the airbag when we wanted.

The remainder of this chapter guides you through creating simulators for the GPS and airbag. The simulators plug into a simple device simulator framework that allows the simulators to be controlled by a web interface. Figure 10-1 shows the device simulators and the device simulator framework along with the web interface used for controlling the simulators.

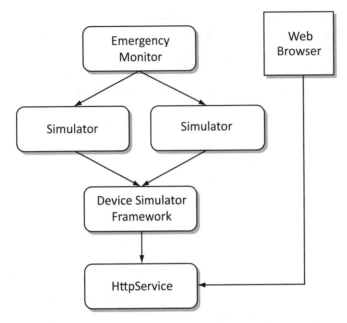

Figure 10–1   Device simulators and the simulation framework

10.2.2 The Device Simulator Framework

The device simulator framework allows other bundles to contribute simulators for particular frameworks—it is itself extensible. Since the internals of the device simulator framework are unimportant here, it's simplest to just load the device simulator rather than develop it from scratch.

○ Use the Samples Manager to load the org.equinoxosgi.toast.devsim project as described in Section 3.4.2, "Comparing."

The bundle has a component.xml, so that's a great place to start exploring the framework.

The component provides a single service called IDeviceSimulator. Each simulator registers itself with the framework by way of this service. The simulator framework serves up a web page for each simulator and processes commands that ultimately control the corresponding simulator. To achieve this, the component references a single service, HttpService, and uses this service to publish the DeviceSimulatorServlet. Figure 10-2 gives you a peek at the device simulators we are building.

Figure 10–2 The airbag and GPS simulators

10.3 Simulated Devices as Pluggable Services

With the device simulator framework installed, we need to implement a device simulator for the airbag and another for the GPS. Each of these implements the corresponding service.

10.3.1 The Simulated Airbag

Follow these steps to create the simulated airbag:

○ Create a new project for the simulated implementation called `org.equinoxosgi.toast.dev.airbag.sim`.

○ In the manifest editor, add the following bundles to the **Automated Management of Dependencies** list:

```
org.equinoxosgi.toast.dev.airbag
org.equinoxosgi.toast.devsim
```

○ Save the manifest.

Now create the component class:

○ Create a new class in this bundle called `AirbagSimulator` and place it in a new package called `org.equinoxosgi.toast.internal.dev.airbag.sim`. Fill in the code with the following snippet:

```
org.equinoxosgi.toast.internal.dev.airbag.sim/AirbagSimulator
public class AirbagSimulator implements IAirbag,
    IDeviceSimulatorListener {
  private static final String AIRBAG = "Airbag";
  private static final String DEPLOY = "Deploy";
  private List listeners;
  private IDeviceSimulator sim;

  public void setDevSim(IDeviceSimulator value) {
    sim = value;
  }

  public void startup() {
    listeners = new ArrayList(3);
    sim.registerDevice(AIRBAG, AIRBAG, this);
    sim.addRepeatableActionSensor(AIRBAG, DEPLOY, DEPLOY, DEPLOY);
  }

  public void shutdown() {
    sim.unregisterDevice(AIRBAG);
  }

  public void addListener(IAirbagListener listener) {
    listeners.add(listener);
  }

  public void removeListener(IAirbagListener listener) {
    listeners.remove(listener);
  }

  public void performAction(String parameterName, String actionName) {
    if (DEPLOY.equals(parameterName) && DEPLOY.equals(actionName))
      airbagDeployed();
  }

  public void valueChanged(String name, int newValue) {
  }

  public void valueChanged(String name, boolean newValue) {
  }

  private void airbagDeployed() {
    for (Iterator i = listeners.iterator(); i.hasNext();) {
      IAirbagListener listener = (IAirbagListener) i.next();
      listener.deployed();
    }
  }
}
```

The IDeviceSimulator service is injected in setDevSim. Then, in startup, the
simulator registers itself with the device simulator framework, providing a unique
device name and a label for the user interface. It adds a single sensor for the airbag deployment, providing the device name (AIRBAG), the sensor name (DEPLOY),

a label for the user interface (DEPLOY), and an action for the servlet (DEPLOY). It unregisters itself in shutdown.

When the developer at the web interface clicks the deploy button, the simulator framework calls performAction, which in turn calls airbagDeployed to notify the listeners that the airbag has deployed.

Now finalize the manifest by following these steps:

- ○ Click the **add dependencies** link at the bottom of the manifest editor.
- ○ Edit the version range on the imported Toast packages to be 1.0.0 inclusive to 2.0.0 exclusive.
- ○ On the **Runtime** tab of the bundle's manifest, add the newly created package to the list of exported packages, leaving it hidden from other plug-ins. Then save the manifest.

Now create the service component:

- ○ Create a new service component in OSGI-INF/component.xml of this bundle. Use AirbagSimulator for the class of the component and startup and shutdown as the activate and deactivate methods.
- ○ Add IAirbag as a provided service.
- ○ Add a referenced service of type IDeviceSimulator named devSim with setDevSim as its bind method.

10.3.2 The Simulated GPS

The simulated GPS bundle is structurally comparable to the simulated airbag bundle, but because it's more internally complex, we won't bother to walk through creating it by hand. Instead, just use the Samples Manager to load the org.equinoxosgi.toast.dev.gps.sim bundle into your workspace.

Again, a good place to start exploring any bundle is its component.xml. Here you can see that this component is similar to the airbag bundle. It requires the IDeviceSimulatorService and provides the IGps service. From that information alone, you can see how this component fits into the system without delving into the internals. You'll see how it functions once we run Toast with the simulators.

10.4 Running with Simulated Devices

Before we run Toast with the simulated devices, we need to update the client product to include both the simulator framework and required infrastructure, and to put in our new API and implementation bundles. Follow these steps to make the changes:

○ Since the existing client.product in the ToastClient project still uses the fake airbag and GPS, make a copy of it first and name it fake-client.product.

○ On the **Dependencies** tab of client.product, add the following bundles to the list. The first two are needed by the device simulator framework because it provides a web interface. The rest are our new simulator bundles.

```
javax.servlet
org.eclipse.equinox.http
org.equinoxosgi.toast.dev.airbag.sim
org.equinoxosgi.toast.dev.gps.sim
org.equinoxosgi.toast.devsim
```

○ On the **Launching** tab, add this line to the **VM Arguments** to assign the port number for the web interface. We don't want it to conflict with the back end's use of port 8080.

```
-Dorg.osgi.service.http.port=8081
```

We're ready to try out the new Toast with the simulated devices. First launch the back end and then the client:

○ Use **Ctrl-Shift-R** to open backend.product in the ToastBackEnd project.

○ Click the run button in the top right corner.

○ Now do the same for the client.product.

You should see an indication on the back end's console that the EmergencyServlet has come to life. Then, on the client's console, you should see an indication that the DeviceSimulatorServlet has started at client/devices.

Let's try deploying the airbag by using the airbag simulator:

○ Open a web browser on http://localhost:8081/client/devices.

○ Click on **Airbag** to see the airbag simulator page.

○ Click the blue button to deploy the airbag once. Clicking the green button starts the airbag deploying every five seconds. Use the red button to stop the repetition.

Now let's try using the GPS simulator to change the location of the vehicle:

○ Click the **Return** button to return to the main simulator page.

○ Click on **GPS** to see the GPS simulator page.

○ Try clicking the various blue buttons to change the vehicle's location. If you deploy the airbag again, you should see the new location reflected on the back end's console.

10.5 Summary

Toast now runs with a simulated airbag and GPS with a web interface to manually control them. While you stepped through the refactoring of the airbag and GPS bundles, you did more than just learn about the PDE tooling. The larger theme at work in this chapter was the importance of separating interface from implementation. It was that initial refactoring that enabled the pluggability of the simulators.

Using OSGi services is the key to enabling this pluggability, and the pluggability in turn enables parallel development on a large scale. While the real device drivers are being developed, development can proceed on the higher layers of domain logic and user interface. With the simulators in place and the domain logic functioning, we next turn our attention to the user interface.

CHAPTER 11

Extensible User Interface

If a picture is worth a thousand words, then Toast is long overdue for something more visually interesting than just logging to the console. Toast's functionality has continued to grow with each chapter, but now it's high time to get down to the business of creating a user interface.

User interfaces come in a wide variety, from desktop-style widgets to a dashboard of simple indicator lights. While these two extremes are certainly possible, this chapter walks you through the creation of a bitmap-based graphical user interface—the kind of thing that makes sense on an in-vehicle telematics platform like Toast. During this walk-through we show you the following:

○ A pluggable SWT-based user interface framework and a set of handy bitmap-based widgets

○ The refactoring of the domain layer to better accommodate a user interface

○ Various application screens that control vehicle climate, audio, emergency, mapping, and guidance facilities

○ The use of an embedded browser to integrate with Google Earth and JavaScript for mapping and guidance functionality

○ The OSGi and Equinox application models and how to set up and run an Equinox-based system with a UI

11.1 Crust

Crust is a user interface framework that provides a pluggable application shell, some graphical widgets, and some other useful utilities for running Crust-based applications. We won't delve into too many details of the inner workings of Crust, but we will take a closer look at how Toast's user interface sits atop this framework.

Let's begin the tour by loading the Crust framework into the workspace:

○ Use the Samples Manager as described in Section 3.4.2, "Comparing," to load the following projects:

```
org.equinoxosgi.crust.widgets
org.equinoxosgi.crust.display
org.equinoxosgi.crust.artwork.toast
org.equinoxosgi.crust.shell
```

11.1.1 Crust Shell

If you've been paying attention, you've learned that a great way to familiarize yourself with a new bundle is to look at its component.xml. So take a look at the component.xml in the org.equinoxosgi.crust.shell project. You can see that the shell requires one service, ICrustDisplay, and provides one service, ICrustShell.

Since Toast's user interface plugs into this framework, let's take a look at ICrustShell. The most important APIs, installScreen and uninstallScreen, are shown in the following snippet. They allow different screens to install and remove their icons from the shell.

org.equinoxosgi.crust.shell/ICrustShell
```
public interface ICrustShell {
    public Composite installScreen(int slot, Class clazz,
        String offImage, String onImage, String depressedImage,
        ICrustScreenListener screenListener);
    public void uninstallScreen(int slot,
        ICrustScreenListener screenListener);
}
```

Figure 11-1 shows the top portion of the Crust shell with various application icons installed.

Figure 11-1   The Crust shell with Toast icons

The org.equinoxosgi.crust.display project is used internally by the CrustShell. We'll cover this in more detail in Section 11.4, "The OSGi Application Model." Finally, the org.equinoxosgi.crust.artwork.toast project is a fragment whose host is org.equinoxosgi.crust.shell. This fragment provides two images needed by CrustShell for the window background and for the pop-up background. All the other artwork in Toast resides in Toast projects.

11.1.2 Crust Widgets

The Crust framework also provides a set of SWT widgets for use in bitmap-based user interfaces like Toast's. The org.equinoxosgi.crust.widgets project contains the three widget classes ImageButton, ImageProgressBar, and ImageSlider. Figure 11-2 shows a sample of each of these widgets as they appear in the Toast user interface.

Figure 11–2   Crust widgets ImageButton, ImageProgressBar, and ImageSlider

---

SWT

SWT is the Standard Widget Toolkit, a graphical widget toolkit that ships as part of Eclipse. Programs that use SWT are portable, but SWT's implementation is unique for each platform. Because SWT uses native widgets on each platform, user interfaces using SWT adopt the platform's native look and feel. SWT is provided as a bundle and a fragment for each supported platform.

11.2 Emergency

With the Crust framework installed, we're ready to turn our attention to putting a user interface on the emergency scenario. When the airbag deploys, the EmergencyMonitor communicates with the back end. The UI should display any response messages that may come back. It should also provide the user with a way to make an emergency call to the service center manually, without the airbag deploying.

11.2.1 Making the User Interface Pluggable

Before we implement the user interface, we need to think about how the emergency user interface bundle will fit into Toast's architecture. Figure 11-3 shows how the emergency user interface bundle plugs into the Toast bundle ecosystem.

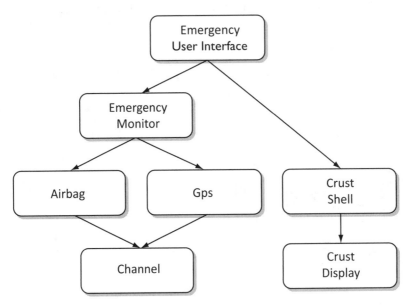

Figure 11–3   Emergency user interface

It is important that the user interface depends on the domain logic and not vice versa. Adopting this approach makes the user interface pluggable in two ways. First, it enables us to run Toast with a variety of possible user interfaces or none at all. We can simply plug any user interface on top of the EmergencyMonitor and the CrustShell. Second, it means that the user interface can be divided up by scenario, with each piece of user interface functionality being independent of the others. This will come in very handy when we get to Chapter 14, "System Deployment with p2."

11.2.2 Refactoring the Emergency Domain Logic

The emergency user interface depends on the EmergencyMonitor, but the EmergencyMonitor does not yet implement any service, so we'll need to add one. The service needs to provide APIs for the two situations mentioned earlier: listening for relevant events from the EmergencyMonitor and manually causing an emergency message send without the airbag deploying.

Modifying a component to provide a service is a common development scenario, so it's worthwhile to review the changes in detail. Rather than stepping you through making the changes yourself, we'll take a guided tour of the refactoring. Start by loading the modified EmergencyMonitor into your workspace:

❍ Use the Samples Manager to load the org.equinoxosgi.toast.client.emergency project.

First, notice in the component.xml that the component now provides a new service called IEmergencyMonitor. Open this new interface and take a look at the service API:

```
org.equinoxosgi.toast.client.emergency/IEmergencyMonitor
public interface IEmergencyMonitor {
   public void addListener(IEmergencyMonitorListener listener);
   public void removeListener(IEmergencyMonitorListener listener);
   public void emergency();
}
```

You can see that it uses the Observer Pattern to allow the user interface, or any other interested party, to add itself to and remove itself from the service's listeners. Then look at IEmergencyMonitorListener, shown here:

```
org.equinoxosgi.toast.client.emergency/IEmergencyMonitorListener
public interface IEmergencyMonitorListener {
   public void failed(Exception e);
   public void succeeded(String reply);
   public void started();
}
```

This interface defines the three methods used to notify listeners as interesting events transpire during an emergency session. We won't show it here, but take a few minutes to use the Samples Manager and compare the current EmergencyMonitor to the same class in "Chapter 10 Pluggable Services." Notice how the domain logic has changed to implement the new service. The changes consist mostly of a handful of methods for notifying the listeners at various points during the session.

Immediate Components and the Food Chain

Previously the emergency component did not provide any services—it was at the top of the food chain. As such, DS automatically treated it as immediate and proactively activated it. Now that the component is providing a service, DS assumes it should defer activation of the component until the provided service is acquired. Since we want the EmergencyMonitor to start listening to the airbag right away, the component's immediate attribute must be set to true.

Finally, the manifest also changed. On the **Runtime** tab of the manifest editor, notice that the bundle now exports the API package that contains the service interface and the listener interface.

To Split or Not to Split?

You've probably noticed that while this bundle now defines a service, it also still contains an implementation. This appears to fly in the face of our own recommended practice of separating interface from implementation.

The reality is that the rule is not hard-and-fast. In fact, it is quite common to leave the interface and implementation together. When you expect that there will only ever be a single implementation, you can leave the two together. Once you have or expect to have more than one implementation, it's best to split them apart.

11.2.3 The Emergency User Interface

The emergency user interface is contained in a single bundle. Again, here we tour the code since the actual UI code is not central to our OSGi theme.

○ Use the Samples Manager to load the `org.equinoxosgi.toast.swt.emergency` project.

Reviewing the `component.xml`, you'll discover that the component requires two services, `IEmergencyMonitor` and `ICrustShell`, and is implemented by the `EmergencyScreen` class.

As shown in the snippet that follows, `EmergencyScreen`'s `startup` method registers with the shell by calling `installScreen`. The first argument is a slot index to determine where the screen's icon is to appear on the shell's icon bar. The second argument is the `EmergencyScreen` class, which is used to acquire the image files from this bundle. The next three arguments are relative paths to images for the up, down, and depressed states of the icon. The final argument is the `EmergencyScreen` itself, used for notifications from the shell. The `startup` method also registers as a listener to the `IEmergencyMonitor` service, so it can receive notifications as the emergency session transpires. The `shutdown` method unregisters from both the `ICrustShell` and the `IEmergencyMonitor` services.

```
org.equinoxosgi.toast.swt.emergency/EmergencyScreen
public void startup() {
  screenComposite = crustShell.installScreen(SLOT, this.getClass(),
      TOPBAR_ICON_OFF_IMAGE, TOPBAR_ICON_ON_IMAGE, null, this);
  monitor.addListener(this);
  new DisplayBlock() {
```

```
                public void run() {
                  f = new ScaledWidgetFactory(this.getClass(),
                    screenComposite.getSize(), REFERENCE_HEIGHT, REFERENCE_WIDTH);
                }
              }.sync();
              Rectangle bounds = f.getScaledBounds(0, 0, POPUP_WIDTH,
                POPUP_HEIGHT);
              popupShell = crustShell.createPopupShell(SWT.NO_TRIM |
                SWT.APPLICATION_MODAL, bounds.width, bounds.height);
              new DisplayBlock() {
                public void run() {
                  populatePopupShell();
                }
              }.sync();
            }

            public void shutdown() {
              new DisplayBlock() {
                public void run() {
                  unpopulatePopupShell();
                }
              }.sync();
              monitor.removeListener(this);
              crustShell.uninstallScreen(SLOT, this);
            }
```

11.2.4 Running the User Interface

Before we run Toast with the emergency user interface, we need to modify the
client.product. Follow these steps to make the necessary changes:

○ Use **Ctrl-Shift-R** to open the client.product file.

○ On the **Overview** tab in the **Application** field, select
   org.equinoxosgi.crust.display.CrustApplication. We'll talk about the
   application support in Section 11.4, "The OSGi Application Model."

○ On the **Dependencies** tab, add SWT, the application support, Crust, and the
   Toast UI to the product. The required bundles are listed here. If you're not
   running on Windows, you'll need to replace the Windows SWT fragment
   with the appropriate one for your platform.

```
org.eclipse.equinox.app
org.eclipse.equinox.registry
org.eclipse.swt
org.eclipse.swt.win32.win32.x86
org.equinoxosgi.crust.artwork.toast
org.equinoxosgi.crust.display
org.equinoxosgi.crust.shell
org.equinoxosgi.crust.widgets
org.equinoxosgi.toast.swt.emergency
```

○ On the **Launching** tab, remove `eclipse.ignoreApp` and `osgi.noShutdown` from the **VM Arguments** for **All Platforms**.

○ Before you run the client, first bring up the `backend.product` and click the **run** button in the top right corner of the editor. Then do the same for the `client.product`.

TOAST ON THE MAC

On the Mac there are a number of issues with running Toast. Most of these relate to SWT and the Google Earth integration and the cross between 32- and 64-bit Java, and Carbon and Cocoa window systems. These issues will be resolved over time. For the most up-to-date steps and setup, see http://equinoxosgi.org/mac.

The Toast user interface appears with the emergency icon in the top left corner. Try clicking that button. A pop-up dialog asking for confirmation appears. After confirmation, another dialog appears showing the back end's response. Figure 11-4 shows the final dialog.

Figure 11–4 The emergency user interface

Try using the airbag simulator we added in Chapter 10, "Pluggable Services," by pointing your web browser at http://localhost:8081/client/devices and deploying the airbag. Then close the user interface to shut down the client. Leave the back end running, since we'll need it again later on.

11.3 Climate and Audio

Let's bring in two more screens to the user interface—one to control the vehicle's climate and another to control the audio system. Both of these are made up of two layers, a device layer and a user interface layer. Interestingly, these illustrate a case where there is no need for a domain logic layer, since the device layer provides a rich enough API to allow the user interface to sit directly on top.

11.3.1 *Climate and Audio Devices*

The richness of the device API is captured in a set of bundles representing the individual devices and fake implementations of each device.

❍ Use the Samples Manager to load the following projects into your workspace:

```
org.equinoxosgi.toast.dev.amplifier
org.equinoxosgi.toast.dev.amplifier.fake
org.equinoxosgi.toast.dev.cdplayer
org.equinoxosgi.toast.dev.cdplayer.fake
org.equinoxosgi.toast.dev.climate
org.equinoxosgi.toast.dev.climate.fake
org.equinoxosgi.toast.dev.radio
org.equinoxosgi.toast.dev.radio.fake
```

Let's start with a quick look at the climate device. The first thing to notice is that we have chosen to separate interface from implementation. The org.equinoxosgi.toast.dev.climate bundle contains just the service interface, whereas the org.equinoxosgi.toast.dev.climate.fake bundle contains a fake implementation of that interface. We fully expect there to be many different device drivers, so this will pay off in the end.

As shown in the following snippet, the IClimateControl interface provides various APIs for controlling the climate device as well as the now-familiar Observer Pattern APIs to register and unregister as a listener:

org.equinoxosgi.toast.dev.climate/IClimateControl
```
public interface IClimateControl {
  public void addListener(IClimateControlListener listener);
  public void removeListener(IClimateControlListener listener);
  public int getMaxTemperature();
  public int getMinTemperature();
```

```
    public void driverTemperatureUp();
    public void driverTemperatureDown();
    public int getDriverTemperature();
    public void setDriverTemperature(int temperature);
    public void passengerTemperatureUp();
    public void passengerTemperatureDown();
    public int getPassengerTemperature();
    public void setPassengerTemperature(int temperature);
    public int getMaxFanSpeed();
    public int getMinFanSpeed();
    public void driverFanSpeedUp();
    public void driverFanSpeedDown();
    public int getDriverFanSpeed();
    public void setDriverFanSpeed(int speed);
    public void passengerFanSpeedUp();
    public void passengerFanSpeedDown();
    public int getPassengerFanSpeed();
    public void setPassengerFanSpeed(int speed);
    public void turnOnAirConditioning();
    public void turnOffAirConditioning();
    public boolean isAirConditioningOn();
    public void turnOnRecirculation();
    public void turnOffRecirculation();
    public boolean isRecirculationOn();
    public void turnOnRearDefrost();
    public void turnOffRearDefrost();
    public boolean isRearDefrostOn();
    public void setAirFlow(short airFlow);
    public short getAirFlow();
}
```

The `IClimateControlListener` interface defines the contract by which listeners are notified of changes on the device. It is shown in the following snippet:

org.equinoxosgi.toast.dev.climate/IClimateControlListener
```
public interface IClimateControlListener {
    public void driverTemperatureChanged(int temperature);
    public void passengerTemperatureChanged(int temperature);
    public void driverFanSpeedChanged(int speed);
    public void passengerFanSpeedChanged(int speed);
    public void airConditioningChanged(boolean isOn);
    public void recirculationChanged(boolean isOn);
    public void rearDefrostChanged(boolean isOn);
    public void airFlowChanged(short flow);
}
```

The `FakeClimateControl` implementation does just enough to be able to store the device's state and notify listeners of state changes. The details are not important here, so the source code is not shown.

The audio system consists of three devices: an amplifier, a CD player, and a radio. All of these devices follow the identical pattern as the climate device, with separate bundles for interface and implementation, interface APIs for control and observation, and a minimal fake implementation.

11.3.2 Climate and Audio Screens

With the device layer in place, let's look at the user interface for the climate and audio:

❍ Use the Samples Manager to load the two required UI bundles into your workspace:

```
org.equinoxosgi.toast.swt.audio
org.equinoxosgi.toast.swt.climate
```

These bundles follow the same pattern as the emergency user interface. The climate bundle requires the IClimateControl service and the ICrustShell service. Similarly, the audio bundle requires the IAmplifier, ICdPlayer, and IRadio services as well as the ICrustShell service. Each bundle listens to its required device services and plugs its UI screen into the CrustShell.

11.3.3 Running the User Interface

Let's run Toast again with the new screens and devices. Follow these steps to make the necessary changes to the product definition:

❍ On the **Dependencies** tab of the client.product, add the following bundles to the list:

```
org.equinoxosgi.toast.dev.amplifier
org.equinoxosgi.toast.dev.amplifier.fake
org.equinoxosgi.toast.dev.cdplayer
org.equinoxosgi.toast.dev.cdplayer.fake
org.equinoxosgi.toast.dev.climate
org.equinoxosgi.toast.dev.climate.fake
org.equinoxosgi.toast.dev.radio
org.equinoxosgi.toast.dev.radio.fake
org.equinoxosgi.toast.swt.audio
org.equinoxosgi.toast.swt.climate
```

❍ Now click the run button in the top right corner.

Toast now includes icons for audio and climate on the icon bar, as shown in Figure 11-5. Click around on the new screens. The figure shows the audio screen.

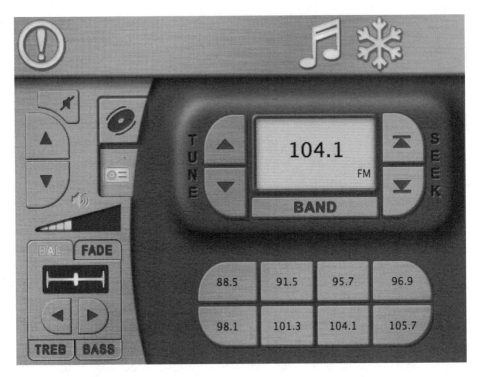

Figure 11–5   The audio user interface

11.4 The OSGi Application Model

In Section 11.2.4, "Running the User Interface," we updated the client product to identify the CrustApplication. Many OSGi-based systems have no top and no bottom and no main method. Rather they are a community of collaborating bundles. There are, however, circumstances where you want to create and manage particular tasks or function sets. In OSGi we talk about these sets as *applications*.

The OSGi Mobile Expert Group (MEG) specification includes an application management setup whereby applications register themselves as ApplicationDescriptors. An application container can then discover these applications and can launch, lock, or schedule them. Launching an ApplicationDescriptor also gives you a chance to capture and process command-line arguments—in effect, this is the standard main method entry point. Running applications are represented by ApplicationHandles that allow for the inspection and control of the application.

The original driver for this facility was mobile phone scenarios. Mobile devices typically have many applications installed but only a few running at any given time. They also have some sort of UI that shows the user the available applications and allows them to start and stop them. This sounds perfect for Toast and Crust.

Equinox includes an implementation of this specification in the `org.eclipse.equinox.app` bundle. This provides an application container and some additions to the application model. Here we touch on the detail but focus mainly on how to hook into this capability.

The Equinox application model allows you to control how and where the application runs. For example, for Toast to run on the Mac, it is important that the UI run on the `Main` thread created by the JVM. Without this the UI would paint but all events would be lost. This is a quirk of the Mac but must be accommodated. The model also allows for giving exclusive control to an application and controlling the number of applications that can be launched.

To see how this works, open the `plugin.xml` file in `org.equinoxosgi` `.crust.display` and flip to the **plugin.xml** tab to see the markup shown here:

`org.equinoxosgi.crust.display/plugin.xml`
```xml
<plugin>
   <extension id="CrustApplication"
       point="org.eclipse.core.runtime.applications">
    <application
        cardinality="singleton-global" thread="main" visible="true">
      <run
          class="org.equinoxosgi.crust.internal.display.CrustDisplay"/>
    </application>
   </extension>
</plugin>
```

Here we use an Equinox extension to declare the Crust application. Extensions are detailed in Chapter 16, "Extensions." The key parts of the markup are highlighted. First is the `id`, `CrustApplication`. This is based on the value you entered in the product definition. It identifies the application itself.

The `cardinality` and `thread` attributes of the `application` tag indicate that there can be only one `CrustApplication` running at any time and that it should run in the main thread created by the JVM.

Finally, the `class` attribute in the `run` element identifies the class that implements the application. In the Equinox model, this class must implement `IApplication`, shown here:

`org.eclipse.equinox.app/IApplication`
```java
public interface IApplication {
  public Object start(IApplicationContext context) throws Exception;
  public void stop();
}
```

For UI applications there must be some thread that sits listening for and processing UI events. Further, to address the main-thread issue on the Mac, that UI thread must be the main JVM thread. Setting thread="main" in the application declaration gets the application on the right thread, so we just have to ensure that the application does the UI processing. The application class is shown in the following snippet. The code is a little daunting but is largely generic, so we'll just highlight the key parts.

org.eclipse.equinox.app/CrustDisplay

```
public class CrustDisplay implements IApplication, ICrustDisplay {

  // IApplication methods
  public Object start(IApplicationContext context) throws Exception {
    display = Display.getDefault();
    context.applicationRunning();
    BundleContext bundleContext = Activator.getBundleContext();
    serviceReference = bundleContext.registerService(
        ICrustDisplay.class.getName(), this, null);
    try {
      runDisplayEventQueue();
    } finally {
      display.dispose();
    }
    return IApplication.EXIT_OK;
  }

  public void stop() {
    shutdown();
  }

  // ICrustDisplay methods
  public void shutdown() {
    // this needs to be passed to another thread if the
    // ui thread were to do this work it would deadlock
    new Thread(new Runnable() {
      public void run() {
        if (!isRunning)
          return;
        serviceReference.unregister();
        isRunning = false;
        display.wake();
      }
    }).start();
  }

  public Display getDisplay() {
    return display;
  }

  private void runDisplayEventQueue() {
    isRunning = true;
    while (isRunning && !display.isDisposed())
      try {
```

```
            if (!display.readAndDispatch())
              display.sleep();
        } catch (Throwable t) {
          t.printStackTrace();
        }
      isRunning = false;
    }
}
```

The main entry point for the application is the `start` method; it's given an application context from which the command-line arguments and various properties can be retrieved. In the Crust case we need to register the `CrustDisplay` as a service and then run the UI's *read-eval* loop. When the application is stopped, either by closing the last window or by stopping the framework, the display service must be unregistered.

Notice in the code that there are a number of threading issues. In particular, unregistering the display service will cause all of the contributed UI parts to be stopped—one of their required services will disappear. In their cleanup code they will likely want to use the display service to free resources and so forth. Since this cleanup is done synchronously with the `unregisterService` call, and all UI manipulation must be done on the UI thread, we must ensure that deregistration is *not* done on the UI thread—otherwise deadlock would occur.

Despite its apparent complexity, `CrustDisplay` is relatively simple. It is the core of any UI application but really needs to be written only once and then can be reused wherever needed.

11.5 Navigation and Mapping

While OSGi itself is predominantly a Java technology, it can integrate tightly with the underlying platform and systems done in other languages. To illustrate this, we will add navigation and guidance support to Toast using Google Earth facilities. You will have seen this sort of functionality in modern cars and handheld GPS devices. The device displays a map, your location, points of interest, and the like and provides routing information for getting from point to point.

11.5.1 Google Earth Integration

Google Earth is a system that uses Google's map facilities combined with satellite imagery and 3D modeling techniques to present a pseudo-realistic view of the environment. It comes as both a stand-alone application and a web browser plug-in. We will use the latter and embed a browser in a new Toast mapping screen. As with the other UI screens, here we tour the code:

○ Use the Samples Manager to load the following projects into your workspace:

```
org.equinoxosgi.toast.client.nav.guidance
org.equinoxosgi.toast.dev.google
org.equinoxosgi.toast.swt.nav.guidance.google
org.equinoxosgi.toast.swt.nav.mapping.google
```

The interesting parts of this are in the device- and SWT-related bundles. Let's start with `org.equinoxosgi.toast.dev.google`. This is the main interface to the Google Earth *device*. Again, an interesting spot to start looking is in the DS components. Here the bundle supplies two, `component.xml` and `google.xml`.

The first of these is responsible for setting up and maintaining a `Browser` service. `Browser` is an SWT class that interfaces Java to an underlying web browser such as Firefox or Safari. To create a `Browser`, we need an SWT `Shell` and a `URLConverter`:

org.equinoxosgi.toast.dev.google/component.xml
```xml
<?xml version="1.0" encoding="UTF-8"?>
<scr:component xmlns:scr="http://www.osgi.org/xmlns/scr/v1.1.0"
    activate="startup" deactivate="shutdown"
    name="org.equinoxosgi.toast.dev.google.browser">
  <implementation class=
      "org.equinoxosgi.toast.internal.dev.google.bundle.Component"/>
  <reference bind="setShell" name="shell"
      interface="org.equinoxosgi.crust.shell.ICrustShell"/>
  <reference bind="setConverter" name="converter"
      interface="org.eclipse.osgi.service.urlconversion.URLConverter"/>
</scr:component>
```

The code for this component is in the `Component` class shown in simplified form in the next snippet. The `startup` method uses the discovered `CrustShell` to create a `Browser`. The browser is then initialized with some content that loads Google Earth, and finally it is registered as a service. The initialization requires two steps: First, the required web page is made available, and second, the page is loaded.

Notice the use of `toFileURL`. OSGi bundles typically ship as JARs. This particular bundle includes a file, `index.html`, that needs to be loaded directly by a browser. Since browsers do not generally understand JAR files, we have to do something to make `index.html` available in the normal file system. The Equinox `URLConverter` service does this for us. By calling `toFileURL`, we are saying, "Find the content at the given URL and ensure that it can be accessed via a `file:` URL." If the input URL is already a `file:` URL, it is returned. Otherwise the content at the URL is read and stored in a cache. The net result is a URL that browsers understand. The last line of startup sets the browser's content to this URL.

org.equinoxosgi.toast.dev.google/Component
```java
public class Component {
  public void startup(final BundleContext context) {
    browser = new Browser(shell.getShell(), SWT.NONE);
```

```
      browser.setBounds(new Rectangle(115, 22, 510, 318));
      browser.setVisible(false);
      URL url = this.getClass().getResource("index.html");
      try {
        url = converter.toFileURL(url);
      } catch (IOException e) {
        LogUtility.logDebug("Unable to find home page: " + url);
        return;
      }
      browser.addProgressListener(new ProgressAdapter() {
        public void completed(ProgressEvent event) {
          browser.removeProgressListener(this);
          browserRegistration = context.registerService(
            Browser.class.getName(), browser, null);
        }
      });
      browser.setUrl(url.toExternalForm());
    }

    public void shutdown(BundleContext context) {
      if (browserRegistration == null)
        return;
      browserRegistration.unregister();
      browserRegistration = null;
      browser = null;
    }
}
```

Simply setting the content in the browser does not mean that the browser is fully initialized and ready to use with Google Earth. Loading and processing all the content may take quite some time. Here we defer the registration of the `Browser` service until the page has completed loading. Note that we do not want to wait synchronously as that would block other unrelated components from activating.

On `shutdown` we are careful to unregister any `Browser` that we registered.

With Google Earth up and running in a browser, we can expose its functionality as a GPS, hook it into the device simulator, and expose a higher-level `IGoogleEarth` service for routing and viewpoint control. This is done in the component as shown here:

org.equinoxosgi.toast.dev.google/google.xml
```xml
<scr:component xmlns:scr="http://www.osgi.org/xmlns/scr/v1.1.0"
    activate="startup" deactivate="shutdown"
    name="org.equinoxosgi.toast.dev.google">
  <implementation
      class="org.equinoxosgi.toast.internal.dev.google.Simulator"/>
  <service>
    <provide interface="org.equinoxosgi.toast.dev.gps.IGps"/>
    <provide interface=
        "org.equinoxosgi.toast.dev.google.IGoogleEarth"/>
  </service>
```

```
<reference bind="setSimulator" name="simulator"
    interface="org.equinoxosgi.toast.devsim.IDeviceSimulator"/>
<reference bind="setBrowser" name="browser"
    interface="org.eclipse.swt.browser.Browser"/>
</scr:component>
```

Most of this is quite conventional. The interesting part is the implementation of the two services, IGps and IGoogleEarth. The actual computation for these is done using JavaScript running in the browser. So here we have to call from Java to JavaScript both to effect changes and to get values. It turns out that this is quite straightforward using SWT's Browser support. The following snippet shows the implementation of IGps.getSpeed and the routing device simulator's driveRoute method:

```
org.equinoxosgi.toast.dev.google/Simulator
private Object run(final String script) {
  final Object[] result = new Object[1];
  final Browser b = browser;
  new DisplayBlock() {
    public void run() {
      result[0] = b.evaluate(script);
    }
  }.sync();
  return result[0];
}

public int getSpeed() {
  String script =
      "if (DS_simulator) return DS_simulator.currentSpeed; return 0;";
  Object result = run(script);
  if (result == null)
    return 0;
  return (int) Math.round(((Double) result).doubleValue());
}

private void driveRoute(int speed) {
  if (isDriving())
    return;
  driving = true;
  controlSimulator(COMMAND_START);
}
```

The main work of getSpeed is to create a little JavaScript code fragment that does the needed functionality and then run that code in the browser. Here the fragment accesses the Google driving simulator to get the speed of the vehicle. If the simulator has not been initialized, 0 is returned. The call to run eventually calls Browser.evaluate with that script and returns the result. The inner class blocks and indirection are needed because Browser calls must be done on the SWT UI thread. The implementation of driveRoute is very much the same, but the script is created and run in controlSimulator.

11.5.2 Mapping Support

Introducing mapping support now is mostly a job of laying out the UI and hooking controls to the IGoogleEarth service. This is done in the org.equinoxosgi .toast.swt.nav.mapping bundle.

Starting with the component definition shown here, we see that we need the ICrustShell, IGps, and IGoogleEarth services and that we need to provide an IMappingScreen service:

org.equinoxosgi.toast.swt.nav.mapping/component.xml
```
<scr:component xmlns:scr="http://www.osgi.org/xmlns/scr/v1.1.0"
    name="org.equinoxosgi.toast.swt.nav.mapping.google"
    immediate="true" activate="startup" deactivate="shutdown">
  <implementation class=
    "org.equinoxosgi.toast.internal.swt.nav.mapping.google.MappingScreen"/>
  <service>
    <provide
      interface="org.equinoxosgi.toast.swt.nav.mapping.IMappingScreen"/>
  </service>
  <reference bind="setShell" name="shell"
      interface="org.equinoxosgi.crust.shell.ICrustShell"/>
  <reference bind="setGps" name="gps"
      interface="org.equinoxosgi.toast.dev.gps.IGps"/>
  <reference bind="setGoogleEarth" name="googleEarth"
      interface="org.equinoxosgi.toast.dev.google.IGoogleEarth"/>
</scr:component>
```

For the most part the implementation of this component is quite conventional. The screen is laid out. When activated, the Google Earth service is told to become visible within a particular bounding box, and the current location is set to the location reported by the GPS service. This is shown in the snippet of the component's implementation class, MappingScreen:

org.equinoxosgi.toast.swt.nav.mapping/MappingScreen
```
public void activate() {
  LogUtility.logDebug(this, "activated");
  ...
  ge.setVisible(mappingComposite,
      f.getScaledBounds(115, 22, 510, 318));
  ge.flyTo(gps, zoom);
}
```

11.5.3 Application Extensibility and Navigation Support

So far these applications have been plugging into the ICrustShell service and using one of the predefined slots on the top toolbar to expose their functionality. In the case of navigation support, routing from point to point, this is really a subfunction of the mapping facilities. In the previous section we did not look at why the mapping support exposed an IMappingScreen service.

The mapping screen is extensible and allows others to augment its appearance with new buttons and sub-screens in much the same way as the CrustShell. The extensibility API is shown in the following code snippet:

```
org.equinoxosgi.toast.swt.nav.mapping/IMappingScreen
public interface IMappingScreen {
    public void setGuidanceLabel(String label);
    public void clearGuidanceLabel();
    public Composite installSubscreen(Class clazz, String offImage,
        String onImage, String depressedImage,
        IMappingSubscreen subscreen);
    public void deactivateSubscreen(IMappingSubscreen subscreen);
    public Font getFont(String fontName);
    public void setSubscreenButtonSelection(
        IMappingSubscreen subscreen, boolean state);
    public void uninstallSubscreen(IMappingSubscreen subscreen);
}
```

The rest of the guidance support is laying out the UI screen and ultimately interaction with Google's route-planning support, IGoogleEarth.loadDirections, when the user selects a destination.

11.5.4 Running the User Interface

Running the Toast Client with Google-supported navigation and guidance is largely the same as the cases we've already seen. There are two important differences:

1. Prior to running you must install the Google Earth browser plug-in.

2. After the client starts, the mapping application takes some time to initialize Google Earth and the browser service.

With that in mind, do the following to set up and run the client with mapping and navigation support:

○ Open the standard web browser on your platform—IE on Windows, Firefox on Linux, Safari on Mac—and access the following URL: http://earth-api-samples.googlecode.com/svn/trunk/demos/drive-simulator/index.html. This offers to install the required plug-ins if they are not already installed.

○ On the **Dependencies** tab of the client.product, add the following bundles to the list:

```
org.equinoxosgi.toast.client.nav.guidance
org.equinoxosgi.toast.dev.google
org.equinoxosgi.toast.swt.nav.guidance.google
org.equinoxosgi.toast.swt.nav.mapping.google
```

○ Run the product. Once it is up and the mapping button shows in the toolbar, click on it to get a UI that looks like Figure 11-6.

Figure 11–6 Google Earth–based mapping

To access the guidance screen, click on the guidance button, in the bottom left of the screen, to get the screen shown in Figure 11-7. The method for inputting destinations is quite simplistic but not particularly material here. When you pick a destination, directions are loaded and the screen closes. The route is then plotted in the map.

MAC COCOA

As of this writing, there is a problem running the Google Earth browser plug-in on the Mac Cocoa windowing system. Mac users should either use Carbon as their IDE or adjust their target platform's **Environment > Window System** setting to be Carbon.

You can then tell the car to drive the course plotted using the routing device simulator. This is analogous to the simulator we saw in Chapter 10, "Pluggable

Figure 11–7   Google Earth–based guidance

Services," and earlier in this chapter. Access the UI by opening a web browser on http://localhost:8081/client/devices and opening the routing simulator page shown in Figure 11-8.

Figure 11–8   Toast routing simulator

11.6 Summary

We covered a lot of ground in this tour of the Toast UI. First we saw Crust, the extensible base UI platform, and laid out the overall architecture. We then looked at the refactoring required to surface Toast's emergency, climate, and audio functions in the UI.

Diving a little deeper, we investigated the OSGi and Equinox application models to see how coherent sets of bundles can be started, stopped, and run on particular threads. Circling back to add more applications, we saw how native UI controls like web browsers can be integrated to create a rich user experience. This drove us to talk about Google Earth integration and Java-to-JavaScript integration. Finally, we observed that notions of extensibility can surface at all levels of an application.

At the end of this chapter the Toast Client is complete. Future chapters tweak a bit here and there, but no substantially new functionality is added to the client—it is already pretty full-featured.

CHAPTER 12

Dynamic Configuration

If you've ever had the strange feeling that someone is watching you, after this chapter you'll have no doubt that it's true. In this chapter we add a new feature to Toast that quietly tracks the vehicle's location.

Like all the functionality we've added to Toast so far, the tracking code is pluggable. But unlike the prior scenarios, this one is *headless*; that is, it has no user interface. We wouldn't want you to think that the only way to add functionality to Toast is via an icon on the user interface.

Most important, the tracking scenario gives us the opportunity to demonstrate OSGi's support for dynamic configuration to change how the tracking scenario operates on the fly.

In this chapter you will learn

○ How to build a headless tracking application that reports to the back end

○ How to use OSGi's `ConfigurationAdmin` service to control the frequency of reports to the back end

○ How to run Toast with the new tracking application

12.1 The Tracking Scenario

Trucking companies, car rental agencies, and especially parents of teenagers are very interested to know the location of their vehicles. The Toast tracking scenario wakes up every ten seconds, fetches the vehicle location from the `IGps` service, and then uses the `IChannel` service to send the readings to the back end. Figure 12-1 shows how the `TrackingMonitor` and `TrackingServlet` fit into the client and back end architecture.

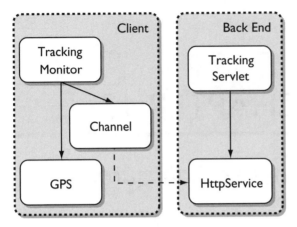

Figure 12–1   The tracking scenario on the client and back end

12.2 Installing the Tracking Code

The tracking scenario consists of one bundle for the client, one for the back end, and one core bundle that is used on both the client and the back end. The details of the tracking functionality are not particularly interesting here, so we will do a quick tour of the setup and then look at configuration issues.

12.2.1 The Core Tracking Bundle

Since the core bundle is required by both the client and the back end, we can avoid compilation errors by loading it first:

○ Use the Samples Manager to load the bundle `org.equinoxosgi.toast` `.core.tracking` into your workspace.

As in the emergency scenario, this bundle defines some constants in `ITrackingConstants` that are used by both the client and the back end. These constants are used throughout the chapter and are shown here for reference:

```
org.equinoxosgi.toast.core.tracking/ITrackingConstants
public interface ITrackingConstants {
    public static final String TRACKING_FUNCTION = "tracking";
    public static final String LATITUDE_PARAMETER = "latitude";
    public static final String LONGITUDE_PARAMETER = "longitude";
    public static final String HEADING_PARAMETER = "heading";
    public static final String SPEED_PARAMETER = "speed";
    public static final String TRACKING_PID =
        "org.equinoxosgi.toast.client.tracking";
    public static final String TRACKING_DELAY_PROPERTY = "delay";
```

```
public static final int TRACKING_DELAY_DEFAULT = 10;
public static final int MAX_TRACKING_HISTORY = 4;
}
```

12.2.2 The Back End Tracking Bundle

The back end portion of the scenario uses a servlet to listen for vehicle location messages from the client. For now, the back end just logs the information to the console.

○ Load the org.equinoxosgi.toast.backend.tracking bundle into your workspace using the Samples Manager.

The structure of this bundle is similar to the back end portion of the emergency scenario in the org.equinoxosgi.toast.backend.emergency bundle. From its component.xml file, shown in the following snippet, you can see that it provides no services and references only the HttpService. This is an immediate DS component that is activated upon acquiring the HttpService.

org.equinoxosgi.toast.backend.tracking/component.xml
```
<?xml version="1.0" encoding="UTF-8"?>
<scr:component xmlns:scr="http://www.osgi.org/xmlns/scr/v1.1.0"
    activate="startup" deactivate="shutdown"
    name="org.equinoxosgi.toast.backend.tracking">
  <implementation class=
   "org.equinoxosgi.toast.internal.backend.tracking.bundle.Component"/>
  <reference bind="setHttp" cardinality="1..1"
     interface="org.osgi.service.http.HttpService" name="http"
     policy="static"/>
</scr:component>
```

The Component class provides the implementation with startup and shutdown methods for activation and deactivation. Upon activation, the Component instantiates the TrackingServlet and registers it with the HttpService. Recall that the rationale for using a separate Component class as opposed to using the TrackingServlet as the component's implementation is based on the desire to keep the TrackingServlet as a pure HttpServlet. This way the Component class deals with the URL and the servlet alias that servlets should not know about. This is nearly identical to the EmergencyServlet shown in Section 7.1.2, "The Back End Emergency Bundle," so it is not shown here.

12.2.3 The Client Tracking Bundle

Let's move on to the client side, where things get more interesting. Here we need a TrackingMonitor to poll the GPS every ten seconds and report the vehicle location to the back end via the IChannel service:

❍ Copy the org.equinoxosgi.toast.client.tracking bundle into your workspace using the Samples Manager.

The component.xml reveals that this component references the IGps and
IChannel services. You can also see the usual startup and shutdown methods that
handle component activation and deactivation. But this time, there are two new
entries in the component. These are highlighted in the following snippet:

org.equinoxosgi.toast.client.tracking/component.xml
```xml
<?xml version="1.0" encoding="UTF-8"?>
<scr:component xmlns:scr="http://www.osgi.org/xmlns/scr/v1.1.0"
    activate="startup" deactivate="shutdown" modified="delayChanged"
    name="org.equinoxosgi.toast.client.tracking">
  <implementation class=
    "org.equinoxosgi.toast.internal.client.tracking.TrackingMonitor"/>
  <reference bind="setGps"
    interface="org.equinoxosgi.toast.dev.gps.IGps" name="gps"/>
  <reference bind="setChannel" name="channel"
    interface="org.equinoxosgi.toast.core.channel.sender.IChannel"/>
  <property name="delay" value="10" type="Integer"/>
</scr:component>
```

At the end of the code, notice that there is a new <property> element that
defines a property called delay with a default value of 10. This property determines the number of seconds the client should delay between sending tracking
updates to the back end. Later on in this chapter we will dynamically configure
the tracking component by changing this property.

The other thing to notice is that the <component> element now has its modified
attribute set to delayChanged. This is the name of the component method that DS
invokes when the component's properties change. Later, you'll see how this plays
out. In the meantime, take a look at TrackingMonitor's startup and updateDelay
methods, shown in this snippet:

org.equinoxosgi.toast.client.tracking/TrackingMonitor
```java
public void startup(Map properties) {
  id = PropertyManager.getProperty(ICoreConstants.ID_PROPERTY,
    ICoreConstants.ID_DEFAULT);
  updateDelay(properties);
  startJob();
}

private void updateDelay(Map properties) {
  Integer delaySpec = (Integer) properties
    .get(ITrackingConstants.TRACKING_DELAY_PROPERTY);
  delay = delaySpec == null ?
    ITrackingConstants.TRACKING_DELAY_DEFAULT : delaySpec.intValue();
  LogUtility.logDebug(this, "Tracking every " + delay + " seconds");
}
```

DS invokes the startup method with a Map of properties as an argument. This Map includes an entry for each property defined in the component. In this case, the Map contains just an entry for delay with a default value of 10. In the private updateDelay method, the TrackingMonitor gets the delay property from the Map and sets its delay field to this value. The startup method then starts a Job that sends a tracking message to the back end. It then uses the value of the delay field to determine how long to wait before repeating the Job.

12.3 Running the Basic Tracking Scenario

Let's checkpoint our progress by running Toast with the basic tracking scenario installed. The dynamic configuration is not happening yet, but it's worth seeing that the tracking runs without it for now. Follow these steps to update the two product files:

❍ Add both the org.equinoxosgi.toast.core.tracking and org.equinoxosgi .toast.backend.tracking bundles to the backend.product.

❍ Add both the org.equinoxosgi.toast.core.tracking and org.equinoxosgi .toast.client.tracking bundles to the client.product.

❍ Now run the back end and the client. Watch the console to see that the client is reporting its location to the back end every ten seconds.

12.4 Configuration

With the basic tracking scenario in place, we turn our attention to dynamic configuration.

12.4.1 OSGi's Configuration Admin

OSGi's ConfigurationAdmin service provides a mechanism for programmatically configuring component properties. Specifically, it means we can use it to change the TrackingMonitor's delay property at runtime. ConfigurationAdmin does not provide a user interface but rather a set of APIs that our code can invoke to change the properties.

12.4.2 The Client Tracking Bundle

Since OSGi's ConfigurationAdmin service provides the capability for the delay property to be dynamically changed at runtime, we need a way to surface this to the user. The simplest way is to use a web interface based on the trusty HttpService. We'll implement a servlet that serves up a web page that allows the user to change the tracking delay. This servlet uses the ConfigurationAdmin APIs to push the update to the TrackingMonitor. Figure 12-2 shows the modifications to the client side of Toast to support dynamic configuration.

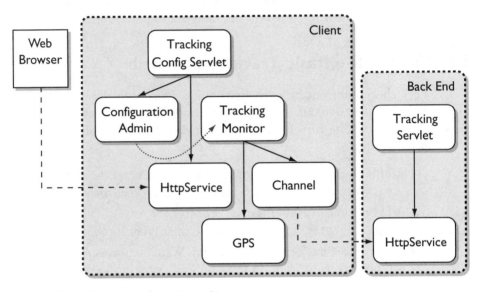

Figure 12–2   Dynamic configuration architecture

❍ Use the Samples Manager to load the
org.equinoxosgi.toast.client.tracking.config bundle.

The plumbing on this bundle is very similar to that of the back end emergency and tracking bundles. When the org.equinoxosgi.toast.client.tracking.config component is activated, the Component class's startup method registers the TrackingConfigServlet with the HttpService. A simplified version of the servlet's doGet method is shown in this snippet:

org.equinoxosgi.toast.client.tracking.config/TrackingConfigServlet
```
protected void doGet(HttpServletRequest request,
    HttpServletResponse response)
    throws ServletException, IOException {
  response.setContentType(CONTENT_TYPE_HTML);
  String delayString =
      request.getParameter(TRACKING_DELAY_PARAMETER);
  if (delayString != null) {
    int delay = Integer.parseInt(delayString);
    if (delay > 0)
```

```
        updateDelay(delay);
    }
    generateResponse(request, response);
}
```

When an HTTP request comes in from the web browser to change the delay, the new value for the delay is parsed from the request parameter and passed to the private updateDelay method shown here:

```
org.equinoxosgi.toast.client.tracking.config/TrackingConfigServlet
private void updateDelay(int delay) {
    try {
        Configuration config = configAdmin.getConfiguration(
            ITrackingConstants.TRACKING_PID, null);
        Dictionary properties = config.getProperties();
        if (properties == null) {
            properties = new Hashtable();
            properties.put(SERVICE_PID, ITrackingConstants.TRACKING_PID);
        }
        Integer delayInteger = new Integer(delay);
        properties.put(ITrackingConstants.TRACKING_DELAY_PROPERTY,
            delayInteger);
        config.update(properties);
    } catch (IOException e) {
        LogUtility.logError(this,"Unable to update tracking config: ", e);
    }
}
```

The servlet's updateDelay method uses the ConfigurationAdmin service to look up the Configuration for the tracking component using its *PID* and its bundle's *location*.

The component's PID is the unique *persistent ID* that ConfigurationAdmin uses to persistently store its Configuration. When configuring a DS component, the PID is the component's name as specified by its <component> element's name attribute.

The bundle location is used by ConfigurationAdmin as a rather weak, and optional, security feature that helps ensure that while all bundles can modify their own configuration data, only privileged bundles can modify another bundle's configuration data. Passing null as the location parameter bypasses the security check, which is exactly what we are doing here.

The updateDelay method gets the properties Dictionary from the Configuration, creating a new one if one does not exist. Then it puts the new delay value into the properties and calls the ConfigurationAdmin service's update API, which in turn updates the tracking component.

Because of its close integration with ConfigurationAdmin, DS is notified when a Configuration has been updated. DS then invokes the delayChanged method on the TrackingMonitor, passing in a Map of changed properties. Remember that the

delayChanged method is the `org.equinoxosgi.toast.client.tracking` component's `modified` method. This method is called when the component's properties
have been modified, so long as its configuration remains satisfied and it is activated.

Here the `delayChanged` method fetches the new value for the `delay` property
and restarts the `Job` so the new value can take effect.

If we had chosen not to set the `org.equinoxosgi.toast.client.tracking`
`<component>` element's `modified` attribute, DS would instead have deactivated
and reactivated the component. In our case, this would not make a noticeable difference, but if other components were dependent upon ours, the deactivation/
reactivation would percolate all the way up the dependency chain. In some cases,
this might have some undesirable side effects, such as the disappearance and reap-
pearance of screen icons.

12.4.3 Running Configurable Toast

With a slight modification to the client product, we can run Toast with configurable tracking:

- ○ Add the bundles `org.eclipse.equinox.cm`, Equinox's implementation of the
  `ConfigurationAdmin` service, and `org.equinoxosgi.toast.client`
  `.tracking.config` to the `client.product`.

- ○ Run the back end and the client. Again, watch the console to see that the client is reporting its location to the back end every ten seconds.

- ○ Now point your web browser at the following URL: http://localhost:8081/
  client/tracking-config.

  Figure 12-3 shows the web interface provided by the `TrackingConfigServlet`.
  Try clicking on the links to change the delay between tracking messages.

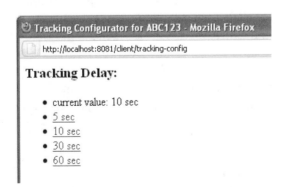

Figure 12–3   Tracking configuration web interface

12.4.4 Running with Persistent Configuration

Each time you change the property from the web browser, the ConfigurationAdmin service persists the value. But if you run the client again by clicking the **Run** button in the client.product, the tooling clears the local storage, effectively resetting the tracking delay to its default value of ten seconds.

There is a way to run the client again without resetting local storage. If you select **Run > RunConfigurations...**, you will find a launch configuration under **Eclipse Application** called client.product. This launch configuration is created automatically when you click the **Run** button in the client.product. Ensure that the **Clear the configuration area before launching** option on the **Configuration** tab is unchecked, to leave the persistent storage from the previous run intact—the tracking delay should be unchanged from the previous run.

12.5 Summary

This chapter showcases OSGi's ConfigurationAdmin service as the mechanism for managing the configuration of available services. We walked you through adding a vehicle-tracking mechanism to Toast. ConfigurationAdmin was used to manage the frequency of location updates. The implementation follows the same client and back end pattern as the emergency scenario and presents a simple web UI for adjusting the tracking frequency.

ConfigurationAdmin makes it easy to define properties in a component, update them dynamically, and persist them between runs. Tracking is only one small example of how ConfigurationAdmin can be used for dynamic configuration. Chapter 15, "Declarative Services," goes into more detail on the other capabilities and uses for ConfigurationAdmin.

CHAPTER 13

Web Portal

So far the Toast Back End has been largely headless—content is written to the console, but there is no user interaction. In this chapter we add a web-based user interface to Toast. The goal here is not to create a fancy UI but rather to talk about some commonly used extensibility mechanisms and metaphors set in the context of providing a UI for Toast.

We use this context to introduce the Whiteboard Pattern, a powerful style of using OSGi services to aggregate operations. In building the portal we also look at how to insulate our domain code from OSGi in cases where explicit OSGi use is inevitable.

In this chapter we do the following

○ Introduce and explore the Whiteboard Pattern

○ Build on our current back end infrastructure and create an extensible servlet structure by composing request handlers

○ Use the extensibility infrastructure to create a simple web UI portal for fleet management

○ Demonstrate the use of higher-order cardinality and dynamicity in Declarative Services

○ Implement a strategy for isolating domain code from OSGi infrastructure

13.1 Portal

Our modest Toast Back End has already demonstrated some of the value of OSGi on servers—we are able to reuse bundles on the client and server, and composing collections of servlets is straightforward. In the larger context, the benefits of OSGi

seen on desktops are at play on servers. In this chapter we explore some of these
and create a simple extensible web UI portal using techniques similar to those
used in other scenarios.

In the Toast context we have a rich client UI. To create a similarly rich server
UI would require significant effort and the use of technology such as the Eclipse
Rich Ajax Platform (RAP). Here, we will create a simple portal that can be
dynamically extended with new actions. For the most part we focus on the portal
extensibility mechanisms and leave aside the details of web design and compelling
workflows. Figure 13-1 shows a screen shot of the portal and the list of vehicles
being managed.

Figure 13–1   Toast Back End portal

The Toast Back End manages a set of vehicles. A UI on the back end should
allow users to browse and interact with the vehicles. Since we are using web
browsers and HTTP, Java servlets are a convenient means of implementing this
functionality. We could have each new piece of functionality implemented as an
independent servlet, but this gets challenging to coordinate, not to mention that
it makes it harder to demonstrate interesting OSGi capabilities. Instead, the Toast
Portal uses one servlet, the `PortalServlet`, and the Whiteboard Pattern to enable
extensibility.

The bulk of this chapter is a tour of the web portal code. As such, you should
load the Chapter 13 sample from the Samples Manager to help in the exploration.

13.2 The `PortalServlet`

The `PortalServlet` acts as a request dispatcher. Incoming requests are inspected
and matched with, and dispatched to, a suitable handler. It is a subclass of
`javax.servlet.http.HttpServlet`, and the following snippet shows its `doGet`
method—the only significant functionality in the class. The two most important
lines are highlighted in the snippet.

```
org.equinoxosgi.toast.backend.portal/PortalServlet
public void doGet(
    HttpServletRequest request, HttpServletResponse response)
    throws ServletException, IOException {
  response.setContentType(CONTENT_TYPE_HTML);
  String id = request.getParameter(ID_PARAMETER);
  String actionParameter = request.getParameter(ACTION_PARAMETER);
  if ((id == null || id.length() == 0)
      && (actionParameter == null || actionParameter.length() == 0)) {
    handleRootRequest(request, response);
    return;
  }
  try {
    IPortalAction action = lookup.getAction(actionParameter);
    if (action == null) {
      handleDefaultRequest(response, id, actionParameter);
      return;
    }
    action.execute(request, response);
  } catch (Exception exception) {
    handleException(exception);
  }
}
```

The portal servlet accepts HTTP GET requests and uses the information supplied to determine an *action* to execute. To make the portal extensible, an action lookup mechanism is introduced. This isolates the servlet from the details of how actions are contributed. As we see in the first highlighted line, the portal servlet gets the relevant action from the action lookup mechanism. Once the action is found, handling of the request is delegated to the action. The portal is not involved in producing the response to any requests other than requests to the root of the servlet URL space or unrecognized requests.

As with the other cases in Toast, a DS component is needed to get the HttpService and register the required servlets. From an architectural point of view the portal is a configuration of the portal servlet and an action lookup mechanism. Together they define how actions are contributed, discovered, and executed.

The portal component combines the action lookup mechanism, business logic, and the control center to create a PortalServlet that is then registered with the HttpService. The key code for the Portal component is shown in the following snippet. In practice, center, lookup, and http are all fields containing services statically referenced by the portal component's portal.xml.

```
org.equinoxosgi.toast.backend.portal/Portal
protected void startup(ComponentContext context) {
  HttpServlet servlet = new PortalServlet(center, lookup);
  String servletRoot = PropertyManager.getProperty(
      ICoreConstants.BACK_END_URL_PROPERTY);
  UrlBuilder urlBuilder = new UrlBuilder(servletRoot);
  servletAlias = urlBuilder.getPath();
```

```
  try {
    http.registerServlet(servletAlias, servlet, null, null);
    LogUtility.logDebug(this, "Registered servlet: " + servletAlias);
  } catch (Exception e) {
    LogUtility.logError(this, "Error registering servlet", e);
  }
}
```

13.3 Action Lookup Using Services

There are many possibilities for implementing the action lookup mechanism. All must implement the interface shown in the following IActionLookup snippet. Here getAction allows for the lookup of an action, and getAvailable and getActionProperty let clients interrogate the structure of the available actions.

org.equinoxosgi.toast.backend.portal/IActionLookup
```
public interface IActionLookup {
  public IPortalAction getAction(String id);
  public Collection getAvailable(String id);
  public String getActionProperty(String id, String key);
}
```

In this chapter we will implement an OSGi service-based action lookup mechanism. In particular we introduce the Whiteboard Pattern as a means of discovering actions registered as services. The Whiteboard Pattern inverts the typical service orientation. In the registration approach used so far in the book, clients of, say, the HttpService discover the service and register their interests and capabilities. In the Whiteboard Pattern, the interested parties leverage the OSGi service registry by registering services, and the *event sources* discover them by querying the service registry. The registered services neither know nor care how they are used.

In keeping with our use of Declarative Services, we implement an IActionLookup that uses DS and the OSGi services following the Whiteboard Pattern. Using the whiteboard approach, action providers register their actions as services with the OSGi service registry. The action lookup mechanism then discovers all available action services and makes them available to the portal. Chapter 15 gives much more detail on the Whiteboard Pattern and dives deeply into the implementation detail of the portal.

SEPARATION OF CONCERNS

Notice that using the IActionLookup intermediate service isolates the portal from the details of how actions are discovered. We can use services with the Whiteboard Pattern or the Registration Pattern or both. In fact, Chapter 16,

"Extensions," shows how to use the Equinox Extension Registry to create an IActionLookup service. This approach is also in keeping with our overall strategy of POJO programming, dependency injection, and separation of concerns.

So far we have used DS in one way—to discover single services to which our components are statically bound. For a whiteboard component we need to allow both multiple service object discovery and dynamic service contribution. The following snippet shows the markup for the service-based IActionLookup component that meets these needs:

org.equinoxosgi.toast.backend.portal/serviceActionLookup.xml
```
<scr:component xmlns:scr="http://www.osgi.org/xmlns/scr/v1.1.0"
  name="org.equinoxosgi.toast.backend.portal.serviceActionLookup">
  <implementation class= "org.equinoxosgi.toast.internal.backend.portal
    .bundle.ServiceActionLookup"/>
  <service>
    <provide interface=
      "org.equinoxosgi.toast.backend.portal.spi.IActionLookup"/>
  </service>
  <reference
    name="action"
    interface="org.equinoxosgi.toast.backend.portal.spi.IPortalAction"
    cardinality="0..n"
    policy="dynamic"
    bind="addAction"
    unbind="removeAction"/>
</scr:component>
```

The snippet declares that the component references 0 or more IPortalAction services. By allowing for 0 references, the component says the referenced service is optional—the portal can run without any actions. With the upper bound set to n, the component allows for many services to be bound to it.

As we are building a dynamic system, the IPortalAction service reference has its policy set to dynamic. This allows referenced services to come and go without affecting the activation state of the component—the service action lookup component, and thus the portal, keeps running even if the actions change.

NAMING CONVENTIONS

Since the action lookup component may be bound to many service objects, the set* and clear* naming convention for the bind and unbind methods that we have been using does not quite work. Instead, in components with a multiple cardinality, we use the add* and remove* naming convention to get methods such as addAction and removeAction.

As IPortalAction services come and go, addAction and removeAction maintain a catalog of the discovered services. To get a sense of how this works, take a look at the addAction snippet:

org.equinoxosgi.toast.backend.portal/ServiceActionLookup
```
public void addAction(ServiceReference reference) {
  Object id = reference.getProperty(ACTION_PARAMETER);
  synchronized (actions) {
    PortalAction data = new PortalAction(reference);
    actions.put(id, data);
  }
}
```

The first thing to notice is that the addAction method's parameter is of type ServiceReference, whereas normally it has been the actual service type, for example, IPortalAction. One of the advantages of using DS is that it enables laziness—declared services are not instantiated until they are actually referenced. By using a ServiceReference, we tell the DS runtime to delay the instantiation of the service object even further until we programmatically dereference the ServiceReference object by calling the DS component's ComponentContext.locateService(String, ServiceReference) method. If the service represented by the ServiceReference is never used, it is never instantiated. Since typically only a few portal actions are used, this saves time and space.

The second point of interest in this code is the PortalAction wrapper class. A PortalAction is an IPortalAction that wraps a ServiceReference discovered by DS. The PortalAction presents an opaque façade that lazily gets the real service when the action is to be executed. The following snippet illustrates the IPortalAction.execute method:

org.equinoxosgi.toast.backend.portal/PortalAction
```
class PortalAction implements IPortalAction {
  ...
  public void execute(HttpServletRequest request,
      HttpServletResponse response) throws IOException {
    ComponentContext context = ServiceActionLookup.this.context;
    if (context == null)
      throw new IllegalStateException("component is not activated");
    IPortalAction action =
        (IPortalAction) context.locateService("action", reference);
    if (action == null)
      throw new IOException("Action has been invalidated: " + id);
    action.execute(request, response);
  }
}
```

Notice that the ComponentContext is used to look up the cached ServiceReference. The execute request is then delegated to the real action implementation. Readers interested in more detail on these points should review the ServiceActionLookup and PortalServlet code and look at Section 15.2.6, "The Whiteboard Pattern."

The final key element of the addAction method is the use of service properties. The first line of the method retrieves the *action property* from the service reference. When the service provider registered or declared the service, it supplied a value for this property. The portal uses the value as an identifier for the action. Incoming HTTP requests identify the action to run by including the related ID as a parameter in the HTTP request. The PortalServlet extracts the parameter and passes it to the IActionLookup. Refer back to the servlet code in Section 13.2, "The PortalServlet," to see the control flow.

DELAYED COMPONENT INSTANTIATION

In addition to the delayed instantiation of IPortalAction objects, the instantiation of the provided IActionLookup service is also delayed until the first HTTP request is received and handled by the portal servlet. This is a characteristic of every DS component that provides a service and is not explicitly declared as an immediate component. For more on DS and component immediacy, see Chapter 15, "Declarative Services," and Chapter 24, "Declarative Services Reference."

13.4 Declaring a Portal Action

Adding an action using the Whiteboard Pattern is as easy as registering an IPortalAction service with the OSGi service registry. This can be done using declarative or traditional service techniques. Since we've adopted DS, we declare a DS component for each portal action.

Action implementations need only implement the simple interface shown in the following snippet:

```
org.equinoxosgi.toast.backend.portal/IPortalAction
public interface IPortalAction {
  public void execute(
      HttpServletRequest request, HttpServletResponse response)
      throws IOException;
}
```

Shown next is the code for the *browse* action. This action presents a UI allowing users to browse aspects of a particular vehicle. This action simply generates a web page with all the browsing actions for a particular vehicle.

```
org.equinoxosgi.toast.backend.portal/BrowseAction
public class BrowseAction implements IPortalAction {
```

```
public void execute(
    HttpServletRequest request, HttpServletResponse response)
    throws IOException {
  generateBrowseVehicle(request, response);
}
}
```

The browse service is contributed to the system using the following DS component declaration:

org.equinoxosgi.toast.backend.portal/browse.xml
```
<scr:component xmlns:scr="http://www.osgi.org/xmlns/scr/v1.1.0"
  name="org.equinoxosgi.toast.backend.portal.browseAction">
  <implementation class=
      "org.equinoxosgi.toast.internal.backend.portal.BrowseAction"/>
  <service>
    <provide interface=
        "org.equinoxosgi.toast.backend.portal.spi.IPortalAction"/>
  </service>
  <property name="action" value="browse"/>
  <property name="label" value="Browse vehicle"/>
  <reference
    bind="setActionLookup"
    interface="org.equinoxosgi.toast.backend.portal.spi.IActionLookup"
    name="actionLookup"/>
</scr:component>
```

The key part of this markup is the two <property> elements—the action and the label. As we saw, the portal uses the action property value to identify actions. Similarly, the label property is used to affect the appearance of the action in the UI—the value of this property is presented to the user.

DECLARING MULTIPLE DS COMPONENTS

Bundles may contribute many actions to the portal to implement their UI. While it is technically possible to declare more than one component, and thus action, in a DS component file, we find it more modular and flexible to use separate files for each component. In addition, the PDE DS component editor currently supports only one component per file.

To add a bit more flexibility to action contributions, IActionLookup includes a simple action hierarchy model using paths in the action property. For example, the action property for the set of actions related to browsing a vehicle all start with browse/. The portal UI can then dynamically identify the browsing capabilities by looking only for the actions with that prefix.

Of course, actions can be contributed from any bundle. For example, the following snippet shows how the UI for tracking a vehicle is contributed by the `org.equinoxosgi.toast.backend.tracking.ui` bundle. Notice the path in the `action` property value.

org.equinoxosgi.toast.backend.tracking.ui/tracking.xml
```
<scr:component xmlns:scr="http://www.osgi.org/xmlns/scr/v1.1.0"
      "org.equinoxosgi.toast.backend.tracking.trackingAction">
  <implementation class=
    "org.equinoxosgi.toast.internal.backend.tracking.ui.TrackingAction"/>
  <service>
    <provide interface=
        "org.equinoxosgi.toast.backend.portal.spi.IPortalAction"/>
  </service>
  <property name="action" value="browse/tracking"/>
  <property name="label" value="Track vehicle"/>
</scr:component>
```

13.5 Running the Portal

Once you have setup the new backend, run the system as follows:

❍ Launch the `backend.product` and open your favorite web browser on the URL http://localhost:8080/toast. You will see something similar to that shown in Figure 13-1 but with no vehicles listed. In Toast, vehicles are dynamically discovered. Since no vehicles are running, there is nothing for the portal to show.

❍ Start a client by running the `client.product`. Wait a few seconds for the client to report its position to the server. At this point the server knows about the client and will show it in the portal. Refresh your browser.

❍ Click on the vehicle shown and navigate to its tracking page. There you will see a map of Washington DC with a series of concentric red circles at the current vehicle location. Since the vehicle is not moving, the circles will not move. You can use the device simulator discussed in Chapter 10, "Pluggable Services," to move the vehicle about and see its position change on the portal map.

13.6 Whiteboard Pros and Cons

This example portal is not intended to be comprehensive or even sophisticated. It serves two purposes: First, it gives the Toast Back End a UI; and second, it motivates a discussion around the Whiteboard Pattern and domain code isolation issues. The approach taken here is very similar to that of several OSGi console implementations. As with those systems, there are a number of pros and cons.

Pros:

○ Contributing new actions is relatively easy.

○ Contributed actions can be consumed by any number of subsystems in any way they choose.

○ Using DS, the contributing bundles need not be started for action contributions to be recognized.

○ The actions can be POJOs and so are testable using standard testing techniques.

Cons:

○ In this example, it is the action providers, the producers, that determine the relative positioning of the actions.

○ Internationalization of the action labels is not directly supported.

○ The OSGi service registry is not scoped. As a result, it does not directly support multiple portals running in one framework having different sets of actions or the simultaneous use of the action service interface in other contexts.

○ Actions contributed to the portal may be used by unintended consumers.

In the end, none of these individual topics should drive your adoption or rejection of the approach. In some cases a pro is a con and vice versa. The needs of your system should drive the mechanism you choose. For more discussion of module collaboration, see Chapter 15, "Declarative Services," and Chapter 16, "Extensions."

13.7 Summary

In this chapter we added an extensible web-based UI portal to the Toast Back End. The portal uses the Whiteboard Pattern to enable the contribution of new UI actions and content. Using the Whiteboard Pattern makes it easy for portal contributors to add functionality but introduces some subtleties that need to be handled by the portal.

As we saw, overall it was quite straightforward to add an extensible web UI to Toast. The example portal is simplistic but suitable for our purposes. From these modest beginnings it is easy to see how you can benefit from the same modular approaches used in RCP development when building the back end UI. Technologies such as Rich Ajax Platform take this a step further and enable rich server-side UIs using client-side programming models.

CHAPTER 14

System Deployment with p2

One of the main goals of Toast is to be a highly modular base for building dynamic software solutions. By now the Toast Client includes a great deal of functionality, from entertainment to navigation and guidance. Running the client as a preconfigured collection of all available functions is convenient, but it still falls short of being a truly dynamic system.

In this chapter we use the provisioning and management facilities in Equinox p2 to create a system for managing Toast Clients from the Toast Back End. By the end of the chapter Toast will be able to dynamically create and install new vehicles, and users will be able to install and uninstall software on the vehicles using the UI portal on the back end.

This chapter covers the following major topics:

❍ An overview of p2 components and architecture

❍ Structuring of Toast for use with p2

❍ Integration with the p2 mechanisms

❍ Extending the web UI to manage Toast Clients from the back end

14.1 Introduction to Equinox p2

p2 is the provisioning system developed by the Equinox project at eclipse.org. It is a powerful replacement for the original Eclipse Update Manager included with the Eclipse Platform. While retaining much of the original functionality, p2 allows system designers greater flexibility in how they define, structure, and deploy their systems.

Fundamentally p2 is a provisioning platform; that is, it is not just one provisioning system but rather a collection of provisioning technologies on top of which you can build a fit-for-purpose provisioning solution. Of course, p2 comes with quite a number of preconfigured pieces to make the creation of your solution as straightforward as possible.

This section gives you a quick overview of the major elements of p2 and how they interact. You will use this background knowledge later in the chapter to structure Toast deployments and implement the Toast deployment mechanism.

14.1.1 Architecture

The centerpiece of the architecture is the *agent*. The agent is a notional concept—there is no actual agent object. Rather the agent is the logical entity that reasons about *metadata* to manage *profiles* by coordinating the downloading of *artifacts* from *repositories* and using an *engine* to manipulate the profiles. Figure 14-1 shows an overview of the agent, the large box in the middle, and how the various parts fit together.

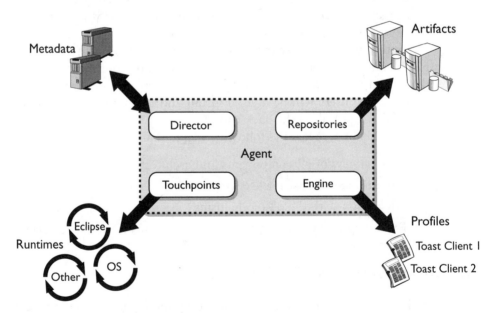

Figure 14–1   Architecture of p2

In the Toast context, the client is represented by a profile, a runnable configuration of software. The artifacts being installed and updated are mostly bundles, and the metadata being reasoned about is the dependency information extracted from the constituent bundle manifests and product configuration files. Runtimes include the OS, application servers, and, of course, OSGi frameworks such as Equinox.

The p2 architecture is quite loosely coupled, allowing the overall agent function to be split up and run separately. The metadata and artifact repositories are independent, the director and engine can be remote, profiles can be distributed, and so on. This allows for great flexibility in putting together provisioning solutions. This chapter shows you how p2 fits together and how the different parts interact to provision Toast.

14.1.2 p2 Metadata—Installable Units

One of the key characteristics of p2 is its separation of metadata from the artifacts being manipulated. Think of it as if the bundle manifests, the metadata, had been extracted from all the bundles, the artifacts, being provisioned. Managing these separately allows p2 to reason about vast numbers of artifacts without having to download any. It also allows for the addition of nonfunctional information, such as configuration information or license information, to the provisioning setup without modifying the artifacts themselves.

All metadata is captured in *installable units* (IUs). Figure 14-2 shows the structure of an IU. An IU has an ID and a version, the combination of which must be globally unique. IUs also have an open set of key/value properties used to capture information such as name and vendor.

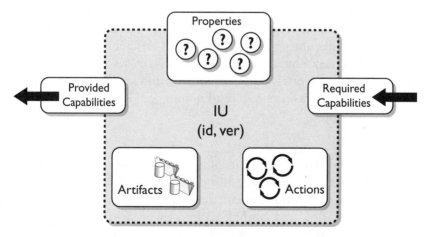

Figure 14–2 The structure of an installable unit

The basis of the p2 dependency structure is an IU's generic *capability* mechanism. IUs provide and require capabilities. A capability is simply an ID and a version number in a *namespace*. For example, a bundle that exports the `org.equinoxosgi.toast.emergency` package at version 1.0 is said to *provide* a capability with the ID `org.equinoxosgi.toast.emergency` and version 1.0 in the `java.package` namespace. Similarly, a bundle that imports that package is said to *require* the corresponding capability. IUs requiring capabilities can specify a version range. Since the set of namespaces is open, the p2 metadata structure can be used to represent all manner of relationships.

In addition to the dependency information, each IU has a number of related artifacts that are installed when the IU is installed and a set of actions that are executed when the IU goes through an install/configure/unconfigure/uninstall lifecycle.

14.1.3 Artifacts

p2 treats artifacts as opaque blobs of data and knows only about the metadata used to describe them. That being said, p2 is able to store the same artifact in multiple forms and do a number of interesting optimizations to reduce bandwidth and disk space requirements.

14.1.4 Repositories

All artifacts and metadata are stored in repositories in a p2 system. p2 specifies an API for repositories but not their internal representation. A repository may be on disk, in memory, structured using XML, in a database, or pretty much in any other form. For example, p2 includes repository definitions that integrate legacy Eclipse update sites unchanged. Metadata and artifact repositories are often colocated for convenience but need not be. p2 includes several tools for publishing to and mirroring repositories. For more information see the online Eclipse Help and the p2 wiki at http://wiki.eclipse.org/Equinox_p2_Repository_Mirroring.

14.1.5 Profiles

As mentioned before, p2 defines profiles to represent runnable configurations of software. Technically profiles are just descriptions of the system; that is, they list the IUs installed in them. During an actual install operation the relevant artifacts are fetched, installed, and configured into the system. On completion, the fact that the artifact has been installed is recorded in the profile. A p2 agent can manage many profiles representing many different systems.

14.1.6 Director

The director is the brains of the p2 operation. It is responsible for working with the metadata available in the known repositories, the profile being managed, and the provisioning request supplied to it to come up with a set of install, uninstall, and update operations. These operations are then passed to the p2 engine for execution.

CONSTRAINT RESOLUTION IS HARD

On the surface the director's job seems reasonably straightforward, but it turns out to be one of those very challenging (i.e., NP-complete) computer science problems. Fortunately, p2 includes a pseudo-Boolean constraint solver, SAT4J, to help with formulating provisioning solutions.

14.1.7 Engine

The engine's job is simply to execute a given set of install, uninstall, and update operations. The engine walks through a set of *phases* and executes the relevant part of each operation in each phase. For example, when an IU is installed, its related artifacts must first be fetched, then installed, and finally configured. The engine executes each phase for all involved IUs before proceeding to the next phase.

The engine is assisted in executing these phases by a set of *touchpoints*. A touchpoint is the interface between p2 and some runtime or configuration system. For example, when a bundle is installed into an Equinox system, its start level and auto-start state need to be configured. This is done by the Equinox touchpoint. If p2 were being used to install a web archive (WAR) or RPM, the relevant operations would be carried out by, say, a Tomcat or RPM touchpoint, respectively.

As long as the touchpoints support rollback, the engine offers a transactional way of modifying a system.

14.2 Refining the Toast Structure

Now that you have a basic overview of how p2 works, let's relate that to Toast and refine its structure to tell p2 all it needs to know. As we have seen, Toast is made up of the back end and the client. Generally there is only one back end, but there may be many clients. Here we want to extend the back end and enable it to install and uninstall various units of functionality on clients that have almost no p2 awareness.

14.2.1 Defining Products Using Features

In the code base for Chapter 13, "Web Portal," the client and back end products are essentially monolithic. They are defined in terms of discrete bundles, but there is no particular structure to enable the (re)configuration of the system.

One of the main problems is the number of bundles. Each product definition is simply a large list of bundles—more than 20 for the back end and more than 60 for the client! In this chapter we want to ship a bare-bones back end and client shell and incrementally add functionality such as navigation, climate control, and audio as required.

Pragmatically, each of these functions may consist of several bundles. Technically it is not a problem for p2 to manage large sets of bundles—it is simply difficult for humans to grasp. Any provisioning solution must hide this detail just as our natural tendency is to abstract out the detail. Here we create lists or groups of bundles that supply some functional element—audio, climate control, or emergency support.

The traditional grouping notion in Eclipse is the *feature*. A feature simply lists a set of bundles and other, nested, features—essentially a bill of materials for some coherent function. You then compose a running system by identifying the relevant set of features rather than laboriously listing the individual bundles. Want audio support? Add the audio feature.

FEATURES ARE STILL INTERESTING

While features originated as a concept in the Eclipse Update Manager infrastructure, they are largely independent of any particular mechanism. With p2, developers still define groupings using features. p2 then maps the features onto IUs that are marked as *groups*, thus providing equivalent functionality.

As with Update Manager, features and groups play no role in the Equinox runtime—they are purely a provisioning and management construct.

So to move toward a dynamically configurable system, we need to break the Toast Client and Toast Back End into sets of features.

14.2.2 Back End Features

To get started on the restructuring, let's change the back end product to be defined in terms of features using the following steps:

○ Open backend.product and on the **Overview** page, change the product configuration to be based on features, as shown in Figure 14-3.

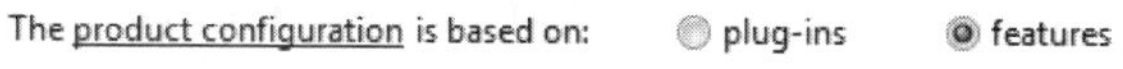

The product configuration is based on: ○ plug-ins   ◉ features

Figure 14–3 A feature-based product configuration

○ Next, flip over to the **Dependencies** page and click on the new feature button at the top right to start the **New Feature** wizard shown in Figure 14-4. You can also create features using **New > Project... > Plug-in Development > Feature Project**. Enter org.equinoxosgi.toast.backend.feature for the project name. By default, the project name matches the feature ID just as with bundles.

○ Fill in the **Feature Properties** as shown in the figure. Leave the **Feature ID** matching the project name. The **Feature Name** should be a human-readable string that is reasonably descriptive. Remember, it will be shown to the user at various points during development and when provisioning. Similarly, the **Feature Provider** should be the readable name of your organization.

Figure 14–4 Defining the Toast Back End feature

Choosing Feature IDs

The feature and bundle ID namespaces are distinct. As a result, you can have a bundle and a feature with the same ID. This can be convenient, but it can also be confusing if at development time you want to have both the feature and bundle projects in your workspace at the same time—if you are following the recommended practice of matching the project names to the IDs, the bundle and feature projects will collide and cannot be loaded together.

There are various conventions for naming features and feature projects. In this book, we avoid overlapping the feature and bundle namespaces by using a naming convention that puts the word `feature` at the end of the feature ID and matches project names to feature IDs. For example, using `org.equinoxosgi.toast.backend.feature` for both the ID and the project name keeps it simple and distinguishes the back end feature from the related bundles.

○ Click **Next,** and the **Referenced Plug-ins and Fragments** page comes up, as shown in Figure 14-5. This page allows you to add bundles to the feature being created. You can either manually select the set of bundles to include or use the **Initialize from a launch configuration** option. Since we have been launching the back end, your workspace should have a `backend.product` launch configuration. Use that configuration as the basis for the new feature.

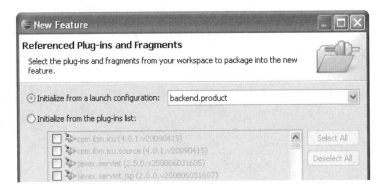

Figure 14–5   Listing feature bundles

The back end feature project is created and opened in a feature editor. Here you see the values that you just entered in the wizard. If you go back to the back end product editor, you will notice that the `org.equinoxosgi.toast.backend.feature` you just created is listed in the **Features** section of the **Dependencies** page, as in

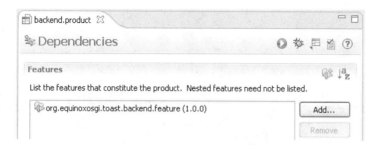

Figure 14–6 The Toast Back End product with its feature

Figure 14-6. We will add more to the product later, but now let's turn to decomposing the client.

14.2.3 Client Features

Restructuring the client is a little more challenging. The Toast Client is very much of a *platform*—the shell of a vehicle system onto which sets of vehicle function are installed. Until now we have run this all together. Here we need to tease it apart.

14.2.3.1 The Shell Feature

First, we need to create the shell feature. This is the base for the Toast UI.

○ Follow the same process as for the back end feature to create a shell feature called `org.equinoxosgi.toast.client.shell.feature`. This time use the `client.product` launch configuration as the basis for the new feature. After following the steps, you should have a new feature with all the client bundles in it. That is too many, but it is easier to trim extras out than to add new ones.

○ Go through the list of bundles in the feature and keep only the bundles that start with `org.eclipse` or are in the following list:

```
org.equinoxosgi.core.autostart
org.equinoxosgi.crust.artwork.toast
org.equinoxosgi.crust.display
org.equinoxosgi.crust.shell
org.equinoxosgi.crust.widgets
org.equinoxosgi.toast.core
org.equinoxosgi.toast.core.channel.sender
org.equinoxosgi.toast.devsim
```

The resulting feature identifies approximately 20 bundles. After the feature is saved, notice that the client product has been updated to point to the new feature. Launch the product as before. Since we just removed all the vehicle function, you should see only an empty Crust shell, as shown in Figure 14-7.

Figure 14–7 Bare Crust shell

Now let's add back the vehicle function by creating a new feature for each of the functional elements of the Toast Client.

14.2.3.2 Audio Support

The pattern for creating the add-on Toast features is very similar to that for the other features, but we have to list the features manually. Create a feature for these bundles using the following steps:

○ On the **Dependencies** page of the `client.product` editor, click the new feature button at the top right to open the **New Feature** wizard. As with the other features, set the project name and feature ID to be the same—`org.equinoxosgi.toast.client.audio.feature` in this case. Fill in a useful feature name and description and click **Next**.

○ In the bundles list on the next wizard page, select all the bundles listed here:

```
org.equinoxosgi.toast.dev.amplifier
org.equinoxosgi.toast.dev.amplifier.fake
org.equinoxosgi.toast.dev.cdplayer
```

```
org.equinoxosgi.toast.dev.cdplayer.fake
org.equinoxosgi.toast.dev.radio
org.equinoxosgi.toast.dev.radio.fake
org.equinoxosgi.toast.swt.audio
```

○ Click **Finish** to complete the wizard and create the audio feature. Since you launched the wizard from the product editor, the new feature is automatically added to the product's feature list.

14.2.3.3 Climate Control

Next create the climate control feature:

○ Follow the same steps as for the audio feature, but use the ID `org.equinoxosgi.toast.client.climate.feature` and include the following list of bundles in the feature:

```
org.equinoxosgi.toast.dev.climate
org.equinoxosgi.toast.dev.climate.fake
org.equinoxosgi.toast.swt.climate
```

14.2.3.4 GPS

The GPS feature is similarly simple:

○ Create the GPS feature using the ID `org.equinoxosgi.toast.client.gps.feature` and include the following bundles in the feature:

```
org.equinoxosgi.toast.dev.gps
org.equinoxosgi.toast.dev.gps.sim
```

14.2.3.5 Mapping

The mapping feature is a little different, as the mapping function depends on the GPS function:

○ Create the mapping feature as before, using the ID `org.equinoxosgi.toast.client.nav.mapping.feature`, and include the following bundles in the feature:

```
org.equinoxosgi.toast.dev.google
org.equinoxosgi.toast.swt.nav.mapping.google
```

As an additional step for this feature, add a dependency to the GPS feature you created in the previous section:

○ Flip over to the **Dependencies** page in the feature editor and use the **Add Feature...** button in the **Required Features/Plug-ins** section to add the GPS feature, `org.equinoxosgi.toast.client.gps.feature`. This tells the system that the mapping feature works only if the GPS feature is installed.

14.2.3.6 Guidance System

Like the mapping feature, the guidance feature depends on another functional unit—in this case, the mapping feature:

❍ Create the guidance feature in the same way as the others but using the ID org.equinoxosgi.toast.client.nav.guidance.feature and including the following bundles:

```
org.equinoxosgi.toast.client.nav.guidance
org.equinoxosgi.toast.swt.nav.guidance.google
```

Again, here we have to add a prerequisite feature:

❍ Add org.equinoxosgi.toast.client.nav.mapping.feature to the list on the **Dependencies** page of the new feature. Note that the dependencies are transitive—guidance requires mapping, which requires GPS, so guidance needs GPS.

14.2.3.7 Emergency Management

Adding a feature for the emergency management facilities is quite similar:

❍ Create the emergency feature as before, using the ID org.equinoxosgi.toast.client.emergency.feature, and include the following bundles:

```
org.equinoxosgi.toast.client.emergency
org.equinoxosgi.toast.core.emergency
org.equinoxosgi.toast.dev.airbag
org.equinoxosgi.toast.dev.airbag.sim
org.equinoxosgi.toast.swt.emergency
```

❍ Add org.equinoxosgi.toast.client.gps.feature to the list on the **Dependencies** page.

14.2.3.8 Client Tracking

Finally, package the client tracking code we added in Chapter 12, "Dynamic Configuration":

❍ Create the tracking feature using the ID org.equinoxosgi.toast.client.tracking.feature, and include the following bundles:

```
org.equinoxosgi.toast.client.tracking
org.equinoxosgi.toast.client.tracking.config
org.equinoxosgi.toast.core.tracking
```

14.2.4 Restructuring Summary

Congratulations. You are now back in exactly the same position you were a few minutes ago! Both the client and the back end products define exactly the same set of bundles as before and run exactly the same way. Run the products and confirm that everything looks and works the same.

There is one very important difference, however. Now each product is described in terms of logical features rather than just a big list of bundles. While p2 can manage bundles independently, logical functions such as audio support are easier for humans to handle and talk about. By creating these groupings, the features, you have laid the groundwork for manipulating Toast configurations.

To get a sense of where we are going, delete the audio or climate feature from the client product definition and launch the client. The function is no longer there. Add the feature back and run. The function is back. The next step is to automate this *provisioning* by enhancing the back end to install and uninstall features in the client dynamically.

14.3 Writing a Provisioner

There are many different provisioning scenarios. Some have control at the client, some at the server, while still others have blended control. For the Toast example here we want a central management system with the p2 function in the back end and very little p2 awareness in the client.

To make this work, the back end needs a p2 profile representing each vehicle and its installed software. Each vehicle is then managed as a separate install of the Toast Client and any added functions. This models the vehicles as physically distinct software platforms.

Rather than having you write the provisioning code, the following section takes you on a tour of the sample code for this chapter. To take the tour, load the back end provisioning projects from the Chapter 14 sample using the Samples Manager.

○ Using the Samples Manager, compare the workspace to the sample for Chapter 14 and load any project that has `backend` in the name, including `ToastBackEnd`.

14.3.1 The Provisioner

The first stop is the `org.equinoxosgi.toast.backend.provisioning` bundle and the `IProvisioner` interface. Our provisioning requirements are quite simple—a provisioner manages a set of vehicles and software features available to be installed on vehicles. Available software can be installed or uninstalled on each vehicle. This is essentially the p2 agent discussed in Section 14.1, "Introduction to Equinox p2." The shape of the provisioner is captured in `IProvisioner`, as shown here:

```
org.equinoxosgi.toast.backend.provisioning/IProvisioner
public interface IProvisioner {
  void addProfile(String id, String environment);
  Collection getAvailableFeatures();
  Collection getAvailableFeatures(String id);
  Collection getInstalled(String id);
  Collection getProfiles();
  IStatus install(String id, String feature, IProgressMonitor monitor);
  void removeProfile(String id);
  IStatus uninstall(String id, String feature, IProgressMonitor monitor);
}
```

An implementation of this interface can be found in Toast's `Provisioner` class. The `Provisioner` is a DS component that references the following services from p2:

○ **IProfileRegistry**—Manages the list of profiles

○ **IPlanner**—Creates the provisioning plans needed when manipulating profiles

○ **IEngine**—Executes provisioning plans to effect the actual install/uninstall of software

○ **IMetadataRepositoryManager**—Tracks metadata repositories

○ **IArtifactRepositoryManager**—Tracks artifact repositories

Notice that the `component.xml` in the bundle has all the appropriate entries for a conventional component requiring these services, and the `Provisioner` class has all the related `set*` methods. The `startup` method in the following snippet does a bit of setup and adds the metadata and artifact repositories given to the component:

```
org.equinoxosgi.toast.internal.backend.provisioning/Provisioner
protected void startup() {
  String location = PropertyManager.getProperty(PROFILE_LOCATION);
  if (location != null)
    dataLocation = new File(location);
  String spec = PropertyManager.getProperty(REPO_LOCATIONS);
  if (spec != null)
    repos = addRepositories(spec);
}
```

"DISCOURAGED ACCESS" WARNINGS

By now you have likely noticed a large number of "discouraged access" warnings in the code. These are caused by references to p2 classes. Most of p2's API is *provisional*; that is, while it is solid and functional, the p2 team has not signed up to support it forever. As such, the PDE tooling is warning you that such references are discouraged. You can ignore these or turn off the warnings using the **Java Compiler > Errors/Warnings** project properties.

As a best practice we recommend leaving the warnings on. Turning them off can lead to other, unintended, non-API references creeping into your code.

Note also that since these packages are internal, PDE's Automated Management of Dependencies facility does not find or add imports for these packages.

In this setup each vehicle is represented by a p2 profile. Profiles are added to the Provisioner using addProfile, as shown in the next code snippet. The arguments specify the ID of the profile and the computing environment—OS, window system, and chip architecture—for the profile. The method creates profiles by capturing the environment and file system location in a series of properties and adding the result to the profile registry.

org.equinoxosgi.toast.internal.backend.provisioning/Provisioner
```
public void addProfile(String id, String environment) {
   String location = new File(dataLocation, id).toString();
   Map props = new HashMap();
   props.put(IProfile.PROP_INSTALL_FOLDER, location);
   props.put(IProfile.PROP_CACHE, location);
   props.put(IProfile.PROP_ENVIRONMENTS, environment);
   registry.addProfile(id, props);
}
```

The set of software available to be installed is determined using the getAvailableFeatures() method shown next. The result is computed by querying the known set of metadata repositories for any installable units tagged as Toast *roots*; that is, any IU that has its toast.root property set to true is available to be installed.

org.equinoxosgi.toast.internal.backend.provisioning/Provisioner
```
public Collection getAvailableFeatures() {
   Query query = new IUPropertyQuery("toast.root", "true");
   Collector collector = new Collector();
   for (int i = 0; i < repos.length; i++)
      repos[i].query(query, collector, new NullProgressMonitor());
   return collector.toCollection();
}
```

To tag a feature as a Toast root, add the p2.inf file shown in the next snippet to the root of the feature project. When the feature is exported and published to a p2 repository, this file is processed. The content of the snippet causes the property toast.root to be set to true on the published IU. p2 does not interpret these properties.

org.equinoxosgi.toast.client.audio.feature/p2.inf
```
properties.1.name=toast.root
properties.1.value=true
```

CONTROLLING IUS USING THE p2.inf FILE

You can control many advanced aspects of artifact publishing for bundles, features, and products using the p2.inf file. The file should be placed in the associated development-time project directly beside the "description" of the artifact—MANIFEST.MF for bundles, feature.xml for features, and the .product file for products. p2.inf can direct the addition of properties, capabilities, requirements, and install actions. For a complete guide to the tagging of IUs using a p2.inf file, see http://wiki.eclipse.org/Equinox/p2/Customizing_Metadata.

The getAvailableFeatures method is useful for a global view of the available features, but in practice users need to know what features are yet to be installed on a given profile. getAvailableFeatures(String) does this by taking the list of all available features and removing those that have already been installed in the given profile:

```
org.equinoxosgi.toast.internal.backend.provisioning/Provisioner
public Collection getAvailableFeatures(String id) {
   Collection result = getAvailableFeatures();
   result.removeAll(getInstalled(id));
   return result;
}
```

The next snippet shows the install method. Given a profile ID and feature ID, the code looks up the profile, finds the IU for the feature, and then proceeds to install the IU in the profile. The first step in doing the installation is to create a change request. This describes, in abstract terms, the operations you want to do to a profile—install this, uninstall that, update something else. Once you have the change request, you can ask the planner to create a plan for carrying out the request. If planning is successful, the resulting plan is executable by the engine and the installation is completed.

```
org.equinoxosgi.toast.internal.backend.provisioning/Provisioner
public IStatus install(
      String id, String feature, IProgressMonitor monitor) {
   IProfile profile = registry.getProfile(id);
   IInstallableUnit unit = findFeature(feature);
   ProfileChangeRequest request = new ProfileChangeRequest(profile);
   request.addInstallableUnits(new IInstallableUnit[] {unit});
   request.setInstallableUnitProfileProperty(unit, ROOT_TAG, "true");
   ProvisioningContext context = new ProvisioningContext();
   ProvisioningPlan result =
      planner.getProvisioningPlan(request, context, monitor);
   if (!result.getStatus().isOK())
     return result.getStatus();
   return engine.perform(profile, new DefaultPhaseSet(),
      result.getOperands(), context, monitor);
}
```

Notice the addition of a ROOT_TAG to the IU being installed. The profile contains many IUs. By adding the ROOT_TAG profile property to the IU requested by the user, we are remembering what the user did. This way we can later offer the tagged IUs back to the user for uninstalling.

PROVISIONING DOES MORE THAN YOU THINK

p2 is always trying to create a runnable system by recursively finding matches for all dependencies. As a result, installing one IU may cause other IUs to be installed, uninstalled, or updated to satisfy the new constraint equation. Similarly, uninstalling something may cause replacements or alternatives to be installed or other dependent functions to be uninstalled.

The uninstall and update processes are exactly the same as installing but with a different provisioning request. For now the provisioner does not do explicit update operations.

14.3.2 Configuring the Back End

Before the back end can provision anything, p2 and the provisioner must be added to the backend.product. Since p2 is a provisioning platform, there are many different configurations of the basic infrastructure. As of the Galileo release of Equinox, the p2 team did not supply an easy-to-consume feature for people looking to create a basic provisioning agent. We have included such a feature in the Samples Manager. Load the org.equinoxosgi.toast.backend.p2.feature project now.

This feature is purposely "bare-bones." It is the basic function needed by a conventional provisioning agent. Depending on your requirements, you may need to add optional p2 functionality such as legacy or UI support or additional ECF transports. Here we are going to programmatically manage vehicle profiles on the same machine as the back end and the repositories, so no additional support is needed.

Next, open the org.equinoxosgi.toast.backend.feature feature and flip to the **Plug-ins** page. Ensure that the org.equinoxosgi.toast.backend.provisioning bundle is listed—it is now part of the back end function. Again, if it is missing, add it or get the final feature definition from the Samples Manager.

14.3.3 Back End Summary

That's it. That is all that is needed on the back end to provision client profiles—just over 100 lines of code. We started this section by observing that there are many different provisioning scenarios. This example strikes a balance of simplicity with a hint of sophistication—provisioning the current running profile is even easier, and provisioning and synchronizing with remote systems requires somewhat more effort.

14.4 Adding a Deployment Web UI

Now that the back end is able to manage vehicle software, we need to expose this function to the user. In this case the user is the back end administrator using the portal defined in Chapter 13, "Web Portal." As you may recall, the portal is extended by adding *actions*. To add a provisioning UI, we need actions to create vehicles and install, uninstall, and list software features. Again, rather than having you write the code, we take you on a tour of the code to implement this function.

Look in the `org.equinoxosgi.toast.backend.provisioning.ui` bundle to find the various actions discussed in the following sections. Each of them is a DS component that implements the `IPortalAction` and requires the `IProvisioner` service.

FORESHADOWING

The following actions will not work as described until you have completed the exporting steps outlined in Section 14.5.1, "Populating a p2 Repository." They are described here to paint the UI picture.

14.4.1 The Create Action

So far with Toast the back end has dynamically added vehicles that have reported position information and the like. With the addition of provisioning and the management function, the portal needs a little more lifecycle around the existence of vehicles. In addition, by providing a *create* action and including provisioning operations, it is possible for users to create vehicle installations from scratch from the back end.

Vehicle creation is implemented by `CreateAction`, and its DS component is declared in `create.xml`. It is positioned on the root page by setting the `action` property to have just one segment, `create`. The following snippet shows the meat of the class, `createvehicle`. Ultimately it simply analyzes the request and asks the control center to add a vehicle as specified. You will see how this operates in Section 14.5.3.

```
org.equinoxosgi.toast.internal.backend.provisioning.ui/CreateAction
public class CreateAction implements IPortalAction {
  private IControlCenter center;
```

```
    private void createVehicle(HttpServletRequest request,
        HttpServletResponse response, String id) throws IOException {
      String config = request.getParameter(
          ICoreConstants.CONFIG_PARAMETER);
      String[] segments = config.split(",");
      String configSpec = "osgi.os=" + segments[0] + ",osgi.ws="
          + segments[1] + ",osgi.arch=" + segments[2];
      center.addVehicle(id, configSpec);
      String home = request.getRequestURI() + "?action=browse&id=" + id;
      response.sendRedirect(home);
    }
  }
```

14.4.2 The Manage Action

The UI for installing and managing a vehicle's software is supplied by ManageAction. This action supplies the **Software Management** page shown in Figure 14-12. The page summarizes the installed and available features for the given vehicle. Features are installed or uninstalled by clicking on the appropriate links. The links themselves are further portal actions, described in the following sections.

The **Software Management** page is implemented by ManageAction. Its corresponding DS component is declared in manage.xml. The component positions the action under the built-in browse action by setting the action property to browse/ manage.

14.4.3 The Install and Uninstall Actions

The implementations of the install and uninstall actions presented on the **Software Management** page are nearly identical. You can see the component markup in install.xml and uninstall.xml respectively.

The key code for the actions is shown in the next snippet. Here the request is reviewed and the feature in question identified. Then the requested operation is run on the provisioner. Finally, the response causes the web UI page to update.

```
org.equinoxosgi.toast.internal.backend.provisioning.ui/InstallAction
public void execute(HttpServletRequest request,
    HttpServletResponse response) throws IOException {
  String id = request.getParameter(ICoreConstants.ID_PARAMETER);
  String feature = request.getParameter("feature");
  provisioner.install(id, feature, null);
  ticler.tickle(id);
  String home = request.getRequestURI() + "?action=manage&id=" + id;
  response.sendRedirect(home);
}
```

14.4.4 Installing the Provisioning UI

The provisioning UI needs to be added to the back end product in the same way as the provisioning function itself. To review, take a look at the **Plug-ins** page of the org.equinoxosgi.toast.backend.feature editor and spot the back end provisioning UI bundle, org.equinoxosgi.toast.backend.provisioning.ui, in the list. If it is missing, add it. Remember, this feature is part of the backend.product, so adding it to the feature adds it to the product.

14.5 Exporting, Running, and Provisioning

To recap, so far we have refactored the client and back end products to be feature-based, implemented a provisioner on the back end that can manage clients (vehicles), and put in place a web-based UI for our provisioning function. Now is the time to export the components, run the system, and do some provisioning.

14.5.1 Populating a p2 Repository

As was mentioned in Section 14.1.4 "Repositories," everything in p2 is stored in a repository. Currently the Toast Back End and Client are in your workspace. In Chapter 9, "Packaging," you exported the client and back end. Here we will follow some very similar workflows but with a focus on populating p2 repositories with the products and features needed.

UPDATE LAUNCHING PATHS

Before exporting any of the products, ensure that the paths on its Launching tab work for your configuration. For example, if you are not on Windows, consider deleting the "c:" from the VM Arguments section. Be sure to check that all paths are changed consistently.

○ Open the backend.product to the **Overview** page and notice the **Exporting** section at the bottom right. Click the **Eclipse Product export wizard** link. The **Export** wizard shown in Figure 14-8 will appear.

○ Set the wizard fields as shown and export the backend.product by clicking **Finish**.

The wizard allows you to identify a number of values. The only values of interest here are the **Archive file** field and the **Generate metadata repository** check box. The archive location determines not only where the runnable product will go but also the repositories. By selecting the repository box, you are saying that

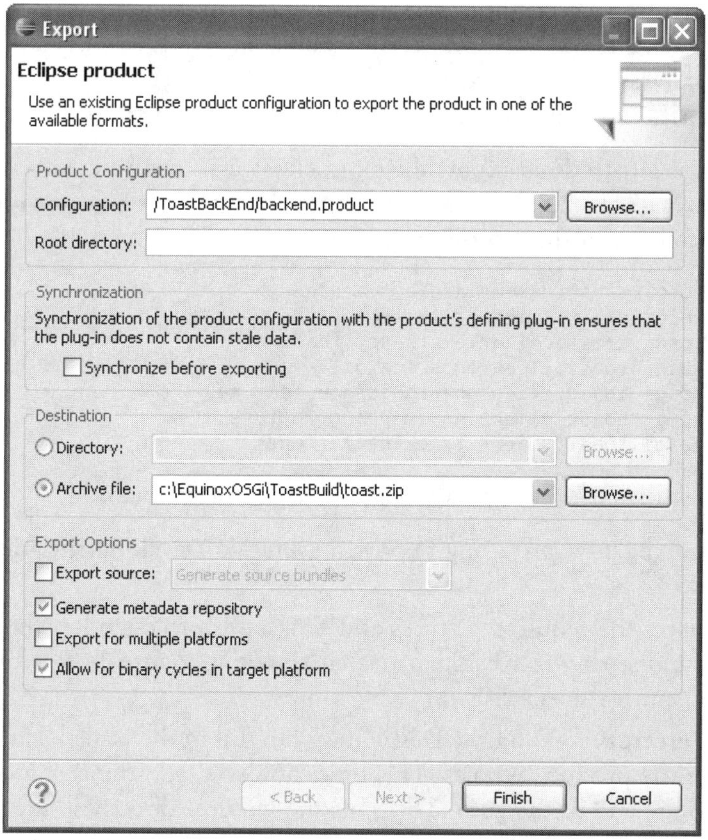

Figure 14–8 The **Product Export** wizard

you want PDE to publish the product content into a p2 repository. PDE automatically creates a metadata and artifact repository in a `repository` folder that is a sibling of the location specified in the archive location field.

When the export is finished running, check that there is indeed a `repository` folder beside the archive location you specified.

Before exporting the `client.product`, let's review its content. In Section 14.2.4, "Restructuring Summary," we saw that the content of the client can be controlled by adding and removing features to the product definition. If you export the client product, including all the client functionality, there will be no way of adding or removing that functionality.

To address this, the client product should be a *platform* onto which more software is deployed:

○ Open `client.product` and ensure that it contains **only** the `org.equinoxosgi.toast.client.shell.feature` in its **Dependencies** list.

○ Having done that, go ahead and export the client using the same settings as for the back end but with a different archive file name, say, `client.zip`. Here we actually don't even need the archive but rather just the contents of the p2 repositories to be used in subsequent provisioning operations.

All that is left to do is export the extra client features we created in Sections 14.2.3.2 through 14.2.3.7 to the repository. Ensure that you have added the `p2.inf` file to each of these projects, as described in Section 14.3.1:

```
org.equinoxosgi.toast.client.audio.feature
org.equinoxosgi.toast.client.climate.feature
org.equinoxosgi.toast.client.emergency.feature
org.equinoxosgi.toast.client.gps.feature
org.equinoxosgi.toast.client.nav.guidance.feature
org.equinoxosgi.toast.client.nav.mapping.feature
org.equinoxosgi.toast.client.tracking.feature
```

These features can be exported directly using these steps:

○ Run the export wizard using **Export... > Plug-in Development > Deployable features**.

○ Multi-select the required features and click **Finish** to complete the wizard. You should see a wizard similar to that shown in Figure 14-9 with all seven of the client features selected.

○ In the **Directory** field on the **Destination** tab, fill in the same location as you used for the product exports. This time, however, add the `repository` segment to the end of the path. This puts the features directly in the repository.

○ On the **Options** tab, be sure to select both the **Package as individual JAR files** and the **Generate metadata repository** check boxes.

○ Click **Finish** and let PDE publish the features and bundles to p2 repositories.

14.5.2 Running the Toast Back End

If you look around the repository you've created, you will see all of the bundles and features from the workspace as well as the various branded executables and such. These are all waiting to be deployed and run. During the export, PDE deployed the back end for you, so it is ready to run—expand the back end archive, `toast.zip` if you used the values in Figure 14-8, and run the `backend` executable.

For advanced users who need to deploy their systems independently or headlessly, follow the instructions here.

To help you along, the `ToastBackEnd` project contains a product definition, `backendDeployer.product`, that runs a mini p2 agent and deploys the back end

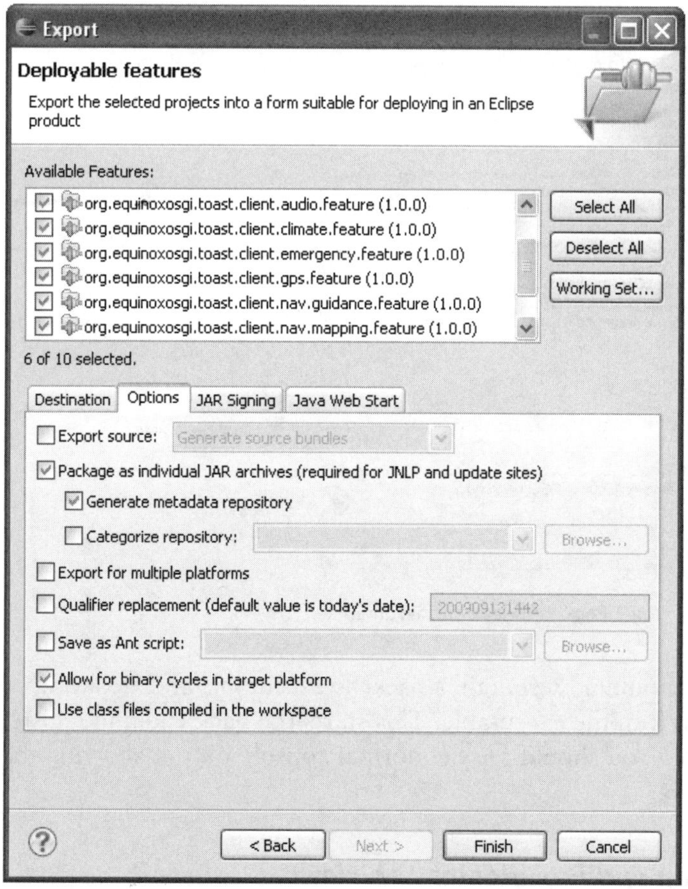

Figure 14–9   Feature Export wizard

for you. You can use it to deploy any product in a p2 repository, but here the launch values shown in Figure 14-10 are set up for the back end.

What is not shown is that this product runs the p2 *director application*, `org.eclipse.equinox.p2.director`. The repository locations given should match the locations to which you have been exporting your products and features. The `destination` and `bundlepool` arguments can point to any location. This is where the back end will be installed. Note that the `eclipse.p2.data.area` VM argument value must match the destination value, and generally the bundle pool is the same as well.

Once you are satisfied with the argument settings, run the product. The console should show the time taken to complete the install. Next navigate to the destination

Launching Arguments
Specify the program and VM arguments to launch the product with.
Platform-specific arguments should be entered on their respective
tabs.

All Platforms | linux | macosx | solaris | win32

Program Arguments:

```
-console -consolelog
-metadataRepository file:///c:/EquinoxOSGi/ToastBuild/repository
-artifactRepository file:///c:/EquinoxOSGi/ToastBuild/repository
-installIU org.equinoxosgi.toast.backend
-version 1.0.0
-destination c:/EquinoxOSGi/backend
-bundlepool c:/EquinoxOSGi/backend
-profileProperties org.eclipse.update.install.features=true
-profile backend
-roaming
```

VM Arguments:

```
-Declipse.p2.data.area=c:/EquinoxOSGi/backend
```

Figure 14–10   Toast Back End deployer arguments

directory. It should now contain a backend executable and a collection of bundles
and features. Run the executable. This starts the back end and registers the servlets as before. You should see the normal console output showing that the back
end is running.

14.5.3 Creating and Provisioning Vehicles

Fire up your favorite web browser and open the back end web UI at http://
localhost:8080/toast. Since this is the first run, the list will be empty. Create a
vehicle by clicking on the **Create Vehicle** link. That gets you to the form shown
in Figure 14-11. There you can enter a name for the vehicle and specify its operating system. Entering an operating system allows you to install for different
machines and then run the clients via shared drives or virtualization technology.
In most cases it will be the same operating system as the back end.

Create a Vehicle

Create New Vehicle: [   ]   Windows ▾   Create

Figure 14–11   Vehicle creation web UI

Complete the form and click **Create** to add the vehicle to the system and then go to the new vehicle's details page. From there you can track the vehicle or go to the **Software Management** page by clicking on the **Manage software** link.

The **Software Management** page allows users to install and uninstall the software on a particular vehicle. The page summarizes the installed and available features for the profile and will be similar to what is shown in Figure 14-12. Since the vehicle was just created, the car has no software installed. In fact, if you look on disk, you will not even see a location for your car. Select the **Toast Client** entry in the **Available Features** list to install the base client software—the client product.

Now check the disk. There should be a ToastClients folder beside the folder containing the back end. This is where the Provisioner installs the client profiles. Notice that there is a directory in there with the same name as your vehicle. Navigate to that directory and run the client executable. The regular Toast Client should start as an empty shell, as shown in Figure 14-7.

Try installing some more functionality into your vehicle using the web UI. Notice that nothing happens in the vehicle UI. There is currently no mechanism to tell the client running in a separate process, or potentially a separate machine, that there are changes in its profile. If you close the vehicle window and restart the client, the provisioning changes should show up. In the next section we talk about how to enable dynamic deployment.

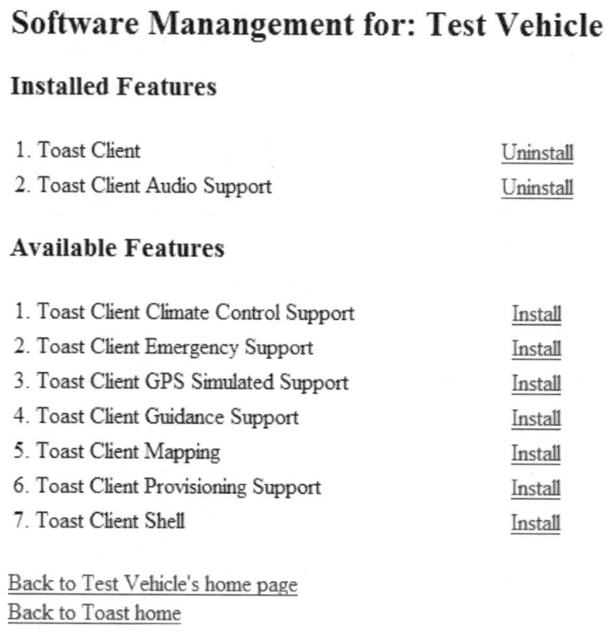

Software Manangement for: Test Vehicle

Installed Features

1. Toast Client   Uninstall
2. Toast Client Audio Support   Uninstall

Available Features

1. Toast Client Climate Control Support   Install
2. Toast Client Emergency Support   Install
3. Toast Client GPS Simulated Support   Install
4. Toast Client Guidance Support   Install
5. Toast Client Mapping   Install
6. Toast Client Provisioning Support   Install
7. Toast Client Shell   Install

Back to Test Vehicle's home page
Back to Toast home

Figure 14–12 Vehicle management web UI

14.6 Client-Side Dynamic Deployment

To make the client respond to changes in its profile immediately, the back end needs a way of *tickling* the client to tell it about the changes. There are many different possibilities here. For a quick and dirty solution we'll put an HTTP service on the client and have it wait for messages from the back end.

Load the following projects from the Samples Manager content for Chapter 14. The back end part of the tickle mechanism should already be in place.

```
org.equinoxosgi.toast.client.provisioning
org.equinoxosgi.toast.client.tickle
org.equinoxosgi.toast.core.tickle
```

Open the `FeatureSync` class. This is a DS component that uses the tickle mechanism to listen for messages and, when told, reloads the OSGi configuration defined by p2. The key method here is `processSync()`, shown here:

org.equinoxosgi.toast.client.provisioning/FeatureSync
```
private void processSync() {
  try {
    configurator.applyConfiguration();
  } catch (IOException e) {
    logSyncFailed(e);
  }
}
```

The call to `applyConfiguration` is the signal that the lineup of OSGi bundles installed in the underlying OSGi framework should be reloaded dynamically. The rest of the code in `FeatureSync` is related to threading to ensure that the long-running apply call does not abuse the thread broadcasting the notification. To package this up, create a feature and add it to the back end product as follows:

○ Create a client provisioning feature to capture the set of bundles listed here. We have called this new feature

```
org.equinoxosgi.toast.client.provisioning.feature.
```

```
javax.servlet
org.eclipse.equinox.http
org.equinoxosgi.toast.client.provisioning
org.equinoxosgi.toast.client.tickle
org.equinoxosgi.toast.core.tickle
```

○ Add the feature to the `client.product` definition and add the bundle `org.eclipse.equinox.simpleconfigurator` at `Start-level` = 1 with `Auto-start` = `true` on the Configuration page of the product editor. The simple configurator must be started to enable processing configurations created by p2.

○ Re-export Toast by deleting the repositories and rerunning the steps from Section 14.5.1, "Populating a p2 Repository."

Now when you modify the software on a running Toast Client, it is immediately notified and the new function is activated or the removed function discarded without the client being restarted.

DELETE REPOSITORIES BEFORE EXPORTING

You have to delete the existing repositories when you re-export because we have not set up our bundle and product version numbers to change each time they are built. As a result, the new bundles have the old version numbers. The export operation will not overwrite the existing content, and the new bundles will not be published into the repositories.

14.7 Summary

In this chapter you were introduced to the overall architecture of p2, the Equinox provisioning platform. We then refactored Toast into features, logical collections of code that go together to implement some function. This formed the basis of creating a manageable modular software structure. From there we showed how you can easily put together a powerful and flexible provisioning mechanism to manage multiple profiles. This was tested by publishing all of the needed bundles into p2 repositories and then using the provisioning solution in both static and dynamic provisioning scenarios.

You should leave this chapter with a clear impression that p2 has a huge amount of functionality and value in a wide range of scenarios. Having a flexible and functional provisioning mechanism brings to life the overall dynamic modularity story behind Equinox and OSGi.

PART III

Deep Dives

OSGi and Equinox provide a wide array of capabilities. These building blocks make OSGi-based systems easy to construct, scale, and extend. One of the main advantages of using OSGi is the reuse of components—it allows you to focus on your domain without having to reinvent the wheel. This is evident from the fact that the Toast system developed in Part II required relatively little code.

But the tutorial only scratched the surface of what is possible. There is much more to OSGi. The standard includes specifications for many services, and most services are very comprehensive. The OSGi specification for all of this comprises hundreds of pages. Rather than attempting a broad partial coverage of the various services, the next few chapters focus on the parts of OSGi and Equinox that are essential for building sophisticated OSGi-based systems—server side, Declarative Services, and release engineering. We dive into the APIs and use them to solve problems motivated by Toast in various real-world scenarios.

You should come away from this part of the book with a solid understanding of OSGi and Equinox technology and how you can use them to accelerate and enhance the creation of flexible systems.

CHAPTER 15

Declarative Services

As we have seen, the OSGi service mechanism greatly improves modularity and flexibility. But the programmatic API for registering and acquiring services is often challenging, as are the complexities of managing dynamic services. OSGi Release 4 introduced the Declarative Services (DS) specification to address these issues.

In Chapter 6, "Dynamic Services," we introduced DS, and the subsequent chapters have assumed their use throughout Toast. This chapter presents a deep dive into the capabilities and use of the DS mechanism. In particular, we

○ Recap the Declarative Services model and programming techniques

○ Identify common usage scenarios for Declarative Services

○ Discuss how to launch and debug an OSGi application that uses Declarative Services

○ Take a look at the PDE tooling for Declarative Services

15.1 The Declarative Services Model

Working with the OSGi service model using the programmatic APIs can be complex and error-prone. In an attempt to simplify their code, developers tend to make optimistic assumptions regarding the availability of services, resulting in runtime exceptions at one extreme and object retention issues at the other.

In large-scale scenarios, using the programmatic API to work with the service model can also result in premature class loading and object instantiation, contributing to delayed application startup and unnecessary memory consumption.

An alternative is to be lazy and declarative. Equinox has supported such techniques for some time through mechanisms such as extension points and delayed bundle activation. DS brings laziness to the OSGi service model and simultaneously makes it much easier for developers to work with services, increasing the quality, scalability, and startup performance of their applications.

When using DS, a bundle declares *components* that can reference and provide services. A component is declared by a bundle in an XML document that is processed at runtime by OSGi's *Service Component Runtime* (SCR) to create a component instance. A bundle can have multiple XML documents, and each document can contain multiple component declarations.

SERVICE COMPONENT RUNTIME VERSUS DECLARATIVE SERVICES?
The Service Component Runtime (SCR) is the name given to the runtime implementation of the Declarative Services (DS) specification. These terms are often used interchangeably, and we use DS in this discussion.

It is interesting to note that DS implementations are add-on bundles to the OSGi framework; that is, DS capabilities can be added to any R4.1 framework implementation—there is no need to build it into the framework.

DS IS NOW PART OF THE ECLIPSE SDK
With the release of Eclipse 3.5, the DS runtime is included in the Eclipse SDK. Now it's easier than ever to build bundles for the Eclipse IDE that are loosely coupled via OSGi services.

15.2 Common Scenarios

Let's review some of the most common design scenarios and how they are implemented with DS. We'll start with the simplest component and then move to more typical scenarios of providing services, referencing services, and both referencing and providing services. Finally, we discuss some advanced scenarios, namely, component factories and the Whiteboard Pattern.

COMPONENT XML SCHEMA 1.1.0
Chapter 24, "Declarative Services Reference," discusses the XML schema used by DS, so don't worry for now if the XML seems confusing.

15.2.1 *The Simplest Component*

The following snippet shows how to declare the simplest possible component, the DS equivalent of "Hello, World":

```
org.equinoxosgi.ds.hello/component.xml
<?xml version="1.0"?>
<scr:component xmlns:scr="http://www.osgi.org/xmlns/scr/v1.1.0"
  name="org.equinoxosgi.ds.hello">
  <implementation class="org.equinoxosgi.ds.hello.Hello"/>
</scr:component>
```

A component XML document must be XML 1.0–compliant and must be UTF-8 encoded. Each component XML document must be added to the bundle's `Service-Component` manifest header:

```
org.equinoxosgi.ds.hello/MANIFEST.MF
Manifest-Version: 1.0
Bundle-ManifestVersion: 2
Bundle-Name: Hello DS
Bundle-SymbolicName: org.equinoxosgi.ds.hello
Bundle-Version: 1.0.0
Bundle-RequiredExecutionEnvironment: J2SE-1.4
Service-Component: OSGI-INF/component.xml
```

The value of this header is a comma-separated list of bundle-relative file name paths. The last segment of each path may include a wildcard, for example:

```
Service-Component: OSGI-INF/browse.xml,
 OSGI-INF/portal.xml,
 OSGI-INF/tracking*.xml,
 OSGI-INF/serviceActionLookup.xml
```

You must use only forward slashes as path separators. Backslashes are illegal, even if they are doubled up. If a file path does not refer to a component XML document, DS will log an error to the `LogService`, if available. The `Service-Component` header is ignored for fragment bundles, but a fragment bundle may contribute XML documents to its host. Clearly this is a case where using a wildcard in the file path is useful. The XML describes the component and the POJO class that implements its behavior. Storing component XML documents below the OSGI-INF folder is a reasonable choice but is not required.

As the component does not provide any services, DS instantiates and activates it immediately. The component's implementation class can be any public class that has a public default constructor. The component's implementation class should already be familiar to you:

```
org.equinoxosgi.ds.hello/Hello
public class Hello extends Object {
```

```
  public Hello() {
    System.out.println("Hello, World");
  }
}
```

The implementation class can hook into its component's lifecycle by adding two methods as shown in the following snippet:

org.equinoxosgi.ds.hello/Hello
```
public class Hello extends Object {
  public Hello() {
    System.out.println("Hello, World");
  }

  public void activate() {
    System.out.println("Activated");
  }

  public void deactivate() {
    System.out.println("Deactivated");
  }
}
```

The symmetry of the component class's `activate` and `deactivate` methods is important in that it reflects the lifecycle of a component. In this example the `activate` method is called immediately upon the component's configuration being satisfied; then once the `activate` method has been called, the `deactivate` method is called when the component's configuration is no longer satisfied, or when its hosting bundle stops. The concept of a component's configuration being satisfied, or not, is discussed in Section 24.1.2 of Chapter 24, "Declarative Services Reference."

Notice that the component's implementation class is simply an `Object`—it does not have to extend or implement another type. DS discovers the component implementation class's `activate` and `deactivate` methods using reflection. While `activate` and `deactivate` are the default method names, you can specify different methods by setting the `<component>` element's `activate` and `deactivate` attributes. In this way DS adapts to work with your POJO class rather than the other way around. The tutorial chapters in Part II often do this, using the method names `startup` and `shutdown`, since they're more POJO-friendly than `activate` and `deactivate`. The next section also includes an example of this.

15.2.2 Referencing Services

A component can reference services by specifying nested `<reference>` elements. A component that references other services is activated only when every reference is satisfied based on its policy and cardinality.

In the following example, the <reference> elements do not specify the policy and cardinality attributes. This implies that the default policy of static and the default cardinality of 1..1 should be used. As such, an IEmergencyMonitor service and an ICrustShell service must be available before the component's configuration is satisfied and the component can be activated.

org.equinoxosgi.toast.swt.emergency/component.xml
```xml
<?xml version="1.0" encoding="UTF-8"?>
<scr:component xmlns:scr="http://www.osgi.org/xmlns/scr/v1.1.0"
  name="org.equinoxosgi.toast.swt.emergency"
  activate="startup" deactivate="shutdown">
  <implementation class=
    "org.equinoxosgi.toast.internal.swt.emergency.EmergencyScreen"/>
  <reference bind="setEmergency"
    interface="org.equinoxosgi.toast.client.emergency.IEmergencyMonitor"
    name="emergency"/>
  <reference bind="setShell"
    interface="org.equinoxosgi.crust.shell.ICrustShell"
    name="shell"/>
</scr:component>
```

When a referenced service is available, DS binds it to the component's implementation by calling the method named in the <reference> element's bind attribute. Likewise, when a reference service becomes unavailable, DS unbinds it from the component's implementation by calling the method named in the <reference> element's unbind attribute.

Both the bind and unbind attributes are optional, and as this snippet shows, unbinding is often not necessary, such as when it involves simply setting a field to null. Specifying the unbind attribute is necessary only when there is real work to be done, such as removing a listener from the soon-to-be-unbound referenced service. Of course, specifying an unbind attribute can assist with debugging since it gives you a place to log a message or set a breakpoint and observe that the referenced service has been unbound.

When using the static policy, the bind method is always called *before the component is activated*, and the unbind method is always called *after the component is deactivated*.

Once the component's configuration is satisfied, DS activates it by instantiating the EmergencyScreen implementation class and calling its startup method. When the component's configuration is no longer satisfied, or when the bundle stops, DS deactivates the component by calling the EmergencyScreen's shutdown method:

org.equinoxosgi.toast.swt.emergency/EmergencyScreen
```java
public class EmergencyScreen implements
    IEmergencyMonitorListener, SelectionListener, ICrustScreenListener {
  private IEmergencyMonitor monitor;
  private ICrustShell crustShell;
```

```
    public void setShell(ICrustShell value) {
      crustShell = value;
    }

    public void setEmergency(IEmergencyMonitor value) {
      monitor = value;
    }

    public void startup() {
      screenComposite = crustShell.installScreen(...);
      monitor.addListener(this);
      ...
    }

    public void shutdown() {
      ...
      monitor.removeListener(this);
      crustShell.uninstallScreen(...);
    }
    ...
}
```

When referencing a service, a component can specify one of four *cardinality* values to describe how many referenced services are required and desired. Similarly, they can specify one of two *policy* values to describe how the component handles referenced service changes. While these combinations result in eight possible pairings, the two most common parings are

1..1 and static—It is not a coincidence that these are the default attribute values and the pairing that you'll use most often. With a cardinality of 1..1 and a static policy, the referenced service is bound before the component is activated, and the component is deactivated before the referenced service is unbound. Toast uses these values in all but a couple of cases.

0..n and dynamic—The 0..n cardinality implies that the referenced service is *optional* and *multiple*, so the dynamic policy makes sense—you don't want the activated component to be deactivated before a referenced service is bound and the component reactivated. And you don't want the activated component to be deactivated before one of the many referenced services is unbound and the component reactivated. Toast uses these values in the back end portal's service action lookup component.

Again, since in our example the <reference> elements do not specify the policy and cardinality attributes, the defaults of static and 1..1 are used.

15.2.3 Providing Services

In addition to referencing OSGi services, DS components can provide services to the OSGi service registry. This is done by listing the provided services in the component's XML document and having the component class implement each provided service. The following snippet shows an example from the GPS bundle:

org.equinoxosgi.toast.dev.gps.fake/component.xml
```
<?xml version="1.0" encoding="UTF-8"?>
<scr:component xmlns:scr="http://www.osgi.org/xmlns/scr/v1.1.0"
    name="org.equinoxosgi.toast.dev.gps.fake">
  <implementation class=
    "org.equinoxosgi.toast.internal.dev.gps.fake.FakeGps"/>
  <service>
    <provide interface="org.equinoxosgi.toast.dev.gps.IGps"/>
  </service>
</scr:component>
```

Notice that the <provide> element is nested within the <service> element and that each element describes a single provided service. The component provides the IGps service, so the implementation class FakeGps must implement IGps, and DS will register the component object as an IGps service.

org.equinoxosgi.toast.dev.gps.fake/FakeGps
```
public class FakeGps implements IGps {
  public int getHeading() {
    return 90; // 90 degrees (east)
  }

  public int getLatitude() {
    return 3776999; // 3776999 N
  }

  public int getLongitude() {
    return -12244694; // 122.44694 W
  }

  public int getSpeed() {
    return 50; // 50 kph
  }
}
```

While a component can have only one implementation class, it can provide multiple services. To support this, the component class must implement each of the provided service interfaces, and each service must be described by a <provide> element. Note that the same component implementation instance will be registered for each provided service.

15.2.4 Referencing and Providing Services

It is common for a component to both reference and provide services. This is effectively a merge of the previous two scenarios. The component lifecycle ensures that a component's services are provided only while its configuration is satisfied. By default a component's implementation class is instantiated and the component activated on the first use of a provided service; that is, the component is lazily instantiated when it is referenced. The following snippet shows this in action:

org.equinoxosgi.toast.client.emergency/component.xml
```xml
<?xml version="1.0" encoding="UTF-8"?>
<scr:component xmlns:scr="http://www.osgi.org/xmlns/scr/v1.1.0"
    name="org.equinoxosgi.toast.client.emergency"
    activate="startup" deactivate="shutdown">
  <implementation class="org.equinoxosgi.toast.internal.client.
      emergency.EmergencyMonitor"/>
  <service>
    <provide interface=
      "org.equinoxosgi.toast.client.emergency.IEmergencyMonitor"/>
  </service>
  <reference bind="setGps"
    interface="org.equinoxosgi.toast.dev.gps.IGps"
    name="gps"/>
  <reference bind="setAirbag"
    interface="org.equinoxosgi.toast.dev.airbag.IAirbag"
    name="airbag"/>
  <reference bind="setChannel"
    interface="org.equinoxosgi.toast.core.channel.sender.IChannel"
    name="channel"/>
</scr:component>
```

The emergency component references the services IGps, IAirbag, and IChannel and provides the service IEmergencyMonitor, which is implemented by the component's implementation class.

org.equinoxosgi.toast.client.emergency/EmergencyMonitor
```java
public class EmergencyMonitor implements
    IAirbagListener, IEmergencyMonitor {
  private IAirbag airbag;
  private IChannel channel;
  private IGps gps;
  ...

  public void addListener(IEmergencyMonitorListener listener) {
    ...
  }

  public void deployed() {
    startJob();
  }
```

```java
  public void emergency() {
    startJob();
  }

  public void removeListener(IEmergencyMonitorListener listener) {
    ...
  }

  public void setAirbag(IAirbag value) {
    airbag = value;
  }

  public void setChannel(IChannel value) {
    channel = value;
  }

  public void setGps(IGps value) {
    gps = value;
  }

  public void shutdown() {
    stopJob();
    airbag.removeListener(this);
  }

  public void startup() {
    airbag.addListener(this);
  }
}
```

15.2.5 Immediate Components

In an OSGi application it is common for DS components to provide services. Such components are considered lazy, and DS delays the loading and instantiation of each component's implementation class until one of its provided services is requested. The performance and scalability benefits that this brings are compelling reasons for using DS. But not all components can or want to be lazy.

Most applications include a few components whose implementation class must be eagerly loaded and instantiated. DS calls these *immediate components*. Immediate components often reside at the top of the food chain, while others need to perform initialization behavior before the first service request, or are independent of services altogether.

To request that DS treat a component as immediate, set the <component> element's immediate attribute to true. DS will respect this request unless the component is a factory component; see Section 15.2.7, "Factory Components," for more details. Setting the immediate attribute to false never affects the immediacy of a component.

The Toast component org.equinoxosgi.toast.swt.emergency is an example of an immediate component. Once the implementation class EmergencyScreen has been instantiated, it registers itself with the ICrustShell. Since this component does not provide any services, it must be immediate since there is no way for it to be activated otherwise.

AVOID IMPLICITLY IMMEDIATE COMPONENTS

A component that does not provide services and is not a factory component is *implicitly immediate*, meaning that DS will treat it as immediate without the <component> element's immediate attribute being set to true.

Implicit component immediacy not only is confusing, but it can be problematic if later the component is changed to provide a service and is quietly no longer immediate. We recommend that if a component needs to be activated immediately, its <component> element's immediate attribute should be explicitly set to true.

Relying on implicit component immediacy can lead to difficult-to-spot regressions in behavior and to some late-night debugging.

The Toast component org.equinoxosgi.toast.backend.portal is another example of an immediate component. Once the implementation class Portal has been instantiated, it creates and registers an instance of the PortalServlet class as a servlet with the org.osgi.service.http.HttpService. This component's only interaction is via HTTP, so being lazy is not an option.

Other examples of immediate components include those that wish to start a thread, add a listener to a referenced service, communicate with hardware or an external system, or simply need the chance to perform initialization behavior prior to the first request for a provided service.

Immediate components can present a performance and scalability risk to an application since they often cause other components to be activated, classes to be loaded, and objects to be created earlier than is absolutely necessary.

15.2.6 The Whiteboard Pattern

As an alternative to the traditional Observer Pattern, the Whiteboard Pattern[1] has been proposed for use in OSGi applications. The Whiteboard Pattern is not inherently OSGi-specific and could be implemented without OSGi, but it does

---

1. See www.osgi.org/wiki/uploads/Links/whiteboard.pdf.

require a publish/subscribe mechanism through which interested parties are discovered. The OSGi service registry is perfect for this.

With the Whiteboard Pattern, the *event source* bundle and the *event listener* bundles are completely decoupled via the OSGi service registry: An event listener expresses its interest in the event source by providing a service, and an event source then discovers the event listener services through which change events are dispatched.

In addition to the loose coupling of the event source and the event listeners, the virtues of the Whiteboard Pattern include a simplified implementation of both the event source and the event listeners. There is no need for the event source to maintain a list of event listeners, and each event listener needs no knowledge of the event source. The OSGi service registry takes care of this by maintaining the set of interested event listener services and notifying the event source when the services are changed.

An additional benefit is the reduced possibility of object retention caused by an event listener neglecting to unregister its interest in the event source; the OSGi framework guarantees that all services are automatically unregistered when the registering bundle stops. Poorly coded event sources can, however, still incorrectly retain references to uninterested event listeners.

Despite these improvements over the Listener Pattern, there are some disadvantages of the Whiteboard Pattern:

○ The OSGi service registry consists of a single namespace, making the set of event listeners global.

○ Without care the application can become unnecessarily coupled to the OSGi framework.

○ Given the active nature of the service registry, applications with many listeners may not scale well.

Since event listeners are services and the OSGi service registry maintains a global, flat list of services, listeners will hear all events regardless of the source. Of course, this can be highly desirable, but it can also unnecessarily complicate system configuration.

Domain objects using the Whiteboard Pattern typically rely on the OSGi service registry to maintain the event listeners. This is counter to the POJO and dependency injection approach that we have used throughout this book. In particular, it inhibits reuse in non-OSGi scenarios and complicates testing.

Of course, this coupling can be avoided by introducing the notion of a lookup mechanism and then supplying a service-based implementation. This allows us to retain the benefits of the Whiteboard Pattern while allowing the code to run without the OSGi framework.

We saw an example of this in Chapter 13, "Web Portal," where the back end `Portal` registers the `PortalServlet` that handles HTTP requests by dispatching to a matching `IPortalAction`. In this way the portal servlet is easily, and infinitely, extendable. Here we take a closer look at the setup, starting with the back end portal component:

`org.equinoxosgi.toast.backend.portal/portal.xml`
```xml
<?xml version="1.0" encoding="UTF-8"?>
<scr:component xmlns:scr="http://www.osgi.org/xmlns/scr/v1.1.0"
    name="org.equinoxosgi.toast.backend.portal"
    immediate="true">
  <implementation class=
    "org.equinoxosgi.toast.internal.backend.portal.bundle.Portal"/>
  <reference
    bind="setHttp"
    interface="org.osgi.service.http.HttpService"
    name="http"/>
  <reference
    bind="setControlCenter"
    interface=
      "org.equinoxosgi.toast.backend.controlcenter.IControlCenter"
    name="controlCenter"/>
  <reference
    bind="setLookup"
    interface="org.equinoxosgi.toast.backend.portal.spi.IActionLookup"
    name="lookup"/>
</scr:component>
```

The back end portal is an immediate DS component whose implementation class, `Portal`, creates the `PortalServlet` and registers it with the `HttpService`.

When the `PortalServlet` is created, it is given an `IActionLookup` service. The `PortalServlet` handles an HTTP request by locating an `IPortalAction` using its `IActionLookup` service and then executing it. The `IActionLookup` service has a `getAction` API that returns the `IPortalAction` object matching a specified ID. The code is roughly as follows:

`org.equinoxosgi.toast.backend.portal/PortalServlet`
```java
public class PortalServlet extends HttpServlet {
  private IActionLookup lookup;
  ...

  public PortalServlet(IControlCenter center, IActionLookup lookup) {
    ...
    this.lookup = lookup;
  }

  public void doGet(
      HttpServletRequest request, HttpServletResponse response)
        throws ServletException, IOException {
    String actionParameter =
      request.getParameter(IPortalConstants.ACTION_PARAMETER);
```

```
    ...
    IPortalAction action = lookup.getAction(actionParameter);
    action.execute(request, response);
  }
  ...
}
```

This action lookup behavior is defined by the IActionLookup service and is completely independent of OSGi. To hook in OSGi services using the Whiteboard Pattern, we have a ServiceActionLookup class that implements the IActionLookup interface *in terms of OSGi services* using the Whiteboard Pattern. This action lookup service is then injected into the Portal and used to handle portal web requests. The next snippet shows the service-based action lookup mechanism. The code looks a little complex but is reasonably straightforward.

The PortalAction inner class is a wrapper for user-supplied actions to ensure that the real action services are not accessed until required. Given the lazy nature of DS components, this defers the instantiation of DS-supplied IPortalAction services. The rest of ServiceActionLookup implements a cache of PortalAction wrappers and the required getAction method.

org.equinoxosgi.toast.backend.portal/IActionLookup
```
public interface IActionLookup {
  public IPortalAction getAction(String id);
  public Collection getAvailable(String id);
  public String getActionProperty(String id, String key);
}
```

org.equinoxosgi.toast.backend.portal/ServiceActionLookup
```
public class ServiceActionLookup implements IActionLookup {
  private class PortalAction implements IPortalAction {
    private final ServiceReference reference;

    PortalAction(ServiceReference reference) {
      ...
      this.reference = reference;
    }

    public void execute(
        HttpServletRequest request, HttpServletResponse response)
          throws IOException {
      IPortalAction action = locateService();
      if (action == null) {
        Object id = getActionId(reference);
        throw new IOException("Action has been invalidated: " + id);
      }
      action.execute(request, response);
    }

    String getProperty(String key) {
      return (String) reference.getProperty(key);
    }
```

```java
    IPortalAction locateService() {
      ComponentContext context = ServiceActionLookup.this.context;
      if (context == null)
        throw new IllegalStateException("component is not activated");
      return (IPortalAction)
        context.locateService("action", reference);
    }
  }

  private final Map actions = new HashMap();
  private ComponentContext context;

  public void activate(ComponentContext context) {
    this.context = context;
  }

  public void addAction(ServiceReference reference) {
    Object id = getActionId(reference);
    if (id == null)
      return;
    synchronized (actions) {
      PortalAction data = new PortalAction(reference);
      actions.put(id, data);
    }
  }

  public void deactivate(ComponentContext context) {
    this.context = null;
  }

  public IPortalAction getAction(String id) {
    synchronized (actions) {
      return (IPortalAction) actions.get(id);
    }
  }

  private Object getActionId(ServiceReference reference) {
    return reference.getProperty(IPortalConstants.ACTION_PARAMETER);
  }

  public String getActionProperty(String id, String key) {
    synchronized (actions) {
      PortalAction result = (PortalAction) actions.get(id);
      if (result == null)
        return null;
      return result.getProperty(key);
    }
  }

  public Collection getAvailable(String id) {
    ...
  }

  public void removeAction(ServiceReference reference) {
    Object id = getActionId(reference);
```

```
      if (id == null)
        return;
      synchronized (actions) {
        actions.remove(id);
      }
    }
    ...
}
```

Notice that the addAction method takes a ServiceReference argument rather than an IPortalAction. This is the key to delaying the loading and instantiation of each bound IPortalAction until it is needed by the PortalServlet to fulfill an HTTP action request.

To hook this into DS using the Whiteboard Pattern, we need a component with a <reference> element for the IPortalAction service and have it use the dynamic policy and the 0..n cardinality. This allows any number of IPortalAction services to be referenced by the component. As IPortalAction services are registered, the ServiceActionLookup is notified by DS calling addAction, which creates and caches a corresponding PortalAction that wraps the ServiceReference. As action services are unregistered, they are unbound from the ServiceActionLookup component via removeAction. The component XML required to describe this is shown in the following snippet:

org.equinoxosgi.toast.backend.portal/serviceActionLookup.xml
```
<?xml version="1.0" encoding="UTF-8"?>
<scr:component xmlns:scr="http://www.osgi.org/xmlns/scr/v1.1.0"
    name="org.equinoxosgi.toast.backend.portal.serviceActionLookup"
    immediate="true">
  <implementation class="org.equinoxosgi.toast.internal.backend.
      portal.bundle.ServiceActionLookup"/>
  <reference
    bind="addAction"
    cardinality="0..n"
    interface="org.equinoxosgi.toast.backend.portal.spi.IPortalAction"
    name="action"
    policy="dynamic"
    unbind="removeAction"/>
  <service>
     <provide interface=
       "org.equinoxosgi.toast.backend.portal.spi.IActionLookup"/>
  </service>
</scr:component>
```

The <reference> element for the IPortalAction service uses a cardinality of 0..n because many services are expected but none are required. In this case using a policy of dynamic makes sense since we do not want changes in the available IPortalAction services to affect the activation of the ServiceActionLookup component.

While this certainly requires more code and is not quite how you would write your POJO servlet, it is very reasonable when you are trying to make the set of portal actions extensible while decoupling your business logic from OSGi.

The following snippet shows how the tracking action is contributed to the portal using DS by providing an IPortalAction service:

org.equinoxosgi.toast.backend.portal/tracking.xml
```
<?xml version="1.0" encoding="UTF-8"?>
<scr:component xmlns:scr="http://www.osgi.org/xmlns/scr/v1.1.0"
    name="org.equinoxosgi.toast.backend.portal.trackingAction">
  <implementation class=
    "org.equinoxosgi.toast.internal.backend.portal.TrackingAction"/>
  <service>
    <provide interface=
      "org.equinoxosgi.toast.backend.portal.spi.IPortalAction"/>
  </service>
  <property name="action" value="browse/tracking"/>
  <property name="label" type="String" value="Track vehicle location"/>
</scr:component>
```

The implementation of the tracking action is as follows:

org.equinoxosgi.toast.backend.portal/TrackingAction
```
public class TrackingAction implements IPortalAction {
  public void execute(
    HttpServletRequest request, HttpServletResponse response)
      throws IOException {
    generateTracking(request, response);
  }

  private void generateTracking(
    HttpServletRequest request, HttpServletResponse response)
      throws IOException {
    String thisAction =
      request.getParameter(IPortalConstants.ACTION_PARAMETER);
    String id = request.getParameter(ICoreConstants.ID_PARAMETER);
    StringBuffer buffer = new StringBuffer(2048);
    WebPageGenerator.writeHeader(buffer, WebPageGenerator.TITLE + id);
    ...
    WebPageGenerator.writeFooter(buffer);
    PrintWriter writer = response.getWriter();
    try {
      writer.print(buffer.toString());
    } finally {
      writer.close();
    }
  }
}
```

15.2.7 Factory Components

So far we have discussed how to use DS to describe components that are statically and automatically created once their configuration has been satisfied. When components need to be created dynamically, or when multiple instances of a component are needed, a DS *factory component* should be used. A factory component implicitly provides an `org.osgi.service.component.ComponentFactory` service that is used by other bundles and components to create and dispose of instances of the component.

To help explain factory components, we show you how to declare an airbag factory component for Toast that allows multiple airbags of varying kinds that reside throughout the vehicle to be dynamically configured.

To keep things simple, the scenario presented here starts with the code in the Samples Manager for Chapter 6, "Dynamic Services," and walks you through editing the `org.equinoxosgi.toast.dev.airbag` bundle to make its DS component a *factory component*. We then implement a second DS component that configures Toast using the factory-component-provided `ComponentFactory` service to create six distinct airbag components.

15.2.7.1 Updating the Airbag Domain Logic

While all cars have airbags hidden within the steering column and behind the front console, it's common these days to also see curtain airbags. Let's start by enhancing the Toast domain logic to support different kinds of airbags, mounted on the left and the right, throughout the vehicle.

```
org.equinoxosgi.toast.dev.airbag/IAirbag
public interface IAirbag {
  // Kinds
  public static final String KIND_REGULAR = "regular";
  public static final String KIND_CURTAIN = "curtain";

  // Orientations
  public static final String ORIENTATION_LEFT = "left";
  public static final String ORIENTATION_RIGHT = "right";

  // Property Keys
  public String PROPERTY_KIND = "kind";
  public String PROPERTY_ORIENTATION = "orientation";
  public String PROPERTY_ROW = "row";

  public void addListener(IAirbagListener listener);
  public void removeListener(IAirbagListener listener);
  public String getKind();
  public String getOrientation();
  public int getRow();
}
```

The new APIs `getKind`, `getOrientation`, and `getRow` allow us to query the type of airbag we have and where it is mounted in the vehicle. The `KIND_*` and `ORIENTATION_*` constants are intended to be used to set the state of `IAirbag`

instances. The PROPERTY_* constants will be used to parameterize the creation of
IAirbag instances. The use of these constants will become clear as we proceed
through the example.

Now that we've enhanced the IAirbag interface, it is necessary to update the
FakeAirbag implementation. To support airbags of varying characteristics, we
have added three fields (one each for kind, orientation, and row) and the methods to satisfy the new IAirbag interface APIs. We have also overridden the
toString method to allow a FakeAirbag to describe itself appropriately on the console or the log. Besides these domain logic changes, the most important changes
are to the FakeAirbag's startup method:

org.equinoxosgi.toast.dev.airbag/FakeAirbag
```
public class FakeAirbag implements IAirbag {
    ...
    private String kind;
    private String orientation;
    private int row;

    public String getKind() {
        return kind;
    }

    public String getOrientation() {
        return orientation;
    }

    public int getRow() {
        return row;
    }

    public synchronized void startup(Map properties) {
        System.out.println("Starting FakeAirbag");
        kind = (String) properties.get(IAirbag.PROPERTY_KIND);
        orientation = (String)
            properties.get(IAirbag.PROPERTY_ORIENTATION);
        Integer rowWrapper = (Integer)
            properties.get(IAirbag.PROPERTY_ROW);
        row = rowWrapper != null ? rowWrapper.intValue() : 0;
        ...
    }

    public synchronized void shutdown() {
        System.out.println("Shutting down FakeAirbag");
        ...
    }

    public String toString() {
        StringBuffer buffer = new StringBuffer(250);
        buffer.append("FakeAirbag: kind=").append(kind);
        buffer.append(", orientation=").append(orientation);
        buffer.append(", row=").append(row);
```

```
        return buffer.toString();
    }
}
```

Remember, the `startup` method is the component's activation method. The declaration of the `startup` method has been changed to take a `Map` argument, which is called by DS at runtime when the component's configuration is satisfied and activated. At that time DS will pass in the `FakeAirbag`'s properties as created by the airbag factory component. This is discussed in the next section. The `Map` contains keys such as those defined by the `IAirbag` constants `PROPERTY_KIND`, `PROPERTY_ORIENTATION`, and `PROPERTY_ROW`.

15.2.7.2 Declaring a Factory Component

The existing airbag DS component needs to be updated to change it to a *factory component*. The `<component>` element has an optional `factory` attribute that is used to identify the component as a factory component.

When this attribute is set, DS ignores the `<component>` and instead registers a `ComponentFactory` service through which instances of the component can be manufactured. This is rather subtle and is one of the most confusing aspects of the DS component schema. When declaring a factory component, you can think of the `<component>` element as a *blueprint* for what the factory will manufacture.

org.equinoxosgi.toast.dev.airbag/component.xml
```xml
<?xml version="1.0" encoding="UTF-8"?>
<scr:component xmlns:scr="http://www.osgi.org/xmlns/scr/v1.1.0"
    name="org.equinoxosgi.toast.dev.airbag"
    factory="org.equinoxosgi.toast.dev.airbag.IAirbag"
    activate="startup" deactivate="shutdown">
  <implementation class=
    "org.equinoxosgi.toast.internal.dev.airbag.fake.FakeAirbag"/>
  <service>
    <provide interface="org.equinoxosgi.toast.dev.airbag.IAirbag"/>
  </service>
  <property name="kind" type="String" value="regular"/>
</scr:component>
```

While uniqueness is not required or enforced for the `<component>` element's `factory` attribute, it is certainly recommended since this is used later by others that need to locate the `ComponentFactory` service in the OSGi service registry.

We have chosen to use the fully qualified `IAirbag` interface name as the component's factory identifier. Not only does this uniquely identify the factory, but as the factory will be manufacturing components that provide an `IAirbag` service, it certainly appears to be intention-revealing.

We have also added a `<property>` element that defines the default value for the `kind` property of the airbag components that the factory manufactures. We'll see shortly how this is used.

The factory component in this example happens to include a `<service>` element since it provides an `IAirbag` service. This is not a necessary part of being a factory component. It is perfectly legal for the components manufactured by a factory component to be immediate, providing no services of their own.

15.2.7.3 Registered Properties of a `ComponentFactory` Service

DS automatically registers a factory component's `ComponentFactory` service with the following properties:

> `component.name`—The value of this property is defined by the `<component>` element's `name` attribute, which in this example is
> `org.equinoxosgi.toast.dev.airbag`.

> `component.factory`—The value of this property is defined by the `<component>` element's `factory` attribute, which in this case is
> `org.equinoxosgi.toast.dev.airbag.IAirbag`; this is the type of the service provided by the component.

Since there can be many registered `ComponentFactory` services, these properties serve to identify this particular `ComponentFactory` service, ideally uniquely. Bundles and components that wish to use a `ComponentFactory` service can use these properties to select the one they want.

15.2.7.4 Using a `ComponentFactory` Service

So far we've seen how to declare the airbag factory component, but we've still not seen how to use its provided `ComponentFactory` to dynamically create multiple parameterized airbag components. For this we need a new DS component that is responsible for using the `ComponentFactory` to configure the Toast airbag components—we call it the *configurator* for short. The `configurator.xml` file is as follows:

```
org.equinoxosgi.toast.dev.airbag/configurator.xml
<?xml version="1.0" encoding="UTF-8"?>
<scr:component xmlns:scr="http://www.osgi.org/xmlns/scr/v1.1.0"
   name="org.equinoxosgi.toast.dev.airbag.configurator"
   activate="startup" deactivate="shutdown"
   immediate="true">
   <implementation class=
       "org.equinoxosgi.toast.internal.dev.airbag.AirbagConfigurator"/>
     <reference
       interface="org.osgi.service.component.ComponentFactory"
       name="factory"
       cardinality="1..1" policy="static"
       bind="setFactory"
       target="(component.factory=org.equinoxosgi.toast.dev.airbag.
           IAirbag)"/>
</scr:component>
```

The first thing to notice about the configurator component is that it does not provide any services and is an explicitly immediate component. DS activates immediate components as soon as their configurations are satisfied, which for the configurator means once its referenced ComponentFactory service is available.

The configurator has two responsibilities: When activated, create Toast's airbag components via the airbag ComponentFactory service, and when deactivated, dispose of the airbag components it previously created.

Since DS registers a distinct ComponentFactory service for each factory component it finds, the configurator component cannot use *just any* ComponentFactory! By specifying the <reference> element's target attribute, it is able to select the ComponentFactory service with a component.factory property of org.equinoxosgi .toast.dev.airbag.IAirbag.

The configurator component's implementation is the AirbagConfigurator class, which for simplicity resides in the org.equinoxosgi.toast.dev.airbag bundle—this gives the effect of the bundle configuring itself. Of course, this behavior could equally well reside in a separate bundle that is responsible for configuring all Toast components using all manner of ComponentFactory services.

Since the AirbagConfigurator class uses the OSGi-defined ComponentFactory interface, the bundle must import the package org.osgi.service.component.

org.equinoxosgi.toast.dev.airbag/AirbagConfigurator
```
public class AirbagConfigurator {
    private ComponentFactory factory;
    private List components; // ComponentInstance objects.

    // ComponentFactory bind method
    public void setFactory(ComponentFactory factory) {
        this.factory = factory;
    }

    // Component activation method
    public void startup() {
        System.out.println("Creating components...");
        components = new ArrayList(6);
        components.add(createComponent(null,
            IAirbag.ORIENTATION_LEFT, 0));
        components.add(createComponent(null,
            IAirbag.ORIENTATION_RIGHT, 0));
        components.add(createComponent(IAirbag.KIND_CURTAIN,
            IAirbag.ORIENTATION_LEFT, 0));
        components.add(createComponent(IAirbag.KIND_CURTAIN,
            IAirbag.ORIENTATION_RIGHT, 0));
        components.add(createComponent(IAirbag.KIND_CURTAIN,
            IAirbag.ORIENTATION_LEFT, 1));
        components.add(createComponent(IAirbag.KIND_CURTAIN,
            IAirbag.ORIENTATION_RIGHT, 1));
    }
```

```
    private ComponentInstance createComponent(
        String kind, String orientation, int row) {
      Dictionary properties = new Hashtable(3);
      If (kind != null) {
        properties.put(IAirbag.PROPERTY_KIND, kind);
      }
      properties.put(IAirbag.PROPERTY_ORIENTATION, orientation);
      properties.put(IAirbag.PROPERTY_ROW, new Integer(row));
      ComponentInstance instance = factory.newInstance(properties);
      Object airbag = instance.getInstance();
      System.out.println("\tCreated component " + airbag);
      return instance;
    }

  private void disposeComponent(ComponentInstance instance) {
      Object airbag = instance.getInstance();
      System.out.println("\tDisposing component " + airbag);
      instance.dispose();
    }

  // Component deactivation method
  public void shutdown() {
      System.out.println("Disposing components...");
      for (int i = components.size() - 1; i >= 0; i--) {
        ComponentInstance instance =
          (ComponentInstance) components.get(i);
        disposeComponent(instance);
      }
      components = null;
    }
}
```

The startup method is the component's activation method. This method calls its private createComponent method six times to create six distinct airbag components. Each call to createComponent returns an OSGi-defined ComponentInstance object that represents an airbag component. These objects are cached in a field for later use.

The createComponent method is simply a helper that constructs a Dictionary and populates it with the properties to be passed to the ComponentFactory's newInstance method. The newInstance method dynamically creates an airbag component, passing along instance-specific properties that DS delivers to the FakeAirbag's startup method upon activation. These properties override any properties declared by the factory component's XML, and since a kind property is declared in its XML, this property is therefore optional.

The AirbagConfigurator's shutdown method, which is the component's deactivation method, does the reverse of the startup method: It iterates through the list of components, calling dispose on each ComponentInstance. The dispose method causes DS to deactivate the airbag component represented by the ComponentInstance and call the FakeAirbag's shutdown method. Finally, the

`AirbagConfigurator`'s `shutdown` method sets the `components` field to `null`, which while not strictly necessary allows the method to preserve symmetry with the `startup` method.

15.2.7.5 Launching Toast

When the `org.equinoxosgi.toast.dev.airbag.configurator` component is activated, it creates six airbag components using the `ComponentFactory` service provided by the `org.equinoxosgi.toast.dev.airbag` factory component.

Stopping the `org.equinoxosgi.toast.dev.airbag` bundle using the console's `stop` command demonstrates how the airbag component factory correctly disposes of airbag components when deactivated. Likewise, using the `start` command to restart it causes the airbag components to be manufactured again.

15.3 Launching and Debugging DS Applications

Launching an application that uses DS is like launching any other OSGi application—you just need a few extra bundles. In particular, ensure that the following three bundles are in your launch configuration:

`org.eclipse.equinox.ds`—The DS implementation

`org.eclipse.equinox.util`—Utilities used by the DS implementation

`org.eclipse.osgi.services`—The OSGi standard API

Bundles that use DS often do so entirely via XML and do not specify a static dependency upon the DS implementation bundle `org.eclipse.equinox.ds`. This makes it easy to forget to include this bundle in the launch configuration. It is also important to ensure that the `org.eclipse.equinox.ds` bundle is started, since only then will it detect bundles that use DS and process their XML.

While we do not recommend that you use start levels, using start levels with DS bundles requires special care. Equinox uses a default start level of 4, so if your DS bundles need a start level *lower* than 4, let's say 3, you must remember to set the `org.eclipse.equinox.ds` bundle's start level to 3 or lower to ensure that your bundle's DS components are processed early enough. If you forget to do this, they will be processed at start level 4 after the `org.eclipse.equinox.ds` bundle is started. For this reason some people simply set the `org.eclipse.equinox.ds` bundle's start level to 1 just to be safe.

Given the loose coupling and laziness provided by DS, there can be some additional debugging problems. In particular, problems with parsing XML and other service binding issues can lead to many late-night debugging frustrations. Fortunately, the Equinox DS implementation has a helpful debugging flag that echoes all error messages to the console. Set the following VM argument when you launch your application:

```
-Dequinox.ds.print=true
```

The DS specification says that errors encountered while parsing and processing the component XML documents must be written to the LogService, if available. To use this, install and start the Equinox log bundle, org.eclipse.equinox.log. This bundle registers a memory-based LogService and a LogReaderService that supports the reading of logged events. You can also use the Equinox console's log command to dump recent log events to the console.

Equinox's DS implementation registers a CommandProvider service that extends the available console commands. The following *Service Component Runtime* commands are available that are helpful for controlling, understanding, and debugging a DS application:

list [-c] [bundle id]—List all components, or the components that belong to the bundle with the specified bundle ID. Use -c to display complete component information. Using -c and a bundle ID is useful for debugging a particular bundle. The short form is ls.

component <component id>—Display the details of the component with the specified component ID. Use the list command without parameters to display all components and their component IDs. The short form is comp.

enable <component id>—Enable the component with the specified component ID. The short form is en.

disable <component id>—Disable the component with the specified component ID. The short form is dis.

enableAll [bundle id]—Enable all components. Specify a bundle ID to enable only the components that belong to a particular bundle. The short form is enAll.

disableAll [bundle id]—Disable all components. Specify a bundle ID to disable only the components that belong to a particular bundle. The short form is disAll.

15.4 PDE Tooling

Having been introduced to Declarative Services, seen some of the common usage scenarios, and started to learn about the component XML, you'll be pleased to know that the Eclipse PDE provides some excellent DS tooling. The PDE tooling includes a DS component definition wizard for generating an initial component XML document and an editor for working with components.

The component wizard generates a component XML document after gathering details such as its location and file name, the name of the component it describes, and the component's implementation class name.

In addition, the wizard updates the ServiceComponent header in the bundle's manifest to reference the component XML document. This is particularly helpful since it's easy to forget, and DS cannot find your component without it.

Figure 15-1 shows the **Overview** page of the component definition editor. The **Component** section of the page is used to configure general component settings such as its name, implementation class, and lifecycle methods. Clicking the **Class*:** link opens the **New Java Class** wizard, providing a shortcut for creating the component's implementation class; once created, the link provides a way to quickly navigate to the class. The **Browse...** button provides a way to pick an existing class.

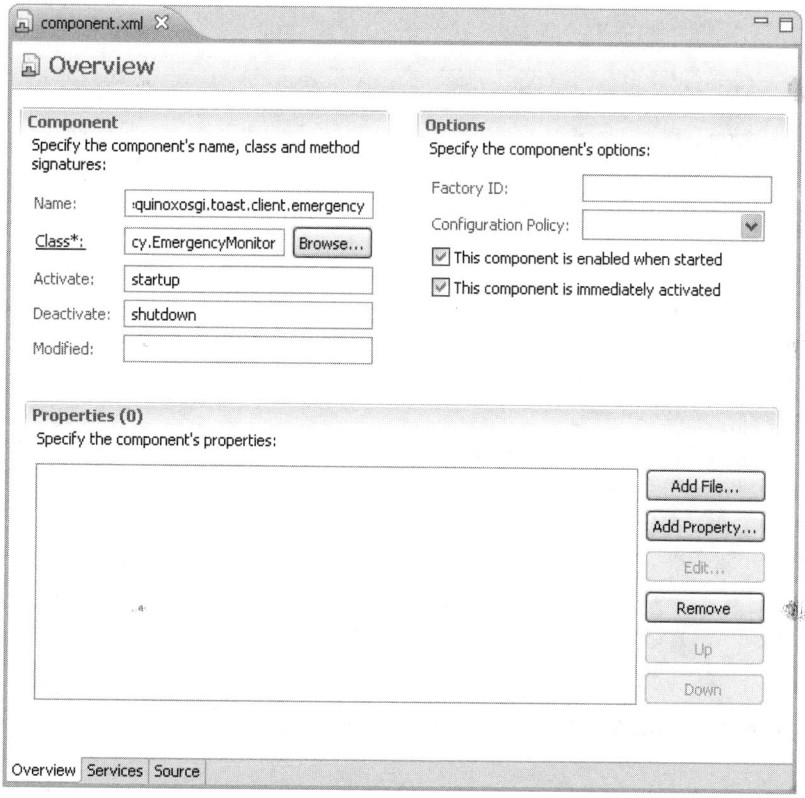

Figure 15-1 The **Overview** page of the component definition editor

The **Options** section is used for less common capabilities such as defining a factory component, setting the component's configuration policy, and controlling its enablement and immediacy settings.

The **Properties** section is where single component properties and component property files are declared. For a single property the **Edit...** button allows the property name, type, and value to be edited, and for a properties file it allows the location and file name to be edited.

Figure 15-2 shows the **Services** page where referenced and provided services are defined. Each referenced service can be edited to set attributes such as its name, interface, cardinality and policy, bind and unbind method names, and its target.

Provided services are shown in the lower half of the **Services** page, and each can be edited to change its interface name.

Figure 15–2   The **Services** page of the component definition editor

Table 15–1 Icons Used to Represent Referenced and Provided Services

Icon	Description
	Provided service
	Referenced service, static policy, cardinality of 1..1
	Referenced service, static policy, cardinality of 1..n
	Referenced service, static policy, cardinality of 0..1
	Referenced service, static policy, cardinality of 0..n
	Referenced service dynamic policy overlay

Table 15-1 shows the various images that are used to decorate a component's services.

Of course, there is also the **Source** page that supports text editing of component XML, but you'll likely find that this is unnecessary.

All this is not to say that the tooling is perfect; having made its debut only in Eclipse 3.5, it is still maturing and will likely be enhanced with future releases. It will likely improve its validation of the component XML and its error reporting. While the form-based editors make composing a component easy, errors reported in the Problems view are currently displayed only as markers on the **Source** page of the editor.

15.5 Summary

Successfully building a service-oriented OSGi application requires that the bundle developer understands the dynamic nature of the OSGi service model. Until the release of Declarative Services in OSGi R4, it was a significant challenge to build an appropriately behaved application, even of moderate complexity. But with the introduction of Declarative Services it is now possible to build a scalable, dynamic, loosely coupled application from OSGi bundles.

In this chapter we have introduced Declarative Services and some of the common scenarios where it can be applied. We taught you enough to be productive with DS, and we discussed the PDE tooling that supports building DS components.

For a deep dive on the component XML schema and the DS component lifecycle, see Chapter 24, "Declarative Services Reference."

CHAPTER 16

Extensions

For the majority of this book we have used OSGi services to facilitate the inter-action between bundles. Services are reasonably lightweight and, with the advent of the Declarative Services mechanism, relatively easy to work with. As mentioned in Chapter 2, "Concepts," services are not the only collaboration game in town. The Equinox Extension Registry can also be used to hook bundles together.

In this chapter we look at how the Extension Registry works and compare and contrast it with the service registry. In particular we will talk about

- Extensions and extension points
- The dynamic behavior of the Extension Registry
- Providing data in extensions
- Scalability and startup performance (event storm, caching)
- Extension and extension point lifecycle
- Relationship with the OSGi service registry

16.1 The Extension Registry

OSGi provides a framework for defining and running separate components. As we have seen throughout this book, it also provides a service mechanism that enables inter-bundle collaboration. Equinox adds to that the *Extension Registry* as a means of facilitating collaboration. The Extension Registry works as follows:

- Bundles open themselves for extension or configuration by declaring an *extension point* and defining a contract. Such a bundle is essentially saying, "If you give me the following information, I will do. . . ."

○ Other bundles *contribute* the prescribed information in the form of *extensions*. These provide data and/or identify classes to run and locations to access.

○ The Extension Registry discovers both extensions and extension points and links them together according to their contributing bundles' lifecycle.

○ Extension point definers are free to access and use contributed extensions in support of their operation.

In this chapter we enhance the back end portal from Chapter 13, "Web Portal," to allow for portal action contribution and discovery via the Extension Registry. In this approach the portal bundle declares an `actions` extension point and a contract that says,

> "Bundles can contribute `actions` extensions that define portal actions with a path, a label, and a class that implements the interface `IPortalAction`. The portal will present the given label to the user organized according to the given path and such that when the user clicks on the label, a particular URL will be accessed. As a result of the URL request, the portal will instantiate the given action class, cast it to `IPortalAction`, and call its execute method."

Figure 16-1 shows this relationship graphically.

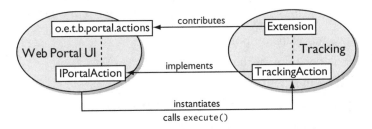

Figure 16–1   Extension contribution and use

Extension-to-extension-point relationships are defined using XML in a file called `plugin.xml`. Each participating bundle has one of these files. In this scenario, `org.equinoxosgi.toast.backend.portal`'s `plugin.xml` includes the following markup:

```
org.equinoxosgi.toast.backend.portal/plugin.xml
<extension-point id="actions" name="Portal Actions"/>
```

A bundle containing an action then contributes an extension using the markup shown in the following `plugin.xml` snippet:

```
org.equinoxosgi.toast.backend.tracking.ui/plugin.xml
<extension point="org.equinoxosgi.toast.backend.portal.actions">
  <action
    action="browse/tracking"
    class=
      "org.equinoxosgi.toast.internal.backend.tracking.ui.TrackingAction"
    label="Track vehicle location">
  </action>
</extension>
```

The `actions` extension point example here plays out as follows: When the portal composes the "browsing" page, it selects and presents the contributed extensions related to this page. Relationships are built using the value of the `action` attribute. In this case the "tracking" action is added to the generated HTML page as a link using the given label and accessing a related URL. When the user clicks on the link, the URL is accessed and the portal instantiates the `TrackingAction` class, casts it to `IPortalAction`, and calls its `execute` method.

This seemingly simple relationship is extremely powerful. The portal has effectively opened itself up as a pluggable web UI framework. It does not need to know about any of the contributions ahead of time, and no code is run to make the contributions—everything is declarative and lazy. These turn out to be key characteristics of the registry mechanism. Here are some other characteristics worth noting:

- ○ The mechanism can be used to contribute code or data.
- ○ The mechanism is declarative—bundles are connected without loading any of their code.
- ○ The mechanism is lazy in that no code is loaded until it is needed. In our example, the `TrackingAction` class is loaded only when a user clicks on the link. If the user does not use the link, the class is not loaded.
- ○ This approach scales well and enables various approaches for presenting, scoping, and filtering contributions.
- ○ Extensions and extension points are well used. Eclipse-based systems use them for everything from contributing views and menu items to connecting Help documents and discovering builders that process resource changes.

The Eclipse IDE includes quite extensive tooling for the Extension Registry. To access the tooling, click on one of the links in the **Extension/Extension Point Content** section of the **Overview** page of a bundle's manifest editor, as shown in Figure 16-2.

The next two sections give the details of how extensions and extension points work and are defined.

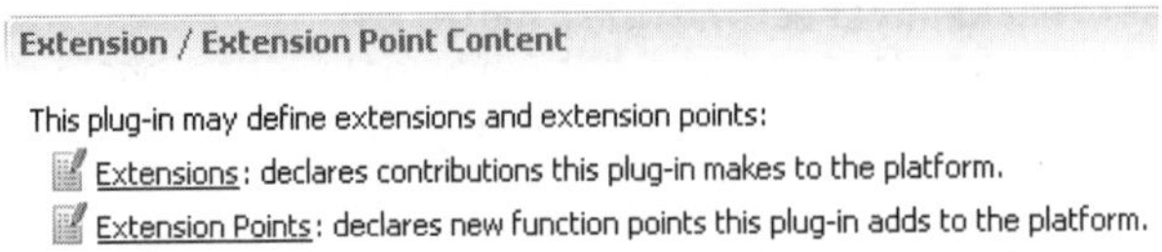

Extension / Extension Point Content

This plug-in may define extensions and extension points:

Extensions: declares contributions this plug-in makes to the platform.

Extension Points: declares new function points this plug-in adds to the platform.

Figure 16–2   Enabling Extension Registry tooling

16.2 Extension Points

In Chapter 13, "Web Portal," the portal was extended using the Whiteboard Pattern to detect adding IPortalAction services. In the example in the preceding section we proposed the use of the Extension Registry for this. Here we show you how to add Extension Registry support to the portal.

In the original design of the portal we purposely set out to isolate the use of OSGi and services from the domain logic of the portal itself. This was done by introducing the IActionLookup mechanism—the portal discovers available actions by consulting a service that manages actions. The original implementation of that service was based on OSGi services and called ServiceActionLookup. Here we'll add ExtensionActionLookup, an IActionLookup service based on the Extension Registry.

The first step in making your system extensible is to define an extension point. This involves both defining the contract and writing the code to implement the contract.

Creating an extension point declaration is done using the **Add...** button on the **Extension Points** page of the relevant bundle editor. Figure 16-3 shows the actions extension point in the org.equinoxosgi.toast.backend.portal bundle.

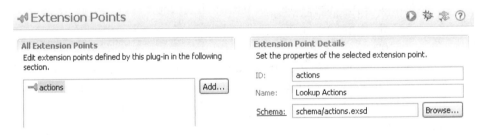

Figure 16–3   New extension point declaration

The **Extension Point Schema** file location field is filled in automatically. Schemas are used at development time to describe the expected structure of extensions contributed to an extension point. They describe everything from the set of tags and attributes to the kinds of values placed in the attributes. See **Plug-in Development Environment Guide > Reference > Wizards and Dialogs > New File Creation Wizard** in the online Help for details on schemas and using the schema editor. Here you can just load the schema file using the Samples Manager.

Now that the extension point structure has been defined, various bundles can contribute extensions that conform to the schema. Section 16.3, "Extensions," details the workflow for doing this.

SINGLETONS MAY BE REQUIRED

Notice that the `Bundle-SymbolicName` header in the bundle manifest now includes the parameter `singleton:=true`. This is needed in all bundles that contribute to the Extension Registry. For more details, see Section 16.4.1, "Contribution IDs."

The bundle contributing the extension point should also include some code that accesses any contributed extensions and implements its side of the contract. All extensions and extension points are maintained in an Extension Registry. The registry allows contributions to be navigated and looked up by name. The following snippet shows how the `ExtensionActionLookup` acquires actions:

```
org.equinoxosgi.toast.backend.portal/ExtensionActionLookup
public IPortalAction acquire(String id) {
  IConfigurationElement[] elements =
    registry.getConfigurationElementsFor(
      "org.equinoxosgi.toast.backend.portal.actions");
  for (int i = 0; i < elements.length; i++) {
    IConfigurationElement element = elements[i];
    if (id.equals(element.getAttribute("action")))
      try {
        return (IPortalAction)element.createExecutableExtension("class");
      } catch (CoreException e) {
        LogUtility.logError("Unable to instantiate action:", e);
      }
  }
  return null;
}
```

Looking through the code, we see that the method first uses the extension point's fully qualified ID to get a set of *configuration elements*. Configuration elements are object representations of the XML elements under the `<extension>` tag in the `plugin.xml` files; for example, the `<action>` markup in the previous example surfaces as a configuration element.

Accessing the registry as shown returns a list of the top-level configuration elements across all extensions contributed to the given extension point. This is convenient where the identity of the extensions and the number of configuration elements per extension are not important, as in this example.

The preceding snippet scans the set of configuration elements and contributed actions, and when it finds the one requested, it instantiates the class identified in the extension by calling `createExecutableExtension`. The result object is then used according to the contract of `IPortalAction`.

ACCESSING CODE IN OTHER BUNDLES

`createExecutableExtension` is a bit of magic code that delegates the loading of the identified class to the class loader associated with the bundle contributing the extension. In this way, bundles can contribute their own code or that of their prerequisite bundles, and the extension point bundle need not have any dependencies on the contributing bundles.

16.3 Extensions

Creating an extension is quite straightforward. As we've seen, each extension point has an associated schema that defines the structure of any contributed extension—the contract. The **New Extension** wizard and **Extensions** page in the bundle editor walk you through the process and validate your entries according to this schema.

To add the extension just described, edit the bundle that will contribute the extension. Here we will have the back-end-tracking UI bundle contribute one of its actions using an extension:

○ Open the `org.equinoxosgi.toast.backend.tracking.ui` manifest editor. On the **Extensions** page, click **Add...** and create an extension of type `org.equinoxosgi.toast.backend.portal.actions`.

○ Right-click on the extension and add an action using **New > action** from the context menu.

○ When you click on the newly added action element, the **Details** pane at the right shows the default values for the action. Update the **action** and **label** fields to match those shown in Figure 16-4.

○ Click on the **Browse...** button beside the **class** field and enter `TrackingAction` to identify the implementation for this action. Conveniently, since we wrote that action as a POJO, we can reuse it here.

Figure 16–4 Adding an action extension to the portal

If you need to create a class for the action, you could use the **class** link. This opens the **New Java Class** wizard with most of the fields, including the interface `IPortalAction`, already filled in. All you have to do is enter a class name.

16.3.1 Running the Sample

Running this new structure is very much the same as running the sample for Chapter 13, "Web Portal." You simply run the `backend.product` and then the `client.product` and wait for them to discover each other. At that point you can access http://localhost:8080/toast and view the backend portal and any active vehicles. The difference here is that at least some of the portal actions are being dispatched using the extension registry rather than the service registry.

16.4 Advanced Extension Topics

The Extension Registry has a number of advanced features put in place to handle specific situations. This section details some of these.

16.4.1 Contribution IDs

Extensions and extension points may have IDs. Traditionally developers needed to provide only a *simple ID*—just one word. The full ID of the contribution was then constructed by prepending the symbolic name of the bundle contributing the element. In this way the flat registry namespace could be managed and uniqueness guaranteed. This assumes, however, that the bundles contributing to the Extension Registry are *singletons*.

A singleton bundle is a bundle whose `Bundle-SymbolicName` header includes the directive `singleton:=true`. This indicates that the framework must resolve at most one bundle with this symbolic name even if multiple bundles with the same symbolic name are installed. All others are left unresolved and so do not participate in execution. As a result, there can be only one bundle of any give symbolic name, and the automatically created full contribution IDs cannot collide.

While beneficial, the automatic full qualification of IDs couples the registry contribution with the bundle making the contribution. This prevents replacement and refactoring. In practice today, developers are able to specify fully qualified extension and extension point IDs, and contributions are no longer tied to their contributor.

16.4.2 Named and Anonymous Extensions

Extensions need not have IDs. IDs are useful where direct and distinct extension access is needed, for example, if one part of the system identifies an extension to be used and another contributes that extension. It is convenient and efficient for the party in the middle to simply take the given ID, look up the corresponding extension, and use the data provided. To name an extension, simply give it an ID attribute as shown in this snippet:

```
some.bundle/plugin.xml
<extension
    id="coolstuff"
    point="org.equinoxosgi.toast.backend.portal.actions">
 ...
</extension>
```

The choice of whether or not to have named extensions is completely up to the party defining the extension point. The benefit of having IDs on extensions is that you can call the optimized IExtensionRegistry method, getExtension(String, String), to fetch a specific extension as opposed to having to traverse or remember the extensions yourself. For example, the previous code snippet repeatedly iterates over all contributed configuration elements to find the appropriate action, whereas if an ID were supplied, it could simply access the registry and directly look up the required extension.

While having a system-managed ID can be convenient and efficient, it can also limit you to one contribution per extension. Using anonymous extensions, for example, allows for any number of <action> elements in an extension to the org.equinoxosgi.toast.backend.portal.actions extension point. This is more concise and eliminates the need to manage a set of IDs that are not used.

There is no one answer here. Both anonymous and named extensions are widely used. Use whichever approach best suits your situation.

16.4.3 Extension Factories

In the previous example, the class to instantiate was given as a fully qualified class in the class attribute of the extension. This requires the identified class to implement a public zero-argument constructor and restricts the initialization that can be done on the resultant object. Another approach is to use an *extension factory* to create or discover the desired object or parameters to inject. Factories are useful as they allow more complex discovery and initialization. For example, one could implement a factory that uses OSGi service lookup or web service discovery to find suitable objects. Factories hide these implementation details from the extension point.

To use an extension factory, ensure that the class identified in the `class` attribute of the extension implements `IExecutableExtensionFactory`. When `createExecutableExtension` is called, this factory class is instantiated and the resultant factory is given the related configuration element. The factory then uses the information given to determine what kind of object to return. Note that the extension factory is free to decide how it creates the requested object. The Javadoc for `IExecutableExtension` and the individual factories details the acceptable syntax of the data following the factory name in the markup.

16.5 Extension Registry Lifecycle

The Extension Registry is tied to the RESOLVED lifecycle of bundles; that is, the extensions and extension points contributed by a bundle are woven into the Extension Registry when the contributing bundle is *resolved*—when all of its dependencies are met. Similarly, if the bundle subsequently becomes unresolved—say, when a prerequisite bundle is removed—its contributed extensions and extension points are removed from the registry. Section 23.6, "Bundle Lifecycle," gives more detail on the lifecycle of bundles.

STOPPING IS NOT ENOUGH

Stopping a bundle does not remove any Extension Registry contributions as the bundle remains resolved. This can be useful but can also lead to some unexpected behavior if you are used to the services lifecycle.

A bundle is generally resolved only once in a given system—when it is installed—and remains resolved between runs of the system; that is, it is resolved once but started many times as the system is stopped and started. Each time a bundle is (un)resolved, its contributions to the registry are updated, and `IRegistryChangeEvent` events containing `IExtensionDeltas` are broadcast to registered `IRegistryChangeListeners`. The API for these players is summarized in the following snippet. These lifecycle events are key to the proper management of dynamic behavior of your system. This is discussed in detail in the next section.

```
org.eclipse.equinox.registry
public interface IRegistryChangeListener extends EventListener {
   public void registryChanged(IRegistryChangeEvent event);
}

public interface IRegistryChangeEvent {
   public IExtensionDelta[] getExtensionDeltas();
   public IExtensionDelta[] getExtensionDeltas(String namespace);
   public IExtensionDelta[] getExtensionDeltas(
       String namespace, String extensionPoint);
   public IExtensionDelta getExtensionDelta(
       String namespace, String extensionPoint, String extension);
}

public interface IExtensionDelta {
   public int ADDED = 1;
   public int REMOVED = 2;

   public int getKind();
   public IExtension getExtension();
   public IExtensionPoint getExtensionPoint();
}
```

Given the infrequency of bundle-resolution-related events, and thus registry changes, it is quite easy for a registry implementation to cache its state and greatly reduce startup and access time. Similarly, the registry generates events only when bundles are resolved or unresolved, so there are relatively few registry change events broadcast, and the ones that are, can be batched to further reduce chatter.

16.6 Dynamic Extension Scenarios

Managing dynamic behavior in a system is challenging. We have dedicated an entire chapter, Chapter 21, "Dynamic Best Practices," to talk about this in detail. Here we talk about the issues specifically related to using the Extension Registry in dynamic environments.

The problems arise as a result of caching information from others in your bundle. Whether it is caching of the extension itself or of any objects created via executable extensions, the cache's coherence must be maintained; that is, where you use executable extensions to provide code, or descriptive extensions to provide data, dynamism is something to think about.

EXTENSIONS ARE DYNAMIC

It is sometimes said that extensions are less dynamic than services. Unfortunately it is just as easy to write a faulty system with services as with extensions. Caching services and not listening to the service registry is directly analogous to caching extensions and not listening to the Extension Registry. Declarative Services helps, as does the infrastructure described in this section.

Extensions are used throughout Eclipse. Equinox includes several extension points for contributed applications, servlets, repository providers, and so on. Section 18.3, "Declarative HTTP Content Registrations," gives an example of contributing Toast servlets and resources via two extension points:

```
org.eclipse.equinox.http.registry.servlets
org.eclipse.equinox.http.registry.resources
```

In that example, contributed extensions identify servlet classes or resource folders to be served by the HttpService. If the HTTP registry bundle was not dynamic-aware for addition, it might miss the addition of these extensions, and the Toast Back End would be unable to handle various client requests. If it was not dynamic-aware for removal, it would miss the removal of the extensions and continue trying to dispatch requests to servlets that are no longer active in the system.

The next three sections enumerate dynamic extension scenarios and how to handle them. In general, they revolve around whether or not the supplied extension is descriptive or executable and whether or not you cache values discovered in the registry or consult the registry each time you need something.

16.6.1 Scenario 1: No Caching

If your bundle consults the Extension Registry each time a value is needed, the burden of being dynamic-aware is substantially reduced. All data lives in and is maintained by the Extension Registry—no work for your bundle. The downside of this approach is that accessing the Extension Registry is likely slower than consulting an optimized, special-purpose data structure or cache in your bundle. If the extensions are accessed infrequently, however, this trade-off is reasonable.

The HTTP registry can use this approach if it registers proxy servlets with the HttpService and then dynamically instantiates the contributed extension servlet class for each request. In this way the HTTP registry never retains an instance of a contributed class. This is fine for small systems, but as the number of contributions increases, it becomes more expensive to find the extension whose alias matches the current request.

16.6.2 Scenario 2: Extension Caching

The performance of extension lookup can be improved by caching the structure of the extensions. For example, the HTTP registry could keep an explicit, in-memory table keyed by servlet alias where the value is the contributing extension. This table needs to be updated accordingly when a bundle contributing a servlet extension is added to the system. Similarly, if an existing bundle is removed, its contributed servlet extension must be removed from the table. Updating this cache is quite trivial—the changed key/value pair is simply added or removed.

This approach improves the time to access the extensions and find the correct servlet or resource class for a given request, but it suffers on two counts: First, it essentially duplicates the extension structure and data; and second, it requires additional infrastructure to implement dynamic awareness.

In some cases, there may be no choice. For example, some extension points such as the Eclipse Help system or the Resources bundle's *markers* extension point are used to create complex graphs of contributed elements. These structures must be computed rather than read directly from the Extension Registry, so they inherently require some level of caching. As such, the defining bundle must implement some dynamic-awareness support to clean up the cache when the set of resolved bundles changes. The cache cleanup is more complicated if the cached data structure is inherently interconnected.

As outlined in Section 16.5, "Extension Registry Lifecycle," the registry supports this need by broadcasting *registry change events* (IRegistryChangeEvent) to registered *registry change listeners* (IRegistryChangeListener) whenever Extension Registry contributions are added or removed. The listeners can then query an *extension delta* (IExtensionDelta) to find out what changed and how. This information is in turn used to update the cached data structures.

Updating the cache need not be a heavyweight operation. For example, if the cache is not critical and rebuilding is not overly expensive, flushing the entire cache on change is reasonable. This approach is sketched in the following code snippet:

```
public class ExtensionManager implements IRegistryChangeListener {
  private Map cache = null;
  public void registryChanged(IRegistryChangeEvent event) {
    cache = null;
  }
  private Map getCache() {
    Map result = cache;
    if (result == null)
      return initializeCache();
    return result;
  }
  public Object getExtension(String id) {
    return getCache().get(id);
  }
}
```

Registry change listeners are notified serially, but you still have to be concerned about threads accessing the cache while listeners are clearing it. The code in getCache gets a reference to the cache and uses that reference. The cache may be flushed at any point after that and the *old* value used. That's acceptable because there were no guarantees about ordering here anyway. Notice that this coding pattern closes the window between getting and testing the cache state, and returning the cache as the result.

Of course, another situation may not be that easy. If cache entries are expensive to rebuild, it is better to add and remove entries incrementally. The following snippet shows how to handle change events and traverse the deltas:

```
public void registryChanged(IRegistryChangeEvent event) {
  // get the changes for one of my extension points
  // and walk through processing the changes.
  IExtensionDelta delta[] = event.getExtensionDeltas(
      "org.eclipse.equinox.http.registry", "servlets");
  for (int i = 0; i < delta.length; i++)
    switch (delta[i].getKind()) {
      case IExtensionDelta.ADDED :
        // add an extension in some application-specific way
        cache.add(delta[i].getExtension());
        break;
      case IExtensionDelta.REMOVED :
        // remove an extension in some application-specific way
        cache.remove(delta[i].getExtension());
        break;
    }
}
```

Here, the listener queries the delta from the change event for any changes to the org.eclipse.equinox.http.registry.servlets extension point. For extension additions, you can choose to aggressively populate the cache with the new extensions or just ignore the additions and look for them later when you have a cache miss. For removals, you need to tear down any data structures and remove the extension from the cache.

16.6.3 Scenario 3: Object Caching

What happens if creating the contributed servlets is expensive? Even with extension caching, the contributed servlet class still has to be looked up and instantiated for each request. Assuming the servlets are properly context-free, one of each type could be cached and used to handle packets as required.

This kind of caching is different from and independent of the extension caching we saw in Scenario 2. Here the HTTP registry would hold on to the servlet class or instances. This prevents the contributing bundles from being properly garbage-collected. Furthermore, the created servlets cannot be left active when the contributor is removed, as they are likely to be invalid because its bundle has been shut down and removed.

LET THE REGISTRY DO THE CACHING

It is instructive to note that the Eclipse UI bundles have various extension points that cover each of these scenarios. Before the dynamic-awareness requirements were placed on the UI, it cached most extension information and created objects. In some cases, this resulted in duplicate information and inefficiencies. It also inhibited the registry's ability to flush its caches and adapt its space requirements to the current usage patterns. And, of course, it meant that the UI bundles would have to do considerably more work to be dynamic-aware. In the end, the approach was to remove the various levels of caching in the UI, whenever appropriate, and to rely on direct access to the Extension Registry or configuration elements.

If the HTTP registry is to be dynamic-aware, the servlets it instantiates must be tracked so they can be cleaned up if their contributor is removed. More generally, cached objects often play a deeper role in your system; that is, they may be woven tightly into the fabric of the application. The challenge is to understand the interconnections and ultimately reduce them so there is less to clean up.

To update the object structure, you can use the same sort of listener as the one described in Scenario 2. This time, however, the cache contains contributor-supplied objects (i.e., servlets). In the case of the HTTP registry, it turns out that there is only one reference to any given servlet. The Extension Registry change listener simply causes the unregistration of all servlets registered on behalf of the deleted extension. The following code snippet shows this in action:

```
public void registryChanged(IRegistryChangeEvent event) {
    IExtensionDelta delta[] = event.getExtensionDeltas(
        "org.eclipse.equinox.http.registry", "servlets");
    for (int i = 0; i < delta.length; i++)
        if (delta[i].getKind() == IExtensionDelta.REMOVED) {
            IExtension extension = delta[i].getExtension();
            IConfigurationElement[] elements =
                extension.getConfigurationElements();
            for (int j = 0; j < elements.length; j++) {
                IConfigurationElement element = elements[j];
                <code for unregistering the servlet>
            }
        }
}
```

To handle more complex situations, Equinox has utility classes that help with tracking and disposal of object references. In the next code snippet, the HttpRegistryManager implements IExtensionChangeHandler and registers itself with an IExtensionTracker to get notification of changes in select extensions.

Extension trackers track objects created for an extension. These objects might
be the result of using `IConfigurationElement.createExecutableExtension` or an
object created manually. Either way, the objects share the common trait that they
should be cleaned up when the related extension disappears.

org.eclipse.equinox.http.registry/HttpRegistryManager

```
public class HttpRegistryManager implements IExtensionChangeHandler {
  private IExtensionTracker tracker;

  public void start() {
    initializeTracker();
  }

  private void initializeTracker() {
    tracker = new ExtensionTracker();
    IFilter filter =
        ExtensionTracker.createNamespaceFilter(HTTPRegistry.ID);
    tracker.registerHandler(this, filter);
  }

  public void stop() {
    tracker.close();
  }

  public void addExtension(IExtensionTracker tracker,
      IExtension extension) {
    // new extensions are accessed on demand.
  }

  public void removeExtension(IExtension extension,
      Object[] objects) {
    for (int i = 0; i < objects.length; i++)
      removeServlet(objects[i]);
  }

  public Object getServlet (String elementName, String namespace,
      String type) {
    String point = "org.eclipse.equinox.http.registry.servlets";
    IConfigurationElement[] decls = Platform.getExtensionRegistry()
        .getConfigurationElementsFor(point);
    for (int i = 0; i < decls.length; i++) {
      IConfigurationElement element = decls[i];
      if (elementName.equals(element.getAttribute("elementName"))
          && namespace.equals(element.getAttribute("namespace"))) {
        try {
          Object servlet = element.createExecutableExtension("class");
          tracker.registerObject(element.getDeclaringExtension(),
              provider, IExtensionTracker.REF_WEAK);
          return addProvider(elementName, namespace, type, provider);
        } catch (CoreException e) {
          e.printStackTrace();
        }
      }
    }
```

```
    return null;
  }
}
```

SIMPLIFIED CODE

The HTTP registry code is actually much more complicated than what is shown here. The snippets used here are intended to show the general idea of how to manage the created objects.

Looking through the code from the top down, we see that `initializeTracker` creates an `ExtensionTracker` and adds the HTTP manager as a handler. Notice that the filter used means that the manager is notified of changes to extension points only in the HTTP registry bundle's namespace. You can narrow this to individual extension points, but this is good enough here.

The manager is notified of changes through `addExtension` and `removeExtension`. Generally it is preferable to create required objects on demand, so there is no work to do when extensions are added.

On removal, however, we do need to ensure that any created servlets are removed. The `removeExtensions` method receives a list of objects that the tracker is tracking relative to the given extension. This list is populated by the HTTP manager whenever it creates a servlet, as shown in `getServlet`. Ignoring the detail of how the servlet contribution is discovered, at some point, a class supplied by an extension is instantiated. The resultant object is then registered with the tracker using `registerObject`. The servlet is then added to the HTTP manager's internal data structure. It is this data structure that needs to be updated if the extension is removed. You saw that code in the method `removeExtension`.

Notice also that the tracker uses weak references (`REF_WEAK`) to track the servlets. This ensures that they do not stay live in the system just because they are being tracked.

The use of extension trackers is to some extent overkill in many cases, but the example gives you an idea of the mechanism's power. You can use one tracker to track many different extension points and many different objects. You can also use it as your primary data structure by calling `getObjects(IExtension)` to access all tracked objects for the given extension.

16.7 Services and Extensions

The OSGi service registry and the Equinox Extension Registry are both mechanisms that enable collaboration between bundles in a loosely coupled way. With the advent of DS, both support declarative specification of this collaboration, and both support dynamic behavior. So the obvious question is "Which do I use?" In short, "It depends."

There are some easy answers. For example, if you are integrating with other components and they already use one approach, consistency is likely a good thing. Some people find one approach simply more appealing than the other. If you can build your system with the level of flexibility and robustness you need, great.

At a purely functional level there are a few characteristics that can help you decide:

Lifecycle—As mentioned previously, the Extension Registry is driven by bundle resolution, whereas the service registry is driven by bundle activation. The former is coarser-grained and somewhat more difficult to control but can be simpler to comprehend and more performant. The latter offers more control but at the cost of more, and more frequent, lifecycle events.

Privacy—An extension point is intended for use by its contributing bundle. As such, extensions contributed to one extension point are not intended for use by other bundles. For example, `IPortalAction` extensions contributed to the portal's `actions` extension point are for use only by the portal. In contrast, the service registry is a global, flat namespace with no formalized partitioning mechanism.

Coupling—Traditionally the IDs attributed to extensions and extension points were automatically prefixed by the `Bundle-SymbolicName` of the contributing bundle. As such, contributing to a particular extension point implicitly coupled your bundle to the extension point bundle and limited your ability to substitute implementations. This default ID structure is not required by the Extension Registry, however. Extension and extension point contributors are free to define IDs in whatever namespace they want as long as the IDs are globally unique.

Singletons—Given the traditional coupling of contribution ID with `Bundle-SymbolicName`, bundles contributing to the Extension Registry are typically marked as singletons. Being a singleton means that only one version of a bundle with the associated symbolic name can be resolved at any given time. This is theoretically limiting but pragmatically seldom an issue.

16.7.1 Integrating Services and Extensions

Choosing either services or extensions is relatively easy. More difficult is the case where you need to use services and extensions together. Here there is a mismatch in expectations as both mechanisms vie for control of object discovery and creation lifecycle. Here we outline a few approaches for integrating the use of services and extensions.

16.7.1.1 Integrating Extensions into Service-Based Systems

Since the Extension Registry is driven by the bundle RESOLVED lifecycle and the service registry by the ACTIVE lifecycle, extensions are generally recognized and available before services. As such, integration is more a matter of surfacing extensions somehow as services.

> **DS enablement**—Declarative Services components can be enabled and disabled from code. Using this in conjunction with Extension Registry listeners, it is possible to surface extensions as components, and thus services, by enabling the components whenever related extensions are available. Factory components can also be used in this context. See Chapter 15, "Declarative Services," for more information on enablement and factory components.

16.7.1.2 Integrating Services into Extension-Based Systems

Integrating the service registry into extension-based systems is relatively easy if the extensions do not consume any services—the executable extension can simply be registered as a service, as we discuss later. If the extension requires some services, however, the lifecycles collide. It is possible to use the factory method to discover required services and inject them into the new object, but what if one or more of the services is not available? Depending on the dynamics of your system, one of the following approaches may work for you:

> **Executable extension factories**—The executable extension factories discussed in Section 16.4.3, "Extension Factories," can be used to look up and return a service from the service registry rather than instantiating a new object. This approach has the drawback that once a service is handed out to an anonymous Extension Registry user, it is hard to manage further service lifecycle events such as when the service is unregistered. This can be handled using transparent or explicit wrappers but may not be viable in all cases.

> **Manual service registration**—Extension implementations that know about the service registry can manually register services. This approach is taken in the Toast Client application. The application itself is contributed as an extension. Under the covers, our application code registers the implementation as an ICrustDisplay service.

> **Dynamic extensions**—The Extension Registry allows extensions and extension points to be contributed programmatically. This capability can be used

from, for example, DS components to register an extension only when its corresponding service is available and to unregister the extension when the service is unregistered.

16.8 Extension Registry Myths

There are a number of misconceptions about the Equinox Extension Registry. While no one tool is good for all purposes, it is worth clarifying the situation somewhat here.

Not pure—Some have argued against the Extension Registry by saying that it is not *pure* OSGi. It is true that the Extension Registry is not part of the OSGi specification spectrum. That is true, however, of 90 percent of any given OSGi system. OSGi is specifically designed to allow and encourage people to augment systems with more function. The purity discussion seems completely out of place.

Equinox-specific—The Extension Registry sees most of its use in the Equinox context. It has, however, been designed and implemented to be run on any OSGi framework implementation. In fact, it does not actually require OSGi at all and can be run as part of a normal Java application.

Tight coupling—Contributing to an extension point does not couple the contributor to the extension point host. Typically the default name qualification does introduce the host's symbolic name; however, it is possible for another bundle to supply an extension point with the same name, thus allowing the system to be reconfigured.

Bundle dependencies—A bundle that contributes an extension does not need to specify a dependency on the extension point host. Dependencies are expressed with respect to class loading. Bundles need only depend on packages and bundles supplying required code.

To be clear, we are not arguing for the use of the Extension Registry but rather for the use of the right tool for the job at hand.

16.9 Summary

The Equinox Extension Registry is a powerful, declarative, and lazy mechanism that facilitates collaboration between loosely coupled bundles. It allows for the clear definition of contracts between collaborators and is well supported by tooling that enforces the contracts. The Extension Registry is designed to support highly scalable systems with fast initial loading and incremental caching.

While the Extension Registry is similar in many respects to the OSGi service mechanism, there are semantic and lifecycle differences that make the technologies more or less applicable in different scenarios. There are a number of strategies for integrating the two stories, but none is perfect or universally applicable. In short, both extensions and services are great tools, and developers should choose what best suits their needs and integrate as necessary.

CHAPTER 17

Logging

The OSGi Log Service specification describes a way for a bundle to log messages. Logging is important for users, application administrators, support teams, and developers, regardless of the application domain. In this chapter we cover the following topics:

○ The logging services defined by the OSGi specification

○ Writing to, reading from, and being a listener of a log

○ How logging is done in Toast

○ Richer logging using Equinox's extended log service

17.1 The Log Service Specification

The OSGi Log Service specification describes two services. The first is the LogService used to *write* log messages, and the second is the LogReaderService used to *read* log messages; these services are a pair, potentially backed by a single implementation. An application may contain zero, one, or many pairs of logging services.

These services were designed when OSGi was conceived, so it was important to define an approach to logging that worked well in embedded applications running on constrained devices such as set-top boxes. The specification does not define how these services are implemented or the destination of logged messages. In fact, applications use these services to ensure that their logging strategy is pluggable and decoupled from logging implementations.

17.1.1 Logging Levels

As with most logging infrastructure, the OSGi `LogService` interface defines levels at which messages are logged.

> `LogService.LOG_DEBUG`—Used for problem determination and may be irrelevant to anyone but the bundle developer. The Log Service specification says that implementations may choose to ignore these messages.
>
> `LogService.LOG_INFO`—Used to log information messages that are considered normal and expected.
>
> `LogService.LOG_WARNING`—Indicates that the application is still functioning but may experience problems in the future because of the warning condition.
>
> `LogService.LOG_ERROR`—Indicates that the application may not be functional and that action should be taken to remedy the situation.

The specification defines loose semantics for the log levels, and it is the application that decides the level at which a message is logged, based on the perceived importance and audience of the message. Readers of the log can use the log level to decide how to handle each message.

17.1.2 Writing to the Log

The `LogService` provides API for writing to a log. Each method takes a level parameter as described in the preceding section. All other parameters may be `null`. The most commonly used methods are shown here:

```
org.osgi.service.log/LogService
log(int level, String message)
log(int level, String message, Throwable e);
```

These methods create an entry in the log that captures the message, the current time in milliseconds, the log level, and an optional exception. If the message being logged is related to an OSGi service, the following logging API can be used to provide additional context for the logged message:

```
org.osgi.service.log/LogService
log(ServiceReference ref, int level, String message);
log(ServiceReference ref, int level, String message, Throwable e);
```

Since these methods take an instance of the OSGi-defined `ServiceReference` class, they are typically inappropriate for use by POJO classes. Bundles traditionally obtained a `ServiceReference` object as a normal part of working with the OSGi service registry, but with the introduction of Declarative Services, `ServiceReference` objects are increasingly rare. For this reason, these methods are seldom used by application bundles.

While the ability to log only string messages might seem surprising, it was done for good reason. Allowing arbitrarily large objects to be logged, and potentially persisted, could be fatal for an application that is running on a constrained embedded device, such as a set-top box. As we will see in Section 17.5, "Equinox's LogService Implementations," the Equinox extended log service addresses this issue.

17.1.3 Reading the Log

A LogService is intended to be a *sink* for logged messages and is not intended to do anything other than store logged messages for eventual distribution to others. The LogReaderService, on the other hand, is intended for reading messages that have been written to the log.

The LogReaderService method getLog is used to poll the contents of the log. The method does not change the contents of the log, but rather it returns an Enumeration of immutable LogEntry objects, each of which describes a single entry in the log. It is not possible to change or remove a log entry, or to empty the log entirely. The LogEntry objects are ordered with the *most recent first*. The following LogEntry methods are available:

getBundle—Returns the Bundle that logged the entry, or null

getException—Returns the Throwable associated with the message, or null

getLevel—Returns the logging level at which the message was logged; see Section 17.1.1, "Logging Levels"

getMessage—Returns the logged message, or null

getServiceReference—Returns the ServiceReference associated with the logged message, or null

getTime—Returns the value of System.currentTimeMillis at the time the LogEntry was created

---

LOGGING AND THE EQUINOX CONSOLE

The Equinox console's log command is a handy way to check for recent problems. It calls the LogReaderService method getLog, writing each LogEntry to the console, ordered from oldest to newest.

Note that the log command uses a single LogReaderService, so you might not see every logged message if there are multiple pairs of logging services. Of course, there must be at least one LogReaderService for the log command to do anything useful.

17.1.4 Listening to the Log

As an alternative to polling the log, the `LogReaderService` allows an application to *listen for messages* by adding a `LogListener`. By listening to the log, the application is notified when a message is added to the log. The API to add and remove a `LogListener` is as follows:

org.osgi.service.log/LogReaderService
```
public void addLogListener(LogListener listener);
public void removeLogListener(LogListener listener);
```

The `LogListener` interface consists of the `logged(LogEntry)` method that is called when a message has been logged. Listeners are free to do whatever processing they like, but, as with all callbacks, care should be taken to return quickly.

17.2 Using the `LogService` in Toast

As an example of how Toast can use the `LogService`, let's look at Chapter 7, "Client/Server Interaction," and change the `FakeAirbag` so that it logs messages when it is started up, deployed, and shut down. Use the Samples Manager to load the code for Chapter 7.

Start by adding a reference to `LogService` in the DS component for `org.equinoxosgi.toast.dev.airbag`:

○ The `LogService` interface is defined by the bundle `org.eclipse.osgi.services`, so use the bundle manifest editor to add it to the **Automated Management of Dependencies** list of the `org.equinoxosgi.toast.dev.airbag` project.

○ Open the `org.equinoxosgi.toast.dev.airbag` component's `component.xml` and add the `LogService` as a referenced service.

○ Set the reference's cardinality to `0..1` and its policy to `dynamic`. Treating the `LogService` as optional makes sense since the `FakeAirbag` can function just fine without it.

○ Since we're using the `dynamic` reference policy, set the component's `bind` callback to `setLog` and its `unbind` callback to `clearLog`.

The component should look like this:

org.equinoxosgi.toast.dev.airbag/component.xml
```xml
<?xml version="1.0" encoding="UTF-8"?>
<scr:component xmlns:scr="http://www.osgi.org/xmlns/scr/v1.1.0"
    name="org.equinoxosgi.toast.dev.airbag"
    activate="startup" deactivate="shutdown">
  <implementation class=
    "org.equinoxosgi.toast.internal.dev.airbag.fake.FakeAirbag"/>
  <service>
```

```
      <provide interface="org.equinoxosgi.toast.dev.airbag.IAirbag"/>
    </service>
    <reference name="log"
      interface="org.osgi.service.log.LogService"
      cardinality="0..1" policy="dynamic"
      bind="setLog" unbind="clearLog"/>
  </scr:component>
```

Having updated the DS component, we now need to update its implementation class to use the LogService. Let's add some logging to the FakeAirbag class; the changes are shown here:

org.equinoxosgi.toast.dev.airbag/FakeAirbag
```
public class FakeAirbag implements IAirbag {
  ...
  private LogService log;

  private void deploy() {
    logInfo("deployed!");
    ...
  }

  public void shutdown() {
    ...
    logInfo("shutdown");
  }

  public void startup() {
    logInfo("startup");
    ...
  }

  ...

  private synchronized void logInfo(String message) {
    message = "FakeAirbag - " + message;
    LogService current = log;
    if (current != null)
      current.log(LogService.LOG_INFO, message);
    else
      System.out.println(message);
  }

  public void setLog(LogService value) {
    if (log != null)
      clearLog(log);
    log = value;
  }

  public void clearLog(LogService value) {
    if (log != value)
      return;
    log = null;
  }
}
```

The first thing to notice is that we've added a logInfo method that handles the class's logging needs. This method is called by startup, shutdown, and deployed. If available, logInfo logs to the LogService; otherwise it falls back to the System.out. The method also adds an identifier to the front of every logged message to make it easy to spot which class logged the message.

WORKING WITH DYNAMIC REFERENCED SERVICES

Did you notice that the FakeAirbag's logInfo method creates a local reference to the LogService that was bound to it? It does this to protect itself against the service being dynamically unbound while using it. This means that a message might get logged to an unbound LogService. It is the LogService implementation's responsibility to be able to gracefully handle such a scenario.

Let's now turn our attention to the component's bind and unbind callbacks. It is important for us to understand how DS behaves when using dynamic 0..1 referenced services. When a unary referenced service is dynamically bound and rebound, the order of events is as follows:

1. Bind a service—setLog(log1).
2. Bind a replacement service—setLog(log2).
3. Unbind the original service—clearLog(log1).

Once a LogService has been bound and the component's configuration satisfied, DS will *always try to rebind a replacement service before it unbinds the current service*. The setLog method takes care to call the clearLog method before allowing the field to be set when the log field is not null. While in this simple case calling clearLog is not necessary, this coding pattern is useful when unbinding from a dynamically referenced service requires cleanup such as removing a listener.

Correspondingly, the clearLog method sets the log field to null only if the service passed to it is *identical* to the service already cached in the log field. This ensures that step 3 does not undo the binding done in step 2.

To try out our changes, run the Toast client. You should see messages logged to the console when the airbag is started up, deployed, and shut down. However, without the org.eclipse.equinox.log bundle installed, Toast was not using logging at all.

Try again after adding the org.eclipse.equinox.log bundle to the launch configuration. This time you will see nothing in the console! Remember, the LogService is a message sink, so to see its contents, you need to use the console's log command or implement a component that uses `LogReaderService`, as discussed in the next section.

Separation of Concerns

Consider carefully before coupling your application to the OSGi Log Service interfaces. Creating a dependency on any OSGi-defined interface typically means that you need to include the OSGi interfaces, and possibly implementations, when packaging your application, even when it is executing outside the OSGi framework.

You should consider defining an application-specific logging API that can be implemented *in terms of* the OSGi service interface, as we do with the Toast `LogUtility`, discussed in Section 17.4, "Toast's `LogUtility` Class."

17.3 Using the `LogReaderService`

As we've just seen, writing to the `LogService` is fruitless unless the `LogReaderService` is available to retrieve logged messages and write them to a file, present them in a user interface, or send them to a server for processing. In this section we build a simple DS component that echoes logged messages to `System.out`.

Start by creating a project called `org.equinoxosgi.toast.core.log.reader` and add the DS component as shown here:

```
org.equinoxosgi.toast.core.log.reader/component.xml
<?xml version="1.0" encoding="UTF-8"?>
<scr:component xmlns:scr="http://www.osgi.org/xmlns/scr/v1.1.0"
    name="org.equinoxosgi.toast.core.log.reader"
    activate="startup" deactivate="shutdown">
    <implementation class="org.equinoxosgi.toast.internal.core.log.
        reader.ToastLogReader"/>
    <reference name="reader"
      interface="org.osgi.service.log.LogReaderService"
      bind="setReader"/>
</scr:component>
```

As soon as the referenced `LogReader` service is available, DS will create an instance of its implementation class, `ToastLogReader`, and activate it by calling the startup method. The class `ToastLogReader` is shown here:

```
org.equinoxosgi.toast.core.log.reader/ToastLogReader
public class ToastLogReader implements LogListener {
  private LogReaderService reader;

  // LogListener callback
  public void logged(LogEntry entry) {
```

```
        StringBuffer buffer = new StringBuffer(250);
        buffer.append(entry.getMessage());
        buffer.append(", Bundle=");
        String name = bundle.getSymbolicName();
        buffer.append(name);
        System.out.println(buffer);
    }

    public void setReader(LogReaderService value) {
        reader = value;
    }

    public void shutdown() {
        reader.removeLogListener(this);
    }

    public void startup() {
        reader.addLogListener(this);
    }
}
```

When activated, the startup method adds the ToastLogReader as a listener of
the LogReaderService. As messages are logged, the LogReaderService notifies its
listeners by calling their logged method, passing a LogEntry that describes the
logged message.

ToastLogReader implements LogListener, and its logged method simply uses
the information from the supplied entry—for example, the message and the bundle from which the message was logged—to build an appropriately formatted
message that it writes to System.out.

When deactivated, the shutdown method removes the ToastLogReader as a listener of the LogReaderService.

Running the Toast Client with Equinox's org.eclipse.equinox.log bundle
and our org.equinoxosgi.toast.core.log.reader bundle included in the launch
configuration gives output similar to what follows. Notice that the LogService is
being used much more than we ever realized. The property manager is logging
accesses and the framework is logging service, bundle, and framework events.

```
[DEBUG] 2009-09-19 23:08:16.640 - Property:
  -Dtoast.backend.url=http://localhost:8080/toast
ServiceEvent REGISTERED, Bundle=org.eclipse.equinox.ds
BundleEvent STARTED, Bundle=org.eclipse.equinox.ds
BundleEvent STARTED, Bundle=org.eclipse.osgi
FrameworkEvent STARTED, Bundle=org.eclipse.osgi
FrameworkEvent STARTLEVEL CHANGED, Bundle=org.eclipse.osgi
FakeAirbag - deployed!, Bundle=org.equinoxosgi.toast.dev.airbag
2009-09-19 23:08:21.687 - Property: -Dtoast.id=ABC123,
  Bundle=org.equinoxosgi.toast.core
2009-09-19 23:08:21.687 - UrlChannel:
  http://localhost:8080/toast/emergency?id=ABC123&speed=50&
```

```
longitude=-12244694&latitude=3776999&heading=90,
Bundle=org.equinoxosgi.toast.core
2009-09-19 23:08:21.687 - UrlChannel: Sending message: emergency,
Bundle=org.equinoxosgi.toast.core
2009-09-19 23:08:22.656 - EmergencyMonitor: Unable to send to back end:
Connection refused: connect,
Bundle=org.equinoxosgi.toast.core
```

Even this is only a partial list. It turns out that org.eclipse.equinox.log, org.equinoxosgi.toast.core.log.reader, and its prerequisite, the DS bundle org.eclipse.equinox.ds, are not starting early enough. As a result, some logged messages are being missed or potentially falling off the back of Equinox LogService's in-memory buffer. To remedy this, launch Toast again, but this time set the start level for these bundles to 1 so that they start before the other bundles. Now the console will show considerably more logged messages, too many, in fact, to show here.

While we generally do not recommend that you use OSGi's start levels, this is perhaps one of the few legitimate reasons for doing so—setting up system utilities that are widely used and need to be in place early.

17.4 Toast's LogUtility Class

Having learned all about the OSGi log services, you might be wondering why Toast does not appear to use the LogService. In fact, it does, but it does so through the singleton class org.equinoxosgi.toast.core.LogUtility. Here are some of the reasons for this structure:

Historical—Toast predates the availability of DS. Toast was originally built using the Service Activator Toolkit (SAT), which provided its own LogUtility singleton. When we moved Toast to use DS, we decided not to change its approach to logging and instead ported SAT's LogUtility to Toast.

Simplicity—Requiring every DS component to reference the LogService is not the simplest thing that could possibly work. We like to keep our code simple, and logging is something that we believe does not fit well as a service.

Logging is pervasive—Logging is needed throughout an application. If Toast were to use the LogService, it would be necessary to pass it from each component's implementation class down into the various domain abstractions, which is more work and more complicated than we need.

Using the LogUtility is simple. Since the class is a singleton, residing in an exported package, every Toast bundle can reference it by importing the package. The LogUtility provides a variety of static methods that make logging easy.

If you look at the bundle org.equinoxosgi.toast.core, you'll see that it contains an immediate DS component that specifies the LogService as an optional and unary referenced service:

org.equinoxosgi.toast.core/component.xml
```
<?xml version="1.0" encoding="UTF-8"?>
<scr:component xmlns:scr="http://www.osgi.org/xmlns/scr/v1.1.0"
    name="org.equinoxosgi.toast.core">
  <implementation class=
    "org.equinoxosgi.toast.internal.core.Component"/>
  <reference name="log"
    interface="org.osgi.service.log.LogService"
    cardinality="0..1" policy="dynamic"
    bind="setLog" unbind="clearLog"/>
</scr:component>
```

This is the same pattern we saw before, but implemented in one place and shared among the Toast bundles. Similarly, the component's implementation class injects the referenced LogService into the LogUtility singleton. The LogUtility's logging methods use the LogService when it is available and falls back to logging to System.out when it is not.

17.5 Equinox's LogService Implementations

The Equinox bundle org.eclipse.equinox.log provides an implementation of the LogService and LogReaderService interfaces. Equinox's LogService is a circular in-memory buffer with a default size of 100 entries. The buffer's size can be configured dynamically at runtime using the ConfigurationAdmin service, which is discussed in Chapter 12, "Dynamic Configuration."

In Equinox 3.5 the ExtendedLogService and ExtendedLogReaderService interfaces were introduced. These interfaces are not part of the OSGi specification but do add some useful logging capabilities:

○ Logging of an arbitrary Object, known as the *context*, rather than just simple message strings; for example, it is now possible to log org.eclipse.core.runtime.IStatus objects

○ Support for multiple named loggers

○ The use of an ExtendedLogEntry to capture the log context, details of the thread on which the log entry was made, and a sequence number for the log entry

○ Enabling integration with other logging frameworks, such as Apache's Commons Logging and log4j and the Equinox logging infrastructure

The `Logger` interface declares the new logging APIs and allows us to have named logs:

```
org.eclipse.equinox.log/Logger
public interface Logger {
  public void log(int level, String message);
  public void log(int level, String message, Throwable e);
  public void log(ServiceReference ref, int level, String message);
  public void log(ServiceReference ref, int level, String message,
      Throwable e);
  public void log(Object context, int level, String message);
  public void log(Object context, int level, String message,
      Throwable e);
  public boolean isLoggable(int level);
  public String getName();
}
```

The `ExtensionLogService` interface extends the `Logger` interface to add API for locating a particular `Logger`, as shown in the following snippet. Note that to use the default, anonymous logger, you can pass `null` to `getLogger` or use `Logger`'s inherited `log` methods.

```
org.eclipse.equinox.log/ExtendedLogService
public interface ExtendedLogService extends LogService, Logger {
  public Logger getLogger(String name);
  public Logger getLogger(Bundle bundle, String name);
}
```

The `ExtendedLogReaderService` interface extends the `LogReaderService` interface with the ability to add a `LogListener` that is notified only of logged messages that match a specified `LogFilter`.

```
org.eclipse.equinox.log/ExtendedLogReaderService
public interface ExtendedLogReaderService extends LogReaderService {
  public void addLogListener(LogListener listener, LogFilter filter);
}
```

```
org.eclipse.equinox.log/LogFilter
public interface LogFilter {
  public boolean isLoggable(Bundle bundle, String name, int logLevel);
}
```

Finally, the `ExtendedLogEntry` interface extends the `LogEntry` interface, adding API for querying the name of the logger, the context, thread details, and sequence number:

```
org.eclipse.equinox.log/ExtendedLogEntry
public interface ExtendedLogEntry extends LogEntry {
  public String getLoggerName();
  public Object getContext();
  public long getThreadId();
```

```
    public String getThreadName();
    public long getSequenceNumber();
}
```

The `ToastLogReader` class from Section 17.3 might use Equinox's `ExtendedLogService`, and specifically its `ExtendedLogEntry` class, as shown here:

```
org.equinoxosgi.toast.core.log.reader/ToastLogReader
public void logged(LogEntry entry) {
    StringBuffer buffer = new StringBuffer(250);
    buffer.append(entry.getMessage());
    Bundle bundle = entry.getBundle();
    buffer.append(", Bundle=");
    String name = bundle.getSymbolicName();
    buffer.append(name);
    if (entry instanceof ExtendedLogEntry) {
        ExtendedLogEntry xEntry = (ExtendedLogEntry) entry;
        Object context = xEntry.getContext();
        if (context != null) {
            buffer.append(", Context=");
            buffer.append(context);
        }
        buffer.append(", Thread=");
        buffer.append(xEntry.getThreadName());
    }
    System.out.println(buffer);
}
```

By querying the actual type of the `LogEntry` object, it is able to handle the case where it's really an instance of `ExtendedLogEntry` and provide enhanced log output.

17.6 Summary

Logging is an important part of every application since it provides a way to communicate important information to developers, support teams, administrators, and users. Logging should not be an afterthought, but rather it should be designed into an application, with the ability to redirect or handle logged messages differently depending on the need.

We showed how the OSGi Log Service specification describes a small-scale, loosely coupled, and pluggable approach to logging. We also showed how to correctly read from and listen to the OSGi log services to ensure that logged messages are observed and handled correctly. This was demonstrated in a DS component that uses the `LogReaderService` to listen to the log and writes each logged message to `System.out`.

Finally, we discussed Equinox's `ExtendedLogService` and saw how it can be used to provide richer log content and to integrate with other logging frameworks.

CHAPTER 18

HTTP Support

In Chapter 7, "Client/Server Interaction," we saw how to set up a simple client/server system using the OSGi HttpService. In Chapter 12, "Dynamic Configuration," Toast used the HttpService to present a simple web UI for configuring the client's tracking frequency. In this chapter we take a deeper look at this service and how to make the most of its capabilities.

The HttpService has been part of the OSGi specification since its inception. It allows applications to register servlets and resources to be served in response to HTTP requests. Since OSGi has always been about network-aware gateway devices, support for HTTP makes sense. In the broader enterprise and distributed application context, HTTP has proved to be a good choice of network protocol since it is lightweight, simple, and stateless.

In this chapter we assume a rudimentary understanding of Java servlets and HTTP and focus on the details of the HttpService. By the end of the chapter you will know about

- The HttpService API
- Registering and unregistering servlets and resources programmatically and declaratively
- Launching and testing HTTP content
- Using HTTP contexts to add security and Java Authentication and Authorization Service (JAAS) integration
- Using the Jetty-based HttpService implementation

18.1 The HttpService

HTTP has become a staple of system design, from web browsing to web services and RESTful interactions—it can be hard to find an application that does not involve HTTP in some way. Applications that act as clients can use the built-in JRE socket and URL support or something like the Apache HttpClient. Systems that need to handle HTTP requests, however, need more support.

Traditionally this support has come in the shape of either embedding an HTTP server such as Jetty in the application or running the application as part of an application server such as Tomcat, Jetty, or WebSphere. These approaches make assumptions about lifecycle and class loading that conflict with the OSGi model—they are not inherently modular.

The OSGi HttpService, however, was designed explicitly to tie into the OSGi modularity story and allow developers to compose server functionality by installing bundles just as they would in a client system. Using the HttpService, developers are insulated from the infrastructure used to service requests and can focus on their domain logic. Chapter 19, "Server Side," talks more about this. Here we show how to use the service to define and manage HTTP-based content.

18.1.1 Concepts

There are three main concepts at play in the HttpService:

Content—The bytes to be served in response to requests. These can be statically or dynamically determined. Static content, *resources*, is just files or other data that is served blindly. Dynamic content is implemented using traditional servlet structures.

Location—HTTP-based content is accessed via URLs. When registering some content, developers must specify the location of that content in URL space, the so-called *alias*.

Context—All requests are processed in a context. The context defines how the request is processed—for example, the mapping from URL to local resource location or security and authentication requirements.

The HttpService surfaces control of each concept by allowing content to be registered at a particular alias in a defined context. The service itself has a simple API, as shown in the following snippet:

```
org.osgi.service.http/HttpService
public interface HttpService {
  public HttpContext createDefaultHttpContext();
  public void registerResources(String alias, String name,
    HttpContext context) throws NamespaceException;
```

```
    public void registerServlet(String alias, Servlet servlet,
        Dictionary initparams, HttpContext context)
        throws ServletException, NamespaceException;
    public void unregister(String alias);
}
```

createDefaultHttpContext—This method creates and returns a default context for processing HTTP requests. This is needed only when implementing your own `HttpContext`. See Section 18.5, "HTTP Contexts and JAAS Integration," for more detail.

registerResources—This method is used to register static content from a bundle under a unique alias.

registerServlet—This method is used to register an instance of `Servlet` with the `HttpService` under a unique alias.

unregister—This method unregisters the previously registered servlet or resource from the given alias.

SUPPORTED HTTP VERSION

The OSGi Service Compendium states that the `HttpService` can be based on either HTTP 1.0 or HTTP 1.1, or some other protocol, so long as it supports the `javax.servlet` API. This is because the `HttpService` must support at least version 2.1 of the Java Servlet API.

18.2 Registering and Unregistering a Servlet

As an example of using the `HttpService`, we're going to look back at Toast's `org.equinoxosgi.toast.client.tracking.config` bundle from Chapter 12, "Dynamic Configuration." The DS component for this bundle references the `HttpService` as follows:

```
org.equinoxosgi.toast.client.tracking.config/component.xml
<?xml version="1.0" encoding="UTF-8"?>
<scr:component xmlns:scr="http://www.osgi.org/xmlns/scr/v1.1.0"
    name="org.equinoxosgi.toast.client.tracking.config"
    activate="startup" deactivate="shutdown">
  <implementation class="org.equinoxosgi.toast.internal.client.
      tracking.config.bundle.Component"/>
  <reference name="http"
    interface="org.osgi.service.http.HttpService"
    bind="setHttp"/>
```

```
  <reference name="configAdmin"
    interface="org.osgi.service.cm.ConfigurationAdmin"
    bind="setConfigAdmin"/>
</scr:component>
```

As this is an immediate component, DS will instantiate and activate it as soon as its configuration is satisfied. The Component class is shown here:

org.equinoxosgi.toast.client.tracking.config/Component
```
public class Component {
  private static final String SERVLET_ALIAS_ROOT_PROPERTY =
    "servlet.alias.root";
  private static final String SERVLET_ALIAS_ROOT_DEFAULT =
    "/client";
  private static final String SERVLET_SUFFIX = "/tracking-config";

  private String servletAlias;
  private String resourceAlias;
  private HttpService http;
  private ConfigurationAdmin configAdmin;

  public void setHttp(HttpService value) {
    http = value;
  }

  public void setConfigAdmin(ConfigurationAdmin value) {
    configAdmin = value;
  }

  protected void startup() {
    try {
      String servletAliasRoot = PropertyManager.getProperty(
          SERVLET_ALIAS_ROOT_PROPERTY, SERVLET_ALIAS_ROOT_DEFAULT);
      servletAlias = servletAliasRoot + SERVLET_SUFFIX;
      String id = PropertyManager.getProperty(
          ICoreConstants.ID_PROPERTY, ICoreConstants.ID_DEFAULT);
      TrackingConfigServlet servlet =
        new TrackingConfigServlet(servletAlias, id, configAdmin);
      http.registerServlet(servletAlias, servlet, null, null);

      resourceAlias = servletAlias + "/images";
      http.registerResources(resourceAlias,
          "/resources/images", null);
      LogUtility.logDebug("Registered TrackingConfigServlet at " +
        servletAlias);
    } catch (Exception e) {
      LogUtility.logError(this,
          "Error registering servlet with HttpService", e);
    }
  }

  protected void shutdown() {
    http.unregister(servletAlias);
  }
}
```

The startup method creates an instance of TrackingConfigServlet and uses the HttpService's registerServlet method to register the servlet under the alias /client/tracking-config. The registerServlet method takes the following parameters:

alias—The location in URL space at which the servlet lives

servlet—The servlet object to register

initparams—Initialization arguments for the servlet, or null if there are none; this argument is used by the servlet's ServletConfig object

context—The HttpContext object for the registered servlet, or null if a default HttpContext is to be created and used

---

SEPARATION OF CONCERNS

The reason for using a separate Component class as opposed to using the TrackingConfigServlet as the component's implementation is the desire to keep the TrackingConfigServlet as a pure HttpServlet. This way the Component class deals with the URL and the servlet alias that servlets should not know about.

The startup method also calls the HttpService's registerResources method to register the path /resources/images as the place in the bundle to look to fulfill resources requested from the URI /client/tracking-config/images (see Figure 18-1). The method registerResources takes three parameters:

alias—The location in URL space at which the resources reside

name—The bundle-relative location of the resources that are being registered

context—The HttpContext object for the registered resources, or null if a default HttpContext is to be created and used

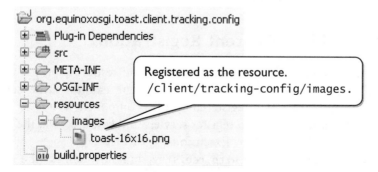

Figure 18–1   The registered bundle resources

The alias parameter is the resource's *logical location*, whereas the name parameter is the resource's *physical location* in the bundle. Separating the resource's logical location from its physical location allows the resources to be reorganized inside the bundle without affecting the URLs used by clients to access them.

When the Toast Client is launched and a web browser is pointed at http://localhost:8081/client/tracking-config, the page shown in Figure 18-2 is displayed.

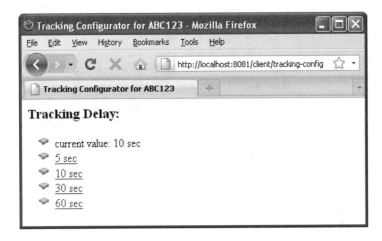

Figure 18–2   Toast's tracking config servlet, with image resources

---

CONFIGURING THE HTTP PORT

By default the HttpService listens on port 80, but in this case we have set the Java system property org.osgi.service.http.port to 8081 using the following VM argument: -Dorg.osgi.service.http.port=8081.

18.3 Declarative HTTP Content Registrations

So far we've discussed how to register a servlet and resources programmatically via the API provided by the HttpService. In our examples the servlet and resources are registered and unregistered by a DS component as it is activated and deactivated. It is also possible to register servlets and resources via the Extension Registry, as seen in Chapter 16, "Extensions."

The org.eclipse.equinox.http.registry bundle defines the following extension points:

`org.eclipse.equinox.http.registry.servlets`—Used to register a servlet, defined by the specified Java class, at the given alias

`org.eclipse.equinox.http.registry.resources`—Used to register a resource, identified by the given path within the bundle, at the given alias

Using extensions has the benefit that registering the servlet and the resources requires no class loading and no object creation. Even the creation of the servlet is delayed until the `HttpService` receives the first HTTP request for the servlet. Now that the registrations are performed declaratively, it is no longer necessary to have a DS component class. This results in fewer dependencies on other bundles and faster loading.

To use the Equinox Extension Registry for contributing to the `HttpService` from within Equinox, the following bundles should be added to your product or launch configuration:

```
org.eclipse.equinox.common
org.eclipse.equinox.registry
org.eclipse.equinox.http.registry
```

18.4 Using Jetty

Equinox supplies a simple HTTP service implementation in the bundle `org.eclipse.equinox.http`. This is a compact and lightweight implementation of the OSGi standard based on the Servlet 2.1 specification. For much of Toast this is sufficient. However, if your requirements go beyond the 2.1 standard—using more modern servlets, JSPs, tag libs, and so on—you need a different HTTP service. Fortunately, the Equinox project also supplies an HTTP service implementation based on Jetty.

Jetty is a highly embeddable, high-performance, open-source servlet engine used by hundreds of thousands of web sites on the internet and countless more internal and embedded systems. The project's focus on integration with the surrounding system makes Jetty an ideal candidate for use in OSGi systems.

JETTY@ECLIPSE

After years of independent development, the Jetty project moved to be part of the Eclipse RT Project in mid-2009. While we anticipate deeper Equinox and OSGi integration, the version of Jetty shipped with Eclipse is used here.

The version of Jetty that comes with the Equinox SDK is available as a set of OSGi bundles—simply drop these into an OSGi system and use the Jetty API. The

Equinox project provides an implementation of the OSGi HttpService based on Jetty in the org.eclipse.equinox.http.jetty bundle. This bundle is included in the Equinox SDK that you have been using in your target platform. The Jetty-based HttpService has been enhanced to support running both static and dynamic JavaServer Pages (JSPs) using Jetty's built-in support.

To add Jetty as the basis for the client's HTTP requirements, open the client.product and replace the old HTTP bundle, org.eclipse.equinox.http, with the following Jetty bundles:

```
org.eclipse.equinox.http.jetty
org.eclipse.equinox.http.servlet
org.mortbay.jetty.server
org.mortbay.jetty.util
```

Now the configuration management web UI can be updated to make use of JSPs, tag libs, and AJAX frameworks such as Dojo. For even more advanced UIs, you can use the Eclipse Rich Ajax Platform (RAP) technology to get RCP-like function in the browser from one code base.

18.5 HTTP Contexts and JAAS Integration

It is quite common in various HTTP scenarios to require users to log in. Fortunately, Equinox includes support of standard JAAS integration. This functionality is found in the org.eclipse.equinox.security.* bundles in the Equinox SDK. In this section we combine JAAS support with the HttpService's HttpContext facilities to add HTTP basic authentication to protect the configuration of the Toast Client.

18.5.1 Basic HTTP Authentication and Login

HTTP manages security through the *HTTP context* used when processing servlet and resource requests. This context is supplied when registering a servlet with the HTTP service. Until now we have just been passing null for the context argument—letting the HttpService use its default context. Here we update the Toast Client's configuration management servlet from Chapter 12, "Dynamic Configuration," to require logins.

SECURITY REQUIRES JETTY

The use of HTTP contexts to add authentication security requires the use of the Jetty-based HttpService. As such, the instructions here assume that you have adopted Jetty as described in Section 18.4, "Using Jetty."

To add security, we need to supply our own context to ensure that the user is logged in for every request. In particular, we need an implementation of `HttpContext.handleSecurity`. The following code snippet sketches an implementation of this method for the HTTP Basic authentication method. For the full code, look at `SecureBasicHttpContext` in the `org.equinoxosgi.toast.core.security` bundle from the sample code.

org.equinoxosgi.toast.core.security/SecureBasicHttpContext
```
public boolean handleSecurity(
        HttpServletRequest request, HttpServletResponse response)
        throws IOException {
  String auth = request.getHeader("Authorization");
  if (auth == null)
    return failAuthorization(request, response);

  StringTokenizer tokens = new StringTokenizer(auth);
  String authscheme = tokens.nextToken();
  if (!authscheme.equals("Basic"))
    return failAuthorization(request, response);

  String base64 = tokens.nextToken();
  String credentials = new String(Base64.decode(base64.getBytes()));
  int colon = credentials.indexOf(':');
  String userid = credentials.substring(0, colon);
  String password = credentials.substring(colon + 1);
  Subject subject = null;
  try {
    subject = login(request, userid, password);
  } catch (LoginException e) {
    // do nothing
  }
  if (subject == null)
    return failAuthorization(request, response);
  request.setAttribute(HttpContext.REMOTE_USER, userid);
  request.setAttribute(HttpContext.AUTHENTICATION_TYPE, authscheme);
  request.setAttribute(HttpContext.AUTHORIZATION, subject);
  return true;
}
```

The method first confirms that the request is using the Basic authentication method. It then decodes the authentication information—user name and password—and attempts a login using these credentials. If the login is successful, the request is configured with the authorization information.

The login code hooks into the JAAS infrastructure, as shown in the following snippet. Here the code first checks to see if there is already a session associated with the request and if that session has already been authenticated. If so, there is nothing more to do. If not, we need to create and configure a login context.

org.equinoxosgi.toast.core.security/SecureBasicHttpContext
```
private Subject login(HttpServletRequest request, final String userid,
    final String password) throws LoginException {
```

```
HttpSession session = request.getSession(false);
if (session == null)
  return null;
ILoginContext context =
    (ILoginContext) session.getAttribute("securitycontext");
if (context != null)
  return context.getSubject();

context = LoginContextFactory.createContext(
    "SimpleConfig", configFile, new CallbackHandler() {
  public void handle(Callback[] callbacks)
      throws IOException, UnsupportedCallbackException {
    for (int i = 0; i < callbacks.length; i++) {
      Object cb = callbacks[i];
      if (cb instanceof NameCallback)
        ((NameCallback) cb).setName(userid);
      else if (cb instanceof PasswordCallback)
        ((PasswordCallback) cb).setPassword(password.toCharArray());
      else
        throw new UnsupportedCallbackException(cb);
    }
  }
});
session.setAttribute("securitycontext", context);
return context.getSubject();
}
```

The login context is used to tell JAAS how and where to get passwords as well as how to validate the credentials. The how and where are defined in the configFile argument to createContext. This file is supplied by the system driving the security policy—in our case the client itself. In more sophisticated systems the configuration would be done in a more centrally managed place. The following text shows the simple configuration file used here:

org.equinoxosgi.toast.client.tracking.config/jaas_config.txt
```
SimpleConfig {
  org.eclipse.equinox.security.auth.module.ExtensionLoginModule
      required
  debug="true"
  extensionId="org.equinoxosgi.toast.core.security.simpleLogin";
};
```

The jaas_config.txt file defines a SimpleConfig element that consists of a class that implements the JAAS LoginModule interface and a set of properties. This login module uses the Equinox Extension Registry to discover further login module implementations to which it delegates. In particular, here we are using the simpleLogin extension supplied by the Toast security bundle.

INDIRECTION YIELDS FLEXIBILITY

The indirection in these definitions is a little confusing but ultimately quite powerful. It allows us to have one bundle that defines, for example, basic HTTP authentication behavior, other bundles that define login modules, and a third that puts it all together to form an authentication solution.

The `simpleLogin` extension identified in the configuration file ultimately points to the `SimpleLoginModule` code shown here:

```
org.equinoxosgi.toast.core.security/SimpleLoginModule
public boolean login() throws LoginException {
  final Callback[] callbacks = {
      new NameCallback("Username"),
      new PasswordCallback("Password", false)};
  handler.handle(callbacks);

  String name = ((NameCallback) callbacks[0]).getName();
  String password =
      new String(((PasswordCallback) callbacks[1]).getPassword());
  if ("user".equals(name) && "password".equals(password)) {
    user = createUser(callbacks);
    return true;
  }
  throw new LoginException("Login failed");
}
```

When `login` is called by the system, it requests the needed information by posting a set of callbacks. The login context we saw before handles the callbacks by filling in the user name and password from the basic authentication credentials of the current request. Our login module then checks the supplied values to see if they are valid. In this simple case we just have a hard-coded "user" with a "password." Clearly other login modules would do more sophisticated validation by consulting the operating system or enterprise directory servers.

18.5.2 Running the Secured Client

It is time to update the client to hook in the new authentication support. Setting up security in the client is easy—just update the place where the configuration management web UI content, the servlet and resources, is registered; that is, update the `Component` class's `startup` method as shown in this snippet:

```
org.equinoxosgi.toast.client.tracking.config/Component
protected void startup(ComponentContext context) {
  ...
```

```
    Bundle bundle = context.getBundleContext().getBundle();
    URL resourceBase = bundle.getEntry("");
    URL configFile = bundle.getEntry("jaas_config.txt");
    HttpContext httpContext = new SecureBasicHttpContext(
        resourceBase, configFile, "Toast Client Configuration");
    http.registerServlet(servletAlias, servlet, null, httpContext);
}
```

The essential change is to instantiate the SecureBasicHttpContext discussed previously and use it in all HttpService register* calls. The context is created using the root of the resource content in the bundle and the example configuration file, jaas_config.txt. At this point it is worthwhile to make sure that the jaas_config.txt file is in the tracking configuration bundle and that the bundle's build.properties file includes it in the list of binary build resources, as discussed in Chapter 9, "Packaging."

Now open client.product and add the bundles required for security:

```
org.eclipse.equinox.preferences
org.eclipse.equinox.security
org.equinoxosgi.toast.core.security
```

Check that you have added the Jetty bundles as discussed in Section 18.4, "Using Jetty" then save everything and run the client product. When you go to the tracking configuration page at http://localhost:8081/client/tracking-config, you should first be prompted to log in to the Toast Client Management realm, as shown in Figure 18-3. Supply "user" and "password" as the credentials to configure the client's tracking behavior as before.

Figure 18–3   Client tracking configuration login dialog

18.6 Troubleshooting

This section discusses some problems that are commonly encountered while working with the HttpService.

18.6.1 `BindException`

During the course of development it is common to see the following exception when launching the OSGi framework:

```
java.net.BindException: Address already in use: JVM_Bind
    at java.net.PlainSocketImpl.socketBind
    at java.net.PlainSocketImpl.bind
    at java.net.ServerSocket.bind
    at java.net.ServerSocket.<init>
    at org.eclipse.equinox.http.HttpServerSocket.<init>
```

This exception means that the `HttpService` was unable to bind to the port on which it was told to listen because the port is already being used by another application. The most common cause of this is another running JVM that you forgot to terminate. The Eclipse Console view can be used to find and terminate previously launched JVM instances.

In cases where the cause is not another JVM, you'll need to rely on some detective work to find which process is using the port. A useful command-line utility that works on Windows, Macintosh, and Linux is `netstat`, which displays the ports that are in use and by which processes. For example, try the following command:

```
netstat -anb
Active Connections
  Proto  Local Address   Foreign Address State     PID
  TCP    0.0.0.0:80      0.0.0.0:0       LISTENING 3188 [javaw.exe]
```

18.6.2 On Which Port Is the `HttpService` *Listening?*

Sometimes it is helpful find out on which port the `HttpService` is listening. The easiest way is to launch the OSGi framework with the `-console` command-line option and use the Equinox console to query the properties of the `org.eclipse.equinox.http` bundle. Use the `bundle` command to display the details of the `org.eclipse.equinox.http` bundle:

```
osgi> bundle org.eclipse.equinox.http
initial@reference:file:plugins/org.eclipse.equinox.http.jar/ [4]
  Id=4, Status=ACTIVE
  Registered Services
    {org.osgi.service.http.HttpService}={
      http.port=80,
      service.pid=org.eclipse.equinox.http.HttpService-http,
      http.address=ALL,
      service.vendor=IBM,
      service.description=OSGi Http Service - IBM Implementation,
      http.scheme=http,
      http.timeout=30,
      service.id=21}
```

```
{org.osgi.service.cm.ManagedService}={
  service.description=OSGi Http Service - IBM Implementation,
  service.pid=org.eclipse.equinox.http.Http,
  service.vendor=IBM,
  service.id=22}
{org.osgi.service.cm.ManagedServiceFactory}={
  service.description=OSGi Http Service - IBM Implementation,
  service.pid=org.eclipse.equinox.http.HttpFactory,
  service.vendor=IBM,
  service.id=23}
```

The output shows that the `HttpService` is listening on port 80.

`HttpService` Properties Are Not Defined by the OSGi Specification

While querying the registered service in this way works for the default Equinox implementation of the `HttpService` as defined by the bundle `org.eclipse.equinox.http`, the OSGi specification *does not* define properties such as `http.port`, `http.address`, `http.schema`, and `http.timeout`. Other implementations of the `HttpService` may or may not register such properties. Note that it is not always possible for the `HttpService` implementation to know the ports on which the application server is listening. For more information, see the following OSGi bug report: https://www.osgi.org/members/bugzilla/show_bug.cgi?id=502.

18.7 Summary

HTTP is a well-known interaction model and protocol. The OSGi `HttpService` is a simple and straightforward approach to exposing HTTP in OSGi. It allows system developers to create web applications by composing bundles that contribute servlets, resources, JSPs, and more, bringing the power of OSGi modularity to the web world.

In this chapter we discussed the `HttpService` interface and how to register servlets and resources both programmatically from a DS component and declaratively using extension points.

We also enhanced the Toast Client configuration management facility to have JAAS integration for login handling. The login support developed is completely generic and can be used in a number of different scenarios. Through the Equinox infrastructure it is also possible to register a number of different login modules, from simple example modules to comprehensive enterprise authentication systems.

Whether it is the basic Equinox implementation or the more comprehensive Jetty-based version, the `HttpService` is a versatile addition to many OSGi-based systems.

CHAPTER 19

Server Side

OSGi has been around for over a decade in the embedded and then the desktop environments. Recently its value and use in the server community have practically exploded. All of a sudden all of the major Java application servers are OSGi-based. WebSphere, GlassFish, Spring DM, and NetWeaver are all adopting or using OSGi.

Why is this happening? Server software is often large and complex and composed of many parts from a variety of sources. Desktop tools are similarly complex. Modularity has brought great value to desktop tools in the form of the Eclipse tooling platform. Now those benefits are being sought in the server world.

OSGi can be used under the covers simply as an implementation mechanism to improve flexibility in server offerings, or it can be exposed to the server application developer. Today we see both approaches. In this chapter we focus on the latter—the full use of OSGi in server environments.

Complete coverage of the server-side software topic is well beyond the scope of this book. Instead, in this chapter we build on previous chapters and look in more detail at how OSGi on the server works. In particular we talk about

- Embedding OSGi in existing web applications
- Running the Toast back end in a WAR on an application server
- Building WARs composed of bundles
- Remote Services

To work with the examples here, start with the sample code from Chapter 14, "System Deployment with p2," and make the changes described in the following sections.

19.1 Servers and OSGi

In Chapter 7, "Client/Server Interaction," we saw how to set up a simple client and server system using HTTP, servlets, and OSGi. Subsequent chapters added a pluggable web interface and provisioning support to the server. These server set-ups were based on an HTTP server embedded in an OSGi framework with serv-lets as the execution model. This was simple and clean but does not suit all use cases. Enterprise applications, for example, require scalability, performance, high-availability characteristics, and integration with existing infrastructure. Other server programming models operate at a level above servlets and are more like distributed systems with inter-object communication. Fortunately, these requirements are not at odds with OSGi.

Broadly speaking, there are three configurations for using OSGi on a server:

Native—One or more OSGi frameworks are run on a server machine. The frameworks interact with one another using remote messaging and mecha-nisms such as OSGi Remote Services and the Eclipse Communications Frame-work (ECF), HTTP, web applications, and other conventional server-side technologies.

Solo—One or more OSGi frameworks are run and include HTTP service implementations such as Jetty. As shown in Figure 19-1, server function is exposed as servlets and JSPs and supplied by bundles hooked together by the HTTP service running directly on an OSGi framework. This is the configura-tion we have been using in Toast.

Bridged—In the Bridged approach, the coding and exposure model is the same as in Solo, but here the OSGi framework is embedded into a web appli-

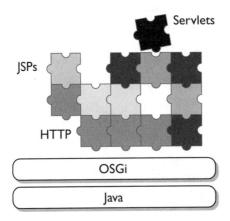

Figure 19–1 Solo server-side configuration

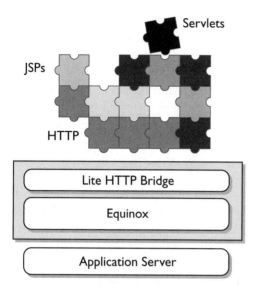

Figure 19–2   Bridged server-side configuration

cation and run inside a traditional web application server such as Tomcat or WebSphere. This is shown in Figure 19-2.

In this chapter we focus on the Native and Bridged scenarios for server-side OSGi. First we change the Toast Back End from using the Solo configuration with Jetty running in Equinox to having Equinox and Toast running inside a web application on Tomcat—the Bridged approach. Details of how this infrastructure works are also covered. Finally, we convert Toast to use OSGi Remote Services and the ECF to manage the communication between the client and back end emergency monitor components without the use of HTTP servers—a Native server-side architecture.

19.2 Embedding the Back End in a Web Application

Many organizations have existing Java web application servers such as Tomcat, Jetty, or WebSphere. These systems are typically run by the IT team and serve business-critical or customer-facing applications. They are secure and managed. With good reason, the IT teams are loath to change from this known infrastructure to running an OSGi framework directly on their servers. They have years of experience with application servers and considerable support infrastructure, load balancing, fail-over, and other technology supporting their needs. Fortunately, the Bridged OSGi server-side story is not "rip and replace" but more of a "co-opt" model.

Rather than having Equinox operate as the overall execution container, the Bridged approach has Equinox running inside a standard web application. As with Solo configurations, server function writers craft bundles and contribute their servlets, resources, and JSPs to an HTTP service, either directly or via the Extension Registry. The Bridged configuration differs in the HttpService implementation. Here the HTTP infrastructure is supplied by the web application server in which the OSGi framework is running. That infrastructure is simply *bridged* into OSGi and surfaced as an HttpService to Toast. Because of the design practices of modularity and separation of concerns that we have followed, Toast doesn't even notice.

The net effect for the system is that the Toast Back End changes from being a stand-alone OSGi-based application to being a standard web application that happens to be implemented with OSGi inside. The application programming model stays the same—bundles, services, and extensions: OSGi. On disk the system changes from being a launcher and set of bundles in a directory structure to being a standard WAR file. Through careful structuring we can use all the same tooling to produce both structures.

19.2.1 Updating the Product

Since the programming model is the same and the function is the same, the only thing in Toast that needs to be changed is the packaging. The version of Toast from Chapter 14, "System Deployment with p2," is described using Eclipse product definitions. These detail the bundles, features, and launcher used for the back end and client. To run the back end code in Bridged mode, we need a product definition that includes the *Servlet Bridge* launcher rather than the conventional launcher.

The Equinox Servlet Bridge is a mechanism for linking the underlying servlet support in a web application server with an OSGi framework running inside a web application. It does this by hooking a set of URLs in the web application URL space and launching an Equinox framework to support the processing of HTTP requests to those URLs. In this way it is both a framework launcher and an HTTP request router. The Servlet Bridge is made up of the following bundles:

> **org.eclipse.equinox.servletbridge**—The bridge itself. While packaged as a bundle, the code in this component is the launcher that instantiates and runs an Equinox framework inside a web application; that is, it runs *under* the framework rather than *in* it. It is packaged as a bundle for consistency and to ease workflows.

> **org.eclipse.equinox.http.servletbridge**—This bundle creates and installs an instance of the HttpServiceServlet to act as a servlet delegate within the application server and capture servlet requests.

`org.eclipse.equinox.http.servlet`—This bundle provides the upper layer of the bridge and defines and registers an `HttpService` instance. The registered `HttpService` behaves like any other HTTP service and supports the registration of servlets, resources, and JSPs.

`org.eclipse.equinox.servletbridge.extensionbundle`—A somewhat magic fragment of the OSGi System Bundle used to export the packages `javax.servlet`, `javax.servlet.http`, and `javax.servlet.resources` as supplied by the underlying application server. The magic comes in that despite being specified and supplied here, the real bundle used at runtime is generated on the fly. We list it here to ensure that all the configuration and dependency information is specified correctly and to smooth workflows.

As of this writing, the bundle needed for the Solo and Bridged configurations is not captured in features shipped by the Equinox project. Let's make the server infrastructure pluggable by refactoring the back end feature to split out the server bundles. You can load this from the Samples Manager or carry out the following steps:

○ Create a feature for the bundles being moved out of the back end. Call it `org.equinoxosgi.toast.server.solo.simple.feature`.

○ Open the `org.equinoxosgi.toast.backend.feature` and look for bits related to the server. Remove all of the bundles listed here from the back end feature and add them to the Solo Simple feature. Save both features.

```
javax.servlet
org.eclipse.equinox.http
```

○ At this point is it also convenient to create a Jetty-based server feature. Create a feature called `org.equinoxosgi.toast.server.solo.jetty.feature` and add the bundles listed here.

○ Open `backend.product`. Now that we have factored out the server code, add the Solo or Solo Simple feature to the list of dependencies.

○ Save the product and run it to ensure that it still works as before.

As with some of the other refactorings we have done, you are now back where you started, but the base structure is more flexible. The next step is to exploit that and make a WAR-based configuration of the back end:

○ Create a feature to capture the Bridged scenario bundles. Call it `org.equinoxosgi.toast.server.bridged.feature`.

○ Add the bundles related to the Servlet Bridge discussed at the beginning of this section and listed here. Notice that we are also including `javax.servlet`. Technically at runtime this bundle is ignored in favor of the servlet classes coming from the application server. We include it here to satisfy the build tools and help you validate your configuration.

```
javax.servlet
org.eclipse.equinox.http.servlet
org.eclipse.equinox.http.servletbridge
org.eclipse.equinox.servletbridge
org.eclipse.equinox.servletbridge.extensionbundle
```

○ Copy backend.product to backend-war.product and open the new product file.

○ On the **Overview** page, update the product **ID** to be org.equinoxosgi.toast.backend.war and uncheck the box beside **The product includes native launcher artifacts**—the framework will be launched by the application server, so native launchers are not needed.

○ Flip over to the **Dependencies** page and swap the Solo Jetty feature for our new Bridged server feature.

○ On the **Launching** page, clear out the **VM Arguments** section. In the Bridged scenario the JVM is already up and running. We'll have to set up the configuration another way.

Now we have to set up the file structure for the web application. The following sections detail the steps required.

19.2.2 The Web Application Root Files

Standard web applications have a particular structure in their artifacts, the WAR files. Figure 19-3 illustrates the layout of a WAR with Equinox inside. This is a conventional structure with a few extra files. Standard are the WEB-INF folder that contains a web.xml file and the lib directory. These are the keys.

The lib directory contains JARs of code that are added to the classpath of the web application as it executes in the application server. The web.xml file is somewhat analogous to the config.ini file in Equinox—it tells the container, the application server, how to install and run the web application.

Figure 19–3 WAR file structure

Here we show the Servlet Bridge base code, `servletbridge.jar`, in the `lib` directory, and a `web.xml` that launches the Servlet Bridge, initializes it, and hooks it into the right spot in the server's URL space:

❍ Use the Samples Manager to load the content of the `rootfiles` folder for the `org.equinoxosgi.toast.server.bridged.feature` project.

The following text walks you through the root files starting with `web.xml`:

org.equinoxosgi.toast.server.bridged.feature/web.xml

```
<?xml version="1.0" encoding="UTF-8"?>
<!DOCTYPE web-app PUBLIC
  "-//Sun Microsystems, Inc.//DTD Web Application 2.2//EN"
  "http://java.sun.com/j2ee/dtds/web-app_2_2.dtd">
<web-app id="WebApp">
  <servlet id="bridge">
    <servlet-name>equinoxbridgeservlet</servlet-name>
    <display-name>Equinox Bridge Servlet</display-name>
    <description>Equinox Bridge Servlet</description>
    <servlet-class>
      org.eclipse.equinox.servletbridge.BridgeServlet
    </servlet-class>
    <init-param>
      <param-name>commandline</param-name>
      <param-value>-console</param-value>
    </init-param>
    <init-param>
      <param-name>enableFrameworkControls</param-name>
      <param-value>true</param-value>
    </init-param>
    <load-on-startup>1</load-on-startup>
  </servlet>
  <servlet-mapping>
    <servlet-name>equinoxbridgeservlet</servlet-name>
    <url-pattern>/*</url-pattern>
  </servlet-mapping>
  <!-- This is required if your application bundles expose JSPs. -->
  <servlet-mapping>
    <servlet-name>equinoxbridgeservlet</servlet-name>
    <url-pattern>*.jsp</url-pattern>
  </servlet-mapping>
</web-app>
```

While this is a standard `web.xml` file, it is worth relating some of the more interesting XML elements to our scenario.

<servlet>—The `id` attribute defines the root of the web application.

<servlet-class>—Identifies the `BridgeServlet` class. This is a servlet that, upon initialization, starts the Equinox framework and ultimately causes an `HttpService` to be registered.

`<init-param>`—There can be any number of `<init-param>` elements. Each defines a key/value pair that is passed into the `BridgeServlet`. For a complete list of the parameters available, see Section 19.2.6, "`<init-param>`s."

`<servlet-mapping>`—Defines the mapping of the given URL pattern in the web application's URL space to the servlet handling requests. The first example in the snippet routes all requests to the `equinoxbridgeservlet`. The second entry is needed to ensure that JSPs are properly routed.

The `lib` directory holds the Servlet Bridge bootstrap code, a copy of `org.eclipse.equinox.servletbridge`. This looks and acts like a bundle, but in fact it is run by the application server as standard Java rather than by Equinox as a bundle. It is the code that will ultimately create and start the Equinox framework.

YOU HAVE TO MANAGE THE BRIDGE

Since `servletbridge.jar` is a binary artifact not managed by the tooling, you need to make sure the correct version of the file is included in the project.

The other file in the `rootfiles` structure is `launch.ini`. This is the functional equivalent of the standard `eclipse.ini`. This file is used to initialize system properties as part of the framework boot process. It is similar to, but takes priority over, the `config.ini` that is discussed in Section 23.10.2, "The Executable." In the Servlet Bridge case the file looks like this snippet:

```
org.equinoxosgi.toast.server.bridged.feature/launch.ini
osgi.*=@null
org.osgi.*=@null
eclipse.*=@null
osgi.parentClassloader=app
osgi.contextClassLoaderParent=app
```

The first three lines are used to clear all existing system properties that match the given pattern. Since we are about to start an Equinox framework nested in an application server, we need to ensure that no Equinox-related property settings leak into the new framework from the external context.

You can also set properties here. The two class-loader-related properties tell the new framework to consult the class loader provided to the web application by the application server when loading system classes. This ensures that classes provided by the application server itself are available to Equinox.

Finally, we have to set up the root files such that the build system copies them to the right spot in the WAR. In Section 20.5.7, "Identifying and Placing Root Files," we detail the root files mechanism. Here it is enough to know that you need to update the `build.properties` file as follows:

○ Open the build.properties file, switch to the **Source** page, and update the contents to look like this by adding the root property:

```
org.equinoxosgi.toast.server.bridged.feature/build.properties
bin.includes=feature.xml
root=rootfiles
```

19.2.3 Building the Web Application

The setup for this structure was a little involved, but we were walking you through all the gory details. In practice, once you have the server features in place, they don't need to be touched. Everything else is done at the product level. To actually create the WAR, you just export the backend-war.product as follows:

○ Open backend-war.product and click the export link or button as in the other chapters. This opens the **Export Product** wizard, as shown in Figure 19-4.

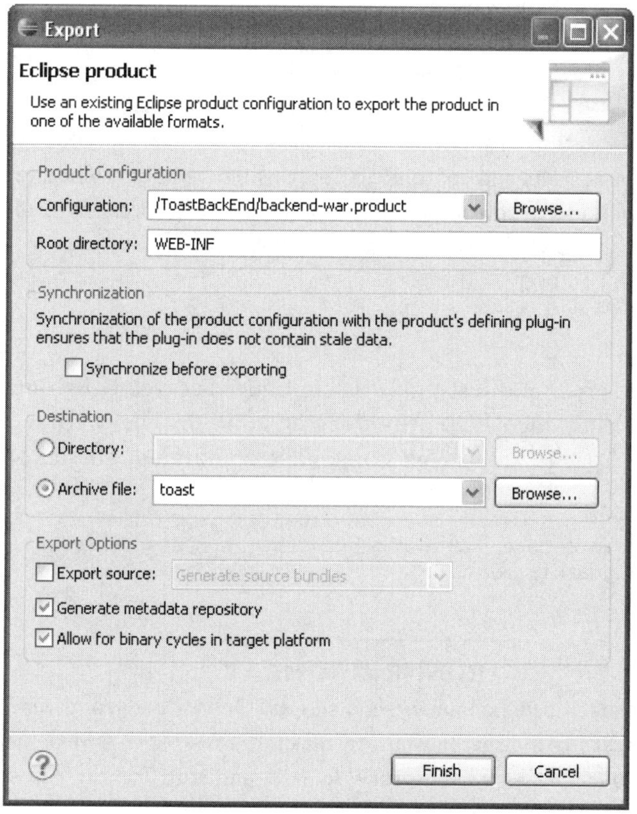

Figure 19–4 Exporting the WAR product

○ In the **Root Directory** field, enter WEB-INF. This tells the export to place all of the generated content in the named folder in the output. This is required for proper structuring of the web application.

○ Uncheck the **Synchronize before exporting** box. We saw this in Section 9.2, "Exporting Toast."

○ Enter toast as the name for the output file in the **Archive file** field.

○ Press **Finish** to export the WAR. When it is done, rename toast.zip to toast.war and install it in an application server as discussed in the next section.

19.2.4 Running the Web Application

Running the Toast Back End WAR is the same as running any WAR. Here we assume the use of Tomcat, but any web application server could be used.

○ Install the WAR into Tomcat by copying toast.war into the webapps directory under the Tomcat install.

POSITIONING TOAST IN URL SPACE

Note that by default, the name of the WAR file surfaces in the URL space as a prefix to all your servlets and content. So Toast would be at http://localhost:8080/toast. This would be a problem for our clients as they expect the back end to be at the root of the URL. To position a web application at the root in Tomcat, rename the WAR to ROOT.war.

Start the web server and test that it is configured correctly by opening a web browser and entering the URL http://localhost:8080. The web server should respond with the Apache Tomcat welcome page containing, among other things, the text

```
If you're seeing this page via a web browser, it means you've setup Tomcat
successfully. Congratulations
```

RUNNING TOMCAT

Tomcat is controlled using command-line scripts. Open a command window and change to Tomcat's bin directory. Ensure that the JAVA_HOME environment variable is set to your JDK or JRE directory. To start and stop Tomcat, run startup or shutdown respectively.

Unfortunately, these scripts spawn another process and the console is not visible. As an alternative, try `catalina run` and `catalina stop`. These run the server in place and give access to the OSGi console.

If you do not see the welcome page, the web server is typically not running or is not listening on port 8080. The shell command `netstat -anb` can be used to list the ports that are in use and by which applications.

CONFIGURING THE TOMCAT PORT

By default Tomcat listens for HTTP connection on port 8080. You can change the port by editing the `<Connector>` element's port attribute in the file `conf/server.xml`:

apache-tomcat-6.0.20/conf/server.xmls
```
<Connector port="8080" protocol="HTTP/1.1"
    connectionTimeout="20000"
    redirectPort="8443" />
```

After changing the port, restart the web server for the change to take effect.

Assuming you called the WAR `toast.war`, accessing the URL http://localhost:8080/toast/sp_test should yield the following response:

```
Servlet delegate registered -
org.eclipse.equinox.http.servlet.HttpServiceServlet
```

By default the `BridgeServlet` provides the following service platform (`sp_`) commands for controlling the OSGi framework. These commands are executed via a URL, as we've just shown.

sp_deploy: Deploy Equinox—This command copies the contents of the web application's WEB-INF folder to the web application's install area, as described by the servlet context attribute `javax.servlet.context.tempdir`.

sp_undeploy: Undeploy Equinox—This command deletes the files that `sp_deploy` copied to the web application's install area. Equinox must first be stopped using the command `sp_stop`.

sp_redeploy: Redeploy Equinox—This command calls `sp_stop`, `sp_undeploy`, `sp_deploy`, and `sp_start`.

sp_start: Start Equinox—Equinox must first be deployed using the command `sp_deploy`.

sp_stop: Stop Equinox—Equinox must first have been started using the command `sp_start`.

sp_test—Test to see if the `BridgeServlet` is registered and is accepting requests.

DISABLING sp_ COMMANDS

The availability of the `sp_` commands is controlled by an `<init-param>` element in the web application's `WEB-INF/web.xml` file that defines the parameter `enableFrameworkControls`. To disable the `sp_` commands, set the `enableFrameControl`'s `<param-value>` to `false` and restart the web server.

Once you are satisfied that the web application is configured correctly, test the Toast Back End by launching the full Toast Client as normal but with the following tweak:

○ Add the following to the **Launching** page's **VM Arguments** section in the product editor:

```
-Dtoast.backend.servlet.container=/toast
```

This instructs the client that the back end URLs should be prefixed with `toast` as this is how the application server positions the application in URL space by default. See the sidebar "Disabling `sp_` Commands" for information on changing this.

○ Once the client is running, click on the emergency button to send an emergency message to the back end.

○ Check the Tomcat console and look for the following message confirming that the emergency request was received by the back end:

```
[INFO] 2008-08-10 23:43:17.274 - EmergencyServlet:
Emergency: ABC123 (38.88746N, -77.02192E) 90deg 50kph
```

19.2.5 Troubleshooting

In the `web.xml` we start the OSGi console using the `-console` command-line argument. This gives you a standard OSGi console and allows you to inspect and control the system as normal. For example, you can use `ss` at the `osgi>` prompt to display the installed bundles and their statuses. You can also use `diag` to investigate any problems with bundle state and the DS console commands described in Chapter 15, "Declarative Services," to introspect your service components.

If your setup is not working or if any bundles are missing, try the following:

○ Open the `backend-war.product` and click the validate button at the top right. Resolve any issues reported and re-export and reinstall the WAR.

○ Look at the exported WAR to ensure that all expected bundles are present.

○ Look at the exported `config.ini` file and ensure that its `osgi.bundles` list has the expected entries. See Section 23.8.3, "`osgi.bundles`," for more details.

○ If Simple Configurator is being used, confirm that the right bundles are listed in the WAR's `bundles.info` file.

○ Check the timestamp and contents of the WAR file in Tomcat's `webapps` directory. If needed, delete the back-end-related directories from `webapps` and the `work/Catalina/localhost` directory.

19.2.6 `<init-param>`s

The Servlet Bridge can be controlled using a number of parameters loaded during initialization. These are defined using the standard `web.xml` `<init-param>` markup. Here is a list of the most interesting parameters and what they control:

commandline—The command line that is passed into the Equinox framework launched inside the Servlet Bridge. Often the `<init-param>` is used to specify `-console` and open the interactive console.

enableFrameworkControls—Enables the `sp_` controls for starting, stopping, and deploying the Equinox framework. The value is `true` or `false`.

extendedFrameworkExports—The `org.eclipse.equinox.servletbridge` package and the Servlet API are exported automatically by the Servlet Bridge bundles. The `extendedFrameworkExports` parameter allows the specification of additional Java package exports. The value is specified as a comma-separated list of exports as specified by the `Export-Package` bundle manifest header. For example:

```
com.mycompany.exports; version=1.0.0, com.mycompany.otherexports;
version=1.0.0
```

frameworkLauncherClass—Specifies the framework launcher class and defaults to `org.eclipse.equinox.servletbridge.FrameworkLauncher`, the launcher supplied by the Servlet Bridge.

19.3 Remote Services in OSGi

Building systems using HTTP and standard web server infrastructure is certainly powerful and widespread. It is not the only way, however. With the OSGi R4.2

Enterprise Expert Group (EEG) specification release, there is a new facility called Remote Services (RFC 119). An early draft of the RFC characterized the work as follows:

> The solution is intended to allow a minimal set of distributed computing functionality to be used by OSGi developers without having to learn additional APIs and concepts. In other words, if developers are familiar with the OSGi programming model then they should be able to use . . . this solution very naturally and straight forwardly to configure a distribution software solution into an OSGi environment.

Put simply, Remote Services extends the normal service discovery and usage model across JVM boundaries.

RFC 119 IS NOT FINAL!

As of the writing of this section, the specification corresponding to RFC 119 was not final. In fact, it is known that the final specification will differ in syntax and form from the structure presented here. This information will be updated in subsequent editions of this book and in the publicly available code samples.

We are including this discussion to demonstrate the range and flexibility of OSGi beyond single-machine scenarios. While the code presented here is real and the underlying mechanisms mature and well used, you should see this discussion as a vision statement for where OSGi is going in the distributed world and how it can help you. Changes to make this code work with the final version of the specification are expected to be minimal.

The code for this section can be found in the Samples Manager as "Chapter 19.3." It is based on the state of Toast at the end of Section 19.2, "Embedding the Back End in a Web Application."

19.3.1 The Eclipse Communication Framework

The Eclipse Communication Framework (ECF) project at Eclipse is all about, well, communication. Whether you are looking for social networking protocols such as XMPP, Twitter, Jingle, and the like or core computing infrastructure such as HTTP, file transfer, ActiveMQ, or Remote Services, ECF is the place to go. As part of the Eclipse community, all ECF functionality is shipped as bundles with few, if any, ties to the specifics of Equinox—it should run on any framework that implements the required parts of the OSGi specification.

The core concept in the ECF API is *container*. A container represents a point to which or from which messages can be sent using a particular protocol. In other contexts these are called *endpoints*. How messages get from one place to another and what happens to them along the way are all details of the container.

System-level programmers extend ECF by plugging in protocol *providers*. A provider generally implements or adapts to a particular messaging protocol or implementation such as XMPP, ActiveMQ, or simple TCP messaging. This is the core of ECF's SPI (System Programmer Interface).

ECF's job, then, it is to marry and map the API-level requests to send a message to some destination to some underlying network location and message format. This all happens under the covers.

To use ECF, you have to add it to your target as follows:

○ Open `toast.target` and **Edit...** the "Galileo" repository entry.

○ In the resultant dialog, uncheck the **Group by Category** box and find and select the **Eclipse Communication Framework SDK** entry.

○ Click **Finish, Save** the target definition, and click **Set as Target Platform**.

19.3.2 Remote Services

Remote Services is independent of ECF. It turns out, however, that ECF inherently implements almost all that is needed to do Remote Services. Roughly speaking, that is two separate elements: distribution and discovery. The RFC characterizes these as follows:

> **Distribution**—The distribution software is responsible for the actual network communication between a remotely available service and its consumer, including the data format (i.e., serialization) and communication protocol.
>
> **Discovery**—The Discovery service is an optional service that enables services running in a framework to be published for remote consumers and the discovery of services running outside a framework.

The RFC comprehensively sets the scene for Remote Services use cases and the interactions between frameworks and services. Here we look at using ECF's Remote Services support to change the way the client and back end interact.

19.3.3 Distributed Toast

Toast became a distributed system in Chapter 7, "Client/Server Interaction," when we introduced the Toast Client and Toast Back End. Since then client and back end interactions have been based on simple HTTP messages and independent servlets. This has been fine for a system of Toast's scale. As the number of inter-acting parties and the complexity of their interactions increase, however, we need a more managed and centralized approach. That is what ECF does for you—all the marshaling, messaging, and management. Adopting ECF then makes sense, but what of distributed services?

Since our initial discussion of Declarative Services, we have found using services to be both easy and natural. Services give us the decoupling we need, and DS deals with many of the complexities around dynamic and unpredictable behavior. Allow-ing services from a remote framework to show up in a local framework blends these advantages. Let's change Toast to use ECF and its implementation of the RFC 119 draft specification to do the tracking and emergency reporting communications.

19.3.4 Remote Service Host

In the back end, the tracking and emergency functions are implemented as serv-lets that process HTTP GET requests containing the relevant information. To switch to Remote Services, we need some services to remote. It turns out that we already have these: `IEmergencyCenter` and `ITrackingCenter`. All we need to do is signal that they should be made available to other frameworks.

The `ControlCenter` component provides both of these services. We need to annotate the component and mark the provided services as remotable:

○ Open the `component.xml` file found in
   `org.equinoxosgi.toast.backend.controlcenter`.
○ On the **Overview** page, click **Add Property...** and fill in the dialog as shown in Figure 19-5. In particular, note that the **Values** field lists each remote inter-face on a line by itself. This list should be the same as or a subset of the ser-vices provided by the component.

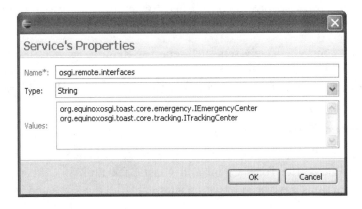

Figure 19–5 Remote interfaces property in DS

That's all we need to do to the Toast Back End proper to enable remote service calls. To make it run, we do need to add the various ECF support bundles to the back end product. There are a great many combinations of ECF message transports and remote interaction mechanisms. For simplicity we have included a feature that groups together the bundles needed for ECF remote messaging using a generic TCP transport:

○ Using the Samples Manager, load the
`org.equinoxosgi.toast.remoteservices.host.feature` project into your workspace.

○ Open `backend.product` and add the new remote services host feature to the list of **Dependencies**. Do the same on the `backend-war.product`.

At this point Toast has the remote services markup and the infrastructure. All that is missing is the initialization of the infrastructure. As ECF is very loosely coupled, we just have to create a container and let Toast and ECF find each other. For our purposes, it is easiest to create the container when the control center component is activated—that is the earliest it would be needed anyway.

○ Update the `ControlCenter` component to depend on ECF's `IContainerManager` service and the `ControlCenter` class to have the appropriate field and setter.

○ Modify the `ControlCenter.startup` method to add the container creation code as shown in the following snippet. The first argument is the type of container to use, and the second is a set of parameters to the container creation.

```
org.equinoxosgi.toast.backend.controlcenter/ControlCenter
public void startup() throws ContainerCreateException {
  containerManager.getContainerFactory().createContainer(
      "ecf.generic.server",
      new Object[] {"ecftcp://localhost:3282/server"});
  discovery.addListener(this);
  Collection profiles = provisioner.getProfiles();
  for (Iterator i = profiles.iterator(); i.hasNext();)
  addVehicle((String) i.next(), null);
}
```

Now that `IEmergencyCenter` and `ITrackingCenter` are exposed directly as remote services, the servlet exposure of the services is no longer needed. In fact, the bundles hosting these servlets do nothing else, so they, too, can be removed:

○ Delete both `org.equinoxosgi.toast.backend.emergency` and `org.equinoxosgi.toast.backend.tracking` from the workspace.

○ Open the back end feature, `org.equinoxosgi.toast.backend.feature`, and delete the emergency and tracking bundles from the **Plug-ins** list. Note that the core emergency and tracking bundles are still needed, as they supply the service interfaces.

Now the back end is functionally equivalent to previous versions but implemented using remote services. Next is converting the client to use remote service calls.

19.3.5 Remote Service Client

The pattern for converting the client to use remote messages is similarly straightforward. Here we look at updating the emergency monitor. Updating the tracking monitor is very much the same.

The EmergencyMonitor originally used the IChannel abstraction to explicitly send messages to the back end. Now the back end surfaces an IEmergencyCenter service for the client's use. Let's assume that that remote service is surfaced in the client's service registry and update the emergency monitor component:

○ Open the emergency monitor's component.xml and change the reference to the IChannel service to reference IEmergencyCenter. Ensure that the name of the reference is set to emergencyCenter and the bind method is updated accordingly.

○ Open EmergencyMonitor and use refactoring to rename the channel field to emergencyCenter and then change its type to IEmergencyCenter.

○ Update the code for runEmergencyProcess to call the emergency center service directly rather than using the channel, as in the following snippet:

```
org.equinoxosgi.toast.client.emergency/EmergenyMonitor
private void runEmergencyProcess() {
  notifyStarted();
  int latitude = gps.getLatitude();
  int longitude = gps.getLongitude();
  int heading = gps.getHeading();
  int speed = gps.getSpeed();
  String reply = emergencyCenter.emergency(
      id, latitude, longitude, heading, speed);
  if (reply == null) {
    notifyFailed(null);
    LogUtility.logDebug(this, "Unable to send to back end: ", null);
  } else {
    notifySucceeded(reply);
    LogUtility.logDebug(this, "Received reply: " + reply);
  }
  job = null;
}
```

○ Organize imports, do other cleanup, and save EmergencyMonitor.

○ Clean up the emergency monitor's MANIFEST.MF by removing the reference to the channel package.

○ Finally, update the test cases to follow the new pattern.

Repeat these steps for the client tracking code to complete the conversion of the code. Once that is done, the coding work is finished. Now we need to initialize the ECF infrastructure as we saw with the back end and update the product definition.

Since multiple bundles need the ECF infrastructure, we chose to put its initialization in a separate bundle. We also created a client-side Remote Services feature to capture all the required ECF functionality.

○ Use the Samples Manager to load the
   `org.equinoxosgi.toast.remoteservices.client` and
   `org.equinoxosgi.toast.remoteservices.client.feature` projects.

○ Open the `client.product` and add the new feature to the list of **Dependencies**.

19.3.6 Service Discovery

Toast now has a remote service host and client and ECF infrastructure for communicating between them—if only they knew about each other. That's where service discovery comes in. The RFC 119 draft defines a generalized mechanism for integrating the services published by one framework's service registry into the registry of other frameworks. ECF includes several implementations of this protocol based on standard technologies such as Service Location Protocol (SLP) and Zeroconf. To keep things simple here, we will use the so-called *local discovery* mechanism.

As the name implies, local discovery reads a local file that describes the remote services available and publishes them in the local service registry. This is a way of externalizing and controlling the location and characteristics of the remote services.

○ Use the Samples Manager to load the local discovery mechanisms. Fetch the
   `org.eclipse.ecf.osgi.services.discovery.local` and
   `org.eclipse.ecf.provider.localdiscovery` projects. As of this writing, these are not part of the official ECF release. With future versions of ECF you can likely skip this step.

○ In each of the client's emergency and tracking bundles, add a remote service definition file, `remote-services.xml`, in the OSGI-INF folder. The following snippet shows the file for the emergency monitor. Be sure to update the service interface type for the tracking monitor.

```
org.equinoxosgi.toast.client.emergency/remote-services.xml
<?xml version="1.0" encoding="UTF-8"?>
<service-descriptions xmlns="http://www.osgi.org/xmlns/sd/v1.0.0">
  <service-description>
    <provide interface=
      "org.equinoxosgi.toast.core.emergency.IEmergencyCenter"/>
    <property name="ecf.sp.cid">
      ecftcp://localhost:3282/server
    </property>
```

```
    <property name="ecf.sp.cns">
      org.eclipse.ecf.core.identity.StringID
    </property>
    <property  name="osgi.remote.interfaces">
      org.equinoxosgi.toast.core.emergency.IEmergencyCenter
    </property>
  </service-description>
</service-descriptions>
```

o Update the MANIFEST.MF for each bundle to point to the new Remote Services declarations by adding the following line:

```
Remote-Service: OSGI-INF/remote-services.xml
```

19.3.7 *Running the Distributed System*

Running Toast with remote service support is the same as running normally. Indeed this whole exercise of converting to Remote Services has been very painless and has left the business logic largely unaffected.

The Value of Our Design Practices

Along the way in the evolution of Toast we have consistently made design choices that are now bearing fruit. The isolation of domain and framework logic—that is, POJO programming—has been particularly valuable. We have also taken care to separate concerns and package the code in a highly modular way. Without exception, whenever Toast was hard to adapt, it was because we had not followed these guidelines. Sometimes that is expedient, but it will certainly surface in future development.

Note that in setting up Toast as a distributed system we have glossed over some key discussions and decisions, namely, how to handle synchronous and asynchronous messaging and whether or not remote method invocation should be implicit or explicit.

Synchronicity is largely a situational decision. In our case the monitors were already set up as stand-alone jobs with nothing to do but send the message, so waiting is OK. To help with asynchronous messaging, the Equinox org.eclipse.equinox.concurrent bundle has support for *futures*. This mechanism allows you to send a message and immediately get back an IFuture object. You can then pass the future around, and only when you need the result of the message send do you need to wait for the value. Equinox futures are quite similar to those found in more recent JREs, but they run on old versions of Java and have support for status values and cancellation.

Here we have used implicit messaging but structured the code with the expectation that the message send may take a long time. Sending remote messages introduces additional chances for failure, which we have not accounted for particularly here. In general, a `RuntimeException` will occur and need to be handled. Of course, explicit remote service calls are also supported. See the ECF project and OSGi specifications for more information.

19.4 Summary

Here we have taken our stand-alone Toast Back End and converted it both to run inside standard web application servers and to use draft Remote Services technology and ECF for remote messaging. Both of these move Toast into the enterprise space.

Shipping the back end as a web application means that it can be deployed without ripping and replacing existing infrastructure while still maintaining the benefits of OSGi and Equinox. Using ECF and Remote Services opens the door to the transparent adoption of enterprise messaging infrastructure such as ActiveMQ.

CHAPTER 20

Release Engineering

Up to this point, you have been using the PDE **Export Product** wizard to publish and create end-user-deliverable versions of Toast. As Toast grows, and as it has more developers working on it and more configurations, there's a pressing need for automated, reproducible, and accessible builds—*release engineering*.

Building modularized systems by hand is somewhat challenging and tedious. The compile-time classpath for any given bundle includes the code from all its prerequisites, in a very particular order and with quite a number of classpath access restrictions. Just computing the classpath and build order is hard. Mix in variations such as projects in the workspace, projects checked out from source control in the file system, or both, and the myriad of output packaging options, and you need help.

There are several build facilities out there, and the landscape is changing all the time. Maven, Ivy, Sigil, and many others all have benefits and drawbacks. Here we focus on the PDE Build infrastructure that comes with the Eclipse tool suite.

PDE Build does not claim to be a general build mechanism but rather a sophisticated OSGi bundle builder that has been in use for many years building Eclipse bundles. Because of that heritage it is well integrated into the Eclipse IDE and workflows.

This chapter dives into PDE Build and guides you through setting up an automated, reproducible build for the various parts of Toast. Here we cover

- ○ Configuring and running a product build
- ○ Running feature-based builds
- ○ Building web archives (WARs)
- ○ The different `build.properties` files associated with building

○ Customizing the build scripts

○ Automatic version number qualification

20.1 What Is PDE Build?

So far, PDE's **Export** wizards have insulated you from most of the details around building and packaging bundles. Unfortunately, those wizards are hard to automate, as you have to click around in a UI to launch a build. They are also hard to make repeatable, as they depend on the contents of the user's workspace. Product teams and communities need *release engineering* builds that are automated and more rigorous. This is where PDE Build comes in.

You have actually been using PDE Build all along. It is the underlying infrastructure used for exporting bundles, features, and products from the workspace. It can also be used to perform release engineering builds of OSGi bundles.

PDE Build takes a product definition or a set of features and bundles and compiles and packages them according to the dependency information in their manifests and a set of control parameters. The output is an archive or directory structure that can be deployed directly or by using Java Network Launch Protocol (JNLP). As you saw in Section 14.5, "Exporting, Running, and Provisioning," you can also export directly into p2 repositories for future provisioning.

At its heart, PDE Build is an Ant script generator. It takes in a collection of bundles and features, their manifests and `build.properties` files, and generates a set of Ant build scripts. These scripts are run to produce a build. The export operations you have been doing throughout this book use PDE Build under the covers.

PDE Build is quite flexible. It can consume hybrid mixes of bundles and features that are prebuilt and those that remain to be built. Some may be included in the final output, and others may not. The output of a build can also vary from bundles in directories to p2 repositories and ZIP archives of JAR'd and signed bundles and features.

The build mechanism builds bundles and features, or cascades of the transitively included features and bundles starting at a root feature or product definition. Cross-platform building is also supported.

The main benefit of PDE Build is that it brings all this together into one relatively simple process. Developers express their normal runtime dependencies in manifest files and a mapping from development-time structure to runtime structure in the feature and bundle `build.properties` files. PDE Build does the rest.

Key to this process is the automatic generation of the build scripts. Using the input manifests and `build.properties`, PDE generates Ant scripts that copy files and compile code using a classpath derived by flattening the bundle dependency

---

Product Files

Product definitions were introduced in Chapter 9, "Packaging." They are build-time configuration files that describe the bundles and features that constitute a running OSGi system. In addition to the bundles and features, product files can be used to specify launch configurations, program and VM arguments, and branding information.

For more information, see the online Eclipse Help at http://help.eclipse.org. Navigate to **Plug-in Development Environment Guide > Concepts > Product**.

---

graph. The runtime classpath for a bundle is defined as a complex graph of bundle dependencies as described in its manifest file. The classes referenced at runtime are also needed at compile time, so the compile-time classpath is similarly complex. PDE Build uses the OSGi bundle resolution and wiring mechanisms to derive the classpath for each bundle being built.

20.2 Bundle `build.properties`

Before we get too far into PDE Build itself, let's recap what you have used as a build process so far in the book. Since the PDE wizards have been doing most of the work, you have seen the `build.properties` file only for the Toast bundles and features. This file is exposed on the **Build** page of the bundle and feature editors.

The role of the `build.properties` file is to map development-time structures in a bundle's project onto the structures described in the bundle's manifest and needed at runtime. For example, by adding elements to the **Binary Build** section, you are stating that the deployable version of the bundle must include those elements.

The various PDE editors and wizards take care of managing binary build entries for most of the common cases. When you add images or other runtime resources to a bundle, you have to update the binary build information in the `build.properties` to ensure that they are included in the build result.

`build.properties` HELP

The various `build.properties` file options are documented in **Help > PDE Guide > Reference > Build Configuration > Feature and Plug-in Build Configuration**.

20.2.1 Control Properties

The bundle editor's **Build** page helps set up common build-related properties. To add more advanced properties, you have to edit the build.properties file directly using the bundle editor's **build.properties** page. When you set up automated builds, these advanced build properties become more relevant. Here we provide an example properties file and Table 20-1 for reference. See the PDE Help for a full list of build properties.

```
build.properties
bin.includes=plugin.xml, META-INF/, ., icons/, html/
bin.excludes=html/private*.html
source..=src/
extra..=library.jar
```

Table 20–1 Bundle Build Properties

Property	Description
bin.includes	A comma-separated list of development-time resources that are copied into the bundle when it is built. This list must include the bundle metadata files MANIFEST.MF and plugin.xml, if present, as well as any code. Use "." when you want a JAR'd bundle or bundle-relative paths to get directory-based bundles. Be sure to list additional files such as icons, message catalogs, and licensing files.
	Entries in the list are expressed using Ant pattern syntax. The most common patterns include * (e.g., *.html) and a trailing "/" (e.g., html/) to indicate that a directory structure is to be included.
	The bin.includes line in the example declares that plugin.xml and the contents of the META-INF, icons, and html directories should be included in the binary version of the bundle.
bin.excludes	A comma-separated list of development-time resources that should *not* be included in the binary version of this bundle. The entries in this list override those in the bin.includes list. Excluded list entries are also expressed as Ant patterns.
	The bin.excludes line in the example declares that all "private" HTML files should not be included in the deployable runtime version of the bundle.
source.<library>	The set of development-time resources to compile to create the Java executable element identified by <library>. Here, <library> is typically "." to indicate the bundle itself. Alternatively, it is the name of a JAR file. The value is a comma-separated list of Ant patterns that identifies files passed to the Java compiler during the build.
	The source.. line in the example declares that the files in the src directory are compiled and the output is placed in the root of the bundle as indicated by the second "." in source...
extra.<library>	A comma-separated list of elements to add to the compile-time classpath when compiling the source as defined in a corresponding source.<library> property. This is commonly needed when you have JARs you compile against but do not ship and do not include in any of the bundles that this bundle requires.

PDE uses this information, in combination with the bundle manifests, to generate a `build.xml` script for each bundle that is then run during the build process.

20.2.2 *Using Custom Build Scripts*

You can opt out of the build script generation by supplying your own `build.xml` and selecting **Custom Build** on the **Build** page of the bundle editor, as shown in Figure 20-1.

Figure 20–1   Custom Build selection

If you opt for a custom `build.xml`, you take complete responsibility for implementing the build script that has all the right targets and that does all the right things. A better solution is to use custom callbacks; see Section 20.5.1, "Customizing the Build Scripts."

20.3 **Setting Up a Builder**

To see how this works in practice, let's set up a managed build process for the Toast Client from Chapter 14, "System Deployment with p2." The client consists of the product definition, several Toast-related features and bundles, and various prebuilt bundles from the target platform.

- ○ Start by creating a simple project for the build scripts using **File > New... > Project > General > Project**. Call it `client.builder`.
- ○ In the file system, navigate to your Eclipse IDE install and go to the `org.eclipse.pde.build` bundle. For example, look in `c:\ide\eclipse\plugins\org.eclipse.pde.build_3.5.1` if your IDE is installed in `c:\ide`.
- ○ Copy both `templates\headless-build\build.properties` and `scripts\productBuild\productBuild.xml` to the `client.builder` project. These are templates for the files used to control builds. In the subsequent sections, the templates are filled in and used to build the product.

The builder's `build.properties` file is quite different from the other `build.properties` files you have seen so far. It contains key/value pairs that define the input parameters to the build itself. The productBuild.xml is an Ant build file that controls the building of products. Having both files here allows you to override or add behavior to the build.

20.3.1 Tweaking the Target for PDE Build

In addition to setting up the builder project, you must also ensure that the required binary dependencies are available. In particular, you need the right executable launcher for the platform you are building—PDE Build cannot assume it's already present or know where it is.

The executables for all supported platforms are available in the *executables feature*. This feature is not intended to be installed; rather it contains native executables for a wide range of platforms. The easiest way to get the executables feature is to get the Eclipse *delta pack*. We saw the delta pack in Section 3.5, "Target Platform Setup." Ensure that your target has the delta pack.

With the target setup, we have everything needed to run PDE Build. Unfortunately, as of this writing, PDE Build does not directly support the use of target definition files in its execution. This means that you must manually manage your binary prerequisites. To help with this we have included a simple tool, the **Target Export** wizard, that collects all of the bundles and features from the current target and places them in a single directory. You can then use the output of this tool in PDE Build. Run it now as follows:

○ Select **File > Export > Plug-in Development > Target definition** to export the bundles and features that constitute the current target.

○ Choose a directory for the Toast binary dependencies—for example, c:\toast_prereqs—and click **Finish**.

20.3.2 build.properties

Now that the build structure is in place, it needs to be customized to build our bundles. Following is a summary of the changes needed to the template build.properties that was copied to the builder project. Some of the properties shown are needed later but are listed here to show the big picture. If a property is not listed here, it does not need to be changed. Of course, you should replace the file system locations appropriately.

client.builder/build.properties
```
# Product and packaging control
product=/ToastClient/client.product
runPackager=true
archivePrefix=toast_shell
```

```
# Build naming and locating
buildDirectory=${user.home}/eclipse.build
buildType=I
buildId=TestBuild
buildLabel=${buildType}.${buildId}

# Base identification and location
skipBase=true
base=C:/toast_prereqs
baseLocation=${base}
baseos=win32
basews=win32
basearch=x86
pluginPath=

# Cross-platform building
configs=win32, win32, x86 & linux, gtk, x86

# CVS Access control
skipMaps=true
mapsRepo=:pserver:anonymous@example.com</path/to/repo>
mapsRoot=<path/to/maps>
mapsCheckoutTag=HEAD
skipFetch=true

# Publish the build to a p2 repository
p2.gathering=true
p2.metadata.repo=${buildDirectory}/repository/toast
p2.artifact.repo=${buildDirectory}/repository/toast
p2.compress=true

# Java class libraries and compile controls
#bootclasspath=${java.home}/lib/rt.jar
compilerArg=
```

Let's look at each of these values and see how they affect the build. There are, of course, many more properties, but understanding these should give you an idea of how the build goes together and the level of control you have. The main information in `build.properties` covers roughly seven areas of concern in the build process. Each of these is detailed in one of the following sections. They are presented roughly in decreasing order of interest; that is, you have to set up the values in the first section but may not have to change things in the last section.

20.3.2.1 *Product and Packaging Control*

These properties describe what you are building, the branding you want, and the shape of the output:

product—The location of the product file that describes what is being built. The value takes the form `/<id>/path/to/.product`, where `<id>` is the ID of the feature or bundle project that contains the `.product` file.

archivePrefix—The specified prefix is added to the beginning of all paths in the output archive. This gives you control over the shape of your product when it is extracted on the user's machine.

20.3.2.2 *Build Naming and Locating*

These properties allow you to control the working directories and names for the build output:

buildDirectory—The absolute file system path where the build is executed. All build input is downloaded to this location, and all compilation and composition are done under this directory. You should keep this path reasonably short to avoid exceeding file system length limits. This is the only directory to which the builder needs to write permissions.

buildType—An arbitrary string used to name the build output and identify the type of build. For example, organizations often have nightly (N) builds, maintenance (M) builds, integration (I) builds, and so on. There is no need to limit this value to a single character.

buildId—The buildId is used in composing the name of the output archives. Typically, the ID conveys some semantics, such as TestBuild or CustomerX, or a full date stamp, such as 20090701.

buildLabel— This is used in the naming of the output directories. The buildLabel is typically a composition of buildType and buildId.

20.3.2.3 *Base Identification and Location*

Most of the time you are building a set of bundles that sits on top of some base. Think of the base as the target for your workspace—it is all the bundles and features that you are *not* developing yourself. This may be the Equinox SDK, or it may be a whole product suite if you are an add-on developer. The properties here allow you to set where the base is, what's inside, and how to get it if it is not present:

base—The location of the product on which the build is based. This is used to determine if the base needs to be installed. If the directory exists, its contents are assumed to be complete. If it does not exist, the build system fetches the base and installs it at this location. In the example, we set the base to be the target platform that was exported using the **Target Definition Export** wizard.

baseLocation—The location of the actual base install against which the bundles being built are to be compiled. This is the logical equivalent of the target used during development—all the bundles and features come from elsewhere.

Note that this can be a full Eclipse install using link directories. This is specified separately from base because different products have different internal structures. For example, the standard Eclipse downloads include an eclipse directory in their structure. In these cases, the baseLocation is just ${base}/eclipse. In our case, we exported our target to c:/toast_prereqs, so we can use that directly as both the base and baseLocation.

baseos, basews, basearch—The os, ws, and arch values for the base set of Equinox components in the install. Eclipse installations may support many platform configurations, so these settings are used to clarify the set of base bundles, fragments, and features to use. If there are several configurations in your base, pick one and assign the properties accordingly.

skipBase—A marker property that, if set, indicates that fetching the base should be skipped.

pluginPath—A list of locations where additional plug-ins and features can be found. Entries in this list are separated with the platform-specific separator.

20.3.2.4 Cross-Platform Building

This property helps control cross-platform building:

configs—An ampersand-separated list of target machine configurations for which you want to build. Each configuration consists of an os, ws, arch triple, such as win32, win32, x86. The build process creates a separate output for each configuration. If the configuration is not set or is set to *, *, *, the build is assumed to be platform-independent. In this example, we are building the Toast Client for Linux GTK and Windows.

20.3.2.5 SCM Access Control

The build process can automatically check out the source for the build from an SCM system. The location of the source is dictated by *map* files, which can themselves be checked out from an SCM system. The following properties let you bootstrap that process by setting basic locations and SCM tags to use:

mapsRepo—The SCM repository that contains the map files needed for the build.

mapsRoot—The path in the SCM mapsRepo to the map files for the build.

mapsCheckoutTag—The SCM tag used to check out the map files. The map files, in turn, control the SCM tags used for checking out the bundle and feature projects.

skipMaps—A marker property that, if set, indicates that the map files are local and should not be checked out.

fetchTag—A property used to override the SCM tags defined in the map files. For example, setting it to HEAD is useful for doing nightly builds with CVS.

skipFetch—A marker property that, if set, indicates that the source for the build is local and should not be checked out.

20.3.2.6 Publishing a Product Build to a p2 Repository

Depending on the way you wish to deploy your software, a p2 repository may be more convenient than platform-specific ZIP files. The following properties control the creation of a p2 repository containing the results of the build. The repositories can be used by others to provision the Toast Client shell and can also be used by PDE Build to build bundles intended to run on top of this product.

p2.gathering—A marker property that, if set, indicates that all the build artifacts should be gathered into a p2 repository

p2.metadata.repo—The location where the metadata repository is written if p2.gathering is on

p2.artifact.repo—The location where the artifact repository is written if p2.gathering is on

p2.compress—A marker property that, if set, indicates that the repositories should be compressed if p2.gathering is on

The artifact and metadata repository properties should identify repository locations under a shared parent. Later, in Section 20.5.2, "Repositories and Additional Dependencies," we may need to use the location of the parent as the repoBaseLocation.

20.3.2.7 Java Class Libraries and Compiler Control

Of course, the build is primarily concerned with compiling Java code. The properties here allow you to define the compilation classpath as well as various arguments passed to the Java compiler:

bootclasspath—The default boot classpath to use when compiling code. This should point to all the classes that are expected to be on the boot classpath when the product being built is run. The value is a semicolon-separated list of file system locations.

compilerArg—A list of arguments to pass to the compiler.

Managing Ant Properties

PDE Build makes heavy use of Ant constructs and in particular Ant properties. The properties listed here are treated as normal Ant properties, so ${variable} substitution is supported. Also, values such as the bootclasspath are passed directly to the associated Ant task.

The so-called *marker* properties are ones that are simply set or not set. The value is irrelevant and not checked. For simplicity, we tend to show the value as true, but setting the value to false does *not* unset the property.

It is often convenient to use build.properties to set up defaults and then override these values for a particular builu. This is done by setting properties from the command line using the -D<prop>=<value> VM argument syntax.

For more advanced settings, see the Ant documentation at http://ant.apache.org.

20.4 Running the Builder

Now that the builder is defined, you are ready to build the Toast Client. For most of this chapter we assume that you are working locally and already have the Toast code in your workspace. For simplicity, we also assume that you exported your target to c:/toast_prereqs. With these assumptions, the builder does not need to access a server. To set this up, make sure that build.properties has the following settings:

```
client.builder/build.properties
skipBase=true
base=c:/toast_prereqs
baseLocation=${base}
skipMaps=true
skipFetch=true
```

Because the bundles and features are not being checked out from CVS, you need to create the build directory by hand. In the following steps replace ${buildDirectory} with the value from build.properties, for example, ${user.home}/eclipse.build:

- ❍ Create ${buildDirectory}.
- ❍ Create ${buildDirectory}/plugins.
- ❍ Create ${buildDirectory}/features.
- ❍ Copy the required feature projects to the features directory and bundle projects to the plugins directory. Figure 20-2 indicates which projects are needed and what the layout should look like in the end.

Figure 20–2   Build layout

COPY FILES EVERY TIME

Since the builder is not checking files out of CVS every time, the projects must be copied every time their content changes.

Now run the builder. The easiest way is to use a command prompt and change your working directory to the location of your builder. For example, if you have been following along, the builder files `build.properties` and `productBuild.xml` are in the `client.builder` project in the workspace. Once there, run Eclipse's AntRunner application using the following command line. The `-buildfile` argument specifies the build file to run. Here we use `productBuild.xml`. The `-consolelog` argument ensures that you can see the output messages as the build progresses.

```
cd <workspace location>\client.builder
c:\ide\eclipse\eclipse.exe
    -application org.eclipse.ant.core.antRunner
    -buildfile productBuild.xml -consolelog
```

CHOOSE THE HEADLESS ANTRUNNER

Make sure you choose org.eclipse.ant.core.antRunner rather than the org.eclipse.ant.ui.antRunner when launching the build.

The build produces the structure shown in Figure 20-3 in the ${buildDirectory}/
${buildLabel} directory. In our example, the output goes in ${user.home}/
eclipse.build/I.TestBuild. This directory contains one archive per configuration that was built and a p2 repository. Each archive is a complete, ready-to-run
Toast Client.

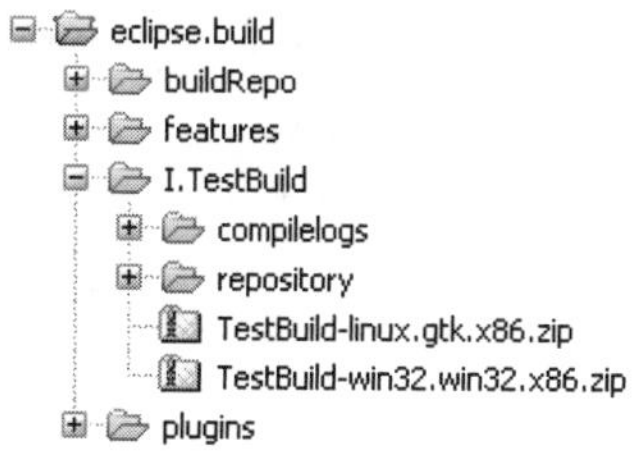

Figure 20–3   Build output

The compilelogs directory contains the build logs for each bundle that was
built. The various assembly and packaging scripts in the build directory are left
over from the build and can be deleted. They are automatically deleted and regen-
erated each time the builder is run.

The repository directory contains the p2 repository from which the Toast
Client can be provisioned.

Debugging the Build

Builds are notoriously hard to get right. Spelling mistakes, commented lines, and
typos all contribute to builders that just do not work. The Eclipse IDE includes comprehensive support both for authoring Ant files and for debugging Ant scripts. There
are a few quirks to setting this up for PDE Build, so the steps are detailed here.

You must have the root build script in your workspace. If you have been following
along, you should have the product build script in your workspace. If not, you can
import it:

○ Use the **Import > Plug-ins and Fragments** wizard to import the
   org.eclipse.pde.build bundle.

○ In the wizard, set the **Bundle Location** to your IDE location (e.g.,
   c:\ide\eclipse) and choose **Import As > Binary projects**.

○ Click **Next**, select the **org.eclipse.pde.build** bundle, and **Add** it to the list.

○ Click **Finish**.

Now you have to set up a launch configuration to run PDE Build's `build.xml`, the root of the build mechanism:

○ Navigate to `org.eclipse.pde.build/scripts/productBuild/productBuild.xml` and use the context menu's **Debug As > Ant Build...** to open the Ant launch configuration dialog.

○ On the **JRE** page, select **Run in the same JRE as the workspace**.

○ On the **Properties** page, uncheck **Use global properties...** and use **Add Property...** to add a property called `builder`, as shown in Figure 20-4.

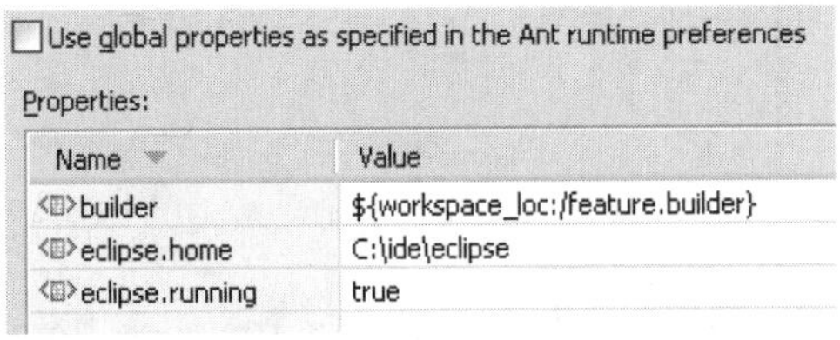

☐ Use global properties as specified in the Ant runtime preferences	
Properties:	

Name ▼	Value
`<▥>builder`	`${workspace_loc:/feature.builder}`
`<▥>eclipse.home`	`C:\ide\eclipse`
`<▥>eclipse.running`	`true`

Figure 20–4   Ant builder properties

○ Click **Debug** and run the build.

Everything should work as before. Now you can open PDE's Ant scripts, such as `productBuild.xml`, and add breakpoints by double-clicking in the left margin or using the **Toggle Breakpoint** context menu. Debug the build again. When the breakpoint is hit, you can inspect Ant properties and step over and into Ant statements.

20.5 Tweaking the Build

Now that you've seen the basics of how to build a system, here are some of the more common and useful customizations. These are not mandatory but are generally useful.

20.5.1 Customizing the Build Scripts

The `templates` directory in the `org.eclipse.pde.build` bundle has many useful script templates. You should copy these into your builder and customize them as needed. Table 20-2 presents an overview of the most relevant templates. For more information on customizing a build, see the Eclipse online Help documentation at http://help.eclipse.org and navigate to **Plug-in Development Environment Guide > Tasks > PDE Build**.

Table 20-1   PDE Build Templates

Script	Description
`headless-build/customTargets`	This script provides Ant targets that are called between the major phases of the build. There are pre- and post-targets for events such as fetching the source, generating build scripts, packaging, etc. Use these callback points to add extra processing during the build.
`customAssembly`	This script provides customization points that will be called during the assembly and packaging phases of the build.
`features/customBuildCallbacks`	The build callbacks template enables features to provide their own custom steps to the build. The feature custom build callback supports only the `gather.bin.parts` target.
`plugins/customBuildCallbacks`	The custom build callbacks template enables OSGi bundles to provide their own custom steps to the build. There are a number of targets that can be customized.

20.5.2 *Repositories and Additional Dependencies*

For the Toast Client we built before, we used the **Target Export** wizard to help create the base against which everything was compiled. However, this approach may not be ideal when configuring a build server. You may have various headless scripts and other facilities to get all the parts you need. If the dependencies end up in different directories, the `pluginPath` and `repoBaseLocation` properties can be used.

The `pluginPath` property points to a separated list of additional locations in which PDE Build can look for prebuilt dependencies.

The `repoBaseLocation` points to a single directory that may contain one or more p2 repositories in either ZIPped or extracted form. When this property is used, you must also specify the `transformedRepoLocation` property and point it to a writable location on disk. PDE Build copies the contents of the base repositories and transforms them into a runnable form. All the bundles and features in the `transformedRepoLocation` are then added to the `pluginPath`.

RUNNABLE REPOSITORIES REQUIRED

Repositories generally come with all their content as JARs. Features, and some bundles, however, need to be expanded on disk to be useful at build time; that is, they need to be in *runnable form*. PDE Build ensures that the given base repositories are transformed appropriately.

20.5.3 Fetching from an SCM System

PDE Build can also be configured to check out the source for the bundles and features being built from an SCM system, such as CVS or SVN. It uses the notion of *map files* to map feature and bundle IDs onto SCM repository locations and tags. This allows you to identify the top-level product or feature and let PDE Build figure out that you really mean "Check out a particular location in a particular repository using a particular SCM tag." A map file contains a series of lines, each of which takes the following form:

```
feature|fragment|plugin@elementId=\
    cvs tag,:method:user@host/path/to/repo \
    [,cvs password][,path/in/repository]
```

CVS IS AN EXAMPLE

In this discussion we use CVS as the example SCM system. The syntax and concepts are equivalent if you are using SVN or some other SCM system.

If the path in the repository, the last element, is not specified, PDE Build assumes that the element to fetch is at the root of the repository and has the same name as the element. If your artifacts are in a different location in the repository, you must specify the complete path from the root of the repository to the directory containing the contents of the element, that is, the full path of the parent directory of the `feature.xml` or `plugin.xml`. Note that this path must *not* start with a "/".

In your `${buildDirectory}`, create a `maps` directory, and in that directory create a `toast.map` file that contains the following entries. Be sure to replace the repository information and the tag. You can use HEAD for the tag if you only ever want to build from HEAD. Note that in this case the qualifier is set to HEAD as well—not very useful. See Section 20.5.6, "Qualifying Version Numbers," for information on how to set the qualifier explicitly.

```
client.map
plugin@org.equinoxosgi.toast.core=tag,:method:user@host/path/to/repo
plugin@org.equinoxosgi.crust.shell=tag,:method:user@host/path/to/repo
feature@org.equinoxosgi.toast.client.shell.feature=\
    tag,:method:user@host/path/to/repo
```

To save space, we have included only two features and one bundle in this map file. In practice, you must add an entry for each bundle and feature that needs to be built. All other elements are assumed to be in the base and do not need to be fetched or built.

Enable fetching by commenting out the `skipFetch` property in `build.properties`. Leave `skipMaps=true` for now. Delete the `plugins` and `features` directories from the `${buildDirectory}` and run the build. Notice that the source listed in the map is checked out and built.

Fetching the Product File

In the case of a product build, there is a bit of a catch-22 situation. The `.product` file drives the list of features and bundles to be built. This file is typically in a bundle or feature project in the SCM, but the map file mechanism does not have a way of indicating which project or where it is. Since the `.product` file drives the fetch phase of the build and the fetch phase cannot fetch it, it must be checked out explicitly.

This can be accomplished using a custom build step early on in the build, for example, by adding the following Ant instructions to the `postSetup` target in `customTargets.xml`:

customTargets.xml
```
  <target name="postSetup">
    <antcall target="getBaseComponents" />
    <ant antfile="${genericTargets}" target="fetchElement">
      <property name="type" value="feature | plug-in"/>
      <property name="id" value="id of feature or bundle project" />
    </ant>
  </target>
```

See Section 20.5.1, "Customizing the Build Scripts," for more information on the `customTargets.xml` file.

Integrating with SCM Systems

Source code repositories and SCM systems figure heavily in the overall release engineering process. PDE Build supports several tools such as CVS and SVN. CVS is supported out of the box, whereas SVN requires the installation of some additional bundles. In both cases standard command-line SCM tools are used to fetch content—PDE Build does not assume the existence of an Eclipse workspace, so the normal Eclipse SCM clients cannot be used.

If you are on a UNIX machine, chances are you have CVS and SVN already installed—type `cvs` or `svn` at the command line to check. If not, consult your OS installer instructions.

On Windows you have to manually download and install the clients. You can get CVS from http://cvsnt.org and SVN from http://tigris.org or http://polarion.com.

SVN users need to augment the standard PDE Build infrastructure with the ability to read SVN-oriented map file entries and use SVN for fetching. See the instructions on the PDE wiki at http://wiki.eclipse.org/PDEBuild.

20.5.4 Fetching the Maps

Sharing the map files in the SCM repository is the next logical step. There may be many map files, for example, each controlled by different teams. The simplest structure is to have a directory in the repository that holds the map files. Different teams then update their map files, and the build automatically picks up their changes.

During the build process, the `getMapFiles` target in `customTargets.xml` is called to download all the map files. The behavior of `getMapFiles` is controlled by setting various properties in `build.properties`, as shown here:

client.builder/build.properties
```
# skipMaps=true
mapsRepo=:pserver:anonymous@example.com/path/to/repo
mapsRoot=path/to/maps
mapsCheckoutTag=HEAD
```

If `skipMaps` is commented out, `getMapFiles` checks out the contents of `${mapsRoot}` from `${mapsRepo}` using `${mapCheckoutTag}` and puts it into a `maps` area in `${buildDirectory}`.

Set this up in the `build.properties`, check your map files into a repository, and delete the entire contents of `${buildDirectory}`. Now, run the builder and watch that first the maps are checked out, then the features and bundles. Then, the build should continue as normal.

20.5.5 Auto-substitution of Version Numbers

Deployed features are full of version numbers—included bundles and features are all identified by precise versions. Listing and managing these specific version numbers at development time is challenging, to say the least. If the version of a bundle changes, all referencing features have to be updated. This is cumbersome and error-prone.

To simplify the process, PDE Build includes support for automatically substituting version numbers during the build. You saw this in Chapter 14, "System Deployment with p2," where included bundles and features were identified as version 0.0.0. The use of 0.0.0 tells PDE Build to substitute the version number of the bundle or feature used in the build. This eliminates the need to change the containing feature definition during development and ensures that the deployed version numbers are always correct. This is the default behavior of PDE Build.

You can lock in version numbers by setting them explicitly in the feature editor. For example, on the **Bundles** page of the feature editor, select **Versions...** in the **Bundles and Fragments** section. There you can select various policies for managing the version numbers. The options specified in the dialog apply to all bundles and fragments. If you want to lock down some bundle numbers but leave some to be assigned at build time, you have to use the **feature.xml** page and edit the file directly.

20.5.6 Qualifying Version Numbers

It is often handy to have output version numbers qualified by a build timestamp or other information. PDE Build supports a mechanism for optionally *qualifying* select bundle and feature version numbers during the build process.

Open the org.equinoxosgi.crust.shell bundle's editor and on the **Overview** page, set the bundle **Version** field to 1.0.0.qualifier. Do the same for the org.equinoxosgi.toast.client.shell.feature. During the build process, the qualifier segment of the version is replaced with a user-selected value. This should be done for all bundles and features.

By default, the qualifier is derived from the context of the build. For example, if the build is based on checking out particular CVS tags using the map files described earlier, the qualifier for each bundle or feature is the CVS tag used to check out the source for the bundle. This way, the bundle's full version number is based on its source.

If the build is not based on SCM tags or is using some sort of default tag—for example, the CVS HEAD tag used in continuous integration builds—the qualifier for the version is the millisecond clock time when the bundle or feature was built.

You can force the value of the qualifier to be uniform across the build by setting the forceContextQualifier property in the builder's build.properties, as shown in the next snippet. You should take care to use qualifier strings that are valid for file and folder names, as the qualifier shows up in the build output disk content. You should also take care to ensure that qualifiers are monotonically increasing so that successive builds have *larger* version numbers.

client.builder/build.properties

```
forceContextQualifier=someQualifierString
```

It is also possible to control the qualification of bundles and features on an individual basis by setting the `qualifier` property in the relevant `build.properties`, as shown here:

```
org.equinoxosgi.crust.shell/build.properties
qualifier=<arbitrary string value here>
```

20.5.7 Identifying and Placing Root Files

In product scenarios it is often required that various files be included in the root of the product distribution. This commonly includes various licenses and legal files and perhaps even a JRE. The PDE Build *root files* mechanism allows you to do this.

The root files mechanism is actually part of the feature build structure. Like bundles, features have their own `build.properties` file that maps the development-time structure onto the runtime structure. This is where you describe the set of files to copy to the root of the final build output. The following snippet shows a typical feature's `build.properties` file. The `bin.includes` property behaves exactly as described for bundles. The remainder of this section details the setup for root files. See the PDE Help for a full list of feature build properties.

```
*.feature/build.properties
bin.includes=feature.xml, about.html, feature.properties, license.html
root=rootfiles
```

The program launcher and related configuration files—for example, `client.exe`, `crust.ini`, and `config.ini`—do appear at the root of an install but are not technically root files if you are building products. Products inherently identify and include the executable and these various configuration files, so they should not be specified again in a feature root file list.

The product definition and export wizards do not give you full control, however. For example, arbitrary root files such as licenses and legal files cannot be directly identified. These files must be enumerated in the `build.properties` for a feature included in the product. The properties relevant to defining the root files are listed here:

> **root**—Files listed here are always copied to the root of the output. If a directory is listed, all files in that directory are copied to the root of the output.
>
> **root.<os.ws.arch>**—There should be one of these lines for each OS, window system, and processor architecture combination that has unique root files. For example, if you need to include compiled libraries or executables, you should identify them on the root lines for the appropriate configurations.

Each property value is a comma-separated list of files to copy to the root of the output. The files are identified using one of the following techniques:

○ The contents of a directory structure are included by listing the parent directory itself. For example, `root=rootfiles` copies the entire contents of the `rootfiles` directory in the feature to the root of the build output. This is the most common setup seen in features.

○ Individual files must be identified by prefixing their location with `file:`. For example, the line

```
root.linux.gtk.x86=file:linux/special_executable
```

copies just the `special_executable` file to the root. Note that the given path is relative to the feature, and the containing directory structure is not copied.

○ Absolute paths can be specified by prefixing the location with `absolute:`.

ROOT FILE PRECEDENCE

Many features can contribute to the root files for a build. The feature root files in parent features overwrite those of their children.

Executable files and libraries often need to have special permissions set when they are placed in the final archive so that when end users unpack the archives, the product is ready to run. You can control the permissions of the root files by defining a property of the form

```
root[.os.ws.arch].permissions.<perm_pattern>=<files>
```

The `os.ws.arch` configuration identification is optional. The `<perm_pattern>` is a UNIX file permissions triple, such as 755, which should be familiar to `chmod` users. The value of the property is a comma-separated list of files to which the permissions should be applied. Ant patterns are supported for identifying files. Since permissions are applied once the files have been copied to their position in the root directory, all paths to permission files should be relative to the output root. Non-existent files are silently skipped, and folders must be indicated with a trailing "/".

20.6 Building Add-on Features

So far this chapter has focused on building stand-alone OSGi systems using Eclipse product definitions. The true utility of OSGi, however, is in the ability to extend a system with additional bundles. Here we show how to build and package some additional bundles, such as audio support, that can be optionally installed into the Toast Client.

In Chapter 14, "System Deployment with p2," we defined a number of features to capture the different functional units that users might install into a Toast Client—audio, mapping, emergency, and so on. The discussion in the chapter showed you how to export these features independently and then provision them dynamically. Here we do basically the same thing but this time using PDE Build in a release engineering context.

20.6.1 Setting Up a Feature Builder

To try this out, let's set up a managed build process for the Toast Client's audio feature. Overall the process is very much like the product builds done previously. As in Section 20.3, "Setting Up a Builder," set up a build project primed with files from PDE itself:

- ○ Start by creating a simple project called `feature.builder` using **File > New... > Project > General > Project** and prime it with template build scripts from your IDE.

- ○ In the file system, navigate to the install location of your Eclipse IDE and go to the `org.eclipse.pde.build`. For example, look in `c:\ide\eclipse\ plugins\org.eclipse.pde.build_3.5.1` if your IDE is installed in `c:\ide`.

- ○ From there, copy `build.properties` and `build.xml` from the `templates\ headless-build` directory into your new builder project.

20.6.2 `build.properties`

The `build.properties` file used to control the building of a top-level feature is similar to one used to build a product. The most significant properties are highlighted next, and we describe the differences between the product `build.properties` and the file we need here.

```
feature.builder/build.properties
# Feature identification
topLevelElementType = feature
topLevelElementId = org.equinoxosgi.toast.client.audio.feature
runPackager=true
archivePrefix=toast_client

# Build naming and location
buildDirectory=${user.home}/audio_feature.build

# Base identification and location
skipBase=true
baseLocation=C:/toast_prereqs
repoBaseLocation=${user.home}/eclipse.build/repository
transformedRepoLocation=C:/transformed_repo
baseos=win32
```

```
basews=win32
basearch=x86

# SCM Access control
skipMaps=true
skipFetch=true

# Publish the build to a p2 repository
p2.gathering = true

# Cross-platform building
configs = *, *, *
```

Let's look at each of these properties and how they affect the build. In particular, we focus on how these properties differ from those specified in a product build.

topLevelElementType—Indicates the type of the top-level element being built—feature or bundle. This property is not used when building products.

topLevelElementID—Indicates the ID of the feature or bundle to build.

repoBaseLocation—This is the parent folder of the repository locations specified when building the client. The contents are used to compile and assemble the result.

transformedRepoLocation—The contents of the repositories used may need to be converted into a runnable form. Runnable components are put in this location. Notice that baseLocation contents may still be needed if the feature being built brings in functionality that is not yet part of the Toast Client.

p2.gathering—Features that are built should be published to a repository from which clients can install the audio feature. In a feature build, unlike product builds, specifying the repository location in p2.metadata.repo and p2.artifact.repo is optional. If the location is not specified, the repository is in the build output location.

configs—Since there is no platform-specific code in the audio feature, we can simply state that we are building for all platforms by setting the configs property to *, *, *.

20.6.3 *Running the Feature Build*

Feature builds are invoked in the same way as the product build in Section 20.4, "Running the Builder"; that is, you must

○ Create ${buildDirectory}.

○ Create ${buildDirectory}/plugins.

○ Create ${buildDirectory}/features.

❍ Copy the required bundles and features to the plugins/ and features/ directories, as shown in Figure 20-5.

❍ Invoke org.eclipse.ant.core.antRunner as shown here:

```
cd <workspace location>/feature.builder
c:\ide\eclipse\eclipse.exe
    -application org.eclipse.ant.core.antRunner
    -buildfile build.xml -consolelog
```

```
audio_feature.build
    features
        org.equinoxosgi.toast.client.audio.feature
    plugins
        org.equinoxosgi.toast.dev.amplifier
        org.equinoxosgi.toast.dev.amplifier.fake
        org.equinoxosgi.toast.dev.cdplayer
        org.equinoxosgi.toast.dev.cdplayer.fake
        org.equinoxosgi.toast.dev.radio
        org.equinoxosgi.toast.dev.radio.am
        org.equinoxosgi.toast.dev.radio.am.fake
        org.equinoxosgi.toast.dev.radio.fake
        org.equinoxosgi.toast.dev.radio.fm
        org.equinoxosgi.toast.dev.radio.fm.fake
        org.equinoxosgi.toast.swt.audio
```

Figure 20–5   Feature build layout

---

build.xml NOT productBuild.xml

When invoking a feature build, the -buildfile argument is build.xml as
opposed to productBuild.xml.

The build produces a structure as shown in Figure 20-6. The content goes in the
${buildDirectory}/${buildLabel} directory or, in our example, in ${user.home}/
audio_feature.build/I.TestBuild. This directory contains an archive that consists of a fully built Toast audio feature. Because the p2.gathering property was
specified, the archive is also a p2 repository. Here we are interested only in the
repository and can delete the archive.

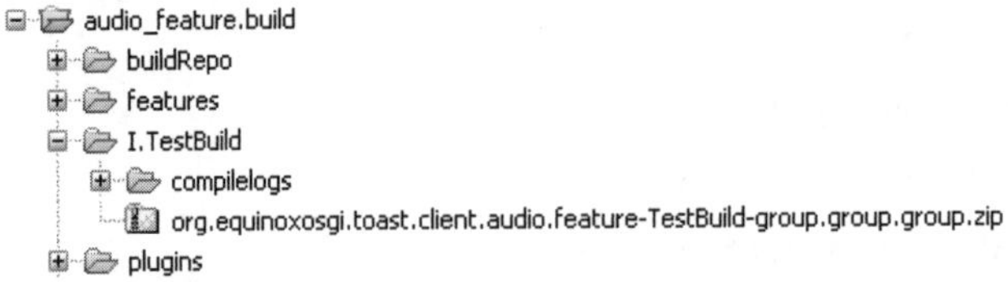

```
audio_feature.build
    buildRepo
    features
    I.TestBuild
        compilelogs
        org.equinoxosgi.toast.client.audio.feature-TestBuild-group.group.group.zip
    plugins
```

Figure 20–6   Feature build output

20.7 Building WARs

In Chapter 19, "Server Side," we saw how the back end could be packaged and delivered as a WAR. We set up a product definition and associated root files and then exported the product from the UI. The result was a `.zip` file that can be used directly as a `.war` after changing the file extension.

Since the Toast web application is described by a standard product, you can use the product build infrastructure discussed previously to build the WAR. All that is missing is the automatic renaming of the output `.zip` file to be a `.war` file. To set this up, you need to modify the builder to have a `customTargets.xml` file and then have it run an Ant task in the `postBuild` target:

- Copy the `client.builder` project to make a `war.builder` project.
- Follow the instructions in Section 20.5.1, "Customizing the Build Scripts," to get the template `customTargets.xml` into the new builder project.
- Modify the `build.properties` in `war.builder` to point to `backend-war.product` and set the `archivePrefix` property to `WEB-INF`.
- Open `customTargets.xml` and update the `postBuild` target to move the build output to `toast.war`:

```
war.builder/customTargets.xml
<target name="postBuild">
  <antcall target="gatherLogs"/>
  <move
    file="${buildDirectory}/${buildLabel}/${buildId}-
      win32.win32.x86.zip"
    tofile="${buildDirectory}/${buildLabel}/toast.war"/>
</target>
```

- Finally, follow the steps in Section 20.4, "Running the Builder," to copy the required features and run the build.

20.8 Summary

Here we covered the basics and got you started using PDE Build to compile and assemble the bundles, features, and products related to Toast. Regular and repeatable automated builds are a critical part of the development process. Without these, teams cannot integrate and have no idea if the system works.

PDE Build offers comprehensive tooling for building OSGi- and Eclipse-related artifacts. It is highly sophisticated and extensible. It is also very specialized. It is not a general-purpose build system. Since it is based on Ant, however, it can be integrated with one of the many build choreographing systems such as Hudson or CruiseControl. We strongly recommend setting up such a build process as early as possible in the life of your project.

PART IV

Reference

The creation of a highly modular system is as much about the actual code that needs to be written as it is about how to structure, package, and deliver it. Part IV of the book introduces you to an array of topics, from integrating non-OSGi code libraries to creating dynamic systems that run in a wide variety of operating environments. In addition, there are a number of pieces of the OSGi and Equinox puzzle that do not fit neatly into a greater topic or compelling scenario. These pieces nonetheless are vital to a full understanding of OSGi and Equinox. As such, this last part of the book includes reference chapters covering the Equinox implementation and information about useful OSGi bundles found in the Eclipse ecosystem.

CHAPTER 21

Dynamic Best Practices

Applications are often dynamic. New functionality is added, old functionality is removed, but the system keeps running. Even if your system is not inherently dynamic in its steady state, it is dynamic at startup and shutdown. Without the ability to handle the incremental addition of collaborators, you have to manually ensure that all prerequisite elements—services, extensions, listeners—are available before they are needed. Managing start order is frustrating, cumbersome, and brittle.

We have seen dynamic behavior and mechanisms throughout the Toast example. OSGi services, Service Trackers, and SAT, discussed in Chapter 6, "Dynamic Services," help considerably. Declarative Services, as discussed in Chapter 15, "Declarative Services," and the Extension Registry covered in Chapter 16, "Extensions," simplify dynamic behavior further. In this chapter we generalize the concept of dynamism and look at how it impacts common coding patterns. In particular, we do the following:

- ❍ Introduce the notion of dynamic awareness and dynamic enablement
- ❍ Outline techniques for handling the arrival and departure of bundles and services
- ❍ Detail the OSGi Extender Pattern and `BundleTracker`
- ❍ Look at the dynamics of OSGi startup and shutdown

21.1 Dynamism and You

This chapter discusses the unique challenges presented to developers as they attempt to handle and facilitate comings and goings in the environment around them. We first recap Toast and look at examples of dynamic tolerance. With that as a base, we identify some common dynamic scenarios and outline coding and design best practices.

Dynamism is more than decoupling and using services. Do not be lured into the belief that simply "using services" will make your system behave correctly in a dynamic environment. Even with all the mechanisms in OSGi and Equinox, it is still possible to get dynamism wrong. Concurrency issues, stale listeners, complex programming patterns, and lost changes all collude to cause system failure in the face of dynamic change. In short, being dynamic does not come for free—you must follow certain practices to make the most of these scenarios.

Lesson from the Past

Equinox and OSGi were introduced to Eclipse in Eclipse 3.0 (June 2004). In the course of describing the evolution to OSGi, we explained to the Eclipse community that OSGi supported the dynamic addition and removal of bundles. People were very excited. When the release came, we got quite a number of bug reports complaining that various tools added on top of the Eclipse IDE did not integrate properly until the system was restarted—this dynamic thing was not working . . .

In actual fact, there was no attempt by the Eclipse teams to make the Eclipse *tooling* platform dynamic. Listening for and handling bundle arrival and departure would be significant work; "Developers would tolerate the restart, and it would be too hard to retrofit dynamism for tools" went the reasoning. Rather, the team adopted the more modest but still significant goal of making the RCP, a subset of the full Eclipse platform, dynamic. This revealed quite a number of assumptions and issues that needed attention. In the end, that goal was largely met, but the effort involved highlights the notion that simply using dynamic mechanisms is not enough. As with concurrency, distribution, transactionality, and persistence, there is no free lunch. Being dynamic takes work.

21.2 Dynamic Aspects of Toast

Toast as an application is dynamic at the domain level; that is, vehicles and users come and go as the system runs. This kind of dynamism is inherent in distributed systems. In addition, in Toast each machine can itself change over time. For example, software can be installed, updated, and uninstalled from vehicles as they are running. We need to ensure that Toast reacts correctly when these changes occur.

The first step is to understand how the elements of the system collaborate—the food chain. Beyond the details of installing functionality, however, are the issues in getting the application to notice the arrival of new functionality and the management of interconnections when functionality is removed from the system—these are the topics addressed in this chapter.

DYNAMISM IS NOT JUST FOR BUNDLES

People often talk about dynamics in terms of bundles coming and going. This is one of the major forces driving dynamism but is by no means the only driver. In reality, dynamic behavior is related to services, extensions, and other contributions changing. The changes can happen at any time for a variety of reasons. For simplicity we talk about "changes in collaborators" as the general category of change that needs to be managed to create a dynamic system.

Figure 21-1 gives a notional outline of the Toast Client bundles and shows how they relate to each other. GPS, Airbag, and Display are all at the bottom of the food chain. Tracking and Emergency are in the middle of the food chain, producing and consuming services, and the various UI bundles are at the top as they consume only services.

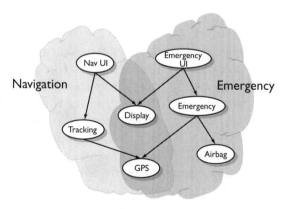

Figure 21–1   Toast bundle structure

Bundles at the bottom of the heap are quite independent of others coming and going. They do, of course, need to clean up after themselves but are otherwise free to be introverted. Bundles in the middle and on top, however, must not only be good citizens and clean up but also carefully watch for other bundles and services coming and going.

Notice that it is sometimes interesting to talk about the grouping of logical functionality. For example, the figure shows that the Navigation application constituent parts interact closely and the elements of the Emergency application interact together, but the applications do not directly interact. Looking at the system more abstractly allows you to talk about the level of interaction between the various applications. This feeds into our food-chain notion but at a coarse grain.

The Toast bundles register services and listeners and contribute extensions to be instantiated by the system. In particular, Toast has the following requirements:

○ Various back end bundles must register servlets with the `HttpService` when it is available.

○ All bundles must clean up listeners on removal.

○ The back end portal must discover and integrate new actions as they arrive and clean up when they are removed.

○ The client UI must react to the coming and going of client applications.

○ All applications must correctly react to the presence or absence of their required services.

The rest of this chapter looks at how to handle each of these requirements, both in the context of Toast and the `HttpService` and in more general scenarios, so that you can apply them to your domain.

21.3 Dynamic Challenges

Being dynamic is all about managing the links between types, their instances, and bundles—collaborators. There are two main challenges when trying to operate in a dynamic world: being *dynamic-aware* and being *dynamic-enabled*.

Dynamic awareness is an outward involvement, ensuring that the links you have to others are updated as collaborators are added to and removed from the system. Awareness is tricky to get right. As such, most of this chapter outlines techniques and helpers for making your bundles dynamic-aware.

Being dynamic-enabled relates to cleaning up after yourself. This is relatively straightforward to achieve because it's a self-centered concern—you just need to do it.

21.4 Dynamic Awareness

Dynamic awareness has to do with updating your bundle's data structures and behavior in response to changes in the set of collaborators; that is, a dynamic-aware bundle is one that can handle *other* elements coming and going or starting and stopping. Dynamic awareness needs to be considered wherever you have a data structure that is based on type, object, or data contributions from other bundles. In the Toast case, everything is dynamic. Vehicle devices such as GPS and airbags, software such as emergency management and audio control, can all come and go at any time. On the back end, portal actions and servlets are also dynamic. In short, all of Toast must be dynamic-aware.

Dynamic awareness comes in two flavors: *addition* and *removal*. We say that a bundle is *dynamic-aware for addition* if it is set up to handle the dynamic addition of collaborators to the system. Similarly, we say that a bundle is *dynamic-aware for removal* if it can handle the dynamic removal of collaborators from the system.

Addition is generally easier to deal with as there is less cleaning up to be done—structures can simply be augmented, caches flushed, or new capabilities discovered on the fly. Handling the removal of relationships may be as easy as flushing a cache, or it may be as complicated as tracking contributed, registered, or constructed objects, deleting them as required, and cleaning up afterward.

This cleanup is important because an uninstalled bundle is not garbage-collected until all instances of its types are collected and all references to its types are dropped; only then can the bundle's classes be unloaded and the bundle be considered truly uninstalled. Technically, you can continue using existing types and objects even after the defining bundle is uninstalled, but the state of the bundle, and thus the integrity of its functionality and services, is not guaranteed—yet another reason why dynamic awareness is important. The OSGi specification calls these *zombie* bundles.

Using OSGi services, in and of itself, does not make your systems dynamic-aware—it is easy to write bad code that ignores the service lifecycle signals given by the framework, or neglects to unget services or unregister listeners. Similarly, the Equinox Extension Registry can be abused to create unstable dynamic systems. The key to being dynamic is using the supplied dynamic management mechanisms effectively.

Chapter 6, "Dynamic Services," highlights several approaches for managing dynamic services. The dynamic service and extension usage patterns outlined in Sections 6.4, "Using Declarative Services," and 16.6, "Dynamic Extension Scenarios," are very powerful approaches. Subsequent sections in this chapter highlight some additional pitfalls and techniques for managing collaboration, such as contributed objects (e.g., listeners) and tracking bundle events.

HIDE OSGi CODE

Keeping your domain- and OSGi-related code separate is a particularly effective element that we have used throughout the book. As we saw in Chapter 13, "Web

Portal," with the IActionLookup class, it is often possible to create an abstraction to insulate your domain code from OSGi. In the discussion here we talk about direct use of OSGi constructs with the understanding that such insulating layers can be introduced as needed.

21.4.1 Object Handling

Many systems include listeners or other objects, observers, that form couplings by being registered with a notifier service, the subject. The HttpService is one example—servlets in effect are registered as clients of the HttpService and are notified when there is a request to process. Every time a listener is added, a link between the listener and the notifier is created. If the listener's contributor disappears or is deactivated, this link needs to be cleaned up.

ANY OBJECT CAN BE A PROBLEM

Here we talk about "listeners" and "observers," but we really mean "any object given to, and held by, another bundle." It could be an actual listener or some other callback handler, a factory, or the implementation of an algorithm. The "notifier" or "subject" is the party that further invokes the listeners. In short, if you register a listener, you should unregister it.

In a perfect world, all clients would be dynamic-enabled and would clean up after themselves. Failure to clean up listeners prevents the uninstalled contributor from being garbage-collected and may cause runtime errors when a decommissioned listener is invoked. Here are a few strategies you can use to handle contributed objects:

Ignore—Assume that everyone is a good citizen and code your notifier robustly to handle any errors that might occur when notifying a stale listener. This tolerates the removal of the contributing bundle but leaves dangling listeners and has the potential to leak memory.

Validity testing—Include a validity test in your listener API. Before notifying any listener, the notifier tests its validity. Invalid listeners are removed from the listener list. The registering client then invalidates all its listeners when it is stopped. This lazily removes the listeners but still has the potential to leak if the notifier never tries to broadcast to, and thus test the validity of, an invalid listener. It also creates a standard test-and-set race condition on the listener's validity flag.

Weak listener list—Using a weak data structure such as WeakReferences or SoftReferences to maintain the listener list allows defunct listeners to simply disappear. Since clients typically have to maintain strong references to their listeners to support unregistering, there is little danger of the listeners being prematurely garbage-collected.

Co-register the contributor—Rather than just registering the listener, have clients register both themselves and the listener. Event sources then listen for bundle events and proactively remove listeners contributed by bundles being removed.

Introspection—Every object has a class. The bundle for a class can be found using FrameworkUtil.getBundle(listener.getClass()). With this information, you can tweak the co-registration approach to use introspection and cleanup. This approach is transparent but can be a bit costly and does not catch cases where one bundle adds a listener that is an instance of a class from a different bundle.

Discovery—The OSGi Whiteboard Pattern discussed in Chapter 15, "Declarative Services," flips the relationship between observer and subject such that observers do not register with the subject but rather the subject discovers the observers when needed. This centralizes the list management and simplifies the cleanup but does not eliminate the issues altogether.

In the end, there is no one right answer. The different strategies have different characteristics. The point is that you must be aware of the inter-bundle linkages and make explicit decisions about how they are managed. You should choose the coding patterns that best suit your requirements (speed, space, complexity) and apply them consistently and thoroughly.

USE SAFE EXECUTION MECHANISMS

In all of these cases, there are windows of opportunity for Toast to accidentally attempt to notify a stale listener. As with any notification mechanism, it is important that the notification code be robust enough to handle any errors that might occur. You should consider using a generalized safe execution mechanism such as SafeRunner and ISafeRunnable from the org.eclipse.equinox.common bundle to help manage such errors.

21.4.2 Bundle Listeners

BundleListeners are a powerful OSGi mechanism for handling change in a running system. Whenever a bundle changes state in the system, all registered BundleListeners are notified. Listeners typically do the same sort of cache management described earlier and as shown in the following snippet:

```
public class Activator implements BundleActivator {
  private BundleListener listener;
  private YourCacheType cache = null;

  public void start(BundleContext context) throws Exception {
    listener = new CacheManager();
    context.addBundleListener(listener);
  }

  public void stop(BundleContext context) throws Exception {
    context.removeBundleListener(listener);
  }

  public void addToCache(Bundle host, Object data) {
    cache.add(host, data);
  }

  public class CacheManager implements BundleListener {
    public void bundleChanged(BundleEvent event) {
      if (cache == null)
        return;
      if (event.getType() == BundleEvent.UNINSTALLED
          || event.getType() == BundleEvent.UNRESOLVED)
        cache.remove(event.getBundle());
    }
  }
}
```

In this case, the listener is registered as soon as the bundle is started. Your code collects and caches references related to bundles as needed. The BundleListener watches for UNINSTALLED and UNRESOLVED bundle events and removes the data related to the affected bundle from the cache it is managing. Notice that this code is a good citizen as it removes its listener when the bundle is stopped.

21.5 The Extender Pattern and BundleTracker

Services are not the only things that come and go in OSGi. As we have seen, bundles also change state. Reacting to these state changes can be quite powerful. The BundleListener described in the preceding section is a simple example of this. Unfortunately, programming raw BundleListeners is fraught with the same sort of complexity as using ServiceListeners, as we touched on in Chapter 6, "Dynamic Services." Enter BundleTrackers.

The BundleTracker class is a direct spin-off of ServiceTracker, complete with customizers. In essence it allows you to describe the kinds of bundles in which

you are interested and then presents you with a collection of the bundles that currently fit that model and a set of events relaying changes in the collection. Very
convenient.

One of the key uses of BundleTracker is to implement the *Extender Pattern*.
The Extender Pattern is reminiscent of the Whiteboard Pattern. It allows an
extender bundle to adapt discovered bundles and configure them into different
contexts. OSGi and Equinox include several examples of this:

❍ The Declarative Services extender watches for active and starting bundles
  that have the Service-Component header in their manifest. When it finds one,
  it parses the listed files and creates the described components.

❍ The Equinox Extension Registry is an extender that watches for resolved
  bundles that contain a plugin.xml file in their root folder. The content of this
  file is loaded and woven into the Extension Registry.

The Extender Pattern itself is very useful, and BundleTrackers make extender
implementation reasonably straightforward.

21.6 Dynamic Enablement

Dynamic enablement means being a good bundle citizen—a dynamic-enabled
bundle is written to correctly handle its own dynamic addition and removal. If
you don't clean up, you become a leak. Leaks bloat the system and eventually
cause it to run out of memory or become intolerably slow. In the case of Toast,
this means that all bundles must correctly unregister their listeners, unget
acquired services, and unregister all their services.

Some of this can be done automatically for you with mechanisms such as
Declarative Services. Being dynamic-enabled may also mean disposing of OS
resources. The OS does not know when a bundle is stopped. To the OS, the JVM
is still running, so it has to maintain all resources allocated to the JVM process.
These include

❍ Open streams

❍ Undisposed graphical objects such as images, colors, and fonts

❍ Unstarted and running threads

❍ Open sockets

For a bundle to be dynamic-enabled, it must clean up any such resources as
they are removed or stopped.

21.6.1 Cleaning Up after Yourself

Developers often assume that when their bundle's stop method is called, the system is shutting down. As such, they do only mild cleanup, if any at all. These bundles are not dynamic-enabled. Bundles can be stopped at any time and actual system shutdown may not occur for quite some time.

A dynamic-enabled bundle is one that

○ Ensures that all objects it registers are unregistered when no longer needed

○ Ensures that all allocated resources are freed

○ Implements a rigorous component deactivate method where Declarative Services are used

○ Implements a rigorous stop method where a BundleActivator is used

Bundles that register listeners, handlers, and UI contributions via code or allocate shared resources must take care to unregister or dispose of such objects when they are obsolete. This is just good programming practice. If you call an add method, ensure that you call the matching remove when appropriate. Similarly, this should be done for alloc and free, create and dispose, as well as for opening and closing streams.

NO MATCH FOR CONSTRUCTOR INITIALIZATION

Problems in this space often come up as a result of registering listeners and the like in object constructors. Since constructors have no natural counterpart, it is often difficult to determine where and when these registrations should be undone.

To implement a backstop, your bundle activator or DS component needs to know which objects to dispose. This can be hard-coded if the set is limited and known ahead of time. For example, if your bundle holds a socket open, ensure that it is closed in the stop method.

More generally, you can track the objects needing disposal. The following code is a sketch of how this works. The activator maintains a weak set of objects that need disposal. Throughout the life of the bundle, various disposable objects are added to and removed from the set. When the bundle is finally stopped, all remaining disposable objects are disposed. The set is weak to avoid leaks in situations where an object is added but not removed, even though it is no longer live.

```
public interface IDisposable {
    public void dispose();
}
```

```
public class Disposer {
  private Map disposables = new WeakHashMap(11);

  public void add(IDisposable object) {
    disposables.put(object, object);
  }

  public void remove(IDisposable object) {
    disposables.remove(object);
  }

  public void dispose(){
    for (Iterator i = disposables.keySet().iterator(); i.hasNext();)
      ((IDisposable) i.next()).dispose();
    disposables.clear();
  }
}

public class Activator implements BundleActivator {
  private static Disposer disposer = new Disposer();

  public static Disposer getDisposer() {
    return disposer;
  }

  public void stop(BundleContext context) throws Exception {
    getDisposer().dispose();
  }
}

public class Listener implements IDisposable, IRegistryChangeListener {
  private IExtensionRegistry registry;
  public Listener() {
    super();
    Activator.getDisposer().add(this);
  }

  public void registryChanged(IRegistryChangeEvent event) {
    // do some processing here
  }

  public void dispose() {
    registry.removeRegistryChangeListener(this);
  }
}
```

This is just an example of an implementation approach. At the end of the snippet, there is an example of a registry change listener that lists itself as a disposable on creation. You can register the disposable at any point as long as it is added before the bundle stops. When the bundle stops, the listener is guaranteed to be removed from the event source—the Extension Registry in this case. If the listener is removed from the source and not the disposal list, it is either removed transparently as garbage or it is unregistered from the source when the bundle is stopped. Unregistering a listener that is not registered is a no-op.

SYNCHRONIZATION OMITTED

For clarity and simplicity, we have omitted the synchronization code and error checking needed to make this pattern robust.

21.7 The Dynamics of Startup and Shutdown

Much of the focus on dynamism tends to be in terms of things being added or removed while the application is running. Some people assume that since their scenario is fixed, dynamic issues do not apply to them. In fact, every system is dynamic since bundles are installed and started in a sequential and more or less random order.

START ORDER IS HARD TO CONTROL

The startup order of bundles is deterministic but is influenced by the install order. Install order is generally not easy to manage or enforce. Therefore, from a system point of view, you have to assume that bundles will be started in an unknown order. Shutdown may be somewhat more orderly, but depending on particular sequences is unlikely to yield good results across the board.

21.7.1 Start Levels

OSGi includes the notion of *start level* to help manage the startup and shutdown order. The start level of a bundle is set using the `StartLevel` service. OSGi start levels are much like UNIX start levels. As the system starts, the start level is increased, and all bundles marked with the current start level are started before moving on to the next level. So, for example, by the time bundles at level 4 are started, all those needing to be started at level 3 have been started. If a level is not specified, the framework uses the default start level. In Equinox the default start level is 4. You can change this by manipulating the value of the `osgi.bundles.defaultStartLevel` system property.

You can inject your bundle into the startup sequence by controlling its start level. This allows you to, for example, add login prompters before the application is run, control the bundles that are installed, or do last-minute cleanup as the system shuts down.

START LEVELS ARE ADVANCED

This mechanism is for advanced and special-case use only. You really have to understand how the system works before looking to manage start levels manually. Do not use start levels to work around bugs in your code. Note also that the current start level values are not API and are subject to change in future releases.

A Word on DS and Simple Configurator

In some of the Toast configurations outlined in this book we use start levels to ensure that two certain bundles are started early, in particular, the Declarative Services implementation, org.eclipse.equinox.ds, and the Simple Configurator, org.eclipse.equinox.simpleconfigurator. These bundles are unique in that they are basic system infrastructure.

The DS bundle must be started before its extender is able to process any contributed DS components. As such, the DS bundle must be started at or before the start level of any bundles expecting to use DS—if DS is not started, their components will not be registered. If you use DS and start levels, we recommend simply ensuring that the DS bundle is started at level 1.

Simple Configurator is part of the p2 provisioning infrastructure and is responsible for installing and managing other bundles. While it is technically possible to start this bundle at any point in the start sequence, earlier is better, as its operation may result in bundles being installed, updated, or uninstalled. It's better to do this before they have started doing work.

21.7.2 *Proper Use of Services*

By far the best approach to startup dynamism is to simply use the available dynamic mechanisms as intended. If your bundle is dynamic-aware for addition, it does not need any special treatment at startup. When the needed services appear, the bundle or component will start operation accordingly. The use of Declarative Services and the Extension Registry with lazy activation greatly ease achieving this goal. Even so, with DS you may need to use immediate components, as discussed in Section 15.2.5, "Immediate Components."

It takes some time for traditional Java programmers to get their heads around the OSGi pattern of interacting bundles. There is generally no main thread or entry point from which you can hang the startup of the various components. Even in situations where there is, that usage pattern is brittle and hard to maintain.

21.7.3 Shutting Down Is Not Always Easy

Many bundles start up and allocate resources that need to be cleaned up on shutdown. HTTP servers, worker pools, network connections, and the like all need to be explicitly shut down. An example from the writing of this book is telling. When putting together the client UI for the radio and CD player applications, we used the Eclipse Jobs mechanism to create workers to manage the operation of each virtual device. These workers wait until an event is discovered, wake and process the event, and then schedule themselves to run and wait again. When the system is shut down, the radio and CD player DS components are deactivated and need to clean up their Jobs. The following snippet outlines this process:

org.equinoxosgi.toast.dev.radio.fake/AbstractFakeRadio
```
public void shutdown() {
  job.cancel();
  try {
    job.join();
  } catch (InterruptedException e) {
  }
}
```

Logically, canceling a Job causes it to stop what it is doing and return. This in turn would allow the join to succeed, and we would be sure that the component's resources were indeed freed. In practice, however, the Job simply uses a wait call and does not check for cancellation, as shown here:

org.equinoxosgi.toast.dev.radio.fake/AbstractFakeRadio
```
private Job createJob() {
  return new Job("Scan") {
    protected IStatus run(IProgressMonitor monitor) {
      try {
        synchronized (this) {
          wait();
          scanUp();
        }
      } catch (InterruptedException e) {
        return Status.CANCEL_STATUS;
      }
      schedule();
      return Status.OK_STATUS;
    }
  };
}
```

Since the Job does not look for cancellation, shutdown's call to cancel has no effect, the Job will never exit, and the join call will never complete—deadlock. Instead, you must be careful to ensure that the component or bundle's deactivation code is robust and complete—resources must be freed and the methods must not fail, do a partial job, or hang. In this case the problem can be addressed by having a volatile boolean field called running that is set and checked in the updated Job code, as shown here:

```
org.equinoxosgi.toast.dev.radio.fake/AbstractFakeRadio
private Job createJob() {
  return new Job("Scan") {
    protected IStatus run(IProgressMonitor monitor) {
      try {
        synchronized (this) {
          wait();
          scanUp();
        }
      } catch (InterruptedException e) {
        return Status.CANCEL_STATUS;
      }
      if (running)
        schedule();
      return Status.OK_STATUS;
    }
    protected void canceling() {
      super.canceling();
      running = false;
      AbstractFakeRadio.this.stopScanning();
    }
  };
}
```

The key here is that the Job itself must be aware that it can be canceled and must clean itself up. The component can then cancel the Job and be assured it is stopped. The same model can be applied to threads, loops, and many other resources allocated and managed by components or bundles.

21.8 Summary

Dynamic update and addition of functionality to running applications is an important part of the total user experience. Toast would be significantly diminished without it, and dynamic server-side applications would be impossible.

OSGi and Equinox include many mechanisms, from Declarative Services to BundleTracker and ExtensionTracker, in support of dynamic behavior. Even with these, being dynamic is not free. It is somewhat akin to concurrent programming. Attention to detail and revisiting and isolating your assumptions are good tactics—and likely good things to do anyway! In many cases, the outcome is a better, more flexible system that is also more dynamic.

CHAPTER 22

Integrating Code Libraries

There are many useful open-source and commercial Java libraries available today, as well as libraries developed by individuals or teams. Using these in an OSGi context can be hampered by two issues: packaging as bundles and the use of historical Java extensibility mechanisms.

The last few years have seen a dramatic increase in the number of Java libraries that include OSGi markup, but even the most OSGi-biased developer would concede that the majority of Java libraries out there are still not shipped as bundles. Even if they were bundles, many libraries use context class loaders and other techniques that clash with OSGi. This chapter discusses the integration of these libraries into the OSGi runtime environment.

Bundling, the generic term for converting a JAR to a bundle, is typically a straightforward process, but there are choices to be made and issues to be resolved. In this chapter we discuss the different bundling variants and common problems that arise when using existing code in an OSGi system. In particular, we show you how to

○ Structure bundles differently

○ Bundle by injection—add bundle metadata to existing JARs

○ Bundle by wrapping—wrap JARs with bundle metadata

○ Bundle by reference—add bundle metadata beside existing JARs without affecting the JARs, their original location, or their surrounding directory structure

○ Find other bundling technology such as *bnd*

○ Solve common class loading problems

22.1 JARs as Bundles

As we saw in Section 2.3, "The Anatomy of a Bundle," a typical bundle is simply a JAR, as shown in Figure 22-1. Such a bundle is like any other JAR with the exception that the MANIFEST.MF contains OSGi headers to define dependencies, classpaths, and the like. In fact, if the bundle's code does not depend on OSGi mechanisms, the JAR will work fine on normal JREs.

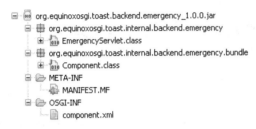

Figure 22–1　A traditional bundle JAR

Looking at it this way, it is natural for library producers to include this extra bundle metadata in their MANIFEST.MF and ship their library as both a stand-alone JAR and a bundle ready for integration into OSGi. If all libraries were shipped this way, you could skip the rest of this chapter! Library producers are increasingly including OSGi metadata, but it is still not the norm. That day may come, but in the meantime, this mind-set should help you in the process of bundling the libraries you want to use in OSGi.

Note also that there is no reason that a bundle has to be a JAR at all; that is just the norm. The Eclipse community has many examples of bundles that are delivered and run as folders. For the most part these folders are just the bundle JAR exploded on disk. Ultimately the installBundle method in OSGi takes an InputStream, so any input stream that the framework implementation understands can be used to supply bundle content. Section 23.3, "The Shape of Bundles," details the benefits and drawbacks of different bundle shapes.

22.2 Bundling by Injection

As you saw in the previous section, JAR files can be used as bundles as long as they contain the required metadata. Here we look at how to bundle existing code library JARs by injecting this information into the manifest. This approach retains all the benefits of JAR'd bundles and increases the chances that the library authors will include the injected metadata directly in their original releases—it directly illustrates the simplicity of the required changes.

Figure 22-2 shows the process of bundling Apache Commons Logging. On the left are some original JARs from Apache and on the right is a bundle composed of the Apache JARs. Note that the original JARs had MANIFEST.MF files—all JARs do—but these did not contain OSGi markup. The operation adds the required OSGi bundle definition information in the MANIFEST.MF file of the output bundle.

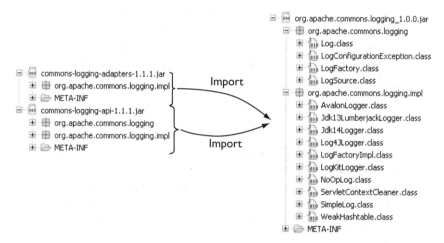

Figure 22–2 Injecting metadata into a code library

Commons Logging comes in a number of different JARs, none of which are bundles. We could bundle these individually, but it turns out that some overlap in different ways. For example, the package org.apache.commons.logging.impl appears in multiple JARs. It would be better to combine these into one bundle.

The process for bundling individual JARs or groups is the same and is outlined here:

○ Create a new bundle project using **File > New > Project... > Plug-in from existing JARs**.

○ Ensure that the **Unzip the JAR archives into the project** box is checked so that the wizard unpacks all the JARs as they are imported into the new project. If more than one JAR is listed, as in Figure 22-2, they are merged as if they were on the classpath in the order specified in the wizard; that is, resources in subsequent JARs *do not* overwrite resources in previous JARs. The wizard then generates a manifest that exports all the packages in the new bundle.

○ Click **Finish**.

The resultant project is just like any other bundle project. You can leave it in the workspace and code against it, you can run with it, and you can export it. A handy trick is to export it and add it to the target platform. You can then delete the project from the workspace—the library becomes just another bundle that you are using. This keeps your workspace clean and allows the new bundle to be shared between workspaces.

ORBIT, A SOURCE FOR BUNDLES

In Eclipse there is a whole project, Orbit, dedicated to the bundling of third-party libraries used by various Eclipse teams. If the library you are using is from an open-source project, chances are that Orbit has a bundled version of it. Check out http://eclipse.org/orbit to see what is available.

Where there are multiple libraries to be bundled, you can merge them as just described or convert each to a bundle individually. This is certainly feasible, but it is not always the best choice. For example, Ant comes as a set of about 28 JARs. Many of these are tiny (<10K). While the overhead of a bundle is small, this feels too fine-grained for most use cases—vast numbers of bundles are harder to manage.

Bundling closely related JARs separately can be a problem when the packages they contain overlap, as we saw previously. If code in these package fragments needs to see package-private members that are in other JARs, bundling separately does not work. Normally these JARs would all be loaded by the same class loader, so there would be only one definition of any given package. In an OSGi-based system, each bundle gets its own class loader, so the package `org.apache.commons.logging.impl` loaded by Bundle A is actually different from the one with the same name but loaded by Bundle B. They do not share package visibility. Whether or not this is an issue is specific to the code being bundled.

Overall the best practice is to bundle each library individually, but in certain cases that may not be possible or optimal.

22.3 Bundling by Wrapping

Since injecting metadata as described in the previous section requires modification of the original JARs, it is not always feasible. The following list outlines the most common problems with that approach:

Licensing—Licenses sometimes explicitly state that the licensed material cannot be modified or that modifications trigger further restrictions or obligations.

Signing—JARs are often signed to prevent otherwise undetected tampering with their contents. In this use of signing, it may be possible to inject the metadata and additional files—these files are either not signed or are signed by a different signer. In other situations, signing is used to imply permissions and rights. In these cases, it is less clear that metadata injection is feasible.

Multiple JARs—Some libraries come as multiple JARs. As discussed previously, the JARs can be bundled separately or they can be combined. Both approaches are feasible but may not be attractive in some cases.

If one of these situations applies to you, consider wrapping the JARs with a bundle definition; that is, create a MANIFEST.MF that describes the dependencies, and then collect the manifest and the JARs together in a single JAR, as shown in Figure 22-3.

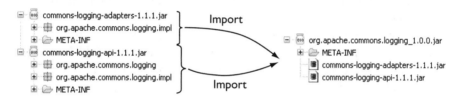

Figure 22–3 Wrapping a code library

The same bundling wizard used to inject metadata can be used to wrap JARs. Simply unchecking the **Unzip the JAR archives into the project** box tells the wizard to copy the JARs into the project without extracting their contents. The JARs are then listed on the bundle's classpath in the order in which you added them to the wizard. Again, the resultant project is just like any other bundle project.

Note that when you export the project, however, you have an additional choice to make. If you export the project as a JAR, you will end up with the original library JARs nested inside the new bundle JAR. Bundles in this layout are usable but are inefficient with respect to disk space, as the nested JARs must be extracted before being used—Java class loaders are not able to load classes directly from nested JARs. Furthermore, standard Java compilers cannot compile against nested JARs.

The alternative is to export the bundle as a folder. Folder bundles are supported by most frameworks, but not all provisioning systems are able to install and manage such bundles. See Section 23.3, "The Shape of Bundles," for details on the pros and cons of various bundle shapes.

22.4 Bundling by Reference

EQUINOX ONLY AND EXPERIMENTAL

This approach is particular to Equinox. It is somewhat experimental and subject to change. It breaks some fundamental notions of bundle encapsulation and is not well supported by tooling. Bundling by reference does, however, address some real use cases. Use with caution and only when absolutely needed.

In some situations, installed JARs cannot be moved, let alone modified. This typically happens when the libraries are delivered as part of another product and are laid down by an installer. The JARs are in a specific spot and are expected to be there to be found by other programs.

The bundling approaches outlined so far do not work because they modify either the JAR itself or its surroundings. For example, wrapping adds bundle metadata beside the JAR being wrapped. If there is only one set of JARs to wrap in a directory, the generated metadata can be directly added to the directory—essentially wrapping in place. If there are multiple libraries in the same directory, the metadata files conflict with each other. Metadata injection can be used only if the issues mentioned earlier are not applicable. For example, the JAR has to be writable.

Even if injection or wrapping is used, there is still the problem of how to get the resultant bundle installed into the framework. Many management systems expect to control bundle location. For example, the traditional Eclipse pattern is to have bundles either in the main `plugins` directory in the Eclipse install or in a `plugins` directory in an extension location. Both approaches require moving the newly bundled library. Some frameworks allow you to explicitly list bundles in configuration files such as `config.ini` in Equinox, but that is cumbersome and hard to manage. See Chapter 23, "Advanced Topics," for a discussion of the `osgi.bundles` property and related topics.

What you really need is to have the metadata *on the side* and break the connection between the OSGi metadata location and the bundle content. For example, suppose you have a façade bundle JAR that contains just the metadata and indicates the location of the code JARs. The façade can be installed, updated, and run using normal OSGi API and management mechanisms without affecting, or being affected by, the referenced code libraries.

To illustrate how this works, consider a mythical Java database connectivity (JDBC) driver JAR that comes with a database product. The product installer puts `jdbc.jar` in `c:\db\drivers\jdbc.jar` and you cannot modify it, move it, or add files to the `drivers` directory.

To set this up, proceed as though you are using the wrapping approach from the previous section. Run the **New Project** wizard and create a JDBC bundle based on `jdbc.jar`. Don't worry about the libraries being copied into the project; you can use them to do your normal development.

When you go to run your application, you need to use the original JDBC libraries. Use the following steps to set up the structure shown in Figure 22-4:

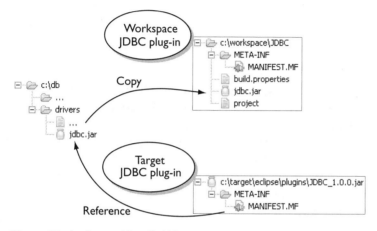

Figure 22–4   External bundle JARs

○ Export the newly created JDBC bundle from your workspace to your target's `plugins` directory.

○ Delete the exported JARs and extraneous files (e.g., `.project`) from the exported target bundle.

○ Edit the exported target bundle's `MANIFEST.MF` and change the `Bundle-Classpath` header to point to the original JARs using absolute file system paths. For example, replace `jdbc.jar` with `external:$JDBC_HOME$/drivers/jdbc.jar`. You can use environment or system properties, or full file system paths, to identify the desired JAR.

○ In the IDE, use **Window > Preferences... > Bundle Development > Target Platform > Reload** to refresh the target and add the new JDBC bundle.

○ Set up an **OSGi Application** launch configuration to run your product. On the **Bundles** page, select the third option, **Choose bundles and fragments to launch from the list....** In the list of bundles, uncheck the JDBC bundle in the **Workspace Bundles** list and check the one in the **Target Bundles** list.

○ Run the launch configuration. It is difficult to tell which JAR is being used, but it should be the original `c:\db\drivers\jdbc.jar`. You can confirm this by renaming the original JAR and running. The application should fail when trying to load JDBC classes.

When it comes time to deploy your application and the JDBC bundle, you have to rely on an installer to set up the bundle's manifest and ensure that jdbc.jar is in fact installed. The task is quite a bit easier if the database product defines environment variables or Java system properties, as shown in the example, to describe the location of its install. For example, if the product defined JDBC_HOME as an environment variable, you can set up the JDBC bundle's manifest to include the line

```
Bundle-Classpath: external:$JDBC_HOME$/drivers/jdbc.jar
```

This mechanism has the added benefit that the JDBC bundle can be built and delivered using standard Eclipse mechanisms. Variables make this even easier.

The real danger in using this setup is the potential for mismatching the metadata and contents of the JARs. For example, you might generate the metadata based on version 3 of the JDBC drivers, but the actual installed drivers are version 2. Tracking down these kinds of bugs is challenging, to say the least. Nonetheless, the mechanism is there, and it solves some real problems. Use it with caution and care and only when absolutely necessary.

22.5 Bundling Using bnd

As an alternative to using PDE or for integration in headless builds, you can use *bnd*. *bnd* is a tool for creating bundles from Java artifacts. It is quite flexible and integrates on the command line, in Eclipse, and in Ant and Maven. *bnd* offers quite a number of directives for how it finds, analyzes, and collects Java artifacts. For full details see www.aqute.biz/Code/Bnd. Here we describe it in high-level detail to give a sense of what it does and how it works.

At its core, *bnd* is similar to the PDE function described previously. It reads the binary class files and looks for references to packages. Your role as the user is to describe the kinds of packages to be in the bundle. *bnd* then finds and exports all such packages. Packages that are referenced in the code, but are not in the export list, are added to the Import-Package list. The *bnd* technique offers some additional flexibility for collecting artifacts from a number of places.

22.6 Troubleshooting Class Loading Problems

Most code libraries are quite straightforward to bundle and then use in OSGi-based systems. You've seen that the wizard to create bundles from existing JARs does most of the work for you. But what happens if there are problems after bundling? At this point there are two main problems that could occur. The first happens at compile time—classes in the bundled JAR may not be visible. This is easily addressed by ensuring that the bundle exports all the necessary packages from the library and contains the correct class versions. But what if something goes wrong at runtime? The classic symptoms are `ClassNotFoundExceptions` and `NoClassDefFoundErrors` showing up in the console or the log file.

This entire section is devoted to helping you understand and troubleshoot these runtime errors. Typically, they relate to the class loading structure inherent in Equinox and OSGi. The OSGi class loading strategy and mechanism are discussed in Chapter 23, "Advanced Topics," but here we detail some standard library coding patterns and how they are handled.

22.6.1 *Issues with* `Class.forName()`

Let's start with the classic example of `ClassNotFoundException`, which occurs while using a bundled code library. Consider adding logging using log4j, a popular library for managing and logging events (http://logging.apache.org/), in Toast. Using the techniques described earlier, you can bundle log4j and add it to either your workspace or target and continue development. At runtime, however, log4j throws a number of `ClassNotFoundExceptions` when trying to configure its *appenders*.

log4j is extensible in that it allows clients to supply log appenders—effectively log event handlers. Appenders are configured by naming their implementation classes in metadata files, much like the Equinox Extension Registry and OSGi Declarative Services runtime. log4j then reads these files and loads the named classes using a code pattern similar to the following snippet:

```
public class AppenderHelper {
  private Appender createAppender(appenderName) {
    Class appenderClass = Class.forName(appenderName);
    return appenderClass.newInstance();
  }
}
```

LOG4J CLASS LOADING VARIATIONS

log4j actually uses a more advanced code pattern that is detailed in the next section. For the sake of this example, assume that log4j is running with the `log4j.ignoreTCL` property set to `true` and that `Class.forName` is its only class loading option.

`Class.forName` is the classic mechanism for dynamic class discovery and loading. It uses the *current class loader* to look for and load the requested class, in this case, an appender. The current class loader is the class loader that loaded the class containing the method executing the `forName` call. In the preceding snippet, the current class loader is the one that loaded `AppenderHelper`. The net result is the same as if a reference to the appender class were compiled into `createAppender`, which is exactly what using `Class.forName` is trying to work around.

In OSGi, this is problematic because the log4j bundle typically does not depend on the bundles providing the appenders. This is actually the point—appenders are log4j's way of allowing its function to be extended without its prior knowledge. As a result, the log4j bundle cannot load these appenders because it does not have them on its classpath.

If log4j were written as a bundle, it could, for example, use the Equinox Extension Registry and define an `appenders` extension point. Bundles wanting to provide extenders would then contribute executable extensions that name their appender classes, and log4j would use `createExecutableExtension` as described in Chapter 16, "Extensions," rather than the code in `createAppender`. log4j could also use the OSGi Whiteboard Pattern discussed in Chapter 13, "Web Portal," to discover available appender services. Unfortunately, neither is true of log4j or libraries in general, so we need an alternative.

Equinox's *buddy class loading* offers an alternative integration strategy that does not require code modification. The mechanism works as follows:

○ Bundles declare that they need the help of other bundles to load classes.

○ They also identify the kind of help they want by specifying a *buddy policy*. The policy defines what kinds of bundles are to be considered to be buddies as well as how (e.g., in what order) they are consulted.

○ When a bundle fails to find a desired class through all the normal routes—`Import-Package`, `Require-Bundle`, and local classes—as outlined in Section 23.9, "Class Loading," its buddy policy is invoked.

○ The invoked policy discovers a set of *buddies* and consults each one in turn until either the class is found or the list is exhausted.

WHAT'S IN A NAME?

The term *buddy class loading* has its origins in the scuba-diving practice of *buddy breathing*. If you run out of air while diving, you rely on your buddy to help out. You never plan to run out of air, but when it happens, you sure are glad you've got a buddy.

Let's apply the built-in *registered* buddy policy to the log4j case and see how it helps. In the log4j scenario, there are a relatively large number of potential clients of the logging API and a small number of clients supplying appenders. For performance and simplicity, it makes sense to limit the buddy search scope to just those supplying appenders. The simplest approach is to make those bundles explicitly register as buddies of log4j.

To set this up, first mark the log4j bundle as needing class loading help and identify the `registered` policy as the policy to use. The following line added to log4j's `MANIFEST.MF` makes that declaration:

```
Eclipse-BuddyPolicy: registered
```

Then in each bundle that supplies appenders, add the following line to the `MANIFEST.MF` to register the bundle as a buddy of log4j (i.e., `org.apache.log4j`):

```
Eclipse-RegisterBuddy: org.apache.log4j
```

At runtime, when log4j goes to instantiate an appender using `Class.forName`, it first tries all of its normal OSGi prerequisites. Then, when it fails to find the appender class, each of its registered buddy bundles is asked to load the class. If all the appender bundles are registered, the appender class is sure to be found.

BUDDIES LOAD AS THEMSELVES

Buddies are consulted as if they were originating the load class request using `Bundle.loadClass`; that is, the buddy's imported packages, required bundles, and, in fact, its own buddies are all invoked as necessary in the search for the desired class.

22.6.1.1 Built-in Buddy Policies

Equinox supplies a number of built-in policies, as summarized in Table 22-1.

Table 22–1 Built-in Buddy Policies

Name	Description
boot	Indicates that the standard Java boot class loader is a buddy.
ext	Indicates that the standard Java extension class loader is a buddy. This policy is a superset of the boot policy.

(*continues*)

Table 22–1   Built-in Buddy Policies (*Continued*)

Name	Description
app	Indicates that the standard Java application class loader is a buddy. This policy is a superset of the ext policy.
parent	Indicates that the bundle's parent class loader is a buddy. By default, the parent class loader is the standard Java boot class loader. Bundle class loader parentage is controlled on a global basis by setting the osgi.parentClassloader system property.
dependent	Consults all bundles that directly or indirectly depend on the current bundle. Note that this casts a rather wide net and may introduce performance problems as the number of bundles increases.
registered	Is similar to the dependent policy, but only dependent bundles that have explicitly registered themselves as buddies of the current bundle are consulted.

One bundle can apply several policies simply by listing them on the Eclipse-BuddyPolicy line in the MANIFEST.MF separated by commas. Equinox invokes each policy in turn until either the class is found or all policies have been consulted.

22.6.1.2 *Buddy Class Loading Considerations*

As powerful and useful as buddy class loading is, it is still a mechanism of last resort. There are a number of issues that you should consider carefully before using buddies in your system:

○ Buddy class loading runs counter to the notion of component that OSGi attempts to maintain and is not particularly well suited to dynamic environments—particularly ones where buddies can be uninstalled.

○ Buddy class loading also incurs various performance costs. For example, buddies are consulted even where they cannot help. Typical Java resource bundle loading causes up to three class load failures and some number of resource load failures before finally getting the desired resource. Each of these failures repeats a fruitless buddy search.

○ Buddy loading is relatively undirected. Normally, the OSGi class loading infrastructure knows exactly where to go to find any given package—using the information gleaned from the MANIFEST.MF files eliminates all searching. Typical buddy loading policies, however, simply search successive buddies.

○ It is possible that the buddy search will find the wrong class with the right name. If two buddies contain the same class, the buddy that ultimately supplies the class depends on the policy used and may in fact be ambiguous.

22.6.1.3 DynamicImport-Package *versus Buddy Class Loading*

Readers familiar with OSGi may be scratching their heads and asking, "What about DynamicImport-Package?" For readers who are not familiar with OSGi, DynamicImport-Package is a mechanism that allows a bundle to state its need to use a given set of packages but not force an early binding to the exporters of those packages. Rather, the binding to package exporters is done at runtime when the bundle tries to load from a dynamically imported package.

So, some Class.forName problems can be alleviated simply by adding

```
DynamicImport-Package: <list of packages or *>
```

to the MANIFEST.MF for the bundle using Class.forName. This has the following drawbacks compared to the buddy loading described previously:

- ○ Dynamic importing is unscoped; that is, all bundles exporting packages are considered. As such, the search may include many irrelevant and unrelated bundles. By contrast, the buddy loading mechanism allows for policies that use dynamic information such as the bundle dependency graph to drive the search for classes.

- ○ Dynamic importing implies inter-bundle constraints. When a Bundle A loads a class from a Bundle B using dynamic importing, A is then considered to be dependent on B. If B is refreshed or uninstalled, A is refreshed. This behavior is valuable for maintaining consistency when A actually uses and retains references to B's classes. However, several serialization scenarios have A simply using B's classes temporarily (e.g., to load some object stream)—there is no lasting dependency.

- ○ Dynamic import considers only packages explicitly exported by other bundles. Again this can be a desirable characteristic, but in various use cases such as serialization, the importing bundle potentially needs access to classes that would normally not be exported, for example, to load instances from an object stream.

This is not to say that DynamicImport-Package should never be used, just that it should be used appropriately. For example, use it when the set of packages needed is well known and the importing bundle has a lasting dependency on the imported packages.

22.6.2 *Issues with Context Class Loaders*

Since Java 1.2, the Class.forName mechanism has been largely superseded by *context class loading*. As a result, most modern class libraries use a context class loader. In the following discussion, we show how Equinox transparently converts the use of context class loaders into something equivalent to `Class.forName`. Doing this allows the buddy loading and `DynamicImportPackage` mechanisms described previously to be used to eliminate `ClassNotFoundExceptions` and `NoClassDefFoundErrors`.

Each `Thread` in Java 1.2 and above has an associated context class loader field that contains a class loader. The class loader in this field is set, typically by an application container, to match the context of this current execution; that is, the field contains a class loader that has access to the classes related to the current execution (e.g., web request being processed). Libraries such as log4j access and use the context class loader with the updated `AppenderHelper` code pattern:

```
public class AppenderHelper {
  private Appender createAppender(String appenderName) {
    ClassLoader loader =
      Thread.currentThread().getContextClassLoader();
    Class appenderClass = loader.loadClass(appenderName);
    return (Appender) appenderClass.newInstance();
  }
}
```

By default, the context class loader is set to be the normal Java application class loader—the one you specify on the Java command line. Given that, the use of the context class loader in normal Java application scenarios is equivalent to using `Class.forName`, and there is only one class loader involved—the normal application class loader. When running inside OSGi, however, the code pattern outlined previously fails, because

○ By default, OSGi frameworks do not consult the application class loader. OSGi-based applications put their code on dynamic bundle classpaths rather than on the normal Java application classpath.

○ OSGi cannot detect bundle context switches and set the context class loader as required—there is no way to tell when execution context shifts from one bundle to the next as is done in web application servers.

These characteristics, combined with the compositional nature of OSGi, mean that the value of the context class loader field is seldom useful in OSGi contexts.

Clients can, however, explicitly set the context class loader before calling libraries that use the context class loader. The following snippet shows an example of calling log4j using this approach:

```
ClassLoader loader = thread.getContextClassLoader();
Thread thread = Thread.currentThread();
thread.setContextClassLoader(this.getClass().getClassLoader());
```

```
try {
    ... log4j library call that calls AppenderHelper.createAppender() ...
} finally {
    thread.setContextClassLoader(loader);
}
```

First the current context class loader is saved. The context class loader field on the current thread is then set to an appropriate value for the current execution, and log4j is called. log4j's `AppenderHelper` uses the context class loader, so in this case it uses the client's class loader (e.g., `this.getClass().getClassLoader()`). When the operation is finished, the original context class loader is restored.

The assumption here is that the client's class loader is able to load all required classes. This may or may not be true. Even if it can, the coding pattern is cumbersome to use and hard to maintain for any significant number of library calls. Ideally, log4j would be able to dynamically discover the context relevant to a particular class loading operation. Equinox enables this using the *context finder*.

The context finder is a type of `ClassLoader` that is installed by Equinox as the default context class loader when the framework is started. When invoked, the context finder searches down the Java execution stack for a class loader other than the system class loader. In the previous `AppenderHelper` example, it finds the log4j bundle's class loader—the one that loaded `AppenderHelper`. The context finder then delegates the load request to the discovered class loader.

This mechanism effectively transforms log4j's call to `getContextClassLoader()` `.loadClass(String)` to the equivalent `Class.forName` call using log4j's class loader to load the given class. Now the buddy class loading techniques discussed in Section 22.6.1 can be applied to help log4j load the needed appender classes.

The net effect is that clients of log4j do not have to use the cumbersome coding pattern outlined earlier, even though the libraries they call use the context class loader. This approach generalizes to other context class loading situations.

22.6.3 Managing JRE Classes

For various reasons, some libraries include packages that are normally found in the JRE. For example, version 2.6 of Xalan, the XML transformation engine, comes with types from the `org.w3c.dom.xpath` package in `xalan.jar`. These types are also included as part of typical JRE distributions. When `xalan.jar` is used as part of a normal Java application, it is added to the classpath, but its `xpath` classes are obscured by those in the JRE. Everything is fine.

When you bundle Xalan, you have to be careful to ensure that you produce `Export-Package` entries for all packages in `xalan.jar`. You should also be sure to add imports for the `org.w3c.dom.xpath` package found in the JRE. Without those imports, Xalan uses its own copies of the xpath types and may conflict with those supplied by the JRE.

This happens because OSGi class loading is highly optimized. These optimizations depend on the bundle manifest information to know which packages come from which bundles. Except for the use of certain buddy policies, the class loaders never search for classes; they always know exactly where to find them.

For the JRE packages, only java.* packages are assumed to come from the boot class loader. All others must be imported in the consuming bundle's MANIFEST.MF. The API packages included in the JRE are typically exported by the OSGi System Bundle. In Equinox, this list is captured in a JRE *profile*. The org.eclipse.osgi bundle includes a number of profiles for common JREs and automatically detects the appropriate one to use. See Section 23.9, "Class Loading," for more details.

So, if the Xalan bundle fails to import the xpath packages, its local copies are used. This may result in ClassCastExceptions because the bundle's copy of the type is not interchangeable with the copy supplied by the JRE. Changing the bundle to import the packages tells OSGi to use the external copy. Alternatively, the offending packages can be removed from Xalan.

22.6.4 *Serialization*

Serialization of objects occurs in many different situations. Some libraries use the built-in java.io.Serializable mechanism directly. Some use it indirectly as a consequence of using Remote Method Invocation (RMI). Others serialize objects using their own marshaling strategies (e.g., Hibernate stores/loads objects to/from relational databases). Regardless of the technique used, these bundles have the following characteristics:

❍ They are typically generic utilities and do not have access to, or knowledge of, your domain classes.

❍ They do not hold on to the classes they request, but rather use them to load objects and then discard their references.

❍ They need access to internal classes if instances of internal classes have been serialized.

Dynamically loading classes using DynamicImport-Package or buddy class loading and context class loading address these problems. In effect, loading a serialized object is equivalent to the log4j appender problem. Appender classes are identified by name to log4j. Classes to load are identified to the serialization bundle by name in the object stream. In both cases, the loading bundle needs to search beyond its prerequisite bundles to find the desired classes.

As with the logging case, the ideal solution is for the library to be OSGi-aware and use services or extensions to allow a bundle with serializable objects to make itself available. This is rarely a pragmatic solution, however.

22.7 Summary

The Java world includes a wealth of useful code libraries. OSGi, Equinox, and PDE provide a number of techniques for integrating these code libraries into the runtime environment. This can be as simple as running a wizard—most of the time it is.

In some cases, however, the code in the library uses certain patterns that are at odds with OSGi's modularity support. Class loading is the most common bone of contention. Equinox includes several mechanisms and strategies for dealing with these cases. In particular, you can use buddy loading policies or `DynamicImport-Package` to provide visibility to classes that would normally not be visible, and the context finder to discover possible sources of classes. In this chapter we described the most significant of these and illustrated their use. The mechanisms outlined here enable you to resolve most remaining class loading issues encountered when integrating code libraries into an OSGi-based environment.

CHAPTER 23

Advanced Topics

Throughout the book we have talked about the essential parts of the OSGi model and the Equinox implementation. That discussion covers 90 percent of what you need to know to build a comprehensive OSGi-based system. This chapter is about the remaining 10 percent of core concepts that crop up infrequently but in key places.

You should think of this chapter as reference material and use it as needed. We cover many advanced topics and explain exactly what your application does from start to finish—the kind of information you need when you have problems and are up late at night troubleshooting. Of course, you are free to read through the chapter and pick up background information and helpful tips and tricks that can be applied every day. In particular, it is useful for people who are

- ○ Curious about how the bundle constructs relate to one another
- ○ Troubleshooting their application, for example, tracking down `ClassNotFoundExceptions`
- ○ Designing a set of bundles and fragments
- ○ Looking to understand more about how Equinox starts, runs, and stops

It is worth pointing out here that the OSGi framework specification is just that, a specification for a framework. The framework is intended to be implemented and run on a wide range of platforms and environments. As such, it does not say anything about, for example, how bundles are installed, how they are started, how they are laid out on disk, or even *if* they are laid out on disk. It is up to implementations to define these characteristics.

Much of this chapter is devoted to mapping the OSGi specification onto the Equinox use case. Readers are encouraged to read the current OSGi Framework Specification from http://osgi.org and treat this chapter as a guide to some advanced detail and the Equinox implementation and use of that specification.

23.1 The Equinox Console

It is quite curious in this day and age of GUIs, web applications, and the like that a simple command-line UI such as the textual Equinox console should be considered a merit. When people first see that there is a console under the covers of the system they are running, the geek in them comes out and they succumb to the need to manually install, start, stop, and uninstall bundles.

This is good fun, but the console is actually quite powerful and useful for both controlling and introspecting a running system. In addition to controlling bundles, you can investigate specific bundles, diagnose problems with bundles not being resolved, find various contributed services, and so on. Figure 23-1 shows an example of the console and a number of bundles in different states.

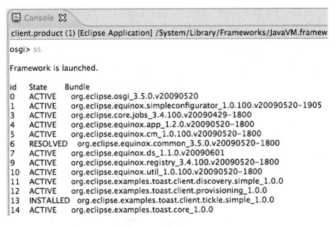

Figure 23–1   Sample console output

In Equinox the console is not started by default. To get a console, start with the -console command-line argument and look for the console's osgi> prompt in either the shell you used to launch Equinox or the new shell created if you launched from a desktop icon. Typing help displays a complete list of available commands.

Of course, the console is extensible, so you can add your own commands. A number of particularly useful built-in commands are listed here:

ss—Displays a short status report of the known bundles, showing their bundle ID and current state. Bundles in the INSTALLED state are missing prerequisites. Use the diag command to find out more.

services—Displays the list of registered services that match the supplied Lightweight Directory Access Protocol (LDAP) filter. For example, to find

all registered ICrustShell services in the client, type services
(objectclass=*Shell).

diag—Displays a diagnosis of why a bundle has failed to resolve. Passes as a
parameter either the bundle ID or the bundle symbolic name of the bundle of
interest. Figure 23-2 shows an example of this.

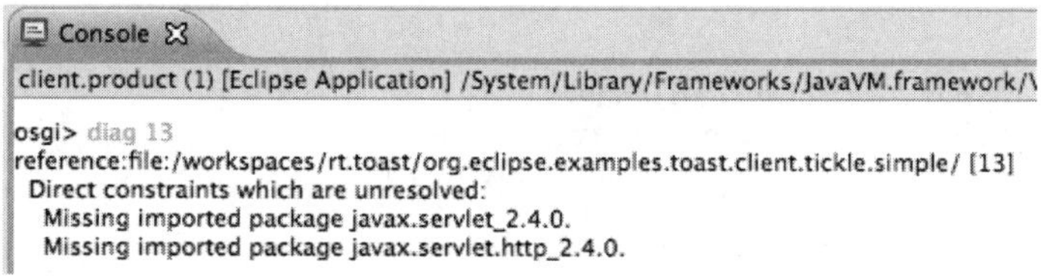

Figure 23–2   Console diag output

23.1.1 Extending the Equinox Console

The Equinox console can be extended by registering an instance of the
org.eclipse.osgi.framework.console.CommandProvider service. This interface
defines just one method, getHelp, that returns an appropriately formatted String
describing the commands it contributes to the console.

Each command that the CommandProvider contributes to the console must be
implemented as a method with the following signature:

```
public void _<name>(CommandInterpreter interpreter);
```

The <name> portion of the method signature is the name of the command that
the user enters at the console's osgi> prompt. Implementing a CommandProvider
is straightforward. Here's how you might implement a listBundles command
that simply lists, in alphabetical order, the names of the installed bundles:

org.equinoxosgi.console/MyCommandProvider
```
public class MyCommandProvider implements CommandProvider {
  private BundleContext bundleContext;

  public void _lb(CommandInterpreter ci) {
    _listBundles(ci);
  }

  public void _listBundles(CommandInterpreter ci) {
    List names = getInstalledBundleNames();
    ci.println("Installed Bundles (" + names.size() + "):");
    Iterator iterator = names.iterator();
    while (iterator.hasNext())
      ci.println("\t" + iterator.next());
  }
```

```
public void activate(ComponentContext componentContext) {
    bundleContext = componentContext.getBundleContext();
}

public String getHelp() {
    StringBuffer buffer = new StringBuffer(60);
    buffer.append("---My Commands---\n");
    buffer.append("\tlistBundles - list the installed bundles\n");
    return buffer.toString();
}

private List getInstalledBundleNames() {
    Bundle[] bundles = bundleContext.getBundles();
    List names = new ArrayList(bundles.length);
    for (int i = 0; i < bundles.length; i++)
        names.add(bundles[i].getSymbolicName());
    Collections.sort(names);
    return names;
}
}
```

Notice that by defining the method _lb we get the command lb as an alias for the listBundles command. This CommandProvider is intended to be registered as a service by DS, for which a service component XML document is required:

org.equinoxosgi.console/component.xml
```
<scr:component xmlns:scr="http://www.osgi.org/xmlns/scr/v1.1.0">
    <implementation class="org.equinoxosgi.console.MyCommandProvider"/>
    <service>
        <provide
            interface="org.eclipse.osgi.framework.console.CommandProvider"/>
    </service>
</scr:component>
```

Launching Equinox with this component installed allows the new command to be used as follows:

```
osgi> listBundles
Installed Bundles (5):
org.eclipse.equinox.ds
org.eclipse.equinox.util
org.eclipse.osgi
org.eclipse.osgi.services
org.equinoxosgi.console
```

Also, the help command displays the usage for our new listBundles command:

```
osgi> help
...
---My Commands---
listBundles - list the installed bundles
...
```

When the user enters a command at the osgi> prompt, the console interprets it by querying the registered CommandProvider services, which it sorts in *descending order* by their service.ranking property and then in *ascending order* by their service.id property. Once the providers have been sorted, the console searches for one that can handle the command.

The console uses Java reflection to find a provider that has a method that matches the name of the command entered by the user. While this scheme allows a command to be handled by a single provider, it is often possible for a bundle to override another provider by registering a CommandProvider service with a higher service.ranking property value. The service.ranking property must be of type Integer with a value up to Integer.MAX_VALUE (2147483647), for example,

```
<property name="service.ranking" type="Integer" value="10"/>
```

To display all the registered CommandProvider services, and to see their service.ranking properties, enter the following console command. Note that there must be *no spaces* within the parentheses.

```
osgi>services(objectClass=*CommandProvider)
```

The Equinox framework's System Bundle, org.eclipse.osgi, registers two CommandProvider services that contribute the core set of console commands, such as help, ss, and diag. These services have service.ranking property values of 2147483647 and, since the System Bundle is always installed first, will always have some of the lowest service.id property values in the registry. This is a clever trick that guarantees that the commands contributed by the System Bundle cannot be overridden.

23.2 Roles in OSGi

Throughout the Toast example we saw elements of the OSGi API—BundleActivator and BundleContext, for example—showing up. Actually, it is a testament to our POJO and dependency injection approach that these classes have seldom surfaced. Here we look at the various roles at play under the OSGi module system:

Identity to others—A module needs some representation in the system so that it can be started, stopped, and otherwise accessed.

Context of the system—Modules need a means of interacting with the system from their point of view so, for example, they can find the services that they are allowed to see.

Lifecycle handler—Modules start and stop and must do initialization and cleanup.

Handy access point—Modules often need *local globals*—collections of constants, values, and functionality that are internal to, but useful across, the bundle.

OSGi separates these roles into different objects, as described here:

`Bundle` == **identity to others**—Other bundles can ask the system for a `Bundle` object, query its state (e.g., started, stopped, etc.), look up files using `getEntries`, and control it using `start` and `stop`. Developers do not implement `Bundle`—the OSGi framework supplies and manages `Bundle` objects for you.

`BundleContext` == **context of the system**—At various points in time, bundles need to ask the system to do something for them, for example, install another bundle or register a service. Typically, the system needs to know the identity of the requesting bundle, for example, to confirm permissions or attribute services. The `BundleContext` fills this role.

A `BundleContext` is created and managed by the system as an opaque token. You simply pass it back or ask it questions when needed. This is much like `ServletContext` and other container architectures.

A `BundleContext` is given to a bundle when started, that is, when the `BundleActivator` method `start` is called. This is the sole means of discovering the context. If the bundle code needs the context, its activator should cache the value.

`BundleActivator` == **lifecycle handler**—Some bundles need to initialize data structures or register listeners when they are started. Similarly, they need to clean up when they are stopped. Implementing a `BundleActivator` allows you to hook these `start` and `stop` events and do the required work.

OSGi does not have explicit support for the role of "handy access point" as outlined here. This role can be filled by any class.

Identity Theft

Of the three OSGi objects outlined here, only your `Bundle` object is meant for others to reference. That, in fact, is its role. Since your `BundleContext` is your identity to the system, you do not really want to hand it out to others and allow them to pretend to be you. Hold your context near and dear, and be careful not to share it via convenience methods or exposed fields.

> Similarly, your `BundleActivator` controls your initialization state. Normally, it is invoked solely by the system. If you give others access to your activator, they can call its `start` and `stop` directly, rather than the corresponding `Bundle` methods, and circumvent any checks and management that the system does.

23.3 The Shape of Bundles

On disk, a bundle is a JAR containing a set of Java-related files. Figure 23-3 shows the example bundle you saw in Section 2.3, "The Anatomy of a Bundle."

Figure 23–3   Standard JAR'd bundle layout

Figure 23-4, on the other hand, shows the bundle as a directory. Notice that everything is the same, except the code is in `junit.jar` rather than in the various `org.*` directories.

Figure 23–4   Directory bundle layout

These two forms are equivalent—Equinox and tooling such as PDE and p2 manage both forms equally well. All frameworks support JAR'd bundles, and several support directory-based bundles.

So what's the difference and why choose one over the other? Following are some useful tips to help you decide which format is better for your bundles:

Use JARs

○ Ninety-five percent of the time people use JARs. It is the de facto standard form of bundles.

○ JARs are useful if the bundle contains many small files that would otherwise fragment the disk and slow installation and searching.

○ JARs are compressed, so sparse files take up much less space.

○ Some systems, such as Java WebStart, require JARs.

○ Standard code signing tools work only on JARs. The Eclipse JAR signer, however, handles both form and nested JARs and directories.

Use directories

○ Use directories if the bundle contains many files that must be directly on the native file system, for example, shared libraries and program executables.

FileLocator IS YOUR FRIEND

Equinox provides the FileLocator mechanism that enables the location and extraction of bundle contents on demand. Many Eclipse facilities such as the class loaders, Intro, Help, and About systems use this to transparently extract the files required by the OS or other external programs. The main concern here is efficiency. Extracting doubles the disk footprint and incurs a one-time cost. If the bundle has many such files or they are large, consider packaging it as a directory.

While the shape of a bundle is transparent to both the user and the developers coding to the API of the bundle, there are a few considerations to note for the developers of JAR'd bundles:

○ JAR'd bundles should generally have a Bundle-Classpath of "." or no classpath specification at all—this implies ".". A "." signifies that the JAR itself is the classpath entry since the JAR directly contains the code.

○ It is technically possible for a JAR'd bundle to have nested JARs on the classpath. Such nested JARs are automatically extracted and cached by the OSGi framework at runtime. As noted earlier, this effectively duplicates the amount of disk space required for the bundle. More significantly, however, tools such as javac and PDE are unable to manage classpaths that include nested JARs. The net result is that while your bundle runs, it takes more space and may not work with your tooling.

○ Similarly, Equinox is able to run JAR'd bundles containing code that is not at the root of the JAR, for example, code in a bin directory such as /bin/org/eclipse/.... Again, tooling is not generally set up for that structure. In particular, standard Java compilers recognize only package structures that are directly at the root of a JAR. As such, developers may not be able to code against JARs structured in this way.

○ The PDE export operations automatically JAR bundles that have "." on the classpath and create directory structures for those that do not.

23.4 Fragments

Sometimes it is not possible to package a bundle as one unit. There are three common scenarios where this occurs:

Platform-specific content—Some bundles need different implementations on different OSs or window systems. You could package the code for all platforms in the bundle, but this is bulky and cumbersome to manage when you want to add another platform. Splitting the bundle into one for common code and others for platform-specific code is another possibility. This is problematic since implementation objects often need to access one another's package-visible members. This is not possible across bundle boundaries.

Locale-specific content—Bundles often need locale-specific text messages, icons, and other resources. Again, it is possible to package the required resources for all locales together in the bundle, but this is similarly cumbersome and wasteful. It would be better to package locale content separately and deploy only what is needed.

Testing—White- and gray-box testing require access to the internals and implementation of the object under test. Here the strong isolation and information hiding of OSGi present a problem.

OSGi supports these use cases using *fragments*. Fragments are just like regular bundles except their content is seamlessly merged at runtime with a *host* bundle rather than being stand-alone. A fragment's classpath elements are appended to its host's classpath, and contributions to the service registry or Extension Registry are made in the name of the host. You cannot express dependencies on fragments, just their hosts. Fragments also cannot contribute new Service-Component manifest entries on behalf of the host.

The next two snippets show examples of both platform- and locale-specific fragments. Both fragments have a manifest file that identifies the fragment, its version, and its host ID and version range. Here is an example of the markup found in the translation fragment for the Equinox common bundle:

```
org.eclipse.equinox.common.nl1/MANIFEST.MF
Bundle-SymbolicName: org.eclipse.equinox.common.nl1
Bundle-Version: 3.5.0
Fragment-Host:
 org.eclipse.equinox.common;bundle-version="[3.5.0,4.0.0)"
Bundle-ClassPath: .
```

The next snippet is from the Windows SWT fragment's manifest file. Notice the highlighted platform filter line. This is an Equinox-specific header that identifies the set of environmental conditions that must be met for this bundle to be resolved. In this case, the `osgi.os`, `osgi.ws`, and `osgi.arch` system properties must match the given values. The syntax of the filter is that of standard LDAP filters and is detailed in the OSGi specification.

```
org.eclipse.swt.win32.win32.x86/MANIFEST.MF
Bundle-SymbolicName: org.eclipse.swt.win32.win32.x86; singleton:=true
Bundle-Version: 3.5.0
Fragment-Host: org.eclipse.swt; bundle-version="[3.5.0,4.0.0)"
Eclipse-PlatformFilter:
 (& (osgi.ws=win32) (osgi.os=win32) (osgi.arch=x86))
Eclipse-ExtensibleAPI: true
Export-Package: org.eclipse.swt.ole.win32,
 org.eclipse.swt.internal.gdip; x-internal:=true
```

In both cases, the fragments directly contain code and resources that are appended to the host's classpath. Adding a fragment's classpath and artifact entries to the host is a vital characteristic of fragments. Fragments generally contain implementation detail for the host. Whether it is code or messages, the contents need to be accessed as though they were part of the host. The only way to do this is to put the fragment on the host's class loader. This gives bidirectional access to the classes and resources as well as enables Java package-level visibility. At runtime, the host and fragment behave as if they were a single bundle.

Fragments are a powerful mechanism, but they are not for every use case. There are several characteristics to consider when you are looking at using fragments:

Fragments are additive—Fragments can only add to their host; they cannot override content found in the host. For example, their classpath contributions are *appended* to those of the host, so if the host has a class or resource, all others are ignored. Their files and resources are similarly added to those of the host bundle.

Multiple fragments can be added—A host can have attached multiple fragments. While the order of the attachment and the fragment contributions to the host's classpath is deterministic, it cannot be controlled. As such, fragments should not have conflicting content.

Fragments cannot be prerequisites—Since they represent implementation detail, their existence should be transparent to other bundles. As such, bundles cannot depend on fragments.

Fragments are not intended to add API—Since you cannot depend on a fragment, they should not expose additional API, since bundle writers are not able to express a dependency on that API.

Fragments can add exports—Normally, fragments are used to supply internal implementation detail. In certain instances, however, such as the previous SWT example and for testing and monitoring, fragments may need to extend the set of packages exported by the host. They do this using normal `Export-Package` syntax. To support development-time visibility, the host bundle should be marked with the header `Eclipse-ExtensibleAPI: true`. This tells PDE to expose the additional fragment exports to bundles that depend on the host.

Figure 23-5 shows the OSGi console of a running Toast Client after the short status (`ss`) command is typed. Notice that the `org.eclipse.swt.win32` fragment (number 25) is shown as installed (and resolved) and bound to the SWT host bundle (number 35).

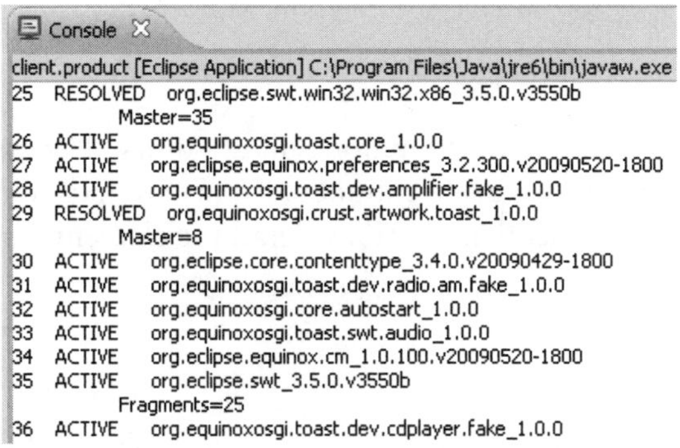

Figure 23–5 Fragment resolution status

23.5 Singletons

In general, OSGi is able to concurrently run multiple versions of the same bundle; that is, `org.equinoxosgi.toast.core` versions 1.0 and 2.0 can both be installed and running at the same time. This is part of the power of the component model. Dependent bundles are bound to particular versions of their prerequisites and see only the classes supplied by them.

There are cases, however, when there really should be only one version of a given bundle in the system. For example, SWT makes certain assumptions about its control over the display and main thread—SWT cannot cohabitate with other

SWTs. More generally, this occurs wherever one bundle expects to have exclusive access to a global resource, whether it be a thread, an OS resource, a Transmission Control Protocol (TCP) port, or the Extension Registry namespace.

To address this, OSGi allows a bundle to be declared as a *singleton*. We saw this in Section 16.4, "Advanced Extension Topics." The bundle in the following example is marked as a singleton. This tells OSGi to resolve at most one version of the bundle. All other version constraints in the system are then matched against the chosen singleton version.

```
org.eclipse.core.runtime/MANIFEST.MF
Bundle-SymbolicName: org.equinoxosgi.toast.backend.portal;singleton:=true
Bundle-Version: 1.0.0
```

The most common reason to mark a bundle as a singleton is that it declares extensions or extension points. The Extension Registry namespace is a shared resource that is populated by bundle IDs. If we allowed multiple versions of the same bundle to contribute to the registry, interconnections would be ambiguous.

23.6 Bundle Lifecycle

OSGi's dynamic capabilities are one of its major selling points. The cornerstone of this is the bundle lifecycle. There are a number of players and events in this lifecycle story. This and some subsequent sections detail the elements and flow of the OSGi lifecycle model.

23.6.1 Lifecycle States

Bundles go through a number of states in their lives. In Section 2.6, "Lifecycle," we introduced the various states and transitions. A deeper understanding of these helps you know when and why various things happen to your bundle and what you can do about them. Section 21.4.2, "Bundle Listeners," details how to monitor any events arising from bundles changing state.

Deployed—When a bundle is deployed, it is laid down on disk and is physically available. This state is not formally represented in the system, but it is used to talk about a bundle that could become installed.

Installed—An installed bundle is one that has been deployed and presented to the OSGi framework as a candidate for execution. Installed bundles do not yet have a class loader, and their service and Extension Registry contributions are not yet processed.

Resolved—Resolved bundles have been installed and all of their prerequisites have been satisfied by other bundles, which are also resolved. If the Equinox Extension Registry is installed and active, the contributions of resolved bundles are added to the Extension Registry. Resolved bundles may have a class loader and may be fully operational. As shown in Figure 23-6, some bundles can stay in the resolved state and never become started.

Starting—A resolved bundle that is started and whose start level has been met transitions to the active state through the starting state. Bundles remain in the starting state while their activator's start method is executing. Bundles that use DS and the lazy activation policy may remain in this state for some time.

Active—An active bundle is one that has been resolved and whose start method has been successfully run. Active bundles have a class loader and are fully operational.

Stopping—An active bundle that is transitioning back to the resolved state passes through the stopping state. Bundles remain in the stopping state while their activator's stop method is executing.

Uninstalled—An uninstalled bundle is a bundle that was previously in the installed state but has since been uninstalled. Such bundles are still present in the system but may behave in unexpected ways.

Figure 23-6 shows the details of the state transitions for bundles. Notice that the deployed state is not shown, as it is outside the scope of OSGi itself. Being deployed simply means that the bundle is available to be installed.

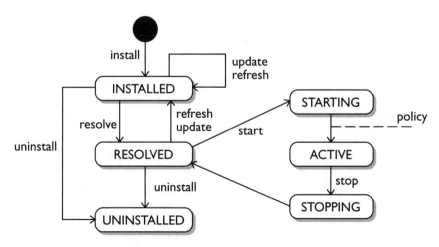

Figure 23–6 Bundle state transitions

The transition between each state is marked by the broadcasting of a BundleEvent to registered BundleListeners. The event identifies the transition or type and the bundle affected. The use of these events, BundleListeners, and BundleTrackers is discussed in Chapter 21, "Dynamic Best Practices."

23.6.2 BundleActivator

In support of the starting and stopping lifecycle transitions, a bundle can supply an *activator* class. Activators are instantiated by the OSGi framework, and their start and stop methods are called when a bundle is started or stopped.

NO THREAD CONTROL

The BundleActivator lifecycle methods are called on whatever thread happens to be executing at the time the bundle changed state. Your start and stop methods should be coded accordingly.

If you define an activator class, you need to tell the framework about it. Use the **Activator** field in the **General Information** section on the bundle editor's **Overview** page, or directly edit the manifest. Clicking the **Activator** link opens the identified class or the **New Java Class** wizard if no class is specified. In the end, this entry corresponds to the following entry in the bundle's manifest:

```
Bundle-Activator: org.equinoxosgi.crust.internal.display.bundle.Activator
```

23.6.3 The Downside of Activators

Having given details and examples of how to write and identify activators, we caution you against using them. Running code on activation is an overused capability. One of the basic tenets of a large system is that laziness is good—"Run no code before its time." In our experience, the start and stop methods rarely need to be implemented.

Bundles can be activated for many different reasons in many different contexts. We commonly see bundles that load and initialize models, open and verify caches, and do all manner of other heavyweight operations in their start methods. The cost of this is added to the startup time and footprint of your application and is not always justified.

We once found a bundle that was loading 11MB of *code* as a side effect of being activated. First of all, that's a lot of code. More critically, however, there were several cases where activation occurred as a result of some trivial processing of some optional UI decorations. This long chain of events caused various bundles to assume that their full function was needed and that they should initialize their data model and do lots of hard work. A better approach is to initialize your caches and data structures as required with more precision.

ACTIVATORS DEGRADE PERFORMANCE

Startup time is a bit of a misnomer in OSGi-based systems. What is really important is the time taken to start individual bundles. An OSGi framework itself starts in milliseconds. The rest of the time is spent executing the start methods and other initialization code for the bundles in the system.

Lazy activation helps but does not solve the problem. With lazy activation, bundles are started only as needed. The initial start time of your application may be fast, but as the user progressively touches more functionality, more bundles are activated—lengthy activations delay users in their quest to use your application.

23.6.4 Uses for Activators

With the advent of Declarative Services components, the need for bundle activators has diminished significantly. Throughout the 100 or so bundles involved in Toast, only a handful have activators. So, if activators are bad and not really needed, why do they exist and when should they be used? Traditionally activators were used to register services, start threads, and the like. These tasks are now typically done using DS component classes. See Section 15.2.1, "The Simplest Component," for more details.

In fact, Toast has only two activators: one in Crust and one in the auto-starter. The Crust activator is required solely to capture the org.equinoxosgi .crust.display bundle's BundleContext for use in registering the ICrustDisplay service. This service must be created by the application in the display bundle to ensure that it is on the right thread, so DS cannot be allowed to instantiate the service.

The auto-starter hooks a BundleTracker in its activator and then allows the system to run its code whenever bundles change—no services are involved so DS cannot help.

23.7 Bundle Activation Policy

The previous section showed how to control when a bundle's start method is called. Traditionally the activator for a started bundle was called as soon as the bundle became RESOLVED. In more recent versions of the specification, each bundle is able to declare an *activation policy* that dictates how and when its activator is called.

Currently the only activation policy defined by the specification is *lazy*:

```
Bundle-ActivationPolicy: lazy
```

The lazy policy works by deferring the call to BundleActivator.start until the first time a bundle is asked to supply a class. A lazy bundle simply exists in the system—it has a BundleContext but does not have a class loader and does not execute any code. When the bundle is asked to load a class, its class loader is created, the bundle's activator is instantiated, and its start method called. This is all done *before* attempting to load the initially requested class. After a successful start call, the requested class is loaded and returned as normal.

WHAT DOES <<LAZY>> MEAN IN THE CONSOLE?

A bundle that uses the lazy activation policy and has not yet been fully activated shows up in the Equinox console with its state listed as <<LAZY>>. This indicates that it is ready to activate and will do so when referenced.

Given that lazily started bundles have a BundleContext, they are able to register services. More accurately, some other bundle is able to register services on their behalf. DS does exactly that—it registers service references on behalf of the lazy bundle. When the service is eventually discovered, the bundle is activated and the service object created.

The net effect is that you can always be sure that your bundle has been activated by the time its code is running (except, of course, the code involved in evaluating the activator's start). This frees you from continually having to check the activation state of your bundle. It also means that the system as a whole can be lazier. There is no need for a central management agent or complicated policy to determine when bundles should be activated—they are simply activated as needed.

It's worth highlighting some of the typical scenarios that do, and do not, cause activation:

○ Using IConfigurationElement.createExecutableExtension *does* cause the bundle supplying the specified class to be activated. Note the subtlety here. It is not the bundle defining the extension but rather the one defining the class specified in the extension. Typically, these are the same but not always.

○ Calling Bundle.loadClass *does* cause activation of the bundle that eventually supplies the requested class. Again, note the subtlety. If, for example, Bundle

A asks Bundle B and B asks Bundle C and C eventually loads and returns the class, Bundle B is not activated. B was simply a step along the way.

❍ Loading a class from Bundle A that *depends on* a class from Bundle B *does* activate B. Here, the notion of *depends on* is derived from the Java language specification. If loading and verifying the class from A requires a class from B, B's class is loaded and B is activated. This can occur if A's class extends B's or references B's in a method signature.

❍ Accessing, traversing, or otherwise using a bundle's extensions, data files, or entries *does not* cause activation.

❍ Bundle activation is not transitive; that is, activating a Bundle A that depends on another Bundle B *does not* in and of itself cause B to be activated. Of course, if classes are loaded from B while activating A, B is activated.

23.8 Controlling Bundle Start

Do not confuse bundle activation with starting bundles—they are related but different. BundleActivators and activation policies all talk about what happens if the framework activates a bundle. They do not control or change when that actually happens.

The distinction is subtle but important. Outside entities such as management agents or users call Bundle.start. Calling start indicates that the bundle can be activated if it is resolved and its activation policy has been satisfied. Calling start has the additional effect of causing a BundleContext to be created. The BundleContext is a key part of the bundle lifecycle, as it is needed when calling the bundle activator and when registering services.

The OSGi specification suggests that there is a management agent of some sort that is starting and stopping bundles according to system requirements. In many modern uses of OSGi this is not the case, and knowing and managing which bundles need to be started and when they should be started is a daunting task. The specification does not include any means of recording or maintaining this information. OSGi programmers then are left with three choices:

Start everything—This is the brute-force approach we saw with the auto-start bundle in Chapter 9, "Packaging." The auto-start bundle simply starts all bundles as they are installed. This is simple and clear and works for small systems that do not have special requirements. For larger systems, however, this incurs a significant overhead at startup time and may bloat the system.

Start specific bundles—Minimalists and people with specific requirements can manage a targeted list of bundles that need to be started in specific situations. Doing this can be brittle and error-prone but may make sense in some cases.

Use lazy activation—Lazy activation allows you to aggressively start all bundles, as with the auto-start bundle, but since the bundles are marked as lazy, they do not run or load any code until they are needed.

In the following sections we talk about mechanisms and techniques for implementing these approaches.

23.8.1 Persistent Starting

The fact that start has been called on a bundle is, by default, persisted such that subsequent restarts of the same framework configuration restore the same set of bundles and their started state. In this case, Bundle.start is only ever called once on a given bundle, though it may be activated many times, once for each start of the framework.

Recent versions of the OSGi specification added the ability to control this persistence—Bundle.start(int) allows a START_TRANSIENT flag to be specified. In this case the bundle is marked as started only for the current run of the framework. This is useful in systems with fluctuating sets of bundles that need to be started. Without this or some agent explicitly stopping bundles, the framework would slowly accumulate bundles marked as started and get slower and slower to start.

23.8.2 Enabling the Activation Policy

Along with the introduction of transient starting and activation policies came the START_ACTIVATION_POLICY flag. This flag is passed to Bundle.start(int) and controls whether or not the activation policy, if any, defined in the target bundle is considered. The default Bundle.start() method does not consider the activation policy and persists the started marking for the bundle—this is the legacy behavior of the method. So if you would like to accommodate lazy bundles, you should use Bundle.start(START_ACTIVATION_POLICY).

23.8.3 osgi.bundles

Equinox pulls together these various elements with a built-in mechanism for driving the lazy activation approach previously outlined. Rather than having to have an external management agent, Equinox includes a simple facility for specifying a set of bundles to start when the framework is started—the osgi.bundles list.

The osgi.bundles property is a comma-separated list of bundles that are automatically installed and optionally started when Equinox is run. It is maintained as a system property set either as a -D VM argument or in Equinox's config.ini file, discussed in Section 23.10.1, "config.ini." You have been unwittingly manipulating these entries in the PDE product editor and launch configurations where various bundles were marked as auto-start and their start level was set. Tweaking those values results in changes to the config.ini used by Equinox. This is a powerful hybrid approach used by most Equinox systems where users are managing their own systems and have no insight into the requirements of the bundles they install.

An example osgi.bundles entry is shown here:

config.ini
```
osgi.bundles=org.equinoxosgi.core.toast@2:start
```

Each entry is of the following form:

```
<URL | simple bundle location>[@ [<startlevel>] [:start]]
```

Simple bundle locations are interpreted as relative to the OSGi framework's parent directory. URLs must be of the form file: or the Equinox-specific platform:/base/. In general, the URLs may include a version number (e.g., .../location_1.2.3). If a version is not specified, the system binds to the location that matches exactly or to the versioned location with the latest version number. If a version number is given, only exact matches are considered.

The :start option indicates that Equinox should start the given bundle after it is installed. The framework starts such bundles persistently and with the START_ACTIVATION_POLICY discussed previously.

In the example osgi.bundles property, the startlevel value indicates the OSGi *start level* at which the bundle should run. Start levels are discussed in more detail in Section 21.7.1, "Start Levels."

23.9 Class Loading

One of the things that sets OSGi apart from other systems is the modularity mechanism. The core of this is the class loading strategy. The following is a deep dive into the guts of OSGi class loading and some Equinox extensions. This section is not for everyone, nor is it for the faint of heart. It is included here for those poor lost souls who, for whatever reason, cannot seem to find the classes they need or are finding classes they don't need.

Traditionally, Java developers put all their code on the classpath and forget about the real dependencies in their systems. This does not make for modular systems. In OSGi, each bundle has its own class loader. This effectively partitions the class namespaces and enables API boundary enforcement, bundle unloading, bundle activation lifecycles, and multiple versions of the same classes being loaded concurrently.

By default, a bundle's class loader is parented by the standard Java boot class loader. This can be changed globally using the `org.osgi.framework.bundle.parent` property. The parent can be one of the following:

boot—The default, the standard Java boot class loader

ext—The normal Java extension class loader

app—The Java application class loader

framework—The framework's class loader

23.9.1 Class Lookup Algorithm

Enumerated in the following pseudo code are the steps OSGi uses for deciding where to look for classes. Here, we assume that a bundle is trying to load some class C in package P.

```
1. if P starts with "java." || P is boot delegated
      return parent.loadClass(C)
2. if P is imported
      return exporter.loadClass(C)
3. if P is exported by some required bundles
      for each exporter
         return exporter.loadClass(C) if found
4. if C is found locally
      return C
5. if C is found in a fragment
      return C
6. if P is dynamically imported
      return exporter.loadClass(C);
7. if buddy loading is enabled for this bundle
      return BuddyLoader.loadClass(c)
8. throw a ClassNotFoundException
```

The next few sections look more closely at how this algorithm works.

BUDDY LOADING IS EQUINOX SPECIFIC

Step 7 is not standard OSGi behavior. Equinox adds this step to facilitate the bundling of code libraries, as outlined in Chapter 22, "Integrating Code Libraries."

23.9.2 Declaring Imports and Exports

The basic premise of the OSGi component model is that all bundles explicitly declare the packages they expose to others and the packages they require from others. Notice that the algorithm outlined in the preceding section does not "search" for class C; the system knows which bundles have which packages, so the exporter is simply looked up. This yields two main benefits:

❍ When bundle dependencies are explicitly declared, bundles are easier to configure and creating valid configurations is easier. For every import, there must be an export, or the bundle does not resolve.

❍ After a bundle dependency graph has been resolved, the system knows exactly where to look for any given package. This eliminates costly searching and greatly improves class loading time for large systems.

Step 1 of the class loading algorithm ensures that all java.* packages are implicitly available to all bundles—they need not be explicitly imported. All other packages from the JRE must, however, be explicitly imported. This implies that there is a matching exporter. The OSGi specification states that the System Bundle must export the additional packages from the JRE.

WHAT IS THE "SYSTEM BUNDLE"?

The System Bundle is the bundle that implements the OSGi framework. The OSGi specification states its symbolic name as system.bundle. In Equinox, it is also known as org.eclipse.osgi.

To implement this, the Equinox implementation maintains a set of *profiles* that lists the standard API packages available in common JRE class libraries such as J2SE1.4, J2SE1.5, and JCL Foundation. These profiles do not include implementation-specific packages such as com.sun.* and sun.*, as they are not standard and are not available in all JREs. The framework automatically finds and uses the profile that matches the current JRE level. You can override this and set your own profile using the osgi.java.profile property.

So, for example, a bundle using the org.xml.sax.Parser class must either import the org.xml.sax package or specifically require the system.bundle. If it does not, the SAX (Simple API for XML) classes are hidden from the bundle. Hiding JRE classes can be useful, for example, if you want to use a particular SAX parser supplied as part of your bundle.

23.9.3 Importing versus Requiring

There is a subtle but important distinction between importing packages and requiring bundles. Imports are undirected in that any suitable bundle exporting the package can be nominated to satisfy the import. This increases flexibility as it separates implementation and API. Typically, you import only API packages and are thus oblivious to what is supplying the implementation—implementations can be replaced without your notice.

Requiring bundles, on the other hand, states that the dependent bundle consumes the packages exported by the specific prerequisite bundle; that is, the consumer is bound to the supplier and its implementation. This is less flexible but is also simpler and more deterministic, as the consumer knows exactly which implementation it is getting.

As you can see, there are benefits and drawbacks to both. Developers from the OSGi world traditionally use only imports, whereas Eclipse developers tend to require bundles—a legacy of the original technologies. As a best practice we recommend importing packages because it encourages looser coupling. As a pragmatic note, using import package without version qualification is, in our opinion, worse than requiring bundles with versions. As there are typically many packages, managing their version numbers can be a daunting task. Some people new to OSGi may find it easier to start by requiring bundles and move to importing packages as their need for flexibility increases.

Either way, the PDE bundle editor allows you to pick how you specify your dependencies. Dependencies are defined using the **Imported Packages** and **Required Bundles** sections of the **Dependencies** page in the bundle editor.

23.9.4 Optionality

OSGi allows prerequisites to be *optional*. Optional prerequisites, whether imports or requires, do not prevent bundles from resolving. Rather, if the prerequisite element is available at resolution time, the dependent and prerequisite are wired together. Otherwise, the dependency is ignored and you must ensure that your code handles the potential class loading errors.

This property is controlled using the **Properties...** buttons on the **Dependencies** page in the bundle editor.

23.9.5 The uses Directive

It is common for API in one package to reference API in another package. For example, say some API method in a class in `com.example.test` returns a type from the package `com.example.util`. Bundles calling this method must express a dependency on both the `com.example.test` and `com.example.util` packages. Similarly, the bundle defining the `test` package must import the `util` package. To ensure class space consistency, the system must ensure that both bundles are wired to the same `com.example.util` package. If they are not, class cast exceptions will occur.

You can declare this relationship and requirement by specifying a uses *directive* on the export of `com.example.test`, as shown here:

```
Export-Package: com.example.test;uses:=com.example.util
```

This says that the `test` package uses the `util` package, so anyone using `test` and `util` should be wired to the exact same supplier of `util`. Specifying uses directives is an important expression of the complete API contract for a bundle.

---

uses IS EXPENSIVE

Defining and maintaining the `uses` information in the manifest can be challenging. Thankfully, PDE and other tools can autogenerate these directives. Unfortunately, adding these declarations increases the complexity of wiring together your bundles to the degree that the OSGi resolver may take minutes to resolve your bundle set. Several OSGi framework implementers are looking for faster algorithms. In the meantime, we do not recommend using the `uses` directive, as it can render system resolution impractically slow.

23.9.6 *Re-exporting*

The OSGi dependency mechanism also supports the *re-exporting* of required bundles. Re-exporting is a structuring where one bundle exposes packages from a prerequisite as its own. For example, the Eclipse UI bundle requires and re-exports JFace and SWT bundles. As a result, UI-related bundles need only to specify a dependency on the UI bundle to get access to all of SWT and JFace.

You should consider using this only when the prerequisite classes somehow form an integral part of your bundle's API. By re-exporting SWT, the UI bundle is effectively adopting the SWT API as its own; similarly for JFace. In a sense, the UI is acting as a façade or wrapper around these bundles. This hides the structuring details, allowing it to evolve over time.

This property is controlled using the **Properties...** button in the **Required Bundles** section of the **Dependencies** page in the bundle editor.

Note that a bundle can export a package it does not contain but rather gets elsewhere via an import or require statement.

23.9.7 x-internal *and* x-friends

There is a healthy tension between designing and defining durable API and enabling advanced exploration and experimentation. If you take a very strict API stance, your bundle should export only the packages that contain API. As we have seen, however, that approach means that other bundles can *never* see the non-API packages—under any circumstances. Depending on your needs and those of your consumers, this approach may be too restrictive in some situations.

Equinox offers two package export directives, x-internal and x-friends, that enable clear API guidance yet still give consumers the power to access internals as needed. We discussed the behavior and uses of these in Section 9.4.2, "Exporting Packages and Friendship."

23.9.8 Boot Delegation

Step 1 of the class loading algorithm mentions the notion of boot delegation. This is an override mechanism that identifies particular packages whose class loads should come from the parent class loader. This is useful for accessing packages that are not java.* and are not otherwise exported by a bundle. For example, some code libraries reference JRE internals or must be on a certain JRE class loader. To get access to such packages, you can either update the JRE profile or use the org.osgi.framework.bootdelegation property in config.ini to list the set of accessible package prefixes as follows:

```
<equinox install>/configuration/config.ini
...
org.osgi.framework.bootdelegation=com.sun
```

23.10 Configuring and Running Equinox

Equinox as a framework implementation is extremely flexible. The entire structure is built on a set of hooks and adapters that allow consumers to replace key operating elements, such as disk storage strategies, to better suit their needs. At a higher level there is a large number of command-line and system property settings that you can use to control many aspects of its operation. The Eclipse Help system at http://help.eclipse.org details these settings in the **Runtime Options** area under **Platform Plug-in Developer Guide > Reference > Other reference information**.

Some of these options must be specified on the command line and others can be specified as system properties. System properties can in turn be specified using –D VM arguments or by putting the settings in Equinox's config.ini file.

23.10.1 config.ini

The config.ini file defines the set of system properties to use when running the framework. Typically this is used to specify a small set of bootstrap bundles to get the system going, the application to run, and a few configuration values. The file is formatted as a standard Java properties file and resides in the configuration area, typically the configuration folder in the Equinox install. At startup its key/value pairs are merged into Java's system properties. By "merged" we mean that if a property with the given key already exists, the value in the config.ini is ignored.

Eclipse uses a number of system properties, and most command-line arguments (e.g., -data, -configuration) have system property equivalents. As such, they can be set in the config.ini file to control how the configuration behaves. As of the Galileo (3.5) release of PDE and Equinox, users generally do not have to edit, see, or touch the config.ini file. Most of the relevant settings can be made in the product or launch configuration editors. Nonetheless, the file is still used at runtime, so it is useful to know what it contains and how to read it. A typical config.ini looks something like this snippet:

Toast/configuration/config.ini
```
osgi.bundles=\
 org.equinoxosgi.core.autostart:start,\
 org.eclipse.equinox.simple.configurator@2:start
eclipse.product=org.equinoxosgi.toast.product.client
osgi.instance.area=@user.home/toast
```

Let's look at these in order:

osgi.bundles—We have already seen the details of this in Section 23.8.3, "osgi.bundles."

eclipse.product—This is the ID of the product extension to run. In the Toast Client we used the Crust display product as the base platform on top of which the client is built. Specifying that product here causes it to start on launch and begin showing the Toast application.

osgi.instance.area—A running Equinox system often needs to write either user data or internal bundle data. The instance area is one location where this information can be written. In the example here, the Toast Client is told to write all such data in the toast subdirectory of the user's home directory. Section 23.11, "Data Areas," contains more information on positioning the instance area.

When editing the config.ini file, it is important to keep the following points in mind:

○ If the list spans multiple lines, follow each comma with a backslash, which is known as the *continuation character*.

○ There must not be any whitespace between the continuation character and the end of the line. Trailing whitespace will effectively terminate the property's value, resulting in a configuration that does not behave as expected.

○ Starting the list of bundles with the continuation character, placing each bundle on a separate line, and indenting each line are not necessary, but these are best practices that make the list easier to read and maintain.

23.10.2 The Executable

Having a native OS launcher seems like a minor thing, but it is extremely powerful. The standard Equinox launcher does a number of important tasks in aid of getting your system running:

○ It finds a JRE and runs it on the Java code contained in the org.eclipse.equinox.launcher bundle. This is the basic bootstrapping of Equinox.

○ It simplifies the running of Equinox. You can just run the executable rather than having to figure out various VM command-line arguments or mess with batch files.

○ It manages the splash screen. The splash screen is essentially a hint that provides feedback to users that they did indeed double-click on the program and something is happening. Having the executable display the splash screen means that it's shown to the user as soon as possible.

○ The executable is the interface with the OS and window system. It dictates ownership and permissions as well as how Equinox is presented in the user's desktop—for example, which icon is shown, the name of the process, and how it shows up in the taskbar or application dock.

The executable takes direction from an initialization file that allows you to define default sets of command-line arguments for both Java and Equinox and thus define how your system operates.

The executable looks for an initialization file of the same name as itself but with .ini appended. For example, the initialization file for toast.exe is toast.ini. The following file tells Toast to start the identified JVM using the given VM arguments:

toast.ini
```
-vm
c:\java 1.4.2\jre\bin\java.exe
-vmargs
-Dtoast.name=Fast
-verbose
```

The initialization file is essentially a standard command line that has been tokenized such that each token is placed on a line by itself. This syntax is a little strange, but it greatly simplifies the parsing required by the executable's C code. Since the file represents a standard command line, order matters—the VM arguments must go last.

Since you can put any VM argument here, you can define system properties using the -D notation shown in the snippet. Properties set this way supersede those set using any other technique.

ONE LINE PER ARGUMENT

Putting all the command-line tokens on one line is a common source of problems with the executable initialization file. If your command-line arguments appear to be ignored, check the format of your file. Also check for invisible characters.

The **Configuration** page in the product editor has a **Launching Arguments** section that exposes both the **Program Arguments** and **VM Arguments**. An example of its use is shown in Figure 23-7. When the product is exported or launched, PDE creates an executable .ini file named and placed according to the product definition. Note that arguments containing spaces must be quoted accordingly.

Figure 23–7 Adding launching arguments

Typically, you should use this mechanism to set VM arguments or supply program command-line arguments that do not have system property equivalents. System properties should be set using the `config.ini` file described in Section 23.10.1, "config.ini."

VM ARGUMENTS WIN

If you use `-Dsystem.property=value`-style VM arguments, such values take precedence over properties set any other way.

23.11 Data Areas

Applications often need to read or store data. Depending on the use case, this data may be stored in one of many locations. Consider preferences as an example.

Typical products use at least some preferences. The preferences themselves may or may not be defined in the product's bundles. For example, if you are reusing bundles from different products, it is more convenient to manage the preferences outside the bundle.

In addition, applications often allow users to change preference values or use preferences to store refresh rates, port numbers, and so on. These values might be stored uniquely for each user or shared among users. In scenarios where applications operate on distinct datasets, some of the preferences may even relate to the particular data and should be stored or associated with that data.

Preferences are just one example, but they illustrate the various scopes and lifecycles that applications have for the data they read and write. Equinox defines four *data areas* that capture these characteristics and allow application writers to properly control the scope of their data:

Install—The install area is where Equinox itself is installed. The install area is generally read-only. The data in the install area is available to all instances of all configurations of Equinox running on the install. See the `osgi.install.area` system property.

Configuration—The configuration area is where the running configuration of Equinox is defined. Configuration areas are generally writable. The data in a configuration area is available to all instances of the configuration. See the `osgi.configuration.area` system property.

Instance—The instance area is the default location for user-defined data (e.g., a workspace). The instance area is typically writable. Applications may allow multiple sessions to have concurrent access to the instance area but must take care to prevent lost updates and related problems. See the osgi.instance.area system property.

User—The user area is where Equinox manages data specific to a user but independent of the configuration or instance. The user area is typically based on the Java user.home system property and the initial value of the osgi.user.area system property. See osgi.user.area system property.

In addition to these Equinox-wide areas, OSGi defines a location specifically for each installed bundle:

Data location—This is a location within the configuration's metadata. See BundleContext.getDataFile.

Each of the Equinox locations is controlled by setting the system properties described before Equinox starts (e.g., in the config.ini). Locations are URLs. For simplicity, file paths are also accepted and automatically converted to file: URLs. For better control and convenience, there are also a number of predefined symbolic locations that can be used. Note that not all combinations of location type and symbolic value are valid. Table 23-1 details which combinations are possible.

Table 23–1 Location Compatibilities

Location/Value	Supports default?	File/URL	@none	@noDefault	@user.home	@user.dir
Install	No	Yes	No	No	Yes	Yes
Configuration	Yes	Yes	Yes*	Yes*	Yes	Yes
Instance	Yes	Yes	Yes	Yes	Yes	Yes (default)
User	Yes	Yes	Yes	Yes	Yes	Yes

* Indicates that this setup is technically possible but pragmatically quite difficult to manage. In particular, without a configuration location, Equinox may get only as far as starting the OSGi framework.

@none—Indicates that the corresponding location should never be set either explicitly or to its default value. For example, an OSGi application that has no instance data may use osgi.instance.area=@none to prevent extraneous files being written to disk. @none must not be followed by any path segments.

@noDefault—Forces a location to be undefined or explicitly defined (i.e., Equinox does not automatically compute a default value). This is useful when you want to allow for data in the corresponding location, but the Equinox default value is not appropriate. @noDefault must not be followed by any path segments.

@user.home—Directs Equinox to compute a location value relative to the user's home directory. @user.home can be followed by path segments. In all cases, the string @user.home is replaced with the value of the Java user.home system property. For example, setting

```
osgi.instance.area=@user.home/toast
```

results in a value of

```
file:/users/fred/toast
```

@user.dir—Directs Equinox to compute a location value relative to the current working directory. @user.dir can be followed by path segments. In all cases, the string @user.dir is replaced with the value of the Java user.dir system property. For example, setting

```
osgi.instance.area=@user.dir/ABC123
```

results in a value of

```
file:/usr/local/toast/ABC123
```

Since the default case is for all locations to be set, valid, and writable, some bundles may fail in other setups, even if they are listed as possible. For example, it is unreasonable to expect a bundle focused on instance data to do much if the instance area is not defined. It is up to bundle developers to choose the setups they support and design their functions accordingly.

Note that each of the locations can be statically marked as read-only by setting the corresponding property osgi.AAA.area.readonly=true, where AAA is one of the area names.

23.12 Summary

The strength of OSGi lies in its robust bundle model. Bundles bring advantages of scale, composition, serviceability, and flexibility. The costs of this power are the rigor and attention to detail required when defining bundles—poorly defined bundles are hard to compose and reuse in the same way as poorly defined objects.

This chapter exposed the essential details of the OSGi component model and the Equinox implementation of the OSGi specification. We touched on some of the framework's configuration options and provided a number of guidelines for building your bundles.

With this information, you will design and implement better components that run more efficiently and have more class loading and composition options.

CHAPTER 24

Declarative Services Reference

Chapter 15, "Declarative Services," introduced DS and the common usage scenarios; this chapter dives deeply into the component XML schema to provide you with a better understanding of how to use DS and how to work with its component lifecycle. In particular, we

- ❍ Detail the Declarative Services XML schema v1.1.0, which is used to describe DS components
- ❍ Discuss the DS component lifecycle and how components interact with the dynamic changes of the OSGi service model

24.1 Component XML Schema v1.1.0

The element structure of a DS component XML document is relatively simple. Every DS component has an implementation class and may optionally define properties and identify services it references and provides. The element structure is summarized in Table 24-1 and is detailed in the following sections.

24.1.1 Declaring the XML Namespace and Schema

In Release 4, version 4.1, of the OSGi specification, the DS XML schema was defined by `http://www.osgi.org/xmlns/scr/v1.0.0`. This is the schema used by Equinox 3.4. For Release 4, version 4.2, a new DS XML schema—`http://www.osgi.org/xmlns/scr/v1.1.0`—was introduced. All DS components in this book use this schema.

Table 24–1   Overview of the Component XML Schema v1.1.0

Element	Use	Occurrences
<component>	Required	Unbounded
<implementation>	Required	1
<property>	Optional	Unbounded
<properties>	Optional	Unbounded
<service>	Optional	1
<provide>	Required	Unbounded
<reference>	Optional	Unbounded

By default a DS component uses the v1.0.0 schema. Since there are now multiple schemas, we recommend that you always define an XML namespace to use the schema with which your component complies. An XML namespace is typically defined using the <component> element and the namespace scr. For example:

```
<scr:component xmlns:scr="http://www.osgi.org/xmlns/scr/v1.1.0" ...>
...
</scr:component>
```

The scr namespace identifier must be specified only on the <component> element. Specifying scr on any nested elements will cause DS to report errors against the XML document.

Contributed XML documents can contain any number of <component> elements nested at any level. An XML namespace must be used if you are declaring multiple components in a single document or are nesting a <component> element in an XML document that uses a different namespace. To use the namespace, the root element must include a namespace declaration, and the recommended prefix for the namespace is scr, for example:

```
xmlsn:scr="http://www.osgi.org/xmlns/scr/v1.1.0"
```

To declare multiple components in a single XML document, make sure that the root element is not a <component> element and that all <component> elements use the declared namespace, which in this case is scr:

```
<?xml version="1.0" encoding="UTF-8"?>
<singleRootElement xmlns:scr="http://www.osgi.org/xmlns/scr/v1.1.0">
  <scr:component>...</scr:component>
  <scr:component>...</scr:component>
</singleRootElement>
```

XML 1.0 COMPLIANCE

For a document to be XML-compliant, it must have a single root element. In this snippet we used `<singleRootElement>` but this is just an example; the root element can have any name.

While it is possible to describe multiple components in a single XML document and to nest DS components inside documents with different XML schemas, the PDE tooling in Eclipse 3.5.x does not support this.

24.1.2 The `<component>` Element

Each `<component>` element describes a single DS component. This element is required. The `<component>` element has the following attributes:

name—A *bundle-unique* name of the component. This attribute is optional, defaulting to the value of the component's `<implementation>` element's `class` attribute. If multiple components share an implementation class, setting this attribute is required to avoid duplicates.

The value of this attribute is used by other components within the same bundle that wish to enable or disable it using the `ComponentContext` API; see the description of the `enabled` attribute for details.

Depending on the value of the `<component>` element's `configuration-policy` attribute, the value of this attribute may also be used as a framework-unique persistent identifier by the `ConfigurationAdmin` service; see Section 24.2.1.2 for more on the `configuration-policy` attribute.

activate—The name of the implementation class method DS calls when the component's configuration is satisfied and the component is activated. This attribute is optional, defaulting to `activate`. See Section 24.2.2 for more on component activation.

deactivate—The name of the implementation class method DS calls when the component's configuration is no longer satisfied and the component is deactivated. This attribute is optional, defaulting to `deactivate`. See Section 24.2.2 for more on component deactivation.

DEFAULT ACTIVATION/DEACTIVATION METHODS ARE OPTIONAL

When a <component> element's `activate` and `deactivate` attributes have not
been set, there is no requirement for methods matching the default attribute values to exist in the component's implementation class. DS requires that the methods exist only if the `activate` and `deactivate` attributes have been explicitly set.

---

modified—The name of the implementation class method DS calls when the
`ConfigurationAdmin` service's `Configuration` for the component has been
modified. This attribute is optional, and there is no default value. Setting this
attribute does not make sense if the `configuration-policy` attribute has been
set to `ignore`. See Section 24.2.5.2 for more on configuration modification.

immediate—Controls whether the component's implementation class should
be instantiated and the component activated immediately upon its configuration being satisfied. This attribute is optional. The default value of the
attribute depends on other characteristics of the component:

> **true**—When the component does not provide any services and is not a
> factory component. In this case the `immediate` attribute is *implicitly* true
> and cannot be set to `false`.

> **false**—When the component is a factory component. In this case the
> `immediate` attribute is *implicitly* `false` and cannot be set to `true`.

It makes sense to explicitly set this attribute to `true` only when the component provides a service and you do not want the component's activation to be
delayed until the first request for a provided service is received. It *never*
makes sense to explicitly set this attribute to `false`. See Section 24.2.4,
"Component Immediacy," for more on component immediacy.

enabled—Controls whether the component is enabled upon creation. This
attribute is optional, defaulting to `true`. It never makes sense to explicitly set
this attribute to `true`.

A component can programmatically enable and disable other components
within the same bundle using the `ComponentContext`'s `enableComponent` and
`disableComponent` methods and passing the component's name attribute as a
parameter. See Section 24.2.1.1, "Component Enablement," for more on
component enablement and disablement.

configuration-policy—Controls whether the component depends on the
availability of a `ConfigurationAdmin` service that has a `Configuration` with a

persistent identifier equal to the component's name attribute. This attribute is optional, defaulting to optional. Legal configuration-policy values are

> **require**—Use this value if the component's configuration can be satisfied only when there is a ConfigurationAdmin service that has a Configuration for the component.

> **optional**—Use this value if the component's configuration can be satisfied regardless of whether there is a ConfigurationAdmin service and regardless of whether it has a Configuration for the component.

> **ignore**—Use this value if the component does not wish to interact with the ConfigurationAdmin service. A component that uses this value does not need its name attribute to be a framework-unique persistent identifier but rather just a *bundle-unique* name.

factory—The component's factory ID. This attribute is optional. When this attribute is set, an org.osgi.service.component.ComponentFactory service is registered. Ideally a component's factory ID should uniquely identify the factory, but there is no requirement for this to be the case. A component factory cannot be an immediate component.

24.1.3 The <implementation> Element

The <implementation> element describes the Java class that implements the behavior for the component. This element is required.

class—The fully qualified name of the class that implements the behavior of the component. This attribute is required. This must be a public, concrete class, with a default constructor, and must be a subtype of *all the types* described by the component's <provide> elements, if any. Section 24.1.7, "The <provide> Element," discusses this further.

24.1.4 The <property> Element

The <property> element describes a single property of the component. Component properties are accessible to the component instance and will be registered with every service provided by the component. This element is optional. See Section 24.2.5, "Component Properties," for more on component properties.

name—The name of the property. This attribute is required.

value—The value of the property. This attribute is required unless the element's body describes the value of the property; this is discussed later.

type—The type of the property. This attribute is optional, defaulting to String. This attribute dictates how the value is parsed. Legal values are

```
Boolean    Double   Long
Byte       Float    Short
Character  Integer  String
```

When using the value attribute, the property will *always* be an object type as specified by the type attribute. For example, specifying a value attribute of 10 and a type attribute of Integer will result in an Integer object. The following snippet declares two single-valued properties:

```
<property name="toast.devsim.host" value="localhost"/>
<property name="toast.devsim.port" value="8083" type="Integer"/>
```

While the value attribute is used to describe a single property value, the body of the <property> element is used to describe *multiple property values*, formatted one per line. In this case the property value is an array of the primitive types as specified by the type attribute. For example, if the type attribute is Long, the property value is a long[]. Multiple values of type String are represented as a String[]. The following declaration results in an int[] property value:

```
<property name="toast.devsim.ports" type="Integer">
   8081
   8082
   8083
</property>
```

It is not possible to externalize and translate a <property> element's value attribute or body content.

24.1.5 The <properties> Element

The <properties> element describes properties of the component, as defined in a properties file. As with the <property> element, these properties are accessible to the component instance and will be registered with each service provided by the component. This element is optional. See Section 24.2.5, "Component Properties," for more on component properties.

entry—A *bundle-relative path* to a properties file. This attribute is required. For portability reasons, favor forward slashes over backslashes as a path separator.

Rather than embedding the properties in the component XML document, this element identifies a file from which properties are loaded. All properties that are loaded using a `<properties>` element are of type `string`. When a bundle contains multiple components, it can be convenient to store common properties in a properties file that is loaded by each component.

DEBUGGING MISSING PROPERTY FILES

If a property file referred to by a `<properties>` element cannot be found, DS logs an error to the `LogService`, if available.

Setting the VM argument `-Dequinox.ds.print=true` will cause DS to log errors to the console.

ORDER MATTERS

The order of `<property>` and `<properties>` elements is significant. Later declarations override earlier declarations.

ONLY A COMPONENT CAN CONTAIN PROPERTIES

Both `<property>` and `<properties>` elements are contained directly within a `<component>` element. All properties are registered with each provided service, and it is not possible to register service-specific properties.

24.1.6 The `<service>` Element

The `<service>` element describes the services to be registered with the OSGi service registry. This element is optional; however, if it exists, it must have at least one `<provide>` nested element, as described in Section 24.1.7, "The `<provide>` Element."

servicefactory—This attribute describes whether the component behaves as a *service factory*. This attribute is optional, defaulting to `false`. A service factory is special in that a unique instance of the component's implementation class is created for each bundle that requests any of its provided services, rather than sharing a single instance with all requesting bundles.

ComponentContext'S getUsingBundle METHOD

When the servicefactory attribute is set to true, the ComponentContext's getUsingBundle method returns the Bundle that is using the component. When the servicefactory attribute is set to false, the getUsingBundle method returns null since the component is shared among all bundles that use the component's provided services.

RESTRICTIONS ON BEING A SERVICE FACTORY

The servicefactory attribute cannot be set to true when the component is immediate or is a factory component.

24.1.7 The <provide> Element

The <provide> element identifies a single Java type under which a component's implementation is registered with the OSGi service registry. This element is required but only as a child of the optional <service> element.

interface—The fully qualified name of a Java type. Despite its name, the attribute's value may be either an interface name or a class name. The component's implementation class must always be a subtype of the Java type named by this attribute. This rule is enforced by DS at runtime when it instantiates the component's implementation class.

FAVOR INTERFACES OVER CLASSES

While it is legal to provide services using Java classes, we recommend that you use only Java interfaces. Using interfaces results in a looser coupling between components. It also allows a component's implementation class to represent a wider variety of service types.

24.1.8 The <reference> Element

The <reference> element describes a single prerequisite service of the component. This element is optional. A referenced service is satisfied when DS has acquired it from the OSGi service registry. Likewise, a referenced service is unsatisfied when it can no longer be acquired from the OSGi service registry.

name—A *component-unique* name for the referenced service. This attribute is optional, defaulting to the value of the interface attribute. The value of the attribute is used by the component's implementation class to programmatically locate the referenced service via the ComponentContext's API. In the rare case where a component has multiple <reference> elements with the same interface attribute, it is necessary to explicitly set the name attribute.

interface—The fully qualified Java type of the referenced service. This attribute is required. The rules for this attribute follow those of the <provide> element's interface attribute. Again, while it is legal to specify a Java class, you should strive to specify a Java interface.

bind—The name of a method in the component's implementation class that is used to bind the referenced service. This attribute is optional. See Section 24.2.3, "Accessing Referenced Services," for more on binding referenced services.

unbind—The name of a method in the component's implementation class that is used to unbind the referenced service. This attribute is optional. See Section 24.2.3, "Accessing Referenced Services," for more on unbinding referenced services.

cardinality—The number of referenced service instances that the component must acquire before its configuration is satisfied. This attribute is optional, defaulting to 1..1. There are only four legal values for this attribute:

> **0..1**—Optional and unary
>
> **0..n**—Optional and multiple
>
> **1..1**—Required and unary
>
> **1..n**—Required and multiple

See Section 24.2.1.3, "Acquisition of Referenced Services," for more on referenced service cardinality values.

policy—This attribute describes how changes in the referenced service are handled by the component. This attribute is optional, defaulting to static. Legal values are

> **static**—When using this policy, the component's implementation sees changes in referenced services only while deactivated. This means that if the component is activated, DS will deactivate the component before it sees the change. If the component's configuration continues to be satisfied, DS will activate the component once more.

dynamic—When using this policy, the component's implementation *dynamically* sees changes in the referenced service. If the component is activated, DS will not deactivate the component before it sees the change. This policy requires the component's implementation to be tolerant of dynamic changes to referenced services.

Using the static policy ensures that a component's activate and deactivate methods are not called asynchronously while a referenced service is being bound and unbound. This is not true when using the dynamic policy.

target—This attribute is an LDAP filter allowing for finer-grained selection of a referenced service. This attribute is optional. If your LDAP filter includes illegal XML characters, such as <, >, or &, you must encode them. For example, use < instead of <, > instead of >, and & instead of &.

ORDER MATTERS

The order in which <reference> elements appear in the XML document is significant since referenced services are bound in the order in which they are described and unbound in the reverse order.

MULTIPLE <reference> ELEMENTS WITH THE SAME INTERFACE

It is legal to have multiple <reference> elements with the same interface attribute, but this makes sense only when using the target attribute to select a particular referenced service.

A service object is bound at most once to a given component. If multiple <reference> elements are specified, multiple services are bound only if their target attributes identify unique referenced service instances.

24.2 The Component Lifecycle

A component has a lifecycle that controls when it is activated and deactivated. A bundle must be started before DS can process its components. When a bundle is in the ACTIVE state, or is in the STARTING state and has its **Bundle-ActivationPolicy** manifest header set to lazy, DS will parse its Service-Component manifest header's list of XML documents and creates the components described by each <component> element.

For each component, DS ensures that its configuration is satisfied before activating it. DS deactivates an activated component when its configuration becomes unsatisfied, or when its hosting bundle is stopped. Unless the hosting bundle is stopped, a component is deactivated and reactivated as its configuration goes from being satisfied to being unsatisfied, to being satisfied once more. The details of how configurations are satisfied are discussed in the next section.

24.2.1 Satisfying a Component's Configuration

A component's configuration is considered satisfied when

- ❍ The component is enabled
- ❍ If the <component> element's configuration-policy attribute is set to require, there is a registered ConfigurationAdmin service that has a Configuration with a persistent identifier equal to the <component> element's name attribute
- ❍ All of the component's referenced services have been acquired per their cardinality attribute

You'll recall from Section 24.1.8, "The <reference> Element," that the <reference> element's cardinality attribute describes whether the service is required or optional and how many instances of the service are required and desired by the component.

24.2.1.1 Component Enablement

The first configuration constraint to be checked is whether the component is *enabled*. By default a component is enabled as soon as it is created. An enabled component's configuration is managed by DS, whereas a disabled component's is not and is effectively dormant. Most components are enabled by default and are never disabled.

Component enablement and disablement are useful when initialization behavior must be performed before a component is enabled, or when the component is enabled only while a condition remains true. For example, perhaps a *roadside assistance* component is enabled only after the *billing* component has queried a remote billing server to check that the driver has paid for roadside assistance.

The automatic enablement of a component can be suppressed by setting the <component> element's enabled attribute to false. Once disabled, a component can be enabled only via another ComponentContext in the same bundle by calling that ComponentContext's enableComponent method and passing as a parameter the name of the component to enable. Passing null to the enableComponent method enables *all components* in the bundle.

A component can disable another component by calling the ComponentContext's disableComponent method and passing as a parameter the name of the component to disable. Unlike the enableComponent method, it is not legal to pass null to the disableComponent method, and doing so will result in an exception being thrown.

The enableComponent and disableComponent methods execute asynchronously, meaning that they may return before the component's enablement or disablement is complete.

24.2.1.2 *Availability of a* ConfigurationAdmin *Service Configuration*

If the <component> element's configuration-policy attribute is set to require, the component's configuration is satisfied only while there is a registered ConfigurationAdmin service that has a Configuration with a persistent identifier that equals the <component> element's name attribute.

If the <component> element's configuration-policy attribute is set to optional or ignore, the satisfaction of the component's configuration is unaffected by the availability of the ConfigurationAdmin service or whether it has Configuration for the component.

24.2.1.3 *Acquisition of Referenced Services*

The third configuration constraint to be satisfied is the *cardinality* of each of the component's referenced services. A referenced service's cardinality is described using the <reference> element's cardinality attribute.

A referenced service's cardinality consists of two values: a lower bound and an upper bound. As discussed in Section 24.1.8, "The <reference> Element," there are four cardinality values: two that describe a *required service*, and two that describe an *optional service*. The two cardinality values that describe a required service have a lower bound of 1:

1..1—The component uses exactly one service.

1..n—The component uses one or more services.

The two cardinality values that describe an optional service have a lower bound of 0:

0..1—The component uses *at most one* service.

0..n—The component uses zero, one, or many services.

Choosing the cardinality is a simple matter of answering two questions:

Is the service required or optional?

Required—Set the lower bound to 1.

Optional—Set the lower bound to 0.

Does the component use one or many instances of the service?

One—Set the upper bound to 1.

Many—Set the upper bound to n.

While the `cardinality` that you choose applies only to a particular referenced service, it takes only a single unavailable *required* referenced service to cause the component's configuration to remain unsatisfied and the component to not be activated.

24.2.2 *Component Activation, Deactivation, and Modification*

The `<component>` element's `activate`, `deactivate`, and `modified` attributes name the methods of the component implementation class that DS calls when the component is activated, deactivated, and modified.

Activation and modification methods can take zero or more arguments, where each argument is of one of the following types:

ComponentContext—A `ComponentContext` is similar to the bundle's `BundleContext` in that it provides an OSGi-defined API for querying and controlling the component and other components defined by the bundle.

BundleContext—The hosting bundle's `BundleContext`.

Map—An immutable `Map` containing the component's properties.

DS searches for activation and modification methods in the component's implementation class in the following order:

1. A one-argument method that takes a `ComponentContext`
2. A one-argument method that takes a `BundleContext`
3. A one-argument method that takes a `Map`
4. A two-argument method that takes a `ComponentContext`, `BundleContext`, or `Map`, in any order; if DS finds multiple matching methods, it will arbitrarily choose one
5. A zero-argument method

If upon calling the `activate` method an exception is thrown, DS will log an error to the `LogService`, if available, and the component is not activated.

Once a component is activated, it remains so until its configuration becomes unsatisfied or its defining bundle is stopped, at which time the component is deactivated.

Deactivation methods can take zero or more arguments, where each argument is of one of the following types:

ComponentContext—Similar to the bundle's BundleContext in that it provides an OSGi-defined API for querying and controlling the component and other components defined by the bundle

BundleContext—The hosting bundle's BundleContext

Map—An immutable Map containing the component's properties

int or **Integer**—The reason the component is being deactivated

DS searches for deactivation methods in the component's implementation class in the following order:

1. A one-argument method that takes a ComponentContext
2. A one-argument method that takes a BundleContext
3. A one-argument method that takes a Map
4. A one-argument method that takes an int
5. A one-argument method that takes an Integer
6. A two-argument method that takes a ComponentContext, BundleContext, Map, int, or Integer in any order; if DS finds multiple matching methods, it will arbitrarily choose one
7. A zero-argument method

When DS calls a deactivation method that takes an int or an Integer, one of the following deactivation reasons is passed as a parameter:

0—Unspecified

1—The component was disabled

2—A reference became unsatisfied

3—A configuration was changed

4—A configuration was deleted

5—The component was disposed

6—The bundle was stopped

Throughout its lifetime a component may be activated and deactivated many times as its configuration becomes satisfied and unsatisfied. Each time a component is activated, a new instance of the component's implementation class and the ComponentContext is instantiated, and the component's referenced services are bound.

The component's `activate`, `deactivate`, and `modified` methods will not be called asynchronously by DS. When the component has a `<reference>` element that uses the `dynamic` policy, DS will call its `bind` and `unbind` methods asynchronously to these methods.

24.2.2.1 Referenced Service Policy

The `<reference>` element's `policy` attribute describes how the component will handle changes in the referenced service. There are two values for the `policy` attribute:

static—This policy ensures that once activated, the component does not see referenced service changes without being deactivated first. Once the component has been deactivated, it will be activated only when its configuration is satisfied once more. This is the default policy.

dynamic—This policy allows the referenced service to change dynamically without deactivating the component first.

The decision regarding the `policy` to choose is often influenced by the `cardinality` of the referenced service. Generally speaking, the most common `cardinality` and `policy` pairings are

1..1 and static—This is the default, simplest, and most common pairing. The component requires exactly one instance of the referenced service, is activated only when the service is available, and is deactivated when the service becomes unavailable.

0..1 and static—Specifying a cardinality with a lower bound of 0 makes the referenced service optional. This is common in scenarios such as logging or where graceful fallback is possible. Note that the component author must carefully handle the case where a service is, or is not, present. The presence or absence of optional referenced services does not affect the activation of the component.

0..1 and dynamic—This variation on the optional service requirement can be useful in highly fluid scenarios. The main difference is that the service can appear and disappear at any time. Pragmatically the coding patterns required here are complicated, so care should be taken.

0..n and dynamic—These settings are common in listener or Whiteboard Pattern cases, as discussed in Chapter 15, "Declarative Services." The component will bind with any number of services and be told of their transitions without affecting the activation state of the component. See the `Portal` component in Chapter 13, "Web Portal," for an example.

When using the dynamic policy, it is common to use bind and unbind methods to manage changes in the referenced services. For the multiple cardinalities (1..n and 0..n) this typically means that the referenced service is added to a collection when bound and removed from the collection when unbound. For the 0..1 cardinality, the referenced service is typically cached in a field when bound and the field is set to null when unbound.

If you use the dynamic policy with one of the unary cardinalities (0..1 and 1..1), when a bound referenced service is unregistered, DS will *always try to rebind a replacement service before it unbinds the current service*. This can come as a big surprise since while the cardinality dictates that only a single referenced service is required, the component must be able to handle it being dynamically switched for another referenced service due to the cardinality constraints. For an example of this, see Section 17.2, "Using the LogService in Toast."

If you use the static policy with one of the optional cardinalities (0..1 and 0..n), the component's configuration can be satisfied with zero referenced services. The static policy dictates that once the component's configuration is satisfied, it will *not be deactivated and reactivated* if a referenced service becomes available later. For this reason we suggest using the dynamic policy with the optional cardinalities.

24.2.3 Accessing Referenced Services

There are two strategies that a component can use to access its referenced services:

Event Strategy—Using this strategy, DS dispatches events to the component as the availability of its referenced services changes. Set the <reference> element's bind and unbind attributes to the name of the implementation class methods that DS calls to handle these events.

Lookup Strategy—Using this strategy, the <reference> element's bind and unbind attributes are typically not set. Instead, the component's implementation looks up each referenced service using its ComponentContext's API.

It is not necessary for a component to use the same strategy for accessing all of its referenced services, since the strategy you pick is influenced by the referenced service's cardinality and policy.

We recommend that you start by using the Event Strategy since it is simple, fits well with POJO APIs, and works well regardless of the referenced service's cardinality and policy. The Toast application uses the Event Strategy in all but a few cases. For an example of the Lookup Strategy, see the org.equinoxosgi .toast.backend.portal bundle where the PortalServlet dynamically looks up IPortalAction referenced services based on an HTTP request.

24.2.3.1 *Using the Event Strategy*

The Event Strategy allows referenced services to be mapped to the API of the component's implementation class via the `<reference>` element's `bind` and `unbind` attributes. The signature of the `bind` and `unbind` method can be one of the following:

void `<method>`(`<service-type>`)—This method takes a simple argument that is typed to the `<reference>` element's `interface` attribute or one of its super-types. At runtime the parameter is the actual service object. This is the most commonly used signature.

void `<method>`(`<service-type>`, `Map properties`)—This method's first argument is as described in the previous signature. The second argument is a `Map` that contains the referenced service's registered properties.

void `<method>`(`ServiceReference reference`)—This method delays the loading and instantiation of the referenced service's class by taking a `ServiceReference` argument.

DS searches for methods in the component's implementation class in the following order:

1. Search for a single-argument method that takes a `ServiceReference`.
2. Search for a single-argument method that is typed to the `<reference>` element's `interface` attribute.
3. Search for a single-argument method that is typed to a super-type of the `<reference>` element's `interface` attribute. If DS finds multiple matching methods, it will arbitrarily choose one.
4. Search for a two-argument method, with the first argument typed as the `<reference>` element's `interface` attribute and the second argument typed as a `Map`.
5. Search for a two-argument method, with the first argument typed as a super-type of the `<reference>` element's `interface` attribute and the second argument typed as a `Map`. If DS finds multiple matching methods, it will arbitrarily choose one.

DS requires that the visibility of these methods be such that they are accessible to the component's implementation class. We recommend that you always make these methods `public`. We say this because they are necessary to use the class outside of OSGi and are really part of the component implementation class's public API in a POJO context. Since these methods are never part of any provided service API, they will never be accessible to consumers of the provided service regardless of their visibility modifier.

Remember, it is desirable for your component implementation classes to remain pure POJOs, independent of OSGi APIs and mechanisms such as DS. For this reason, we recommend that you think carefully before defining `bind` and `unbind` methods that take a `ServiceReference` argument; doing so creates a dependency upon OSGi.

When the `bind` method takes a service instance argument, the referenced service's implementation class clearly must have been loaded and instantiated before being passed as a parameter to the `bind` method. By contrast, when the `bind` method takes a `ServiceReference` argument, the referenced service's implementation class is neither loaded nor instantiated before the `bind` method is called. This laziness is particularly valuable when using the *multiple* cardinalities, 0..n and 1..n, since a component often does not use every referenced service as soon as it is bound, but rather caches each `ServiceReference` and selects one based on criteria such as the referenced service's registered properties. The reference service's class is loaded and instantiated when the `ServiceReference` is dereferenced using the `ComponentContext`'s API `locateService(String, ServiceReference)`.

24.2.3.2 Using the Lookup Strategy

While the Event Strategy involves DS injecting services by binding and unbinding the component's referenced services, the Lookup Strategy involves the component's implementation querying DS for its referenced services.

Of the two strategies, the Lookup Strategy is generally considered the *lazier* since a referenced service is reified into a service object only when a request for it is made. When using this strategy, referenced services are looked up via the component's `ComponentContext` that provides the following API:

`locateService(String name)`—This method locates a referenced service using the `<reference>` element's name attribute.

`locateService(String name, ServiceReference reference)`—This method locates a referenced service using the `<reference>` element's name attribute and a `ServiceReference`. The name argument is necessary because a single `ServiceReference` can represent multiple service types, so specifying the name ensures that you locate a service object of the appropriate type. A component can obtain a `ServiceReference` in a variety of ways, but the most common way is by using the Event Strategy and having the `ServiceReference` dependency injected. When using this method, therefore, the Event Strategy and the Lookup Strategy are used together.

`locateServices(String name)`—This method locates all the referenced services using the `<reference>` element's name attribute. While this method can be used regardless of the referenced service's `cardinality`, it is most commonly used with a *multiple* `cardinality`, namely, `0..n` and `1..n`.

The two `locateService` methods return an `Object` and the `locateServices` method returns an `Object[]`, so it is necessary to cast the services to their actual types before use. Care must be taken to ensure that the `name` parameter passed to the methods is correct; otherwise an exception will be thrown when casting to the actual service type.

Since the `ComponentContext` is available only while the component is activated, locating services is typically done from the component's `activate` method. This method should be typed to take a `ComponentContext` argument. Unfortunately `ComponentContext` is an OSGi class, and this makes it too easy to pollute a perfectly good POJO with an OSGi dependency. We recommend the following alternatives:

○ Implement the component's implementation class as an OSGi-dependent wrapper that delegates to a cached instance of the POJO. For this to work, the wrapper class must implement all the provided service interfaces and delegate to the cached POJO.

○ Resign yourself to the fact that your component's implementation class is OSGi-dependent and will never run as a POJO.

24.2.4 Component Immediacy

The concept of *component immediacy* is important to understand since it controls when a component is activated. Activation causes a component's implementation class to be loaded and instantiated. One of the benefits that DS brings to the OSGi service model is lazy class loading and instantiation of the component's implementation class. This can result in significant performance gains in terms of startup time and memory consumption.

An immediate component is activated as soon as its configuration is satisfied. By contrast, a delayed component has its activation delayed until one of its provided services is requested.

The `<component>` element's `immediate` attribute is used to request the component's activation characteristics, but it is important to remember that this attribute is merely a *hint* to DS rather than a demand. A component is immediate when

○ It does not provide any services. DS considers the component to be *implicitly* immediate.

○ Its `immediate` attribute is explicitly set to `true`.

There is no guarantee that DS will honor a component's immediacy hint. Regardless of the value of its immediate attribute,

○ If the component is a factory component, it will not be immediate. A factory component must *always have its component activation delayed* since its purpose is to provide a service through which component instances are dynamically created and activated.

○ If the component does not provide any services, and is not a factory component, it will always be immediate. Without any provided services, a component is at the top of the food chain and must therefore be activated immediately.

Since many components provide services, immediate components are rare. Examples of immediate components include

○ A user interface component that needs to display a shell when the application starts.

○ A component that registers servlets rather than services. A servlet must always be registered before an HTTP request for it is received.

○ A component that performs asynchronous data collection from a device such as a thermometer, which may or may not provide services.

Remember that the activation of a component may be the cause of a potentially large chain of component activations, class loading, and instantiation of objects across the entire system. For performance reasons, care must be taken before making a component immediate. Since a well-designed OSGi application is composed of many finely grained components, it is important to understand the true cost of activating a single component.

24.2.5 Component Properties

A component's properties can be set in three ways, in order of precedence:

○ A component factory accepts properties passed via the ComponentFactory's newInstance API that is used to create new component instances.

○ If a <component> element's configuration-policy attribute is set to either require or optional, the ConfigurationAdmin service can be used to create and update a Configuration for the component. See Section 24.1.2, "The <component> Element."

○ Finally, a component's properties can be set statically in the component's XML document using <property> and <properties> elements. See Sections 24.1.4, "The <property> Element," and 24.1.5, "The <properties> Element."

This means that when a property is passed to a component by a component factory, it is not possible to configure the property via the ConfigurationAdmin service, since the properties passed by the component factory will always override those of the configuration managed by ConfigurationAdmin. Likewise, when a component is using ConfigurationAdmin to manage its properties, updating its Configuration will override the properties defined in the component's XML document.

Regardless of how a component's properties are set, they are presented to the component as a single immutable Dictionary via its ComponentContext's getProperties method. See Chapter 13, "Web Portal," for an example of using properties.

A component's properties are also registered as properties of any service that it provides. The exception to this rule is that properties whose name starts with a dot (".") are considered private to the component and will not be registered with provided services.

24.2.5.1 Component Properties and the ConfigurationAdmin Service

The DS specification has always included close integration with the ConfigurationAdmin service as a way of remotely and persistently configuring a component's properties.

In v1.0.0 of the DS schema, DS always attempts to acquire the ConfigurationAdmin service to look for a Configuration with a persistent identifier equal to the <component> element's name attribute. If a Configuration is found, its properties are used to override those defined in the component's XML declarations. In this context *properties* are defined as

○ A property described by the <property> element.

○ A property described by a <properties> element.

○ Each referenced service's *target property* as described by its <reference> element's optional target attribute. Target properties are discussed in Section 24.2.5.3, "Referenced Service Target Properties."

This is certainly a useful capability since otherwise there is no other way to configure a component's properties, which are often statically declared in XML and for which there is no programmatic API that allows them to be changed.

In v1.1.0 of the DS schema the <component> element attribute configuration-policy was introduced, which allows a component to more accurately describe its integration with the ConfigurationAdmin service. A component can now

○ Require a ConfigurationAdmin service and a Configuration before its configuration is considered satisfied. If the component is a *factory component* and there is no `ConfigurationAdmin` service and a `Configuration`, the `ComponentFactory` service will not be registered.

○ Optionally use the `ConfigurationAdmin` service with a matching `Configuration`.

○ Ignore the `ConfigurationAdmin` service. In v1.0.0 of the DS schema every component interacted with the `ConfigurationAdmin` service, if available. Now there is a way of opting out.

The `<component>` element's `configuration-policy` attribute is discussed in Section 24.1.2, "The `<component>` Element."

24.2.5.2 Component Configuration Modification

In v1.0.0 of the DS schema, updates to a component's `Configuration` resulted in the component always being deactivated and reactivated regardless of the changes to the properties. In v1.1.0 of the DS schema, the `<component>` element's `modified` attribute was added. This attribute can be set to the name of a method in the component's implementation class that DS calls when the component's `Configuration` has been updated such that its configuration remains satisfied. The signature of the method named in this attribute is discussed in Section 24.2.2, "Component Activation, Deactivation, and Modification."

24.2.5.3 Referenced Service Target Properties

As discussed in Section 24.1.8, "The `<reference>` Element," a `<reference>` element has an optional `target` attribute that is used to finely tune the referenced services that the component acquires. The `target` attribute's value is an LDAP filter that is used by DS to satisfy the constraints of the referenced service based on its registered properties, for example:

```
<reference
  name="http"
  interface="org.osgi.service.http.HttpService"
  target="(http.port=80)"/>
```

In this example the referenced service's `target` property is the LDAP filter (http.port=80). The component's configuration will be satisfied only if an `HttpService` is acquired that has an `http.port` property with the value 80. Recall that the `<property>` and `<properties>` elements are used by a component to describe the properties that will be registered with its provided services.

While a referenced service's `target` property is described statically in XML, it can be configured dynamically, just like any other component property, but by using its *target property key*. A target property key is the concatenation of the

<reference> element's name attribute and the suffix .target, which would be http.target in our example.

USE ComponentConstants

The org.osgi.service.component.ComponentConstants class defines a variety of useful constants, such as REFERENCE_TARGET_SUFFIX, that can be used in the creation of a target property key.

24.3 Summary

The Declarative Services XML schema is certainly not complicated, but to use DS effectively it is helpful to understand its subtleties. In this chapter we dived deeply into the schema to describe every element and attribute, as well as how the various attribute values affect components' behavior.

We have also discussed the DS component lifecycle with the goal of teaching you to build flexible and pluggable applications composed from OSGi services. Toast is built entirely of DS components and services and uses DS to good effect. With the knowledge you have gained from Chapter 15, "Declarative Services," and the discussion in this chapter, we hope that you'll quickly be able to leverage the benefits of building applications composed of loosely coupled and highly cohesive components and services.

Index

The Definitive Guide to Eclipse Rich Client Development— Fully Revised to Reflect Eclipse 3.5's Major Enhancements

Eclipse Rich Client Platform, Second Edition

Jeff McAffer,
Jean-Michel Lemieux,
Chris Aniszczyk

- Builds on the highly successful first edition, the industry's number one source of information on rich client Eclipse development

- Covers Eclipse 3.5's improvements for designing, coding, and packaging RCP applications— information too new to appear in any other book!

- Includes extensive real-world, nontrivial working code examples

In *Eclipse Rich Client Platform, Second Edition,* leaders of the Eclipse RCP project show exactly how to leverage these capabilities for rapid, efficient, cross-platform desktop development. Building on their highly praised first edition, the authors walk step-by-step through developing a fully featured, branded RCP application. They introduce a wide range of techniques, including developing pluggable and dynamically extensible systems; using third-party code libraries; and packaging applications for diverse environments. Readers will build a complete prototype, refine and refactor it, customize user interfaces, add Help and Update features, then build, brand, and ship the finished software.

Learn more at informit.com/title/9780321603784
Available in all major eBook formats and Safari Books Online

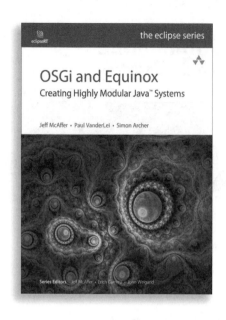